INTERCHANGE
READING AND WRITING CRITICALLY

INTERCHANGE
READING AND WRITING CRITICALLY

Christine Evans Carter
St. Louis Community College—Meramec

John Stilla
Seneca College—King Campus

NELSON

NELSON

Interchange

by Christine Evans Carter and John Stilla

VP, Product Solutions, K–20:
Claudine O'Donnell

Senior Publisher, Digital and Print Content:
Lenore Taylor-Atkins

Executive Marketing Manager:
Amanda Henry

Content Manager:
Jacquelyn Busby

Photo and Permissions Researcher:
Julie Pratt

Senior Production Project Manager:
Imoinda Romain

Production Service:
SPi-Global

Copy Editor:
Karen Rolfe

Proofreader:
SPi-Global

Indexer:
SPi-Global

Design Director:
Ken Phipps

Higher Education Design PM:
Pamela Johnston

Interior Design:
Sharon Lucas Creative

Cover Design:
Sharon Lucas Creative

Cover Image:
ivcandy/Getty

Art Coordinator:
Suzanne Peden

Compositor:
SPi-Global

Library and Archives Canada Cataloguing in Publication

Carter, Christine Evans, author

Interchange : reading and writing critically / Christine Evans Carter (St. Louis Community College—Meramec), John Stilla (Seneca College—King Campus).

Includes index.

Issued in print and electronic formats.

ISBN 978-0-17-676468-5 (softcover)
ISBN 978-0-17-688847-3 (PDF)

1. English language—Rhetoric.
2. Report writing. 3. Reading.

I. Stilla, John, author II. Title.

PE1408.C37 2019
808'.0427 C2018-905727-0
        C2018-905728-9

ISBN-13: 978-0-17-676468-5
ISBN-10: 0-17-676468-2

To our students.

BRIEF CONTENTS

CONTENTS

PREFACE

Christine Carter and John Stilla partnered with Nelson after Humber College's Department of English adopted significant portions of Christine's reading strategy textbook, *Mindscapes: Critical Reading Skills and Strategies*, as its custom text for college composition. Humber's English faculty, of which John was a part, recognized the need to incorporate concrete, explicit reading strategies in order to enhance students' proficiency with analyzing and thinking critically about what they are reading. These reading strategies, in turn, result in greater depth in student writing and the ability for students to analyze and think about their own writing just as they analyze and think about the writing of others. Christine and John discussed partnering on a textbook when Christine was keynote speaker at the College Association for Language and Literacy conference in 2014. With encouragement from Nelson, Christine and John began *Interchange: Reading and Writing Critically*.

Approach

Interchange offers a scaffolded and integrated approach to teaching and learning composition. In essence, the book encourages students to read from a writing perspective and to write from a reading perspective. In this symbiotic approach, the edges of the two fundamental literacy skills are blurred, producing a truly blended approach to understanding writing through reading, and vice versa. Furthermore, borrowing from the tenets of English language pedagogy, *Interchange* encourages speaking and listening along with reading and writing through chapter prompts for writing and discussion as well as other applied exercises throughout each chapter. The chapters are fully thematic—meaning that each chapter not only focuses on specific reading and writing skills, but also compels students to investigate a topic in depth via both reading and writing. Furthermore, grammar is integrated in each chapter, drawing practice and examples from the chapter's readings. Each skill and strategy is followed by hands-on application throughout each chapter. The approach used in this textbook is truly integrated in a variety of ways.

Key Features

- A recursive, metacognitive approach that encourages students to reflect on their own thinking with explicit instruction.
- Each chapter toggles between the two skills, explicitly linking the interchange of reading and writing.
- Each chapter offers two or three high-interest **readings** to deepen topic understanding and generate thoughtful writing.

- The readings in each chapter are overwhelmingly Canadian in origin, making the topics specifically relevant to Canadian learners; however, the broad topics are of high interest to international learners, too.
- Each chapter builds on the last, fusing skills and strategies in both reading and writing in a scaffolded manner.
- **Learning Objectives** at the beginning of each chapter promote a focused experience for maximum comprehension.
- The **Why Is This Information Important?** feature explains the importance of the skills and strategies introduced and developed in each chapter.
- The **Think about It!** feature at the start of each chapter gets students involved in and curious about the chapter theme, encouraging opinions about the broad theme and eliciting reactions to key features in the variety of writing approaches. This reading serves as the basis for many chapter explanations and applications.
- **Figures** visually illustrate key concepts covered in the chapter.
- Pedagogy breaks down each skill with related examples from readings in the chapter rather than random examples. This builds background knowledge on the subject and shows students that writers approach writing in different ways, encouraging learners to *think about* their writing purpose, topic, and audience first.
- Each skill or strategy is followed by an **Apply the Skill** feature that allows practice on skill subsets before assembling them.
- Chapters include a **Review** feature after each broad topic to ensure students understand and can apply key concepts and strategies.
- **Did You Know?** weaves an appropriate grammar, mechanics, punctuation, or strategic writing topic into each chapter. Instead of isolating skills, we set them in context, unfolding these topics in each chapter in a recursive manner.
- **Questions for Writing and Discussion** offer thought-provoking prompts that often integrate ideas from readings in each chapter.
- The appendix, **Documentation**, provides students with useful models and methods to support their writing for their courses.

Instructor Resources

The **Nelson Education Teaching Advantage (NETA)** program delivers research-based instructor resources that promote student engagement and higher-order thinking to enable the success of Canadian students and educators. Visit Nelson Education's **Inspired Instruction** website at www.nelson.com/inspired to find out more about NETA.

The following instructor resources have been created for *Interchange: Reading and Writing Critically*. Access these ultimate tools for customizing lectures and presentations at www.nelson.com/instructor.

NETA POWERPOINT

Microsoft® PowerPoint® lecture slides for every chapter have been created by Brigid Kelso, George Brown College. Many slides feature key figures, tables, and photographs from *Interchange*. NETA principles of clear design and engaging content have been incorporated throughout, making it simple for instructors to customize the deck for their courses.

MINDTAP

Offering personalized paths of dynamic assignments and applications, **MindTap** is a digital learning solution that turns cookie-cutter into cutting-edge, apathy into engagement, and memorizers into higher-level thinkers. MindTap enables students to analyze and apply chapter concepts within relevant assignments, and allows instructors to measure skills and promote better outcomes with ease. A fully online learning solution, MindTap combines all student learning tools—readings, multimedia, activities, and assessments—into a single Learning Path that guides the student through the curriculum. Instructors personalize the experience by customizing the presentation of these learning tools to their students, even seamlessly introducing their own content into the Learning Path.

Student Ancillaries

MINDTAP

Stay organized and efficient with *MindTap*—a single destination with all the course material and study aids you need to succeed. Built-in apps leverage social media and the latest learning technology. For example:

- ReadSpeaker will read the text to you.
- Flashcards are pre-populated to provide you with a jump start for review—or you can create your own.
- You can highlight text and make notes in your MindTap Reader. Your notes will flow into Evernote, the electronic notebook app that you can access anywhere when it's time to study for the exam.
- Self-quizzing allows you to assess your understanding.

Visit www.nelson.com/student to start using **MindTap**. Enter the Online Access Code from the card included with your text. If a code card is *not* provided, you can purchase instant access at NELSONbrain.com.

About the Authors

The authors share a significant history in teaching different levels of postsecondary learners as well as those for whom English is a second language. Christine Evans Carter, raised in Toronto, is a professor of reading in the English department and has taught reading and writing at St. Louis Community College for almost 20 years, as well as teaching reading and ESL along with college anthropology in other states. She holds two master's degrees in anthropology and reading along with a graduate certificate in Gender Studies. She has published two textbooks on reading skills and strategies for college learners with Cengage.

John Stilla was a professor and program coordinator in Humber College's Department of English, focusing on the areas of remedial and developmental English. During his time in the role, he helped move first-semester composition courses toward a curriculum that heavily integrates reading and writing pedagogy. In addition to a master's degree in English, he is an Ontario Certified English Language Teacher, having completed a post-graduate certificate in Teaching English as a Second Language. Currently, he holds the position of Chair, School of English and Liberal Studies at Seneca.

Between them, the authors have presented at international as well as regional conferences and are known as experts in their field. In joining forces, Christine and John bring a unique product to the postsecondary market.

The authors wish to thank the following professionals from Nelson Education for their enormous help in bringing this edition to fruition:

- Lenore Taylor-Atkins, Senior Publisher
- Jacquelyn Busby, Content Manager
- Amanda Henry, Executive Marketing Manager
- Imoinda Romain, Senior Production Project Manager
- Karen Rolfe, Freelance Copyeditor

The authors and publisher also wish to thank those who reviewed this project during its development and provided important insights and suggestions:

Trevor Arkell, Humber College

Francesca Boschetti, Memorial University of Newfoundland

Barbara Buetter, Niagara College

Carrie Dawson, Dalhousie University

Chandra Hodgson, Humber College

Brigid Kelso, George Brown College

Craig McLuckie, Okanagan College

Don Moore, University of Guelph

Amanda Paxton, Trent University

Amanda Quibell, Georgian College

Clayton Rhodes, Durham College

Lara Sauer, George Brown College

William Thompson, MacEwan University

Vanessa Vandergrift, Vanier College

John would also like to acknowledge the faculty in Humber's Department of English who, through research, curriculum review, presentations, and endless dedication to their students, have inspired the pedagogical approach this book takes to reading and writing skills development. He would also like to thank his students for helping to finesse the approaches described in this book and for inspiring him to create new methods to help develop their critical reading and writing abilities.

The authors dedicate this book to their families, whose support and encouragement made this book possible. Christine would like to thank Bryonie, Miranda, Cassandra, Nancy, Hugh, and Jeff, as always, for their interest, feedback, and ongoing support. John would like to thank his children for being so patient and understanding during the many long writing and revision periods that often put playtime on hold. Moreover, he extends his gratitude to his wife, Julianna, without whom he would not have been able to co-author this book. She took on substantially more responsibilities to provide him with the time to write, and for that, he will always be grateful.

They also dedicate this book to their students—present, past, and future.

Lightspring/Shutterstock.com

LAYING THE FOUNDATION: EFFECTIVE READING AND WRITING PROCESSES

BY THE END OF THIS CHAPTER, YOU WILL BE ABLE TO

- Determine the purpose, topic, and audience of your own writing and the writing of others.
- Explain how purpose, topic, thesis, and audience are integral components of the reading and writing processes.
- Write a focused and limited thesis statement and identify the thesis in readings.
- Describe the connection between reading and writing.
- Employ effective reading and writing processes.
- Deconstruct writing prompts to focus your responses.

▶ WHY IS THIS INFORMATION IMPORTANT?

The connection between reading and writing is quite clear. If you learn to read well, recognizing how words, sentences, and paragraphs work together to deliver clear messages, you will become a better writer by employing similar patterns to deliver your own messages. If you learn to write well, others will be able to read and respond to your messages, which helps to facilitate communication.

Good reading and good writing involve two important processes. The reading process, sometimes referred to as *active reading*, helps ensure you understand the complexities of a text so that you can respond to it in meaningful ways. Active reading often includes marking and annotating a text and asking questions about its form and content. The writing process, sometimes referred to as *recursive writing*, involves revising, honing, and clarifying ideas so that your message is understood by your readers. Recursive writing, like active reading, often includes marking your own written drafts and asking questions about form and content to ensure clear communication. Both the reading and writing processes involve visiting the text more than once; in fact, as an active reader or writer, you revisit the writing several times. As a reader, you deconstruct the reading assignment to think along with the writer; as a writer, you construct the writing assignment to clarify your thoughts for the reader. So, thinking about reading as a writer and writing with your reader in mind helps ensure maximum comprehension of ideas.

▶ Think about It!

What Does Being Educated Mean?

In this first chapter, you will read and write about what it means to be educated and how to improve learning. Here are some questions to consider as you move through this chapter and as you read the following essay.

1. What is the value of formal education?
2. Does a person have to go to school to be considered educated, or can someone who learns on his own also be considered educated?
3. What is your definition of an educated person?

Now, read this essay from *The Globe and Mail* and consider these questions:

1. What is the author's main idea or thesis?
2. What is the author's definition of an educated person?
3. After reading this essay, have you changed your view of what it means to be an educated person?
4. How does the author's view of education compare with yours?

AN A+ STUDENT REGRETS HIS GRADES

By Afraj Gill

1   The purpose and meaning of education is widely misunderstood and wrongly presented.

2   This is why the education system needs "reinventing, not reforming," according to Harvard Innovation Education Fellow Tony Wagner. We're creating a culture—reinforced by society and habitually drilled into students from an early age and well into their teens—that revolves around textbooks, lectures, GPAs and exams, where failing or not doing well are either unacceptable or wrongly considered a sign of weakness or a lack of intellect.

3   Education is not confined to the walls of a classroom; it stretches well beyond that. Valuing success above all else is a problem plaguing the schooling systems, at all levels, of many countries including Canada and the United States, and undermining those very qualities that are meant to foster an educated and skillful society.

4   This very issue took a toll on my own educational career, not in terms of academic performance, but other aspects considerably more important.

5   Less than three years ago, I graduated high school. I was a driven student who scored a 100 per cent average, served as the students' council president and class valedictorian, earned over 16 scholarships/awards, etc. The bottom line is that I was a high achiever, but I mistakenly defined achievement in a way most do: with my GPA. It was only until a couple of years ago, when I began to question my own educational career, that I realized something profound: The academic portion of my high school life was spent in the wrong way, with cloudy motivations. I treated schooling and education synonymously. I had been directed not by my inner voice, but by societal pressures that limited my ability to foster personal creativity.

6   The system teaches us that if you get "As" across the board, you'll be successful. And if you fail a course, you'll be labelled incompetent or hopeless. These pressures force students to regard education as a mere schooling tenure where the goal is to input a sufficient amount of work to output the highest possible grades. We sacrifice learning for schooling. One of my professors once said, "Writing exams isn't a measure of intelligence or knowledge, it's about getting inside your prof's head to figure out what'll be on the exam."

7   Information is propelled into students without teaching them how to practically utilize it. This is senseless. Regurgitating facts, memorizing figures and formulas, compressing course material in our short-term memory for the sake of doing well on an exam; they are all detrimental to the learning experience. But students still do it because they don't want to fail. Instead, we should be fostering a culture where, to paraphrase Arianna Huffington, "Failure isn't considered the opposite of success, but an integral part of it."

8   One of the few classes that effectively taught me how to take information from the classroom to the real world was instructed by Doug Wightman at Queen's University. The course covered concepts from how to start a start-up, build business models and prototypes, to venture deals, stock options and term sheets. But it didn't end there. Toward the end of the course, many students had working prototypes, and a few managed to execute and launch their ideas. This course taught me something important: We can't allow learning to become passive. We need to teach students to learn how to learn—to become independent, innovative thinkers capable of changing the world.

9   Finland's nonconformist education system—the best in the world—should serve as an example of how students ought to see their educational experience. Finnish students don't start school until they're 7, they aren't measured for the first six years of their education; and they rarely take exams or do homework until they are well into their teens. These students aren't raised to see school as a measurement cycle where everything comes down to standardized testing, graded assignments and exams worth large portions of their final grade. Their educational culture is substantially different from the evaluation-driven Western world.

10   Culture is a problem, and we need to fix it—from the ground up. There's a psychosocial dynamic of not questioning current practices of education. But we can't

let this get in the way. Embrace education with all your heart, and remember that schooling is only a small part of the puzzle. The remainder is what you'll have to discover and solve through your own journey.

Source: Gill, Afraj. "An A+ Student Regrets his Grades." *The Globe and Mail,* 18 Jan. 2013, www.theglobeandmail.com/news/national/education/an-a-student-regrets-his-grades/article7359620/. Reproduced by permission of the author.

Reading and Writing: Purpose, Topic, Thesis, and Audience

When you read and when you write, you do so for a reason. The purposes for reading and writing are important to consider from the beginning of the activity. Being unclear about your purpose can muddy comprehension of a reading passage and development of a writing activity.

Purpose for Reading

Depending on your purpose for reading, you may customize your reading speed or your level of concentration. If you are reading for entertainment or a general overview, you read quickly. If your purpose is to read for detail and content, such as for a test, you read slowly. Reading for detail and content requires you to read actively.

Purpose for Writing

Whether you are writing in the workplace, writing an application letter, or writing for a job or school, you must consider your purpose. There are four fundamental purposes for writing:

1. **To inform or explain**. In this purpose, you provide information without including your opinion, or you explain an idea to clarify a concept for the reader. Activity guides, policy manuals, materials for university or college orientation, textbooks, and contracts are examples of writing that informs or explains.
2. **To instruct**. In this purpose, you tell the reader how to do something or how to understand something. User guides, procedure manuals, and how-to documents are all examples of writing that instructs.
3. **To persuade.** In this purpose, you aim to convince the reader of an opinion. Newspaper editorials, advertisements, and political speeches are all examples of writing that persuades.
4. **To entertain**. In this purpose, you use humour, description, narrative, or other entertaining techniques to get the reader to enjoy your text. Novels, comics, movie/television scripts, and literature are all examples of writing that entertains.

Sometimes you may have more than one purpose. For example, if you write poetry, you may both entertain and persuade your reader of a perspective or discovery. Typically, however, one purpose will be predominant.

Topic

In order to read with comprehension, the first step is to determine the topic, also known as the subject—whom or what the reading is about. Of equal importance, when you set out to write a passage for whatever purpose, you must have a topic in mind. You need to know about what or whom you are writing.

DETERMINING TOPIC

You can usually determine the topic of a reading through one or more of the following strategies as shown in Figure 1.1:

1. Read the title or headings.
2. Scan the reading for boldfaced words or special print such as italics or coloured print.
3. Look for words repeated throughout the passage or words mentioned and referred to by pronouns.

FIGURE 1.1
CLUES FOR TOPIC

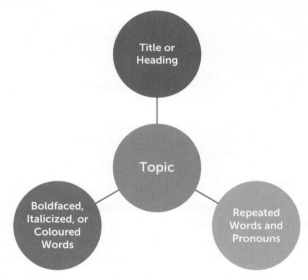

WRITING YOUR OWN TOPIC

When you use prewriting techniques, you focus on your topic. As you select and refine what you want to write about and what you have to say about that subject, you further clarify your topic. To help your reader identify the topic in your writing, state the topic in the title or subheading, use bold or italicized words, and/or use repeated words and synonyms that indicate the topic. Doing so achieves unity and coherence, thus aiding comprehension.

Thesis

In both reading and writing, focusing on the most important point is critical. In writing, you must craft an effective thesis or overall point about your topic. Also, you should ensure that each of your body paragraphs has a clear and unified point. Similarly, when you read another's writing, you must determine the most important point about the topic as well as the supporting points in order to understand the author's train of thought.

MAIN IDEA

The author's most important point about a topic is called a *main idea,* although different terms can be used as indicated in Figure 1.2. For example, the main idea of a longer reading is called a *thesis.* A thesis can be directly stated in one sentence, known as a thesis statement, or it can be implied—suggested but not written in one sentence in the text. The directly stated main idea of a paragraph is called a *topic sentence.* If the main idea of a paragraph is not directly stated but is implied, there is still a main idea. In this case, the main idea is suggested by the supporting details. You will learn more about topic sentences and implied main ideas in Chapter 2.

FIGURE 1.2
TYPES OF MAIN IDEAS

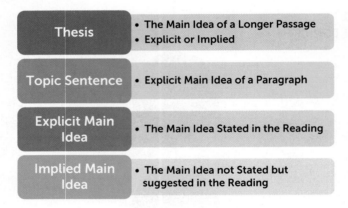

Thesis	• The Main Idea of a Longer Passage • Explicit or Implied
Topic Sentence	• Explicit Main Idea of a Paragraph
Explicit Main Idea	• The Main Idea Stated in the Reading
Implied Main Idea	• The Main Idea not Stated but suggested in the Reading

THESIS STATEMENT

The most important point, or thesis, is the key component to find in a reading; not surprisingly, it is the key component to consider in your writing as well. The thesis is strongly influenced by topic, audience, and purpose. The thesis can be stated directly in the writing, or it can be implied. Your thesis should refer to both your topic and the assertion, or point, you want to make about your topic. A strong thesis statement is both focused and limited. This means your assertion is focused and the topic is limited. For example, consider these three potential thesis statements:

1. Education is declining.
2. Online education at the postsecondary level is creating students who don't master content on a deeper level, don't engage in meaningful dialogue with other learners, and don't engage in a direct exchange of ideas with an instructor.
3. Online education at the postsecondary level robs students of several key learning experiences.

In Example 1, the topic, "education," is too broad. The assertion "is declining" is too vague. This thesis statement is neither limited nor focused. In contrast, the statement in Example 2 has a limited topic, "Online education at the postsecondary level," and a focused point about the topic, ". . . is creating students who don't master content on a deeper level, don't engage in meaningful dialogue with other learners, and don't engage in a direct exchange of ideas with an instructor." Linking the major supporting details in a thesis statement is sometimes known as a "plan of development" thesis since the reader is provided with the key supporting points within the thesis statement. In this case, the three supporting points that back up the thesis are as follows:

- Students don't master content on a deeper level.
- Students don't engage in meaningful dialogue with other learners.
- Students don't engage in a direct exchange of ideas with an instructor.

A thesis statement can also be a general statement, as long as the statement is focused. For instance, Example 3 is a general statement. In this example, the writer doesn't tell the reader what the key points in the essay will be; instead, the writer provides a general point about the topic that is still focused:

Topic: Online education at the postsecondary level

General point: robs students of several key learning experiences.

▶ Apply the Skill

Limited and Focused Thesis Statements

For the following thesis statements, circle the topic and underline the assertion. Next, determine whether the thesis statements have a limited topic and a focused assertion. If the statement is not limited, provide some suggestions about how to limit the topic; if the statement is not focused, provide some suggestions about how to focus the assertion. Discuss your answers with a small group or in class discussion.

Example: (Postsecondary training) is a fast-growing area of concentration.

Explanation:

a. The topic needs to be limited: "Postsecondary STEM training programs in the Health Sciences" is one way of limiting the topic.

b. The assertion needs to be focused: "Have had dramatic enrolment increases since 2015 at Lakeshore College" is one way of focusing the assertion.

Rewrite: Postsecondary STEM training programs in the Health Sciences have had dramatic enrolment increases since 2015 at Lakeshore College.

1. E-books have limited use in school.

2. Hybrid education, where part of the instruction is online, is growing.

3. Publishers are taking action to reduce the cost of textbooks.

Keep in mind that in the drafting stage, there will be many opportunities for you to continue to refine your thesis statement. You need to start with a "working thesis" to guide your writing, but one of the purposes for writing is to learn more as you write. The more you learn as you write, the more you will likely revisit and reshape the thesis statement to accurately reflect your point of view.

LOCATION OF THE THESIS

There are several places writers can position their thesis as shown in Figure 1.3. Some writers place the thesis in the first paragraph, so their reader understands the primary point immediately. Other writers place the thesis in the last paragraph, stating their point after the reader follows along with the major supporting details. Sometimes, writers choose to put the thesis in the middle of the writing. Perhaps a writer began the piece with an anecdote or descriptive scenario to offer a relatable event or story to grab the reader's attention first. Later, then, the writer may state the thesis. Finally, writers may elect not to state the thesis directly in the passage; instead, they may imply the thesis, relying on key details to make the suggested overall point.

For now, if you are at the beginning of your academic studies, you will likely benefit from placing your thesis at the beginning of your writing since this placement is straightforward. You state your overall thesis and then go on to provide the support that defends it. Each body paragraph or group of paragraphs presents one more reason to support your thesis. Upcoming chapters will explore further details about the relative merits of thesis placement.

FIGURE 1.3
THESIS PLACEMENT

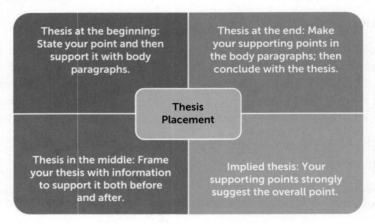

Audience

Being clear about purpose, topic, and thesis are vital for you as both a writer and a reader. Audience is also vitally important to understand in a reading and when you are directing your writing. Who does the writer—you or someone else—have in mind as the reader? This mindset influences a number of qualities in the writing:

1. **The level of vocabulary.** Writers adjust their language to suit the background knowledge and sophistication of their audience. Where the piece is published can often reveal the intended audience.
2. **The style of writing.** Writers use more complex vocabulary and sentence structure with a knowledgeable reader as the audience than they would an unsophisticated or younger reader.
3. **The purpose or aim in writing.** Writers adjust their aim for writing based on their reader. If procedural changes are taking place that Employee Group A would like but Employee Group B would not like, then the communication to Employee Group A would likely be informative while the communication to Employee Group B would likely be more persuasive.

4. **The choice of topic.** If their audience is a postsecondary student, writers choose a subject appropriate to that level of understanding and critical thinking ability.
5. **The most important point or thesis:** Writers have an overall point they want to communicate to their audience. The components of the thesis (topic and assertion) and the vocabulary used in the thesis reflect to whom the writing is directed.

Purpose, topic, thesis, and audience are inextricable from one another; each element supports the others, as seen in Figure 1.4. At the outset of a writing task or a reading task, purpose, topic, thesis, and audience are the primary and immediate considerations.

FIGURE 1.4

PURPOSE, TOPIC, THESIS, AND AUDIENCE

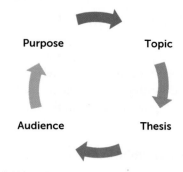

▶ Apply the Skill

Identifying Purpose, Topic, Thesis, and Audience

Identify the purpose, topic, thesis, and audience for each of the following.

1. "An A+ Student Regrets His Grades" by Afraj Gill.

2. A cover letter for your own job application.

3. "There's No Online Substitute for a Real University Classroom" by Clifford Orwin. This reading is located in the middle of this chapter.

4. "Attention, Students: Put Your Laptops Away" by James Doubek. This reading is located at the end of this chapter.

Review

Purpose, Topic, Thesis, and Audience

Answer the following review questions in paragraph form or generate ideas to contribute to a group or class discussion.

1. What are the main purposes an author may have for writing? Explain each type, providing examples.
2. Why is topic one of the first things to consider in reading and writing?

3. How can determining topic and purpose help you to determine the thesis?

4. Why is determining the intended audience so important in reading and writing?

5. Discuss the interconnection of purpose, topic, thesis, and audience.

6. What are some strategies to determine the topic of a reading or clarify your topic when writing?

7. What makes a good thesis?

Reading and Writing Processes

Both reading and writing have processes—sequences or steps as seen in Figure 1.5. Following a step-by-step process while reading yields the best comprehension; likewise, writing following a step-by-step process yields the best writing. Following these methods helps you get your assignments done in the most efficient manner.

FIGURE 1.5

THE READING AND WRITING PROCESSES

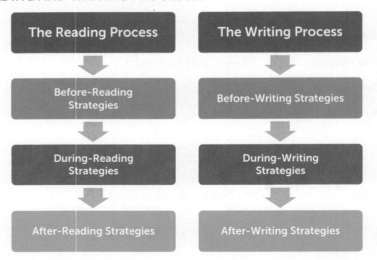

The Reading Process

The *reading process* and *active reading* are terms that refer to understanding and using before-reading, during-reading, and after-reading strategies to enhance your comprehension and retention of information. To be an *active reader*, you interact with the text you are reading; active reading involves thinking along with the author as you read and being aware of what you are thinking as you read. Being aware of your thought process is called *metacognition*. *Meta* means *beyond*; *cognition* means *thinking*. Metacognition, then, is thinking about your own thinking.

BEFORE-READING STRATEGIES

Before you read, consider what you already know about the topic at hand—this is called generating background or prior knowledge. Thinking about what you already know about a topic will prime your brain to accept new information. Next, have a clear purpose for reading: are you reading to carefully analyze the author's argument or are you reading for an overview of general information? Setting your purpose also helps prime your brain.

Depending on why you are reading, you will adjust your speed and degree of concentration. For example, if you are reading to analyze a text, you will read carefully as compared with reading for pleasure in which you could scan—or quickly read—certain parts of the text.

You should also preview a text before you start reading it all the way through, following the steps in Table 1.1. *Previewing* involves looking for key elements that will help you gain a preliminary understanding of the text.

TABLE 1.1
STEPS IN PREVIEWING

STEPS	REASONING BEHIND THE STEPS
• First, read and think about the title.	• The title often indicates the subject or topic.
• Second, read the first paragraph in its entirety.	• The introduction often holds clues to the key points in the reading, including the thesis.
• Next, read the first sentence of each body paragraph and read headings and subheadings if applicable.	• The first sentence of a body paragraph is often the topic sentence or main idea. Like the title, headings indicate what the sub-section is about and how it is organized.
• Last, read the whole concluding paragraph.	• If the thesis is not stated or implied in the introduction, it is likely to be in the conclusion.

After following the process of previewing, you will then read the article through already knowing the thesis and key points that support it; this will enhance your understanding as you read.

▶ Apply the Skill

Previewing

Preview the following editorial from *The Globe and Mail* about online learning. Read the highlighted parts that reflect the previewing strategy. Then answer these questions:

1. What are the purpose, topic, and thesis of the essay? Who is the intended audience?

2. What does the author think about online education?

3. How does the author define education?

4. Read the author's biography at the end and note the publication. Is he a credible voice on this topic? Do the author's credentials and source of publication help you to determine purpose and audience?

5. Now read the essay in its entirety. When you are done, consider how helpful the previewing was. How much of the key information were you able to understand before reading the full essay?

THERE'S NO ONLINE SUBSTITUTE FOR A REAL UNIVERSITY CLASSROOM

By Clifford Orwin

1   You hear a lot of talk about how universities and teachers are expensive dinosaurs and how the future of teaching lies online. Don't believe a word of it. The classroom experience—live—remains the heart of real education.

2   One necessary word of distinction: By "education" I don't mean training or even mere instruction. Widget-making (however complex the widget) may well be teachable online. By education I mean formation of the whole person, to which the humanities have traditionally aspired—as have the natural and social sciences in their noblest conceptions of themselves.

3   Online education of this sort may sound good—false economies often do. One professor and a zillion students—there's a ratio to cheer the heart of a university administrator. And that all those students can remain isolated in their cubicles, from Saskatoon to Shanghai, not even having to spring for bus fare to get to the campus? And can tell everyone they got to study with a famous professor (as the headliners of such courses often are)? How awesome is that?

4   No doubt such courses are a boon to many: shut-ins, desperate housewives, the fully employed and overemployed, deployed soldiers, the incarcerated, technicians at the South Pole—in short, all who lack access to a real education. Something is always better than nothing, and I applaud colleagues who undertake such outreach.

5   Still, don't mistake what's better than nothing for what's best. Real education requires real teachers and students, not disembodied electronic wraiths. Once that condition has been met, by all means bring in the Web, too. Especially where courses are too large (as is common in our universities), an electronic component can be very useful. But so-called education without live dialogue between teacher and student should excite no one.

6   My theory of education is simple: You have to be there. I've been privileged to know both great teachers and outstanding students. Neither could have revealed themselves as such except in person, nor could they have partaken fully of what the other had to offer. The electricity that crackles through a successful classroom can't be transmitted electronically.

7   Recently, someone offered me an online platform for my teaching. He was in a position to promise that under his electronic patronage my lectures would reach legions. I declined. I'm particular about my students. If they want to study with me, they will have to find their way to my classroom. I also know that I'm only at my best with flesh-and-blood students to animate me. Inspired by that command made famous at the Battle of Bunker Hill, my motto is this: Don't teach until you see the whites of their eyes.

8   The *New York Times* of July 19 contained an excellent column by the University of Virginia's Mark Edmundson. He explained why teaching requires the physical presence of the students. Prof. Edmundson likens good teaching to jazz. It is inherently responsive and improvisational. You revise your presentation as it goes, incorporating the students' evolving reception of it. In response to their response, as individuals and as a group, you devise new variations on your theme. You don't address students in the abstract or as

some anonymous throng scattered throughout cyberspace. You always teach these students, in this room, at this time.

9   So, it matters to me to know who my students are, to know their faces and names, to see how they dress and what they're reading. I need to talk to them before and after class and listen to what they're saying among themselves. Above all, it's crucial for me to hear their voices as they answer my questions and ask their own, to heed their inflections and mark the expressions on their faces. In my large introductory course, I devote a third of the time to discussion. That's not just so the students can probe me, but so I can probe them.

10   It's equally important to the students that I'm there. They need a real person with whom to engage. Someone to interrogate. Someone to persuade them. Someone to resist. Someone with whom they can identify or refuse to identify. Because education addresses the whole person, it requires a real person to model it. It matters to the students not just to hear *what* I say but to hear the voice in which I say it—the hesitations as well as the certainties. They need an example of someone who, like them, is learning as he goes along—but just happens to be further along than they are.

11   Live education is expensive, you say? The best things in life tend to be.

Clifford Orwin: a political science professor at the University of Toronto and a distinguished fellow at Stanford University's Hoover Institute. Professor Orwin holds an M.A and a Ph.D. in Political Philosophy from Harvard University and has taught for more than 25 years.

Source: Orwin, Clifford. "There's No Online Substitute for a Real University Classroom." *The Globe and Mail*, 18 Aug. 2012, www.theglobeandmail.com/commentary/theres-no-online-substitute-for-a-real-university-classroom/article4487214/. Reproduced by permission of the author.

DURING-READING STRATEGIES AND ACTIVE READING

During the reading process, you should read actively. *Active reading* involves the following strategies:

- turning headings into questions to focus your reading
- answering questions posed by you, your instructor, or another source (these questions are referred to as *guide questions*)
- writing notes in the margin while reading, including any questions you may have (this is called *annotating*)
- underlining key points (this is called *text marking*)

Also, as an active reader you will use metacognition or metacomprehension, thinking about what you are thinking, to carefully monitor comprehension as you read—asking yourself, "Am I understanding what I'm reading?" If there is a lapse in comprehension, you may reread or slow down. Jot down notes when you come across any confusing passages.

MARKING AND ANNOTATING A TEXT

Part of being an active reader involves marking the text and annotating in the margins. This strategy is effective since it focuses your attention while you are reading for key points. In addition, the annotations in the margins function as notes that you can transcribe and refine after you read. There are no set rules for annotating and marking the text. With practice, you will find the method that works best for you.

If you are unsure where to start with text marking, follow this simple method: underline key points, circle key terms or definitions, and number major supporting details or highlight them. You can refine what works for you by using highlighters if that helps clarify the relationship between ideas. Then, write brief notes in the margins restating main points and inserting your ideas or questions as well. Another strategy for guiding your reading and emphasizing key points is to create guide questions by turning the title or headings into questions. If there are no headings, pose a question of your own and read to answer the question. Then, underline the answer(s) to the question in the text and write the key point(s) in the margin.

Here is a subsection from "There's No Online Substitute for a Real University Classroom" by Clifford Orwin. Take a look at how one writer has marked and annotated the essay:

Why is online education not as effective as in-class education?

THERE'S NO ONLINE SUBSTITUTE FOR A REAL UNIVERSITY CLASSROOM

Thesis: real education happens in a class-room, not online

1 You hear a lot of talk about how universities and teachers are expensive dinosaurs and how the future of teaching lies online. Don't believe a word of it. The classroom experience—live— remains the heart of real education.

*Author's definition of education: forming the whole person. What does that mean? *will need to ask in class*

2 One necessary word of distinction: By "education" I don't mean training or even mere instruction. Widget-making (however complex the widget) may well be teachable online. By education I mean formation of the whole person, to which the humanities have traditionally aspired—as have the natural and social sciences in their noblest conceptions of themselves.

Exaggeration and sarcasm; author seems to be condescending to those who run universities

3 Online education of this sort may sound good—false economies often do. One professor and a zillion students—there's a ratio to cheer the heart of a university administrator. And that all those students can remain isolated in their cubicles, from Saskatoon to Shanghai, not even having to spring for bus fare to get to the campus? And can tell everyone they got to study with a famous professor (as the headliners of such courses often are)? How awesome is that?

Misperceptions of the value of online education: author doesn't think that saving transporta-tion fees and being exposed to famous professors only from a distance are worthy benefits of online education—I agree!

—more sarcasm

---

4   No doubt such courses are a boon to many: shut-ins, desperate housewives, the fully employed and overemployed, deployed soldiers, the incarcerated, technicians at the South Pole—in short, all who lack access to a real education. Something is always better than nothing, and I applaud colleagues who undertake such outreach.

Author thinks online education is helpful only to those without access to in-class education

5   Still, don't mistake what's better than nothing for what's best. Real education requires real teachers and students, not disembodied electronic wraiths. Once that condition has been met, by all means bring in the Web, too. Especially where courses are too large (as is common in our universities), an electronic component can be very useful. But so-called education without live dialogue between teacher and student should excite no one.*

Reiteration of thesis: real education = students and teachers together in the same physical space

Author acknowledges some value of online educational components—he is being fair by conceding some points

Can't you have live dialogue online?

▶ **Apply the Skill**

Text Marking and Annotating

Mark and annotate the second half of Clifford Orwin's essay. Afterward, ask yourself if you represented key points *and* your key reactions in the margins.

---

6   My theory of education is simple: You have to be there. I've been privileged to know both great teachers and outstanding students. Neither could have revealed themselves as such except in person, nor could they have partaken fully of what the other had to offer. The electricity that crackles through a successful classroom can't be transmitted electronically.

7   Recently, someone offered me an online platform for my teaching. He was in a position to promise that under his electronic patronage my lectures would reach legions. I declined. I'm particular about my students. If they want to study with me, they will have to find their way to my classroom. I also know that I'm only at my best with flesh-and-blood students to animate me. Inspired

---

*Orwin, 2012.

by that command made famous at the Battle of Bunker Hill, my motto is this: Don't teach until you see the whites of their eyes.

8   The *New York Times* of July 19 contained an excellent column by the University of Virginia's Mark Edmundson. He explained why teaching requires the physical presence of the students. Prof. Edmundson likens good teaching to jazz. It is inherently responsive and improvisational. You revise your presentation as it goes, incorporating the students' evolving reception of it. In response to their response, as individuals and as a group, you devise new variations on your theme. You don't address students in the abstract or as some anonymous throng scattered throughout cyberspace. You always teach these students, in this room, at this time.

9   So it matters to me to know who my students are, to know their faces and names, to see how they dress and what they're reading. I need to talk to them before and after class and listen to what they're saying among themselves. Above all, it's crucial for me to hear their voices as they answer my questions and ask their own, to heed their inflections and mark the expressions on their faces. In my large introductory course, I devote a third of the time to discussion. That's not just so the students can probe me, but so I can probe them.

10   It's equally important to the students that I'm there. They need a real person with whom to engage. Someone to interrogate. Someone to persuade them. Someone to resist. Someone with whom they can identify or refuse to identify. Because education addresses the whole person, it requires a real person to model it. It matters to the students not just to hear *what* I say but to hear the voice in which I say it—the hesitations as well as the certainties. They need an example of someone who, like them, is learning as he goes along—but just happens to be further along than they are.

11   Live education is expensive, you say? The best things in life tend to be.

Source: Orwin, 2012.

AFTER-READING STRATEGIES

As an active reader, you will rewrite your notes to solidify learning and clarify the most important points after you read. You can rewrite your text annotations, clarifying the relationships between ideas. Writing also helps to store information in your long-term memory, so you can retrieve the information more effectively. You will search for answers to any questions you may have asked while reading. Furthermore, you will review this material over a period of days to solidify the material in your long-term memory. This method of spaced practice has been proven to help in the retention and recall of information.

▶ Apply the Skill

Practising After-Reading Strategies

Look back at the mark-ups you made in the previous Apply the Skill activity and do the following:

1. Rewrite any points you wrote down, but try using different words.

2. Define any terms you may not have understood while reading the passage.

3. Determine and write down potential answers to questions you wrote about the passage.

Table 1.2 summarizes the steps in the reading process.

TABLE 1.2
STEPS IN THE READING PROCESS

BEFORE	DURING	AFTER
Generate prior knowledge	Read to answer questions	Rewrite notes
Set a purpose for reading	Mark text	Define unknown terms
Preview	Monitor your comprehension	Answer questions
	Take notes	Review regularly

The Writing Process

Just as effective reading relies on strategies that enhance comprehension and aid learning, so does writing. The foremost writing strategy is known as the *writing process*, a term that acknowledges the multiple steps involved in writing well.

The *writing process* refers to understanding and using before-, during-, and after-writing strategies for optimum development of your writing.

FIGURE 1.6

STEPS IN THE WRITING PROCESS

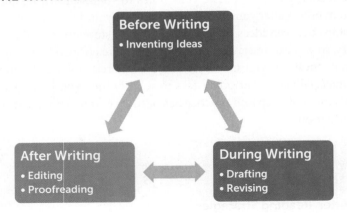

The writing process has three steps, as shown in Figure 1.6. Paying attention to each of these steps improves your writing. This process is *recursive,* which means that you can revisit stages as you work on your writing. For example, you may want to revisit the drafting stage even when you have reached the revision stage if you determine you need to develop your ideas further. By following these steps, you will decrease the likelihood of *writer's block*—the frustrating experience of not knowing what to write.

BEFORE WRITING: INVENTION

The first step in the writing process is generating ideas, often called *prewriting* or *invention. Prewriting* involves generating ideas following a number of possible techniques. The purpose of the prewriting stage is to come up with ideas without being distracted by spelling, grammar, or even the coherence—how ideas relate to one another—of your writing. Prewriting functions to generate ideas and shorten the time thinking about what to write. Prewriting can also involve organizing your best ideas prior to transcribing them into sentence form. Here are some popular prewriting techniques: freewriting, journalling, outlining, and graphic organizing.

1. FREEWRITING

Freewriting involves writing for a fixed period of time about a general topic without lifting your pen or taking your fingers off the keyboard. After the fixed period of time is over, read what you've written to see if there are any intriguing ideas that can be further developed.

2. JOURNALLING

Journalling is a method of unearthing ideas for writing by adopting the daily habit of writing reflections or observations. In other words, it involves regularly writing down what you are thinking, feeling, or seeing. Journalling can help generate content for a specific writing task or become the inspiration for a future piece of writing. It can also help you with the difficult task of putting complex ideas into words, phrases, and sentences your audience will understand.

3. OUTLINING

Outlines are useful to you as both a reader and a writer. You can use outlining for organizing ideas to write a summary of someone else's writing or to plan the key points in your own writing. You are likely used to creating outlines for your own essays. Essay outlines help you organize your ideas, and when you create an outline, you begin to predict the structure and the content of your own essay.

Outlining is useful for both generating ideas as well as organizing them prior to drafting. A prewriting outline provides just the bare bones of your piece of writing, which you then flesh out with plenty of details as you draft your essay.

Figure 1.7 is an example of an outline for a short essay:

FIGURE 1.7
TITLE OF ESSAY

Thesis:
1. Main Idea 1
   a. Major Supporting Detail 1
      i. Minor Detail 1
      ii. Minor Detail 2
   b. Major Supporting Detail 2
      i. Minor Detail 1
      ii. Minor Detail 2
2. Main Idea 2
   a. Major Supporting Detail 1
      i. Minor Detail 1
      ii. Minor Detail 2
   b. Major Supporting Detail 2
      i. Minor Detail
      ii. Minor Detail

Creating an outline of a reading is a good strategy for organizing main ideas and details into a summary or to clarify the relationships between ideas in a reading. Outlining will help you understand the key points and how they relate to one another. Your text marking and annotations as a during-reading strategy are fundamentally an outline of major points that you note as you read. For a reading, an outline can be an end in itself. Additionally, your outline of a reading can be incorporated into a piece of writing you construct using the material in a reading. One product is a literary essay; another product is a summary of a reading. You will learn more about summary writing in Chapter 4. For now, consider this outline from the annotation model of the first section "There's No Online Substitute for a Real University Classroom."

1. **Thesis:** The classroom experience—live—remains the heart of real education.

   A. Supporting Detail: Education of "the whole person" versus training requires direct interaction.

   B. Supporting Detail: Online education may sound good and be cost-effective to administrators but may compromise the educational experience.

   C. Supporting Detail: Online education is commendable for those who physically cannot get to campus since any education is better than no access, but is not ideal.

D. Supporting Detail: Ideal education requires face-to-face interaction between teacher and student.

E. Supporting Detail: Education can benefit from technology, but technology cannot substitute for traditional educational delivery.

The key similarity between a summary outline and an essay outline is that they both capture the main ideas and major supporting details and indicate how they are all related. The key differences are the stage in the process during which the outlines are written, the exclusion of minor supporting details in the summary outline, and how the outlines are actually developed into sentences and paragraphs.

▶ Apply the Skill

Outlining a Reading and Outlining Your Writing

1. Create an outline from your annotations of the second section of "There's No Online Substitute for a Real University Classroom."

2. Choose a writing prompt from the Questions for Writing and Discussion near the end of this chapter. Then, develop an outline of key ideas you would craft into an essay.

---

4. GRAPHIC ORGANIZING

Graphic organizing involves webs or graphic organizers and charts involve jotting down ideas in a visual format. This technique is useful to show connections among ideas and is suitable for differentiating between general and more specific ideas and their relationship to one another.

CLUSTER DIAGRAMS

One type of graphic organizer is a cluster diagram. Cluster diagrams are a plan of action for your own writing (see Figure 1.8) or visual representations of the main ideas and

FIGURE 1.8
CLUSTER DIAGRAMS TO AID WITH WRITING

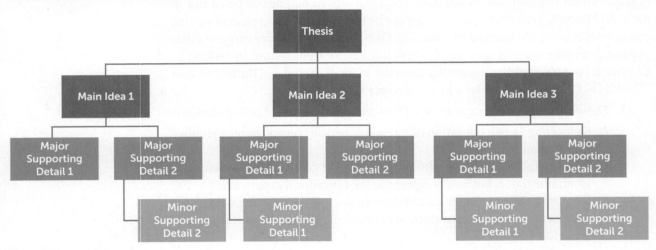

supporting details of a reading (see Figure 1.9). They typically provide the same information that an *outline* would, but they do so in a way that demonstrates the relationship between ideas using shapes and lines, rather than using a linear structure with indentations. Cluster diagrams can help you develop and connect your own ideas for your own piece of writing as part of the prewriting process whether for a summary, an essay, or a written response for a test.

Cluster diagrams can also be used to represent the organization of another person's writing. They improve your comprehension of a reading by visually depicting the relationships between ideas. Consider this cluster diagram (Figure 1.9) from the annotation model of the first section of "There's No Online Substitute for a Real University Classroom."

FIGURE 1.9
CLUSTER DIAGRAMS TO AID WITH SUMMARIZING A READING

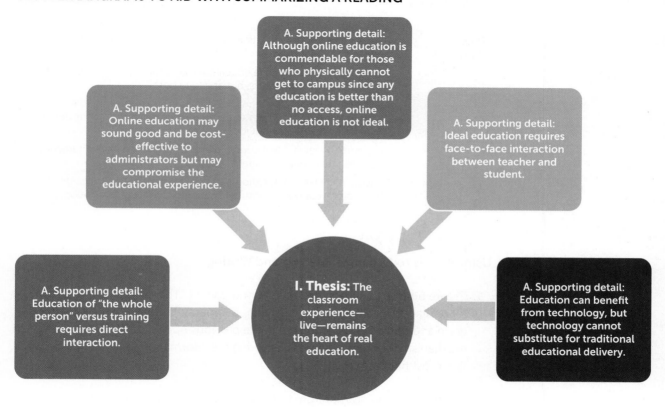

Cluster diagrams can be used for both writing and reading since organization is key to both communicating information and processing information.

▶ Apply the Skill

Using Cluster Diagrams for Reading and Writing

1. Create a cluster diagram for the the second part of "There's No Online Substitute for a Real University Classroom." For help with this task, use the work you've done in the other Apply the Skill features in this chapter as well as the annotation and summary outline models provided. When you are done, compare your cluster

diagram with a peer's. Describe the similarities and differences, and explain to your peer why your particular cluster diagram is helpful to you.

2. Choose a writing prompt from the Questions for Writing and Discussion near the end of this chapter. Then, develop a cluster diagram of key ideas you would craft into an essay.

TABLES

Tables are another type of graphic organizer. Tables are a way to visually represent the information from a reading or to organize material as a prewriting strategy. They can clearly depict the main ideas, major supporting details, and minor supporting details. Here is a table of the key points of Part 1 of "There's No Online Substitute for a Real University Classroom."

Thesis: The classroom experience—live—remains the heart of real education	Supporting Detail: Education of "the whole person" versus training requires direct interaction.
	Supporting Detail: Online education may sound good and be cost-effective to administrators, but at a high cost.
	Supporting Detail: While online education is commendable for those who physically cannot get to campus since any education is better than no access, but is not ideal.
	Supporting Detail: Ideal education requires face-to-face interaction between teacher and student.
	Supporting Detail: Education can benefit from technology, but technology cannot substitute for traditional educational delivery.

▶ Apply the Skill

Using Tables to Organize Reading and Writing

1. Create a table to summarize the second part of "There's No Online Substitute for a Real University Classroom." Then, compare this table with the cluster diagram and outline you completed in the previous Apply the Skill activities. Which mechanism for organizing and classifying the information for the reading do you find most helpful? Why?

2. Choose a writing prompt from the Questions for Writing and Discussion near the end of this chapter. Then, develop a table containing the ideas you would craft into an essay. Next, compare this table with the cluster diagram and outline you completed in the previous Apply the Skill activities. Which mechanism for organizing and classifying the information for the reading do you find most helpful? Why?

CHOOSING METHODS OF PREWRITING

When prewriting, choose a technique based on what works best for you and that will lend itself to your purpose, topic, thesis, and audience:

- If you are writing a narrative in chronological order, you may choose an outline to arrange ideas in sequence.

- If you are writing a descriptive passage, you may find freewriting or journaling to generate sensory details will work best.
- If you are writing a cause/effect paper, you may prefer to use a cluster diagram, showing the relationship between causes and their effects.

▶ Apply the Skill

Choosing Prewriting Methods

Identify and engage in the best prewriting technique for each of the following writing tasks:

1. A description of what you see when you look out the nearest window

2. An essay that asks you to agree or disagree with Clifford Orwin's essay, "There's No Online Substitute for a Real University Classroom"

3. A critique of the last movie or television show you watched

4. A comparison essay on a topic of your own choosing

5. A history essay on the causes and effects of the Cold War

DURING WRITING: DRAFTING AND REVISION

In this stage of the writing process, you are crafting your paragraphs and revising for content (what you are writing about) as well as form (how you write).

DRAFTING

Drafting involves putting ideas down in sentence format. After you have outlined or organized your ideas in the prewriting stage, you will craft these ideas into unified and coherent paragraphs. A *unified* paragraph is one in which all sentences focus on one central idea. A *coherent* paragraph is one that logically takes its readers from one point to the next, usually with the help of repetition and transition words. You will learn more about unity and coherence in Chapter 2.

▶ Apply the Skill

Drafting

Write a draft of one body paragraph that corresponds to one or more of the writing tasks described in the previous Apply the Skill activity.

REVISING

The third step of the writing process is revising. *Revision* involves honing your ideas, and improving your points and their support to better reflect your thoughts in a more concise and precise way. Figure 1.10 indicates three key areas of revision:

1. revising content, which involves adding, cutting, or changing content;

2. revising organization, which involves moving content around; and
3. revising language, which involves changing specific word choices or phrases to ensure they indicate the appropriate tone or attitude.

FIGURE 1.10
REVISION

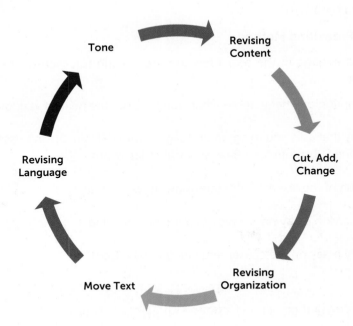

DRAFTING AND REVISING CHECKLIST

As you revise your writing and move through the drafting, revising, and editing and proofreading stages, it is worthwhile to use a checklist. Better still, use a checklist for each drafting stage. For example, if you plan to create three drafts, use checklists that become increasingly specific.

Another useful method of improving your drafts is to use peer review. Peer review means that another writer will provide feedback on your writing. If you are reading a peer's work or if she is reading your draft, follow a checklist to focus the review. Of course, the checklist needs to pertain to the assignment and will need to be customized to suit your aims. However, a general checklist can be helpful in earlier drafting states.

Figure 1.11 is an example of a checklist that can be used by you as a writer or by a peer reviewer in the drafting and revising stages.

▶ Apply the Skill

Revising

Revise one of the paragraphs you wrote in the previous Apply the Skill activities. Follow the revision checklist and try to make revisions corresponding to at least three of the items on the checklist. When you are done, write another paragraph that describes the specific changes you made and how you think they improve the overall quality of your paragraph.

FIGURE 1.11
CHECKLIST FOR DRAFTING AND REVISING

☑ **Purpose:** What is the writer's purpose?

☑ **Topic:** Is the topic of the essay or paragraph limited?

☑ **Thesis:** Is the thesis focused?

☑ **Audience:** Who is the audience?

☑ **Title:** Does the title hint at the thesis but not give it away? Does the title engage the reader?

☑ **Introduction:** Is the introduction effective at capturing the reader's attention?

☑ **Body Paragraphs:** Does each body paragraph have a clear main idea, whether stated or implied?

☑ **Content:** Are the supporting details clear and effective?

☑ **Subtopic Sentences/Unity:** Do the subtopic sentences, or major supporting details, directly relate to the topic sentence or implied main idea?

☑ **Transition Words/Phrases/Coherence:** Do the supporting points in the body paragraphs connect together logically and flow coherently?

☑ **Conclusion:** Is the concluding paragraph effective at ending the essay? Does it encourage the reader to continue thinking about the topic?

☑ **Sentence Structure:** Are sentence structure choices varied and appropriate for the purpose, topic, thesis, and audience?

☑ **Language Choice:** Are the word choices appropriate for the purpose, topic, thesis, and audience?

☑ **Tone:** Do language choices reflect the writer's underlying attitude (tone) appropriately? Is this tone appropriate for the purpose, topic, thesis, and audience?

☑ **Style:** Does the writer use a style of writing that appropriately reflects the purpose, topic, thesis, and audience?

☑ **Add your own ideas:**

Your instructor may provide guidance for reviewing your essay as you focus on your development of ideas. Regardless, a checklist such as this will help you focus on key areas to improve as you move through the drafting process.

AFTER WRITING: EDITING AND PROOFREADING

The final stage of the writing process is editing and proofreading. *Editing* involves refining your draft, carefully considering your word choices, and making final changes to content. *Proofreading* involves paying close attention to improving grammar and mechanics. Like the other stages, the process of editing and proofreading can be quick, or it can be laborious depending on how accurate your drafts have been and to what extent you have paid attention to grammar and mechanics. Editing may involve manipulating ideas; proofreading helps to put the final touches on your writing by checking for typos and finalizing word choice. Consider the following techniques to help you edit and proofread effectively:

- **After you read over your document from start to finish, try rereading from finish to start.** In other words, begin with reading the last sentence slowly. Then, once you've ensured it is accurate, move to the second-last sentence. Continue until you get back to the beginning. Reading in reverse helps to slow your reading pace and focus on just one sentence at a time, making it more likely for you to catch any unintentional grammar or punctuation errors.

- **Use a word processor to catch potential spelling errors.** Keep in mind, however, that you still need to make a judgment call when errors are pointed out. Sometimes computers identify something correct as something incorrect, and vice versa.
- **Engage in peer review.** It is often easier to catch errors in the writing of others than it is in your own writing. The reason has to do with familiarity. The more familiar writing is to you, the more you tend to lose focus of the details on the page and read what you believe to be there rather than what is actually there. When proofreading for others, the writing is unfamiliar, so you tend to focus specifically on the words in front of you to help put together the message in your head. Therefore, both you and a peer benefit greatly from proofreading and editing each other's work.

As you move to polishing your writing, there are several key elements to consider as seen in Figure 1.12. Again, your instructor may provide further explanation of what to look for, perhaps depending on the skill that is highlighted in your assignment. A general checklist can be helpful as you put the finishing touches on your writing, whether you use it for your own reflection as you consider your product, or if you use it in peer review. As you know from active reading, looking for a specific quality as you read can focus your attention.

FIGURE 1.12

CHECKLIST FOR EDITING AND PROOFREADING

☑ **Word choice, sentence structure, and style:** Are the choices about language and expression varied, interesting and appropriate for the purpose, topic, thesis, and audience?

☑ **Grammar:** Are sentences well constructed, using standard grammar? If the writer used non-standard grammar, is this approach used for a reason and well executed?

☑ **Mechanics:** Are punctuation and capitalization used effectively and correctly?

☑ **Style and Tone:** Does the style of the writing suit the purpose, topic, thesis, and audience?

☑ **Sentence Variety:** Are the sentence structures varied and appropriate for the purpose, topic, thesis, and audience?

☑ **Formatting:** Is the presentation of the writing in accordance with the assignment requirements?

☑ **Citations and Other References:** Does the paper reflect the guidelines of citing sources or referencing sources in accordance with the assignment?

☑ **Typographical Errors:** Are there any typographical errors? Have you used a spell-check program?

☑ **Add your own ideas:**

▶ Apply the Skill

Editing and Proofreading

Edit and proofread the paragraph you revised in the previous Apply the Skill activity. Try using at least two of the editing and proofreading techniques described above.

Review

Reading and Writing Processes

Answer the following review questions in paragraph form or generate ideas to contribute to a group or class discussion.

1. Discuss the interconnection of reading and writing.
2. Define active reading and recursive writing.
3. Describe the stages of the reading process.
4. Describe the stages of the writing process.
5. Explain why it is important to engage in the complexities of the reading and writing processes.

Question–Answer Relationships: Essay Responses

At this point, you have a good foundation in fundamentals of reading and writing: you know about key considerations like purpose, topic, thesis, and audience, as well as applied processes such as the reading process and the writing process. The next step is to carefully consider writing prompts to enable you to craft the very best response to a question, whether in a writing assignment or an essay exam. A *writing prompt* is a question or an issue that you are asked to write about. You will want to understand precisely what is being asked of you in a writing prompt. A careful look at the key words in the prompt can help you determine what form and content your response should reflect. For example, writing a summary requires you to pull out key points of a reading and put these points together in the same order as the reading in a clear paraphrased format, using your own words. Primarily, you need to comprehend the original reading and restate the key points in sequence.

However, some writing tasks require that you go beyond basic comprehension and employ *critical thinking* skills such as analysis: breaking ideas into pieces and then explaining how these supporting points reconstruct to support a broader point, like in an argument. Also, you may be asked to show differences or similarities between more than one reading, or to put together researched information from different sources and draw your own conclusions—this is called *synthesis*. Last, you may be asked to find flaws and strengths in another person's argument, or you may need to write your own argument. This requires the thinking skills of *evaluation*. As you can see, *critical thinking* means going beyond literal comprehension to think more analytically about the subject matter. Some writing prompts and essay test responses are designed to elicit critical thinking skills; some are designed to test your mastery of the subject matter. It is very important to be clear about what the writing prompt is asking you to do in your written response. To this end, it is important to know what level of thinking is required to provide the best answer to the writing prompt. It can also be challenging to know how to organize your written response to fully demonstrate your mastery of the material.

In Table 1.3, the left-hand column contains common terminology used in writing prompts, and the denotative—or straightforward—explanation of what you are supposed to do given the terminology to fulfill the assignment. Then, the second column lists the critical thinking level that the prompt implies. Knowing the critical thinking level expected will help you draft an appropriate response and showcase your best understanding of the information. The column on the right suggests appropriate patterns of organization to use with the prompt. Although you will learn more about patterns of organization in Chapter 3, it is useful to consider now precisely what you are being asked to do in a writing prompt.

TABLE 1.3
WRITING PROMPTS

WRITING PROMPT TERMINOLOGY	CRITICAL THINKING LEVEL EXPECTED	POSSIBLE PATTERN OF ORGANIZATION
1. **Summarize:** Provide main points only. Do not include your opinion.	Comprehension	List, classification (other possible patterns of organization depending on the original)
2. **Outline:** Provide main points only.	Comprehension	Simple Listing Sequence
3. **Compare/contrast:** Explore similarities and/or differences.	Analysis	Simple Listing Compare/Contrast
4. **Trace:** Relay the sequence of events in time order.	Comprehension	Sequence
5. **Explain:** Why? Causes/effects. State your point and provide explanatory examples or reasons.	Analysis	Compare/Contrast Sequence Cause/Effect Problem/Solution
6. **Evaluate (or critique):** Explore the arguments for or against and state the strengths and/or weaknesses of each. This may involve summarizing alternative points of view or constructing your own argument and supporting it.	Synthesis and Evaluation	Simple Listing Emphatic Order Compare/Contrast Cause/Effect
7. **Interpret:** Explain the idea. How does it fit in with other, related information? This essay will require that you construct an argument.	Analysis Synthesis Evaluation	Definition and Example Classification Listing Sequence
8. **Describe:** List and exemplify the important characteristics. This may be written in time order or emphatic order. It may require a dominant impression or tracing causes or reasons.	Analysis	Description Classification Definition Listing
9. **Classify:** Put a concept in a category in which the subject belongs. Explain why.	Application, Analysis	Classification Cause/Effect Compare/Contrast
10. **Define:** Explain the concept or key term clearly and carefully. Define the idea. Provide examples of the idea.	Comprehension	Definition and Example Classification

Keep these terms and their explicit meanings in mind as you build on your understanding of critical thinking.

▶ Apply the Skill

Question–Answer Relationships: Essay Responses

Answer the following review questions in paragraph form or generate ideas to contribute to a group or class discussion.

1. Look at the Questions for Writing and Discussion toward the end of this chapter. Analyze the questions for terminology, critical thinking requirements, and possible pattern of organization for a response. Then, compare your answers in class discussion or with a small group.

2. What is the relationship among writing prompt terminology, pattern of organization, and critical thinking level? Why is seeing the relationships among these ideas important in crafting an effective essay response?

3. Can you add to the table? In other words, can you come up with other writing prompt terminology? Can you think of another critical thinking level associated with a particular prompt or another appropriate pattern of organization for a written response? Be prepared to explain your answer.

▶ Did You Know?

IDENTIFYING SUBJECTS AND VERBS

Subjects and verbs are the building blocks for clauses, clauses are the building blocks for sentences, and sentences are the building blocks for most pieces of writing. In order to create clauses and join them correctly in sentences (which you'll learn more about in Chapters 2 and 3), you need to be able to identify subjects and verbs.

A **subject**, is who or what the clause is about.

A **verb**, which can indicate an action or a linkage, indicates the time of the clause (past, present, or future). An *action verb* (e.g., *run, evaluate, ask*) indicates what the subject is doing or what is being done to the subject. A **linking verb** (e.g., *is, feels, seems*) connects the subject to another noun, pronoun, or adjective that renames or describes the subject.

A clause is a group of words that includes both a subject and a verb. If there is more than one subject–verb combination in a sentence, that means there is more than one clause in that sentence.

In the following two sentences, the subjects have been highlighted in yellow, and the verbs have been highlighted in blue:

1. Postsecondary institutions create a skilled workforce for their communities.

   What is the sentence about? Postsecondary institutions

   What do postsecondary institutions do? Create a skilled workforce for their communities

2. <mark>Education</mark> is important for the development of a country.

What is the sentence about? Education

Is education doing anything in this sentence? No. It is just being described by an adjective: *important*. We have a linking verb, *is*, instead of an action verb.

When trying to identify the subject and verb of a clause or sentence, always find the verb first. Remember that the verb indicates the time of the sentence. Consider the following three sentences:

I receive straight As.
I received straight As.
I will receive straight As.

The first sentence is in the present, the second sentence is in the past, and the third is in the future. Notice the form of the word *receive* is what changes when the tense changes. This tells us that *receive*, *received*, and *will receive* are the verbs in those sentences. When you have difficulty finding a verb, simply change the tense of the sentence. Whatever word changes when you change the tense is your verb.

After you find the verb, finding the subject is much easier. Simply ask yourself who or what is involved in the action or linkage of the verb. Just be sure not to confuse a *subject* with an *object*. A subject *performs* the action of a verb, whereas an object *receives* the action. The exception to this rule is in passive sentences, which you will learn about in Chapter 10.

▶ Apply the Skill

Subjects and Verbs

Select one paragraph from one of the readings in this chapter. Then, do the following:

1. Underline all the subjects and circle all the verbs.

2. Define each verb as an action verb or a linking verb.

3. Write a paragraph of your own, on a topic of your own choosing. Then repeat Questions 1 and 2 above. When you are done, switch paragraphs with a class-mate to verify the accuracy of your labelling.

▶ Questions for Writing and Discussion

Preview and then read the article below from NPR (National Public Radio's website) and consider the following questions. You may write a response to these questions as well.

1. Explain the central argument in this essay. What is the thesis, and what major supporting details does the author use to back up his main point?

2. Based on the reading and your own ideas, evaluate the pros and cons of using technology to learn.

3. The three essays in this chapter present views on what comprises effective education and learning. Compare and contrast the main points of these arguments.

4. In "An A+ Student Regrets His Grades," the author states the following: "We can't
allow learning to become passive. We need to teach students to learn how to
learn." Explain how this quote might relate to "There's No Online Substitute for
a Real University Classroom" and "Attention, Students: Put Your Laptops Away."

5. From your own experience or from talking with someone from another educational experience, compare the mainstream Canadian approach to education
with another viewpoint.

6. Drawing from information in the essays in this chapter and your own experience,
trace where education has been and then explain in what direction you think
education is heading. Will we chart a new course with technology or revert to
tried and true methods of learning?

ATTENTION, STUDENTS: PUT YOUR LAPTOPS AWAY

By James Doubek

1   As laptops become smaller and more ubiquitous, and with the advent of tablets,
the idea of taking notes by hand just seems old-fashioned to many students today.
Typing your notes is faster—which comes in handy when there's a lot of information to take down. But it turns out there are still advantages to doing things the
old-fashioned way.

2   For one thing, research shows that laptops and tablets have a tendency to be
distracting—it's so easy to click over to Facebook in that dull lecture. And a study
has shown that the fact that you *have* to be slower when you take notes by hand is
what makes it more useful in the long run.

3   In the study published in *Psychological Science,* Pam A. Mueller of Princeton
University and Daniel M. Oppenheimer of the University of California, Los
Angeles sought to test how note-taking by hand or by computer affects learning.

4   "When people type their notes, they have this tendency to try to take verbatim
notes and write down as much of the lecture as they can," Mueller tells NPR's
Rachel Martin. "The students who were taking longhand notes in our studies
were forced to be more selective—because you can't write as fast as you can type.
And that extra processing of the material that they were doing benefited them."

5   Mueller and Oppenheimer cited that note-taking can be categorized two ways:
generative and nongenerative. Generative note-taking pertains to "summarizing,
paraphrasing, concept mapping," while nongenerative note-taking involves
copying something verbatim.

6   And there are two hypotheses to why note-taking is beneficial in the first
place. The first idea is called the encoding hypothesis, which says that when a
person is taking notes, "the processing that occurs" will improve "learning and
retention." The second, called the external-storage hypothesis, is that you learn by
being able to look back at your notes, or even the notes of other people.

7   Because people can type faster than they write, using a laptop will make people
more likely to try to transcribe everything they're hearing. So on the one hand,
Mueller and Oppenheimer were faced with the question of whether the benefits of
being able to look at your more complete, transcribed notes on a laptop outweigh

the drawbacks of not processing that information. On the other hand, when writing longhand, you process the information better but have less to look back at.

8   For their first study, they took university students (the standard guinea pig of psychology) and showed them TED talks about various topics. Afterward, they found that the students who used laptops typed significantly more words than those who took notes by hand. When testing how well the students remembered information, the researchers found a key point of divergence in the type of question. For questions that asked students to simply remember facts, like dates, both groups did equally well. But for "conceptual-application" questions, such as, "How do Japan and Sweden differ in their approaches to equality within their societies?" the laptop users did "significantly worse."

9   The same thing happened in the second study, even when they specifically told students using laptops to try to avoid writing things down verbatim. "Even when we told people they shouldn't be taking these verbatim notes, they were not able to overcome that instinct," Mueller says. The more words the students copied verbatim, the worse they performed on recall tests.

10   And to test the external-storage hypothesis, for the third study they gave students the opportunity to review their notes in between the lecture and test. The thinking is, if students have time to study their notes from their laptops, the fact that they typed more extensive notes than their longhand-writing peers could possibly help them perform better.

11   But the students taking notes by hand still performed better. "This is suggestive evidence that longhand notes may have superior external storage as well as superior encoding functions," Mueller and Oppenheimer write.

12   Do studies like these mean wise college students will start migrating back to notebooks?

13   "I think it is a hard sell to get people to go back to pen and paper," Mueller says. "But they are developing lots of technologies now like Livescribe and various stylus and tablet technologies that are getting better and better. And I think that will be sort of an easier sell to college students and people of that generation."

Lightspring/Shutterstock.com

MAIN IDEAS: CLARIFYING THE POINT

BY THE END OF THIS CHAPTER, YOU WILL BE ABLE TO

- Identify both explicit (directly stated) and implied main ideas in a reading.
- Draw conclusions about a reading based on inferencing.
- Assess unity and coherence in a reading and in your own writing.

▶ WHY IS THIS INFORMATION IMPORTANT?

Determining the most important point of a reading is always your number one goal, just as crafting a clear main idea is your overriding goal in writing. Once you have sharpened your skill at finding a main idea when reading, you will also be better at expressing clearly and concisely the key points in your own writing. Expressing the important point clearly means that all the information in your writing functions to support the main idea. Unity, then, is an important feature of effective writing. In addition, ensuring that your ideas connect smoothly is a primary goal for a writer in order to communicate clearly to a reader. Coherence, then, is another important feature of effective writing.

▶ Think about It!

In this chapter, you will read and write about the effect of culture on how we see the world. Here are some questions to consider as you move through this chapter and as you read the following essay.

1. To what extent does our culture dictate how we view the world?

2. How important is identifying with certain cultural viewpoints for our own well-being?

3. How can we better understand and communicate with those from a different cultural perspective?

Now, read this essay and consider these questions:

1. What is the author's main idea or thesis?

2. What is the North American culture's view of time? The author refers to a wristwatch as a widespread accessory; how has this changed with the invention of the smartphone? Is this change a beneficial one? Does it negate the author's point about the watch?

3. Do other cultures have different perspectives on time and how we ought to manage it?

4. What are your views on our preoccupation with punctuality, time management, and scheduling?

5. After reading this essay, have you changed your views on the impact of culture on our worldview?

CULTURAL MESSAGES ABOUT TIME

By Joan Fleet and Denise Reaume

A Social Construct

1   A student who is a "New Canadian" was talking one day about the wonders of Canada. "You know," he said, "Canada is such a rich country. It has education, housing, lots of food in the stores and goods to buy. But the one thing that Canada is very short of is—TIME. Everyone here is in such a hurry. No one has much time to talk. They're always rushing off somewhere because they have so much to do. In my country the days were really long and slow. They seemed to go on forever." Does this observation make you stop and think?

2   Canada is very typical of modern industrialized countries of the world. In its main population centres, the pace is fast and time is of the essence. How many people do you know who do not wear a wristwatch? It is probably a very small number. Getting one's first watch is almost what an anthropologist calls a "rite of passage." This is one of those events that indicate that we belong to a particular group. Learning to tell the time is such an important goal of our society that children are often given toy clocks and watches to facilitate early development of the concept of time through play. Even the name *"watch"* is a clear indication of what we expect to do with time!

3   Cultures differ in their beliefs and values about time. On a TV program about dance in religious ceremonies, a Nigerian was explaining the beautiful, gentle movements associated with dances of the old religion in Nigeria. The movements were very rhythmic and unhurried. He said, *"These movements parallel life. They represent patience. In our dealings with people in Nigeria, patience is a very important quality."* There are many other cultures, like that of Nigeria, in which the concept of time is slower than ours: where patience is practised and expected. Cultures have evolved over centuries and the concept of time has been constructed differently by the various societies. The Spanish word *"siesta"* for example, does not have an English equivalent and yet we all know what it means. The term *"afternoon nap"* hardly captures the meaning of the traditional respite from the heat of the day. We may not have the word "siesta" in our language, but how many people in North America experience that slowing down in the early afternoon, especially in the hot weather, as they try to maintain high productivity?

4   Cultures teach values, including values about time. For you to understand fully your own experience with time, it is important for you to put it into the context of the society in which you live. What has your society taught you about time management?

The Society in Which We Live

5   Society sends clear messages about the role that time plays in people's lives. On some TV channels, time is on constant display and viewers can set their watches to within a micro-second. We live in a culture in which time matters and success is often measured by speed. For many people the few weeks of the year when they are on holiday and can enjoy the slower pace of unhurried living are a welcome change from the fast pace of work and school. Others even prefer to vacation at a fast pace and get bored quickly if there is a lull in activities. Whether we choose to fit with society's expectations about time, choose to ignore them, or fight against them, society has influenced the way in which we all view and manage time.

Fast Is Better

6   A pervasive message from our own society is that "fast is better." With transportation, such as cars, trains, planes, bikes, skis and even roller blades, one of the major selling points is speed. How quickly can they get us from point A to point B? We expect tools to do the job as quickly as possible; office computers are getting faster all the time; touch telephones are rapidly making the telephone dial obsolete; the check-out counter at the supermarket uses computer scans to total the grocery bill; the instabank machine has replaced the line up at the bank. Fast is in and those who do not move or think fast can be left behind in our modern society.

Time Is Limited

7   We are also bombarded with the idea that "time is limited." How often do you see signs that proclaim *"for a limited time only,"* *"weekly specials,"* or *"time is running out."* We get the message that we had better make up our minds quickly, otherwise we will miss the boat! As students, we live with the time limits of tests and exams. The academic testing situation evaluates far more than knowledge of the course content; it also tests our ability to work within time limits.

Time Is Money

8   The business concept of "time is money" directs us to save time because, when we waste time, we are wasting something of measurable value. Office desks are located with accessibility in mind. You may have set up your own workspace at home based on the same principle. Also, it costs a lot of money to be a student, and so students will often plan to graduate as quickly as possible for budget reasons. Saving time is always a most persuasive argument, for example, to rationalize driving the car to school instead of walking, cycling, or taking public transportation.

Source: Fleet, Joan and Denise Reaume. "Cultural Messages about Time." Maple Collection, 1994. Accessed 22 June 2016. From Fleet/Reaume. *Power Over Time*, 4E. © 1994 Nelson Education Ltd. Reproduced by permission.www.cengage.com/permissions.

Identifying Explicit Main Ideas

As you learned in Chapter 1, a writer has a purpose for writing. This purpose may be to inform, to instruct, to persuade, or to entertain, or a combination of these purposes. Furthermore, a writer has in mind an audience to whom he directs the writing. Similarly, the writer has in mind a topic or subject. Next, a writer develops a thesis that is the most important point of the writing; the writing functions to communicate the thesis. As you learned in Chapter 1, a thesis can be directly stated (explicit). It can also be implied or suggested (not stated directly). However, most often a thesis will be directly stated, most commonly in the introduction or conclusion. To think this through, ask yourself the following questions:

1. What is the topic?
2. What is the author's most important point about the topic?

To ensure you have understood the main idea, ask yourself the following questions:

1. Is the main idea stated in one sentence?
2. Does the sentence contain the topic?
3. Does the sentence make sense by itself? In other words, if someone were to read the sentence, would he understand both the topic and the assertion?
4. Do all the supporting points support the main idea?

Main Ideas in Subsections

Just as a longer reading has a thesis, a subsection of a longer reading will have a main idea. This type of main idea doesn't have a dedicated name other than *main idea*. A subsection of a reading is most often indicated by headings that divide the longer piece into sections. Sub headings will indicate the topic of the subsection, and when turned into a guide question, this subheading can direct you to the main idea. You learned about the strategy of using guide questions to locate a main idea and major supporting details of a reading in Chapter 1. If a subsection is not indicated by a subheading, you will need to determine the topic and pose a guide question based on this topic. Like a thesis, a main idea of a subsection can be explicit or implied. When you preview, you take note of sub headings within a longer text, and you scan for clues to the main idea of these subsections that, in turn, help clarify the thesis.

Topic Sentences

The main idea of a paragraph, like a thesis or a main idea of a subsection, can be explicit or implied. Most often, the main idea of a paragraph is explicit. A *topic sentence* is a directly stated, or explicit, main idea in a paragraph. This means the writer sums up the point within the paragraph in one sentence. The topic sentence could be anywhere in the paragraph, the most likely place for a topic sentence is the first sentence. Therefore, when you preview a passage you read the first sentence of each body paragraph as you learned in Chapter 1.

The second most likely place for a topic sentence is the last sentence of a paragraph. When a topic sentence is placed last, it is often indicated by summative words. *Summative words* (see Table 2.1) are words that announce the main idea. Words like *clearly, to sum up, in conclusion, in short,* among others, are the writer's way of telling the reader that this is the main idea.

TABLE 2.1
PHRASES AND WORDS INDICATING A MAIN IDEA STATEMENT

IN CONCLUSION	TO SUM UP	CLEARLY
• The point is • In short	• In summary • Overall	• It is clear • It is evident

The topic sentence can also be in the middle of the paragraph, but this is less likely. When a writer begins a paragraph with a question, often the second sentence answers the question. This answer will be the topic sentence. One way to exclude a sentence from being a topic sentence is if it is announced with a transition word that indicates a supporting point. For example, *in addition* or *second* or *finally* are transition words that do not suggest a topic sentence but suggest a supporting detail that backs up the main idea.

Sometimes a topic sentence is stated at the beginning and then restated in different words at the end of the paragraph. In this case, one sentence is usually more detailed while one, still conveying the main idea, is more general. Writers use this technique to ensure the reader gets the point.

Here are some examples of the placement of topic sentences. Most of these examples come from the reading "Cultural Messages about Time" from earlier in this chapter.

Topic sentence at the beginning of a paragraph

<u>Cultures differ in their beliefs and values about time.</u> On a TV program about dance in religious ceremonies, a Nigerian was explaining the beautiful, gentle movements associated with dances of the old religion in Nigeria. The movements were very rhythmic and unhurried. He said, *"These movements parallel life. They represent patience. In our dealings with people in Nigeria, patience is a very important quality."* There are many other cultures, like that of Nigeria, in which the concept of time is slower than ours: where patience is practised and expected. Cultures have evolved over centuries and the concept of time has been constructed differently by the various societies. The Spanish word *"siesta"* for example, does not have an English equivalent and yet we all know what it means. The term *"afternoon nap"* hardly captures the meaning of the traditional respite from the heat of the day. We may not have the word "siesta" in our language, but how many people in North America experience that slowing down

in the early afternoon, especially in the hot weather, as they try to maintain high productivity?*

Topic sentence in the middle of a paragraph

A student who is a "New Canadian" was talking one day about the wonders of Canada. "You know," he said, "Canada is such a rich country. It has education, housing, lots of food in the stores and goods to buy. <u>But the one thing that Canada is very short of is—TIME</u>. Everyone here is in such a hurry. No one has much time to talk. They're always rushing off somewhere because they have so much to do. In my country the days were really long and slow. They seemed to go on forever." Does this observation make you stop and think?*

Topic sentence at the beginning and end of a paragraph

<u>Society sends clear messages about the role that time plays in people's lives.</u> On some TV channels, time is on constant display and viewers can set their watches to within a micro-second. We live in a culture in which time matters and success is often measured by speed. For many people the few weeks of the year when they are on holiday and can enjoy the slower pace of unhurried living are a welcome change from the fast pace of work and school. Others even prefer to vacation at a fast pace and get bored quickly if there is a lull in activities. <u>Whether we choose to fit with society's expectations about time, choose to ignore them, or fight against them, society has influenced the way in which we all view and manage time.</u>*

Topic sentence at the end of a paragraph

Anthropologists learn about the theory of linguistic relativity, which was a movement beginning in the 1800s linking world view to language. This theory was made popular by the Sapir-Whorf hypothesis, which has since been discredited in some arenas. Still, the theory raises interesting questions. The theory states that language influences thought. In other words, how we categorize information through vocabulary has a direct effect on how we think about the world. <u>The Sapir-Whorf hypothesis claiming that words affect thought had broad implications for understanding different cultures.</u>

▶ Apply the Skill

Locating Topic Sentences

Use your skills of determining the topic and locating topic sentences in the following paragraphs from the reading "Cultural Messages about Time" from earlier in this chapter.

Beneath each paragraph, write the topic and then write the main point in your own words. Next, go back and underline the topic sentence.

1. Cultures teach values, including values about time. For you to understand fully your own experience with time, it is important for you to put it into the context of the society in which you live. What has your society taught you about time management?

---

* Fleet and Reaume, 1994.

Topic:

Main Idea:

Underline the topic sentence. If the main idea is stated at the beginning and reiterated at the end, underline both sentences.

2. We are also bombarded with the idea that "time is limited." How often do you see signs that proclaim *"for a limited time only," "weekly specials,"* or *"time is running out."* We get the message that we had better make up our minds quickly, otherwise we will miss the boat! As students, we live with the time limits of tests and exams. The academic testing situation evaluates far more than knowledge of the course content; it also tests our ability to work within time limits.

Topic:

Main Idea:

Underline the topic sentence. If the main idea is stated at the beginning and reiterated at the end, underline both sentences.

3. The business concept of "time is money" directs us to save time because, when we waste time, we are wasting something of measurable value. Office desks are located with accessibility in mind. You may have set up your own workspace at home based on the same principle. Also, it costs a lot of money to be a student, and so students will often plan to graduate as quickly as possible for budget reasons. Saving time is always a most persuasive argument, for example, to rationalize driving the car to school instead of walking, cycling, or taking public transportation.

Topic:

Main Idea:

Underline the topic sentence. If the main idea is stated at the beginning and reiterated at the end, underline both sentences.

4. A pervasive message from our own society is that "fast is better." With transportation, such as cars, trains, planes, bikes, skis and even roller blades, one of the major selling points is speed. How quickly can they get us from point A to point B? We expect tools to do the job as quickly as possible; office computers are getting faster all the time; touch telephones are rapidly making the telephone dial obsolete; the check-out counter at the supermarket uses computer scans to total the grocery bill; the instabank machine has replaced the line up at the bank. Fast is in and those who do not move or think fast can be left behind in our modern society.

Topic:

Main Idea:

Underline the topic sentence. If the main idea is stated at the beginning and reiterated at the end, underline both sentences.

Source: Fleet and Reaume, 1994.

Inferences

You make inferences when interacting with text: when using context clues to determine the meaning of an unknown word; when understanding an overall point of a chart or graph; when anticipating what will happen next in a reading; when using word parts—such as prefixes, root words, and suffixes—to deduce the meaning of an unknown word; and when previewing a text and predicting the main idea and major supporting points based on skimming key parts of a reading. Can you think of other ways you make inferences?

An *inference* is an educated guess based on information in the text. An educated or *reasonable* guess implies that evidence from the text can be provided to support the inference. An inference is not directly stated in the reading. In fact, making an inference requires you to read between the lines and suppose information based on logic and deduction. A reasonable guess is based on reasoning.

A conclusion is a broader judgment that is derived from several inferences. So, inferences can be minor conclusions. For example, determining an implied thesis requires you to draw several inferences that result in your conclusion about what the writer's most important point is. Considering a series of main ideas from the reading's body paragraphs allows you to draw a conclusion about what the overall point is.

To make an accurate inference, look at the supporting evidence and deduce a generalization that makes sense based on that evidence. You cannot make a reasonable inference based solely on your prior knowledge or guesses; like a lawyer in court, you must back up your reasoning with clear evidence for your conclusions. In short, to use the courtroom analogy, a defence lawyer guides the judge or jury to make many inferences—all leading to the overall conclusion he or she wants the judge or jury to accept: the client is not guilty.

In the reading "Cultural Messages about Time," we can infer that the opening paragraph is a statement made by a new immigrant to Canada. Let's make some more inferences and then draw conclusions based on what the author provides in this passage.

Within the first paragraph, the speaker says, "everyone here is in such a hurry. No one has much time to talk. They're always rushing off somewhere because they have so much to do. In my country the days were really long and slow. They seemed to go on forever."*

What is a reasonable inference to make about this passage?

a. The speaker admires Canada's fast pace.

b. The speaker misses his home country.

c. The speaker is experiencing adjustment difficulties.

d. The speaker isn't sure if preoccupation with time is the right way to live.

If you think that all but the first option (a) are reasonable inferences, you are correct. The speaker says that no one has time to talk, everyone is rushing, everyone has so much to do, whereas in his home country, the pace is relaxed. So, it is reasonable to infer that the speaker at least has some nostalgia about his home, that he is having some difficulty adapting to life in Canada's fast-paced society and, as a result of both of these points, he may question if the fast-paced lifestyle is for the best. There is no evidence that the speaker thinks that Canada's fast-paced lifestyle is admirable, despite the country offering many positive benefits.

Now, let's look at those reasonable inferences and draw an overall conclusion based on what we can infer.

Which of the following conclusions is reasonable based on the above information?

a. Canadians should re-examine their priorities and moderate their pace.

b. Canadians need to speed up to keep abreast of modern life.

---

* Fleet and Reaume, 1994.

c. Old ways are better than new ways.

d. The speaker regrets his decision to immigrate to Canada.

The reasonable conclusion to draw from the speaker's reflections is that Canadians should re-examine their priorities and moderate their pace of life. Why? Because the speaker suggests that rushing detracts from some of life's interactions, such as no one has time to talk since everyone is rushing around to keep up with pressing obligations. It is implied that slowing down may help Canadians enjoy life more.

▶ Apply the Skill

Making Inferences and Drawing Conclusions

Look at the following paragraph from "Cultural Messages about Time" and answer the questions about inferences and conclusions.

> Canada is very typical of modern industrialized countries of the world. In its main population centres, the pace is fast and time is of the essence. How many people do you know who do not wear a wristwatch? It is probably a very small number. Getting one's first watch is almost what an anthropologist calls a "rite of passage." This is one of those events that indicate that we belong to a particular group. Learning to tell the time is such an important goal of our society that children are often given toy clocks and watches to facilitate early development of the concept of time through play. Even the name *"watch"* is a clear indication of what we expect to do with time!

Source: Fleet and Reaume, 1994.

1. Which of the following options is *not* a reasonable inference based on this paragraph?

   a. The Western world has the same perceptions about time as do Canadians.

   b. Anthropologists call getting a watch a rite of passage because this means you are inducted into Canadian culture and its obsession with time.

   c. The focus on time is communicated to children, so they can be enculturated into Western society.

   d. Those who do not wear watches are free from the pressures of time.

2. Based on the three reasonable inferences above, which of the two conclusions is logical?

   a. Part of Western society's enculturation is to instill a preoccupation with time.

   b. To overcome early enculturation to time pressure, watches should not be worn.

3. Look back at the reading "Cultural Messages about Time" or choose one of the other readings from this chapter or Chapter 1. Write down three reasonable inferences. Then, based on these inferences, write down a reasonable conclusion. Share your answers in writing, with a small group, or in class discussion.

Implied Main Ideas

As a reader, an *implied main idea* is a sentence you construct summarizing the main idea based on evidence in the text. An implied main idea of a longer passage—the thesis—is an overall conclusion based on evidence. Keep in mind that another person *implies* while you *infer*—these words are frequently misused. So, to imply is to provide hints—writers imply; on the other hand, to infer means to draw a conclusion—readers infer. You are making an inference when you understand another writer's implied main idea.

Look at these examples of implied main ideas:

Example 1: Implied main idea of a paragraph

Consider the main idea from this paragraph from "Cultural Messages about Time." Write the topic of the paragraph and then write the main idea in your own words.

> Canada is very typical of modern industrialized countries of the world. In its main population centres, the pace is fast and time is of the essence. How many people do you know who do not wear a wristwatch? It is probably a very small number. Getting one's first watch is almost what an anthropologist calls a "rite of passage." This is one of those events that indicate that we belong to a particular group. Learning to tell the time is such an important goal of our society that children are often given toy clocks and watches to facilitate early development of the concept of time through play. Even the name *"watch"* is a clear indication of what we expect to do with time!*

> Topic:
> Main idea:

Now, read the sample solutions below.

Topic: Canada and modern industrialized countries and time
Main Idea: Canada, like other modern industrialized countries, is fast paced with time pressure.

Now, look back at the paragraph. Is this main idea stated in one sentence? In other words, is there a topic sentence? No, in this case, the main idea is implied.

Example 2: Implied thesis

What is the thesis of the reading "Cultural Messages about Time"?

First, answer this question: What is the topic of the reading? The answer is "culture and messages about time." Now, ask yourself, what is the author's most important point about the topic? The answer, which is the thesis, is that *Canadian culture sends the message that time is important and in short supply.*

Can you find that thesis stated in one sentence in the reading? If the thesis is stated in one sentence in the reading, it is explicit; if it is not stated in one sentence in the reading, it is implicit or implied. While this message is clearly suggested, it is not stated directly; therefore, the thesis is implied.

---

* Fleet and Reaume, 1994.

Constructing an Implied Main Idea

There are three methods to constructing a sentence that captures a writer's implied main idea. *Method 1* is making an existing sentence in the text more complete, usually by adding a word or a phrase that is the topic. *Method 2* is combining two sentences from the text, usually in the case of contrast patterns of organization; part of the point is in one sentence, and the rest of the point is in another sentence. Combining these sentences states the complete thought. *Method 3* is making a summary sentence based on all the supporting details. All three methods rely on your skill of making inferences. The method you use depends on the degree of information the writer provides. Regardless, Method 3—a summary sentence—will always work. Refer to Figure 2.1.

FIGURE 2.1
IMPLIED MAIN IDEA METHODS

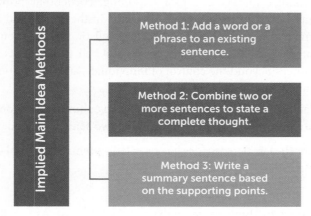

Implied Main Idea Methods

Method 1: Add a word or a phrase to an existing sentence.

Method 2: Combine two or more sentences to state a complete thought.

Method 3: Write a summary sentence based on the supporting points.

METHOD 1: ADD A WORD OR PHRASE TO AN EXISTING SENTENCE

First, a writer may almost state a main idea but leave out critical information like the topic, for example. Instead, the writer may use a pronoun to refer to the topic. To state the main idea, then, you would insert the topic or missing word or words. This is method 1.

Method 1: This comes from Paragraph 3 of "How High Is Your Horizon?"

These scientists were not the first to be fascinated by horizon lines. Several years ago, a team of cross-cultural psychologists, led by Takahiko Masuda, analyzed hundreds of paintings from East Asian and Western cultures between 1500 and 1900. They found that, in landscape art, East Asian paintings consistently had higher horizons.*

Here, you add information to the last sentence and replace "they," a pronoun, with what it replaces; in other words, add "cross-cultural psychologists." Why? Because the

---

* Jackson and White, 2014.

topic of the paragraph is cross-cultural psychologists and analysis of East Asian paintings and horizons. So, the implied main idea is:

> Cross-cultural psychologists found that East Asian paintings consistently had higher horizons.

METHOD 2: COMBINE TWO SENTENCES

Sometimes, especially when the organizational pattern is contrast, the writer may state the main idea in two sentences in the passage rather than one. Method 2, then, requires that you combine these two sentences.

Method 2: This comes from Paragraph 5 of "How High Is Your Horizon?"

> <u>Research over the last two decades has revealed systematic cultural differences in cognitive processes across cultures</u>—and some of the most striking differences are between adults from Western and East Asian cultures. <u>Westerners tend to think more analytically, while East Asians think more holistically.</u> Analytic thinking is marked by logical reasoning, a belief that individuals and their attributes are the primary cause of events in the world, and a focus on objects in the foreground of a visual scene. Holistic thinking, on the other hand, is characterized by dialectical reasoning, a belief that events are caused by external forces beyond the control of individuals, and a focus on the background elements of a visual scene.*

This paragraph contrasts Western and East Asian cultural impact on cognitive processes. So, to state the implied main idea, combine two sentences (underlined above):

> Research over the last two decades has revealed systematic cultural differences in cognitive processes

and

> Westerners tend to think more analytically, while East Asians think more holistically.

So the main idea is:

> Research has revealed systematic cultural differences in cognitive processes in which Westerners think more analytically, whereas East Asians think more holistically.

Note in this example that the pattern of organization is contrast. Notice the transition words and phrases that show contrast: *differences, between, while, on the other hand.*

METHOD 3: A SUMMARY SENTENCE

The third and most universal method is creating a summary sentence based on the supporting details and what they all together demonstrate. So, when in doubt, use Method 3. If your thought process is correct, your main idea summary sentence will succinctly state the overall point.

Method 3: This comes from Paragraph 1 of "How High Is Your Horizon?"

> Not long ago, on an ordinary school day in Japan, a team of researchers crammed themselves into a first-grade classroom. They passed out art supplies to the

---

* Jackson and White, 2014.

students, along with some simple instructions: Draw a landscape, including at least a house, a tree, a person, and a horizon. The children had 30 minutes to complete their drawings.*

In this example, the author provides a list describing steps in the research process. The thought pattern is sequence since the points need to be in this order to make sense (steps over time). So, using Method 3, summarize in a sentence the overall point. Your wording may be different from another's, but the main idea will be the same. Here is one way of stating the implied main idea using Method 3:

Researchers did a study in Japan with children who were tasked with drawing a landscape within 30 minutes.

Keep in mind the following about implied main ideas:

- Determine the topic and formulate a question: What is the author's most important point about the topic? The answer will be the main idea.
- Look for summative words that may indicate the main idea (see Table 2.1)
- When you see a contrast pattern, consider the possibility of using Method 2.
- Since a main idea is a sentence, begin with *there are* or *there is* to ensure your statement is a complete thought.
- When in doubt, use Method 3.

▶ Apply the Skill

Implied Thesis and Explicit Thesis

1. Look back at the thesis for "Cultural Messages about Time."

   Canadian culture sends the message that time is important and in short supply.

   Return to the reading and determine which method for constructing an implied main idea was used for this thesis statement.

2. Choose a reading from this chapter or another reading in this book and determine the following:

   a. What is the thesis of the reading?

   b. Is the thesis directly stated or implied?

   c. If the thesis is implied, analyze what method you used to construct the main idea: Method 1, Method 2, or Method 3.

   Share your answers in writing, with a small group, or in class discussion.

3. Read the following article about culture and thought. Then, complete the following activities.

   a. What is the main idea of the whole reading? Is the thesis directly stated or implied? If it is implied, what method did you use to construct the main idea statement?

   b. What is the topic and the main idea for each body paragraph? Is the main idea directly stated in a topic sentence or is it implied? If it is implied, what method did you use to construct the main idea statement? (Follow the process from the preceding section, "Constructing an Implied Main Idea," where we analyzed Paragraphs 1, 3, and 5)

---

* Jackson and White, 2014.

HOW HIGH IS YOUR HORIZON?
Landscape drawings reflect cultural habits of thought.

by Steven Jackson and Lawrence T. White

1   Not long ago, on an ordinary school day in Japan, a team of researchers crammed themselves into a first-grade classroom. They passed out art supplies to the students, along with some simple instructions: Draw a landscape, including at least a house, a tree, a person, and a horizon. The children had 30 minutes to complete their drawings.

2   Meanwhile, on the other side of the world, the same scene played out in a Canadian classroom. The teacher halted the lesson and the children dutifully set to work on their landscapes. Exactly 30 minutes later, the researchers gathered the artwork and left. After the classroom visit, they analyzed the drawings with an eye for one detail: Where was the horizon line? They repeated the artwork assignment for students in grades 2 through 6, always carefully measuring the placement of the horizon on the page.

3   These scientists were not the first to be fascinated by horizon lines. Several years ago, a team of cross-cultural psychologists, led by Takahiko Masuda, analyzed hundreds of paintings from East Asian and Western cultures between 1500 and 1900. They found that, in landscape art, East Asian paintings consistently had higher horizons.[1]

4   Why do psychologists care about horizon lines in art? To answer that question, we need some context.

5   Research over the last two decades has revealed systematic cultural differences in cognitive processes across cultures—and some of the most striking differences are between adults from Western and East Asian cultures. Westerners tend to think more analytically, while East Asians think more holistically. Analytic thinking is marked by logical reasoning, a belief that individuals and their attributes are the primary cause of events in the world, and a focus on objects in the foreground of a visual scene. Holistic thinking, on the other hand, is characterized by dialectical reasoning, a belief that events are caused by external forces beyond the control of individuals, and a focus on the background elements of a visual scene.

6   This is where art comes in. The placement of the horizon in a piece of art tells us a lot about the culture in which that art was made. If the horizon is high on the page, the field of information is deep, and there's ample room for contextual details in the frame. This kind of visual layout reflects a holistic cognitive style, which is more common in East Asian cultures. If the horizon is low on the page, there's less background space in the frame, and more of the page is taken up by one or two objects in the foreground. This kind of visual layout reflects the analytic style that is more common among Westerners.

7   When the same researchers who analyzed all those classic paintings asked adults to draw landscapes, they found that East Asians tended to draw their horizon lines higher than Westerners—about 19% higher, to be precise.

8   But there's a problem here: Most of the cross-cultural research on cognitive style has used young adults as subjects. As a result, we don't really know how early in the lifespan these differences emerge. That's why the researchers were collecting art from grade-schoolers in Japan and Canada. They wanted

to know if these cognitive styles are learned later in life, or if they are present from a very young age.

9   When they analyzed the children's artwork, they got their answer. Starting in the second grade, Canadian children drew their horizon lines significantly lower than Japanese children did. (First-graders in both countries didn't understand the concept of the horizon at all; their lines were all over the place.) To ensure that drawing ability did not influence the results, the researchers conducted a second study in which the kids used pre-made collage items to create a landscape.

Images courtesy of Sawa Senzaki, Ph.D.

10   In both the drawing and the collage tasks, the results were the same. Once children understand what a horizon is and how it relates to perspective, they begin to make art that is consistent with their culture: Japanese kids make art that is more context-rich, while Canadian kids make art that is more focused on singular objects in the foreground.

11   These studies remind us that works of art are more than just pretty pictures. They're cultural products that reveal diverse ways of thinking and moving through the world.

Sources: Masuda, T., Gonzales, R., Kwan, L., & Nisbett, R.E. (2008). Culture and aesthetic preference: Comparing the attention to context of East Asians and Americans. *Personality and Social Psychology Bulletin*, 34(9), 1260–1275. Republished with permission of SAGE PUBLICATIONS, INC. from Senzaki, S., Masuda, T., & Nand, K. (2014). Holistic versus analytic expressions in artworks: Cross-cultural differences and similarities in drawings and collages by Canadian and Japanese school-age children. *Journal of Cross-Cultural Psychology*, 45(8), 1297–1316; permission conveyed through Copyright Clearance Center, Inc.

[1] By "East Asian," cross-cultural psychologists usually mean Japan, China, and Korea. "Western" usually means the United States, Canada, and the United Kingdom.

Source: Jackson, Steven, and Lawrence T. White. "How High Is Your Horizon? Landscape Drawings Reflect Cultural Habits of Thought." *Psychology Today*, 17 October 2014, www.psychologytoday.com/blog/culture-conscious/201410/how-high-is-your-horizon/. Accessed 21 July 2016. Reproduced by permission of the authors.

Review

Main Ideas

Discuss your response to the following questions in a small group or in class discussion. Alternatively, write a paragraph response to one or more of these questions. Make sure to clearly explain your ideas.

1. Explain the differences between an explicit and an implicit main idea.
2. Describe the three methods for constructing an implied main idea.
3. What is a rationale for putting the section about inferences before the section on implied main ideas?
4. What are summative words and how can they help the reader understand the main idea?

What Makes a Strong Paragraph?

A paragraph is a collection of sentences with one unified, overall point. As you learned, a directly stated main idea in a paragraph is called a topic sentence. The sentences that are major supporting details are called *subtopic sentences*. *Sub* means *below*, and these supporting sentences are figuratively, if not literally, below the topic sentence. In a paragraph with a topic sentence, one sentence functions as the brain of the paragraph and the other sentences function to support that main point (see Table 2.2). A concluding sentence then functions to reiterate or reinforce the topic sentence, if the topic sentence is at the beginning of the paragraph.

TABLE 2.2
BASIC STRUCTURE OF A PARAGRAPH

Topic Sentence:
Transition & Subtopic 1:
Support:
Support:
Transition & Subtopic 2:
Support:
Support:
Transition & Subtopic 3:
Support:
Support:
Conclusion (restate topic sentence in different words):

The same principles that apply to understanding a paragraph when reading also apply to writing a paragraph. When writing, you must consider purpose, topic, and audience and have in mind an overall structure for your paragraph. For it to be effective, your paragraph must stay on topic and must flow easily, so a reader can follow your thoughts. You can connect your ideas in a paragraph using effective transition words and phrases. You must also provide sufficient examples or support for your topic sentence, so the reader is satisfied that your point has been substantiated or proven. For this reason, you need to think through your paragraph before you write. You can use this paragraph structure or a variation of it for stand-alone paragraphs or body paragraphs in an essay. Of course, not all paragraphs will use three subtopics.

Focused and Limited Topic Sentences

As you learned in Chapter 1, an effective thesis has a limited topic and a focused assertion or point about the topic. In the same way, an effective topic sentence needs to be limited (a reasonably narrow topic) and focused (a reasonably narrow point about the topic). At its most fundamental, a topic sentence is a topic plus a point about that topic. Do not announce your *intentions*; instead, state them directly. Consider these examples; which is the more effective topic sentence?

1. Cultural stereotyping is unfair.
2. I am going to write about the unfairness of cultural stereotyping.
3. Dismantling stereotypes based on language and gender is an important writing topic in the English 101 classroom.

Number 3 is the most effective topic sentence for the following reasons: First, it clarifies what type of stereotype is the subject of the statement. Instead of "cultural stereotype," the topic is limited to "dismantling stereotypes based on language and gender." Second, it does not announce but, rather, states a limited topic and the point. Last, the point about the topic is focused: "is an important writing topic in the English 101 classroom."

▶ Apply the Skill

Limited and Focused Topic Sentences

Put a check mark by workable topic sentences. If the topic sentence is flawed, rewrite it to be more focused and limited.

1. _____ Because of my first job interview in December 2018, I learned to prepare and concentrate before stressful events.

2. _____ You can learn from stressful situations.

3. _____ Stressful interviews are the topic of this paper.

4. _____ Capsizing my boat at Georgian Bay one stormy summer night in 2018 made me realize I could rely on my own judgment.

5. _____ Boats that capsize.

6. _____ This is about Georgian Bay and boating accidents.

Transition Words

Transition words usually indicate major or minor supporting details. Transition words can be used within a sentence in order to communicate the relationship between ideas in a sentence. Transition words and phrases can also connect ideas in a paragraph or connect paragraphs in a longer piece of writing. You are already familiar with transition words since you use them in everyday speech as well as in writing. Some common transition words are below in Table 2.3. These words are often associated with a pattern of organization used in the writing.

TABLE 2.3
COMMON TRANSITION WORDS AND THEIR FUNCTIONS

COMMON TRANSITION WORDS	RELATIONSHIP BETWEEN IDEAS
• First, second, third, next, finally, last • In addition, furthermore, also • As a result, in effect, consequently, because • In contrast, on the other hand, but, while	• Show order or sequence or items in a list • Show further examples or subtopics • Show cause or effect • Show comparison or contrast

You will learn more about transition words in Chapter 3. For now, start noticing how transition words function to connect ideas in writing.

Unity and Coherence

In a paragraph, all the supporting details function to support the main idea. This is called *unity*. If you include a detail that does not directly support the overall point, consider removing it or start a new paragraph. Each paragraph must have one controlling idea to be unified.

You can see the relationships between ideas in a passage in Figure 2.2. In a piece of writing, the supporting points function to back up the main idea, which, in turn, backs up the overall topic.

FIGURE 2.2
UNITY: SUPPORTING POINTS BACK UP THE MAIN IDEA

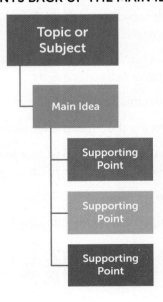

A passage is considered *coherent* when all ideas are connected in a logical and planned manner. In a coherent passage, transition words or phrases function to link ideas in a rational way. For example, when writing, you may choose to organize ideas according to importance—you may deliberately place the most important supporting detail last or first in a paragraph or in an essay for a specific reason. Also, you may choose a transition word or phrase that functions to connect ideas between and among sentences using cause and/or effect words that help lubricate the flow of ideas, enabling the reader to follow your train of thought smoothly.

Look at this paragraph from the reading "How High is Your Horizon":

Research over the last two decades has revealed systematic cultural differences in cognitive processes across cultures—and some of the most striking differences are between adults from Western and East Asian cultures. Westerners tend to think more analytically, while East Asians think more holistically. Analytic thinking is marked by logical reasoning, a belief that individuals and their attributes are the primary cause of events in the world, and a focus on objects in the foreground of a visual scene. Holistic thinking, on the other hand, is characterized by dialectical reasoning, a belief that events are caused by external forces beyond the control of individuals, and a focus on the background elements of a visual scene.*

The main idea is a combination of the first and second sentence; the point of the paragraph is research has uncovered differences in thought processes between Western and non-Western cultures. Read over the supporting sentences. Does each supporting sentence relate directly to the main idea? If so, the paragraph is unified. Do the sentences relate to one another using transition words and phrases that clearly connect ideas? Look back at the paragraph and the underlined words. The transition word *while* shows contrast as does the phrase *on the other hand*. The paragraph logically flows, so the reader can follow the author's train of thought. As a result, the paragraph is coherent as well as unified.

▶ Apply the Skill

Unity and Coherence

1. Write a unified and coherent paragraph using the techniques discussed in this chapter. For topics, consider the Questions for Writing and Discussion near the end of this chapter.

2. As you revise a paragraph draft or do a peer edit, list ways to improve unity and coherence.

Effective Introductions

Introductions in essays often follow a pattern. The primary functions of the introduction are twofold: First, the introduction needs to capture a reader's attention. Second, an introductory paragraph should state the main point or thesis of the writing or hint at it if the thesis is directly stated elsewhere in the essay or is implied. As you learned in Chapter 1, it's often a good idea to consider placing your thesis in your introduction until you become more experienced with different thesis locations and techniques. Also, choose the type of thesis—a general thesis, a plan of development thesis, or an implied thesis. Whatever you decide, consider carefully and make the choice deliberately.

---

* Jackson and White, 2014.

INTRODUCTION FRAMES AND HOOKS

A *hook* is a brief attention-getting device to draw your reader into your introduction and then your essay. A *frame* is a word that describes the organization of your introduction. Typically, the hook or technique you use to grab your reader's attention is related to the framing mechanism you choose. You can also use this frame to round out your conclusion. Table 2.4 shows common elements for framing an introduction and the associated hook.

TABLE 2.4
INTRODUCTIONS: HOOKS AND FRAMES

HOOK	POSSIBLE FRAME
Dialogue	Narrative
Vivid image or description	Description
Startling statement or fact	Cause–effect
Contradictory statement	Compare–contrast
Quote or question	Any frame

▶ **Apply the Skill**

Introductions

Read the five introduction examples below and, in the table, write the number of the example next to the hook and/or frame it seems to follow. Does each example correspond to an idea listed in the table or did the author use a different technique? The first example is completed for you. In Example 1, the author uses a vivid image or description to grab the reader's attention and continues with a narrative frame. Keep in mind that not all introductions will fall neatly into a pre-ordained format.

HOOK	EXAMPLE	POSSIBLE FRAME	EXAMPLE
Dialogue	1	Narrative	1
Vivid image or description		Description	
Startling statement or fact		Cause–effect	
Contradictory statement		Compare–contrast	
Quote or question		Any frame	

1. From "How High Is Your Horizon?"

Not long ago, on an ordinary school day in Japan, a team of researchers crammed themselves into a first-grade classroom. They passed out art supplies to the students, along with some simple instructions: Draw a landscape, including at least a house, a tree, a person, and a horizon. The children had 30 minutes to complete their drawings.

Source: Jackson and White, 2014.

2. **From "Cultural Messages about Time"**

A student who is a "New Canadian" was talking one day about the wonders of Canada. "You know," he said, "Canada is such a rich country. It has education, housing, lots of food in the stores and goods to buy. But the one thing that Canada is very short of is—TIME. Everyone here is in such a hurry. No one has much time to talk. They're always rushing off somewhere because they have so much to do. In my country the days were really long and slow. They seemed to go on forever." Does this observation make you stop and think?

Source: Fleet and Reaume, 1994.

3. **From "Homecoming Trauma: What Do We Really Know about PTSD?"**

Sebastian Junger wants to talk about a paradox. U.S. combat mortality rates have been dropping exponentially for 70 years while disability claims have skyrocketed. The 21st-century army suffers deaths at only a third of the rate of its Vietnam-era predecessor, but files for disability three times more often than Vietnam vets. In part, the opposing trends are entirely predictable: medical advances mean severely wounded soldiers survive more often but are in need of life-long care. But it's the nature of the claims that preoccupies Junger. The American military currently has the highest reported post-traumatic stress disorder rate in its history—probably, Junger reckons, the highest in the world. Roughly half of Iraq and Afghanistan war vets have applied for permanent PTSD disability. Yet combat troops make up only 10 per cent of the army, the prominent journalist adds in an interview, "so the remaining 40 per cent has to be explained by something other than trauma" in combat.

Source: Bethune, 2016.

4. **From "An A+ Student Regrets His Grades" in Chapter 1.**

The purpose and meaning of education is widely misunderstood and wrongly presented.

Source: Gill, 2013.

5. **From "Attention, Students: Put Your Laptops Away" in Chapter 1.**

As laptops become smaller and more ubiquitous, and with the advent of tablets, the idea of taking notes by hand just seems old-fashioned to many students today. Typing your notes is faster—which comes in handy when there's a lot of information to take down. But it turns out there are still advantages to doing things the old-fa

Source: Doubek, 2016.

Effective Conclusions

A conclusion paragraph in an essay is important because it's your last chance to drive your point home to your reader. In a conclusion you restate your thesis in different words if you stated it earlier. Also, many conclusions contain reference to the major supporting points, using different wording than earlier in the essay. Another reason to paraphrase information in your conclusion is to maintain the reader's interest by varying your choice of language. Using the same wording repeatedly gets boring for the reader; varying word choice and sentence structure increases the engagement of your reader—something you, as a writer, should always aim to do.

Conclusions often contain a finishing thought—often referred to as an *expanded thought*—to frame the essay and keep the reader thinking about the topic. Earlier in the section on introductions, you were introduced to the concept of an introductory frame. If you choose to follow one of the frames you see demonstrated in essays in this chapter and Chapter 1, then it's a good idea to somehow allude to it in your conclusion. For example, if you began your essay with a descriptive passage, consider ending your essay with a descriptive passage. If you began your essay with a narrative, end with one. If you began your essay with a startling fact, end with another, and so on. There are no set rules for writing conclusions.

▶ Apply the Skill

Conclusions

Consider these three conclusions from readings in this chapter and Chapter 1. Why do you think the authors decided to end their essays this way? How do these conclusions reflect the introductory techniques the authors use? Do you think these techniques are effective? Why or why not? Discuss your reactions in a small group or in class discussion.

1. **From "How High Is Your Horizon?"**

   These studies remind us that works of art are more than just pretty pictures. They're cultural products that reveal diverse ways of thinking and moving through the world.

Source: Jackson and White, 2014.

2. **From "An A+ Student Regrets His Grades" in Chapter 1.**

   Culture is a problem, and we need to fix it—from the ground up. There's a psychosocial dynamic of not questioning current practices of education. But we can't let this get in the way. Embrace education with all your heart, and remember that schooling is only a small part of the puzzle. The remainder is what you'll have to discover and solve through your own journey.

Source: Gill, 2013.

3. **From "Attention, Students: Put Your Laptops Away" in Chapter 1**

   "I think it is a hard sell to get people to go back to pen and paper," Mueller says. "But they are developing lots of technologies now like Livescribe and various stylus and tablet technologies that are getting better and better. And I think that will be sort of an easier sell to college students and people of that generation."

Source: Doubek, 2016.

Unity, Coherence, Body Paragraphs, Introductions and Conclusions

Discuss your response to the following questions in a small group or in class discussion. Alternatively, write a paragraph response to one or more of these questions. Make sure to clearly explain your ideas.

1. What are the characteristics of a strong paragraph?
2. What is meant by a focused and limited topic sentence?
3. What are unity and coherence, and why are they so important?
4. What characterizes an effective introduction?
5. What characterizes an effective conclusion?

▶ Did You Know?

SENTENCE PARTS: CLAUSES

Every sentence is made up of one or more clauses. A clause is a group of words that contains a subject and its corresponding verb. Most clauses also contain objects and/or complements. There are two types of clauses: independent and dependent.

An independent clause (IC) is a complete thought, while a dependent clause (DC) is an incomplete thought. Therefore, an independent clause can be a sentence all on its own. A dependent clause, however, must be attached to an independent clause; a dependent clause cannot be a sentence on its own.

IC = independent clause = subject + verb + complete thought = sentence

DC = dependent clause = subject + verb + incomplete thought = sentence fragment

Take a look at the following two clauses. Each clause has the same subject and verb, but notice how the first clause makes a statement that is complete, while the second clause begins an incomplete cause-and-effect relationship:

1. Time is a valuable commodity for Canadians
2. Because time is a valuable commodity for Canadians

If someone came up to you and spoke the first sentence, you would understand exactly what he meant. If someone came up to you and spoke the second sentence, however, you would likely ask "what is the result?" or "what is the outcome?" The person has begun a cause-and-effect statement but has included only the because.

▶ Apply the Skill

Sentence Parts and Clauses

Five groups of words are given below. Some of these groups are clauses; others are not. If the group of words is not a clause, write NC. If the group of words is an independent clause, write IC. If the group of words is a dependent clause, write

CHAPTER 02 Main Ideas: Clarifying the Point

DC. If you are having difficulty deciding, try to identify subjects and verbs first. The first one has been done as an example.

__DC__ 1. Although the importance of time differs from culture to culture

_____ 2. People in Canada engage in different cognitive process from people in Japan

_____ 3. In most Western countries

_____ 4. Culture defines the way we think

_____ 5. What your opinion is on the importance of time

Being able to distinguish independent clauses from dependent clauses is important for making your writing clear and complete. You must combine these two types of clauses in specific ways in order to write correct, comprehensible sentences. You will learn these combination techniques in the following chapter. First, though, you need to familiarize yourself with the three types of dependent clauses: noun clauses, adjective clauses, and adverb clauses as depicted in Table 2.5. Each of these dependent clauses has key markers, specific words, that will help you identify them as dependent clauses. Knowing these clauses and their markers will help you combine clauses correctly to create clear, correct sentences.

TABLE 2.5
TYPES OF DEPENDENT CLAUSES

CLAUSE TYPE	FUNCTION	MOST COMMON MARKERS
Noun Clause	Subject or object	5Ws (who, what, where, when, why), how, that, which, who(m)ever, whichever, whatever
Adjective Clause	Describes a noun; usually answers the question which one(s)?	That, which, who(m)
Adverb Clause	Describes a verb or a complete sentence; usually answers the question when? where? why? how? how often? under what condition(s)?	If, because, when, whenever, before, after, although, even though, even if, while, whereas, so that

Here are three sentences from the reading "How High Is Your Horizon?" to help you see these different types of clauses in action:

1. They found that, in landscape art, East Asian paintings consistently had higher horizons.

   Here, the noun clause is an object. Found what? In landscape art, East Asian paintings consistently had higher horizons.

2. This kind of visual layout reflects the analytic style that is more common among Westerners.

   Here, the dependent clause is an adjective. Which analytic style? The one more common among Westerners.

3. <u>When they analyzed the children's artwork,</u> they got their answer.

    Here, the dependent clause is an adverb. When did they get their answer? When they analyzed the children's artwork.

▶ Apply the Skill

Independent and Dependent Clauses

Select one paragraph from one of the readings in this chapter. Then, do the following:

1. For each sentence in the paragraph, identify the independent and dependent clauses. For each dependent clause you find, be sure to

    a. label it as a noun clause, adjective clause, or adverb clause, and

    b. circle the marker word that tells you there is a dependent clause.

2. Write a paragraph of your own, on a topic of your own choosing, that mimics the clause structure of each sentence in the paragraph from the reading.

3. Label the independent and dependent clauses in your own paragraph to double-check that you've followed the clause structure from the reading precisely. For each of your dependent clauses, be sure to

    a. use the label noun clause, adjective clause, or adverb clause, and

    b. circle the marker word that you've used to indicate the dependent clause.

4. Label the subject(s), verb(s), and object(s) in each of your sentences so that you can see the relationship between these sentence parts and clauses.

▶ Questions for Writing and Discussion

Consider the two readings so far in this chapter: "Cultural Messages about Time" and "How High Is Your Horizon?" Also, read the article below from *Maclean's* magazine about post-traumatic stress disorder and the world view of returning service members. Then, consider the following questions. You may write a response to these questions as well.

1. What is the author's central argument in the essay "Homecoming Trauma: What Do We Really Know about PTSD?" What is his main point and what major supporting details does he use to back up his main point? Analyze the thesis as well as the main ideas of each of the body paragraphs. Which main ideas are directly stated and which are implied? If a main idea is implied, what method did you use to construct it?

2. Take a position on this topic: Do you agree that the reason for the rise of PTSD in war veterans is because of "the psychological shock" returning veterans

experience that is "rooted in the vast gulf between the essentially tribal nature of war and modern, individualistic societies"? State clear reasons why you agree with the author or why you disagree.

3. How does the first reading "Cultural Messages about Time" relate to the second reading "How High Is Your Horizon?" Can you draw conclusions from each reading about a culture's influence on perception and cognition? What might be a reasonable inference to draw about how cultures perceive time and how they perceive an individual's place in society? Are there correlations, do you think?

4. Interview someone from a culture different from your own, or consider your own cultural tradition. Share a summary of each of the readings about time and horizons. To which cultural group does your interviewee or your family belong? Does your interviewee or do you agree or disagree with the ideas promoted in those readings? Provide specific examples to back up your interviewee's or your point of view.

5. In the reading "Homecoming Trauma: What Do We Really Know about PTSD?" the author accounts for the rise in emotional and cultural alienation among veterans. Do you think other groups of citizens may also suffer from cultural alienation as a result of trying to fit in with modern society? State your point of view and support your ideas by comparing and contrasting your group with the veterans discussed in the article.

6. Can we elect to join another culture or subculture to the point where our thinking actually changes to that of the new culture or subculture? Or, is it not truly possible to become someone other than who we were enculturated to be from childhood? Take a position and reference the three readings in this chapter to bolster your argument.

HOMECOMING TRAUMA: WHAT DO WE REALLY KNOW ABOUT PTSD?

What if PTSD is located not in the trauma of combat, but in the transition back to modern life?

By Brian Bethune

1   Sebastian Junger wants to talk about a paradox. U.S. combat mortality rates have been dropping exponentially for 70 years while disability claims have sky-rocketed. The 21st-century army suffers deaths at only a third of the rate of its Vietnam-era predecessor, but files for disability three times more often than Vietnam vets. In part, the opposing trends are entirely predictable: medical advances mean severely wounded soldiers survive more often but are in need of life-long care. But it's the nature of the claims that preoccupies Junger. The American military currently has the highest reported post-traumatic stress disorder rate in its history—probably, Junger reckons, the highest in the world. Roughly half of Iraq and Afghanistan war vets have applied for permanent PTSD disability. Yet combat troops make up only 10 per cent of the army, the prominent journalist adds in an interview, "so the remaining 40 per cent has to be explained by something other than trauma" in combat.

2   That something else, Junger argues in *Tribe: On Homecoming and Belonging*, lies in the psychological shock American vets encounter at home, rooted in the

vast gulf between the essentially tribal nature of war and modern, individualistic societies. Contemporary culture's failure to properly reintegrate those who suffer danger and trauma on its account—not just soldiers but emergency personnel and others—is not a matter of misapplied funding or mental health care, but of modernity's inability to offer a communal bond that matches the veterans' intense experiences. Humans don't mind hardship, Junger writes, as much as they mind feeling useless, and "modern society has perfected the art of making people not feel necessary."

3   Junger, 54, is still most famous for *The Perfect Storm,* his 1997 bestseller about Massachusetts fishermen lost at sea, but since then his focus has been on men at war, in the award-winning documentary films *Restrepo* and *Korengal* and his book *War* (2010), all dealing with Afghanistan. Pondering the PTSD claims and his own experiences—including a brief bout of PTSD after he first returned to America in 2000 from Afghanistan, where he was "embedded" with an Afghan leader—have led him to the most personal book of his career. *Tribe* is framed by an event that has remained alive in his memory for 30 years. Hitchhiking outside Gillette, Wyo., in 1986, Junger watched as a dishevelled man walked up the on-ramp from town toward him. The visitor asked Junger if he had any food; fearing robbery, Junger lied and said he didn't. The older man, who explained he lived in a broken-down car in Gillette and had seen Junger pass by, gave the author, then 24 years old, the lunch a local church had provided him: "Just wanted to make sure you were okay."

4   If home is where they have to take you in, Junger now reasons, then tribe may well be defined as "people you feel compelled to share the last of your food with. I don't know why that man put me in his tribe, why he took responsibility for me, but it was a life-long lesson in generosity."

5   In *Tribe*, Junger combines those lessons with not-entirely-random historical facts: the way defection along colonial North America's ever-roiling frontier virtually always went from European to Native; how crime dropped in post-9/11 New York and mental health indicators improved during the London Blitz. He filters them all through the PTSD epidemic, which he uses as a "lens to look at the failures of modern life." The result is jarring, thought-provoking and politically resonant all at once.

6   Junger does not mean to romanticize tribal life, certainly not the endemic warfare, torture and violent death that was as prevalent between Native groups as it was in European-Native conflict. (He's descended from a woman who hid with her baby boy—his ancestor—in a cornfield in western Pennsylvania in 1781 while a raiding party killed her older sons.) But he does want readers to consider its virtues—the way a million years of hominid evolution has suited us to it, psychologically and emotionally—much as colonial-era thinkers did. Benjamin Franklin was not the only one to question why Native children "brought up among us and habituated to our customs" fled to the wilderness at the first opportunity, or why white captives, ransomed home by relatives, also tended to run back.

7   Sometimes observers in racially stratified colonies acknowledged the Native indifference to skin tone as a factor, how white members were accepted as tribal equals in a way Native children rarely were among settlers. For European female captives, whose even greater tendency to prefer Native life troubled colonists, the advantages went further. "I am the equal of all the women in the tribe," one white

woman told a French official. "I shall marry if I wish and be unmarried again when I wish. Is there a single woman as independent as I in your cities?"

8   Tribalism's inherent egalitarianism, its place for everyone in war and peace, compares favourably with modern culture's atomism, argues Junger. Social resilience, as it is known, is a better predictor of trauma recovery, according to studies cited by Junger, than individual resilience. Soldiers find this emotional support, at tribal-level intensity, in a military unit's cohesion, and they miss it achingly when they return home. "Part of the trauma of war is leaving it," he writes.

9   Although soldiers in all First World armies returning from danger zones face the same struggles in reintegrating—a 2015 Canadian Forces study found that deployment abroad was emerging as a significant risk factor in military suicides—Junger thinks Americans face a country of exceptionally low social resilience. Inequality is growing and jobs hard to find: "Instead of being able to work and contribute to society—a highly therapeutic thing—a large percentage of vets are just offered lifetime disability payments."

Source: Bethune, Brian. "New Theory Roots PTSD in the Loneliness of Coming Home." *Macleans.ca,* 8 May 2016, www.macleans.ca/culture/books/new-theory-roots-ptsd-in-the-loneliness-of-coming-home/. Used with permission of Rogers Media Inc. All rights reserved.

03 CHAPTER

SUPPORTING DETAILS AND PATTERNS OF ORGANIZATION: THE RELATIONSHIP BETWEEN STRUCTURE AND SUPPORT

BY THE END OF THIS CHAPTER, YOU WILL BE ABLE TO

- Identify the relationship between structure and support.
- Recognize and use patterns of organization and associated transition words.
- Describe the different categories of patterns of organization and their connection with supporting details.
- Interpret the main ideas and supporting details of graphics.

▶ WHY IS THIS INFORMATION IMPORTANT?

Recognizing the main idea of a reading passage or constructing your own main idea in writing is your primary focus; however, the main idea is only as good as its support. Furthermore, the support for the main idea is only as good as the organization of the support.

Supporting details are facts, reasons, or examples that function to bolster the main idea. *Patterns of organization* refer to the writing structure and thought pattern that connects the supporting details and is reflected in the main idea.

Why is structure so important? First, recognizing structure can make up for a reader's lack of prior knowledge about the topic. Second, patterns of organization are important for comprehension because recognizing structure allows the reader to identify what is important. Third, the pattern of organization also provides insight into the most important point—the main idea. Also, recognizing the pattern of organization allows the reader to know which supporting points are major and which are minor. This helps with effective note-taking, studying, predicting content as well as test questions, and recall.

Similarly, having a pattern of organization in the early planning stages of writing and organizing supporting points according to a logical structure helps focus your writing and greatly aids in coherence and unity between and among ideas. Without a strong structural pattern to unite supporting details, a piece of writing lacks organization and may have questionable connections between ideas. In short, your reader may be lost. Since your aim as a writer is to communicate clearly to your reader, making this task straightforward using an appropriate structure to convey your intention is critical.

▶ Think about It!

In this chapter, you will read and write about topics concerning diversity, policing, and issues that impact both racialized and non-racialized groups. Also, you will think about some differences between Canadian culture and its approach to some complex social issues and other cultures, specifically the United States. Here are some questions to consider as you move through this chapter and as you read the following essay.

1. How well does Canada handle racial tensions? Does the Canadian culture address and resolve racial tensions effectively?

2. How does social unrest in Canada compare with social unrest in the United States?

3. How can we better understand and communicate with those from different cultures, racialized groups, or identity perspectives?

Now, read this essay and consider these questions:

1. What is the author's main idea or thesis?

2. How do Canadian and American perspectives on moral issues compare?

3. Can you categorize general types of agreement and disagreement between Canadians and Americans?

4. What are your views on these issues?

5. After reading this essay, have you changed your view of differences and similarities between the two cultures regarding these issues?

HOW AMERICANS AND CANADIANS DIFFER ON RIGHT AND WRONG

Canadians are more likely to find doctor-assisted death, abortion and gay relationships "morally acceptable."

By Amanda Shendruk

1   We share television programs, movie stars, sports leagues, political organizations and a border. But there's at least one thing Canadians and Americans don't share: our view of what is morally acceptable.

2   Over the weekend, Abacus Data released a poll comparing the Canadian and American moral compass. They found that Canadians are significantly more

likely to find doctor-assisted death, abortion and gay and lesbian relationships "morally acceptable," while our southern neighbours feel more comfortable with medical testing on animals, wearing and buying fur and, only slightly, cloning animals.

3   A particularly interesting find was the lack of differentiation on the question of the death penalty. Fifty-nine per cent of Americans find the death penalty morally acceptable, and 58 per cent of Canadians agreed.

4   Check out the chart below to see how Canadians and Americans compare on questions of right and wrong.

RIGHT OR WRONG: HOW DO CANADA AND AMERICA COMPARE?

Per cent who say "morally acceptable"

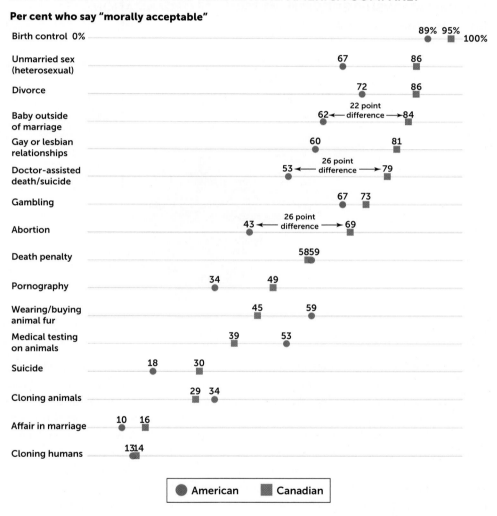

Source: Shendruk, Amanda. "How Americans and Canadians Differ on Right and Wrong." *Macleans.ca,* 11 July 2016, www.macleans.ca/news/how-americans-and-canadians-differ-on-right-and-wrong/. Data: Abacus Data. Used with permission of Rogers Media Inc. All rights reserved.

The Relationship between Structure and Support

There is a strong relationship between the structure of a piece of writing, or the pattern of organization, and the supporting details that back up the thesis. In fact, one is inextricable from the other: there needs to be an organization of the supporting points, and a pattern of organization needs supporting points to organize. Both of these function to support the main idea, which, in turn, provides the most important point about the topic (see Figure 3.1).

FIGURE 3.1
INTERRELATIONSHIP BETWEEN PATTERNS OF ORGANIZATION, SUPPORTING DETAILS AND MAIN IDEA

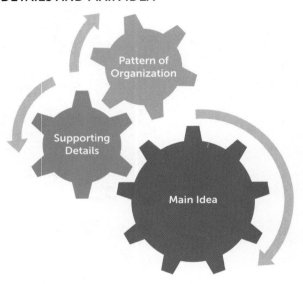

Transition Words

Transition words were mentioned in the first chapter because they are vital for following a writer's train of thought or, in the case of writing, helping your reader understand the connection between your ideas. You know from Chapter 2 that the main idea is the writer's most important point about the topic. In order to prove or support this main idea, readers look for (and writers use) supporting details. Think of supporting details as the structure of a building, necessary to hold up the roof or the main point. Transition words would be the nails holding the structure together and the design of the structure could be likened to a pattern of organization. To connect ideas, writers organize these ideas according to a pattern. The organization of ideas is referred to as *the pattern of organization* and is also known by the following terminology: writing structure, organizational patterns, writing patterns, thought patterns, or rhetorical modes.

Major and Minor Supporting Details

Major supporting details directly support the main idea. If the main idea of a paragraph is explicit, it is called a topic sentence. In writing, major supporting details are called subtopic sentences when explicitly stated in a paragraph. Minor supporting details

▶ Supporting details are the building's structure to hold up the roof (main idea). The transition words are the nails that connect the boards, and the pattern of organization is the design of the structure.

function to support the major supporting details. Topic sentences of body paragraphs support the thesis (see Figure 3.2).

FIGURE 3.2
CHAIN OF SUPPORT

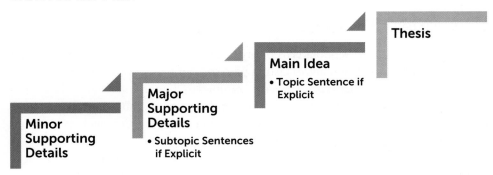

Why Are Patterns of Organization Important to Recognize in Reading?

Understanding patterns of organization is important for several key reasons. First, seeing the structure of a reading helps you understand the main idea, major details, and minor details. Second, using patterns of organization helps you learn information if you lack background knowledge of the topic since you can see the relationship between ideas in a passage and, therefore, you have a tool to recognize important points. Patterns of organization also make studying easier, retention of information more accurate, memorizing more effective, and performance on tests better. For example, if the reading passage you are being tested on is cause and/or effect, the test question will ask about causes or effects.

Why Are Patterns of Organization Important to Recognize when Writing?

Organizational patterns are important for you to consider as a writer because they reflect how you have arranged the information in the passage; focusing on structure allows you to plan and communicate your ideas in a clear and orderly manner for your reader. In addition, using patterns of organization helps keep your writing unified on one topic and improves coherence when employed, as you learned in Chapter 2. For example, if you are writing about causes, you can check to make sure all your major points reflect this within a paragraph. Patterns of organization also help you structure an essay response to a writing prompt, as you learned in Chapter 1. Furthermore, having a pattern for organizing your ideas helps you construct your thesis or main idea and triggers connecting words, or transition words, to connect your ideas. These benefits are summarized in Table 3.1.

TABLE 3.1

HOW DO PATTERNS OF ORGANIZATION HELP YOU AS A READER AND WRITER?

READING	WRITING
1. They help you understand the main idea. 2. They help you recognize major details and how these details relate to the main idea. 3. They help you decide what is important and what to study. 4. They help you predict test questions since the question will be in accord with the organizational pattern of the reading. 5. They help you memorize information more easily since the brain likes organization. 6. They help you organize your notes. 7. There is significant research that shows that recognizing text structure can make up for a lack of background knowledge about a reading passage or subject.	1. They organize your supporting points. 2. They help you fine-tune your thesis and topic sentences or implied main ideas. 3. They help you convey ideas clearly to your reader through related transition words. 4. They suggest how to structure a response to a writing prompt. 5. They help keep you on task by clarifying your backup points.

Categories of Patterns of Organization

There are three categories of patterns of organization: patterns that list, patterns that explain, and patterns that analyze. Listing patterns can be in a random order or in a specific order. Patterns that explain provide examples to support a general idea and clarify this idea. Patterns that analyze look at parts and how they combine to make a whole, and they concern the relationships between two or more entities, such as compare and contrast or cause and effect. These three main categories have several subtypes of patterns. Look at Table 3.2 and notice transition words and text clues (like bullets, dashes, and numbers) that indicate certain patterns of organization. There are other patterns of organization, but these are the most frequently used patterns.

While there are more transition words that may indicate a pattern of organization, they will be variations on the words and clues listed in Table 3.2. As you read these examples of listing, explaining, and analyzing patterns, notice the text clues, such as bullets, parentheses, and numbers, and transition words that indicate each pattern.

Listing Patterns

Listing patterns involve a list of supporting points in either a specific or a random order. Specific-order lists are a type of sequence, whether steps in a process organized according to time, or items arranged in a deliberate order such as putting your strongest point

TABLE 3.2

PATTERNS OF ORGANIZATION, AND TRANSITION WORDS AND TEXT CLUES

LISTING PATTERNS			
TIME/CHRONOLOGICAL	PROCESS ORDER OR STEPS	ORDER OF IMPORTANCE	RANDOM OR SIMPLE LIST
Time order, chronological order Dates	Steps in a process Instructions Stages Phases	Most important point last, first, or otherwise specifically placed Emphatic (emphasis) order also known as *order of importance*	Consider this option last since everything is a list of something Very general main idea sentence Points are organized in a random order
First, second, third, last, before finally, next, then, later, when Dates and times	*First, second, third, last, finally, next, then, also, another, furthermore, moreover* Bullets, numbers, letters Stages, steps	*First, second, third, last, finally, next, most important, least important, most significant, ultimately*	*First, second, third, last, finally, also, another, furthermore, moreover* Bullets, numbers, letters
EXPLAINING PATTERNS			
DEFINITION	CLARIFICATION	DESCRIPTION	
Contains a definition context clue	Contains a point followed by explanation	Describes a person, place, or thing with reference to sensory images	
Means, is defined as, is Colon, parentheses, dashes followed by the definition Bold, italics, coloured words	*The point is, in other words, to restate, to explain*	Adjectives, narrative, detailed description, *to illustrate*	
ANALYZING PATTERNS			
CLASSIFICATION	CAUSE–EFFECT (AND PROBLEM–SOLUTION)	COMPARE–CONTRAST	
Putting things into groups, categories, types, or kinds Contains two or more types Usually contains more than one definition context clue	Causes and/or effects or problems and/or solutions	Similarities or differences among different entities	
More than one boldfaced, italicized, coloured word or term	Cause—*because, the reasons, why, is caused by, is due to* Problem—*the problem is*	Compare—*similarly, likewise, like, both, same, also, just as*	
Groups, types, categories, classes, factors, classifications	Effect—*thus, therefore, consequently, as a result, the effect, leads to, linked to, results in, outcome* Solution—*the solutions are, to solve the problem*	Contrast—*on the other hand, unlike, in contrast, however, but, while, rather than, whereas, although, conversely, nevertheless*	

last in an argument paper. These lists are called time/chronological order, process order or steps, and order of importance. Random or simple listing reflects items or points arranged in a random order.

TIME/CHRONOLOGICAL ORDER

The following example comes from the Ontario Human Rights Commission website recounting a Chilean woman's experience with racial profiling. Notice the underlined transition words.

One account that clearly illustrated this came from a woman who immigrated to Toronto from Chile. She had participated in a demonstration and was arrested along with other demonstrators. When she was taken before a Justice of the Peace for a bail hearing, the Justice of the Peace concluded that she should be denied bail based on a discriminatory assumption that since she was born in Chile and people from Chile are "known" for throwing stones, she must be a public danger. When her lawyer emphasized that she had been a Canadian for 27 years, the Justice of the Peace emphasized that she was born in Chile. As a result, she spent four nights in jail, simply because of racial profiling. The Justice of the Peace Review Council investigated the case and determined that the comments by the Justice of the Peace were inappropriate and he was required to issue an apology. But, this did not change the fact that a decision was made that resulted in this woman spending four days in prison. The initial charges were eventually withdrawn.*

This passage is an example of sequence, specifically time or chronological order since the passage provides events as they occurred in time. In other words, the details can't be taken out of order and still read as a chronological narrative.

PROCESS ORDER OR STEPS

In many postsecondary-level readings, you will find a type of sequence that indicates steps in a process or instructions in a deliberate order. In this example from the Ontario Human Rights Commission website, the author uses language that indicates steps in a process as well as text clues like bullets.

What steps can organizations take to reduce the potential for human rights conflict and competing rights?

- Be familiar with the Ontario Human Rights Code and your obligations under it
- Take steps to educate and train appropriate staff about competing human rights situations and the Ontario Human Rights Commission's Policy on Competing Human Rights.

Having this background knowledge will help organizations act quickly and responsibly when issues arise.

Next, develop a competing rights policy. This policy should:

- Set out the process for resolving competing rights situations
- Inform all parties about their rights, roles and responsibilities
- Commit the organization to deal with competing rights matters promptly and efficiently.

Taking these proactive steps to address competing human rights matters can help protect organizations from legal liability if a human rights complaint occurs.**

---

* Ontario Human Rights Commission. "The Effects of Racial Profiling." *Paying the Price: The Human Cost of Racial Profiling.* Inquiry Report, 21 Oct. 2003, www.ohrc.on.ca/en/paying-price-human-cost-racial-profiling/effects-racial-profiling/. © Queen's Printer for Ontario, 2003. Reproduced with permission.

** Ontario Human Rights Commission. "What Steps Can Organizations Take?" *Competing Human Rights*, www.ohrc.on.ca/en/learning/part-2-reducing-potential-conflict/what-steps-can-organizations-take/. © Queen's Printer for Ontario, 2018. Reproduced with permission.

In this example, words such as *steps* and *next* as well as bullet points outlining the process of reducing conflict and developing a policy that deals with human rights all indicate process order.

ORDER OF IMPORTANCE: EMPHATIC ORDER

This example comes from the Ontario Human Rights Commission website about racial profiling.

> It is also important to note that concerns with profiling relate directly to the concepts of discretion and power. Persons in society who hold positions in which they exercise a large degree of discretion have more of an opportunity to engage in profiling and are also more likely to be perceived to be engaging in racial profiling in the exercise of their discretion. Similarly, those in a position of power may consciously or unconsciously exercise that power differently when dealing with racialized persons. And, because these individuals are entrusted with power over others in society, <u>it is particularly important</u> that they be accountable when widespread concern is being expressed about the way in which that power is exercised.*

This is an example of order of importance since the last point that concerns profiling and those who have discretion and power is the most important outcome, according to the author. As a result, the author offsets this point with the phrase *it is particularly important*. So, the author intends this point to be in a specific place in the paragraph—in this case, at the end.

RANDOM OR SIMPLE LIST

The difference between one of the previous examples—all of which reflect a deliberate order of ideas for a reason—and a random or simple list is that random or simple lists reflect a random order in the supporting details. In other words, the order of supporting details could be rearranged without compromising the author's intentions. This example comes from the Ontario Human Rights Commission website about racial profiling.

> People reported changing their driving habits in a <u>number of ways.</u> <u>Some</u> reported no longer driving a particular type of vehicle, e.g. an expensive car, a sports car or SUV, as they feel that such vehicles, when driven by racialized persons, attract police attention. <u>Some</u> even noted that they believe that particular brands of cars attract more scrutiny because of stereotypes that drug dealers or others involved in illegal activity favour that particular make and model. <u>In addition,</u> many people reported altering the tinting on their car, either by adding tinted glass or buying a vehicle that does not have tinted glass: "I have since gotten a very dark tint on my truck since that incident in the hopes that the fact that I am a Black woman driving a nice vehicle would become a non-issue." (C.B.)**

---

* Ontario Human Rights Commission. "What Is Racial Profiling?" *Paying the Price: The Human Cost of Racial Profiling.* Inquiry Report, 21 Oct. 2003, www.ohrc.on.ca/en/paying-price-human-cost-racial-profiling/what-racial-profiling/. © Queen's Printer for Ontario, 2003. Reproduced with permission.

** Ontario Human Rights Commission. "The Effects of Racial Profiling." *Paying the Price: The Human Cost of Racial Profiling.* Inquiry Report, 21 Oct. 2003, www.ohrc.on.ca/en/paying-price-human-cost-racial-profiling/effects-racial-profiling/. © Queen's Printer for Ontario, 2003. Reproduced with permission.

In this passage, the examples could be arranged in a different order and would still make sense. Notice the choice of wording in the very general main idea statement underlined in the passage. This general main idea reflects random list patterns.

Explaining Patterns

Patterns that explain elaborate on a definition, clarify a general point, or describe something. The passage, then, provides information in the form of supporting points that expand the reader's understanding of the topic. For example, a writer may provide a definition and then back up that statement with examples. Or, a writer may make a point that is complex and then provide further information to clarify the point for the reader. Last, a writer may describe a person, place, or thing to create a mental image in the mind of the reader.

DEFINITION

This pattern is very common in postsecondary texts since one of the functions of an introductory postsecondary course is to introduce you to the vocabulary of the discipline. Notice this example from the Ontario Human Rights Commission website about racial profiling. This passage defines a distinct type of socialization that parents concerned with profiling instill in their children. In this reaction to profiling, parents restrict the actions of their children to minimize the risk of experiences of profiling.

> This is a form of socialization, <u>which is</u> a process by which the child grows up to accept the basic social behaviour that is taught and practiced by his or her family. This teaching provides the child with an understanding of its world and forms the concept of identity. This socialization determines for our entire lives, our every day behaviour, our reflex-reactions, our moral values and how we see the world.*

In this example, the author defines socialization in the first and second sentence and then proceeds to explain and provide examples of the terminology in the rest of the paragraph.

CLARIFICATION

Clarification is a pattern in which a writer makes a point and then proceeds to explain or clarify the point. It is similar to definition and example insofar as a concept is explained. It is different from definition, however, because nothing is specifically defined. Instead, an idea is clarified. Look at this example from the OHRC website:

> The perception of racialized groups that they are being profiled must also be addressed due to the psychological impact of this belief. <u>In other words,</u> the impact of racial profiling, as discussed below, has a social cost whether profiling can be proven to be occurring or whether it is based on people's beliefs. It is therefore imperative that steps be taken to address the concerns raised.**

Note in this example that the author introduces a point in sentence 1. Then, "in other words" follows in sentence 2, supported by an explanation or clarification.

---

* Ontario Human Rights Commission. "The Effects of Racial Profiling." *Paying the Price: The Human Cost of Racial Profiling.* Inquiry Report, 21 Oct. 2003, www.ohrc.on.ca/en/paying-price-human-cost-racial-profiling/effects-racial-profiling/. © Queen's Printer for Ontario, 2003. Reproduced with permission.

** Ontario Human Rights Commission, "The Existence of Racial Profiling." *Paying the Price: The Human Cost of Racial Profiling.* Inquiry Report, 21 Oct. 2003, www.ohrc.on.ca/en/paying-price-human-cost-racial-profiling/existence-racial-profiling/. © Queen's Printer for Ontario, 2003. Reproduced with permission.

DESCRIPTION

Another type of explanatory structure is description. In this pattern of organization, a writer describes a person, place, or thing by providing sensory images. The main idea is referred to as the dominant impression in a description. The *dominant impression* is the mood or tone that permeates the descriptive passage. In this example from Ontario Human Rights Commission website, a person describes how he or she feels about being racially profiled.

> It shakes [your] whole idea that you have become a Citizen of this country. In fact, you are told blatantly that you will never be a citizen, as when he said that because I was born in Chile, it didn't matter how many years I had been a Canadian citizen. You are told point blank that you don't belong here, no matter if you work, you know, how productive you are in society, etc., etc., you will not belong here. And so . . . suddenly you are again reminded that you are an outsider, and as an outsider, you don't have the same rights . . . (M.S.M.)*

Notice in the example that the speaker expresses feelings and describes them. What is the dominant impression? In other words, how does the writer feel about the topic? The speaker is upset and angry. These emotions are apparent from words like *shakes* and *bluntly*, and *point blank*. These words underscore the speaker's feelings of frustration. Description is a common structure in literature but also in prose.

Analyzing Patterns

Analysis is showing how parts fit together into a whole; this may take place when deconstructing an argument, looking at the structure of a paragraph, or in other ways. These analyzing patterns show the relationships between parts. For example, classification shows subcategories of a superordinate (general idea). Cause–effect shows reasons and/or outcomes relating one to another. Comparison–contrast shows similarities and/or differences between two or more things.

CLASSIFICATION

Classification is a structure that clarifies and analyzes content by putting it into types, kinds, classifications, characteristics, or categories, or otherwise dividing something into parts or divisions. In the following example from the Ontario Human Rights Commission website, notice the number of references to category or group.

> Many members of First Nations, Métis and Inuit communities object to being referred to as another "<u>minority group</u>" or "<u>ethnic group</u>." Using this <u>terminology</u> when referring to Aboriginal peoples fails to appropriately respect what it means to be an indigenous person in Canada. Monique Lariviere of Montreal, Quebec explained it clearly and simply when she wrote to the Toronto Star: "[As] an aboriginal person and a member of the Cree nation, I belong to the Cree people and am not a member of a "minority". <u>Characterizing</u> Aboriginal people as "ethnic minorities" fails to take into account the very important fact that her "people have been here since time immemorial."**

---

* Ontario Human Rights Commission. "The Effects of Racial Profiling." *Paying the Price: The Human Cost of Racial Profiling.* Inquiry Report, 21 Oct. 2003, www.ohrc.on.ca/en/paying-price-human-cost-racial-profiling/effects-racial-profiling/. © Queen's Printer for Ontario, 2003. Reproduced with permission.

** Ontario Human Rights Commission. "The Impact of Racial Profiling on the Aboriginal Community." *Paying the Price: The Human Cost of Racial Profiling.* Inquiry Report, 21 Oct. 2003, www.ohrc.on.ca/en/paying-price-human-cost-racial-profiling/impact-racial-profiling-aboriginal-community/. © Queen's Printer for Ontario, 2003. Reproduced with permission.

In the first sentence, there are two classifications. Later, the quote shows further classifications. Finally, the last sentence disputes a categorization.

CAUSE–EFFECT (PROBLEM–SOLUTION)

This pattern is very commonly used. Both causes *and* effects can be discussed, but usually the focus is on causes *or* effects. A subtype of this structure is problem and solution where one problem and multiple solutions or many problems and one solution are typically outlined. Keep in mind that *why* indicates cause as does *reason*; *results* and *outcomes* are effects. Look at the following example for the OHRC website.

> The American Psychological Association notes that research psychologists have studied the psychological <u>effects</u> of racial profiling and found that "victim <u>effects</u>" of racial profiling include post-traumatic stress disorder and other forms of stress-related disorders, perceptions of race-related threats and failure to use available community resources.*

In this example, the signal words *effects* and *victim effects* indicate an effect pattern—the focus is on outcomes rather than causes.

COMPARE–CONTRAST

Compare–contrast is also a very common pattern of organization. Look at this passage at the underlined words that indicate compare–contrast.

> Representatives of Muslim, Arab and South Asian communities also pointed out that one of the chief complaints has been that it has been treated as a community to be looked into, <u>rather than</u> invited to help solve the problem. This community is <u>just as</u> concerned about Canadian safety and security <u>as</u> everyone else and would like to be invited to the table to offer assistance or advice on improving security for everyone, <u>rather than</u> to just be treated as a security threat.*

Later in the chapter you will learn different methods of constructing comparison and/or contrast essays.

MIXED PATTERNS

As you have noticed, passages may well have words that indicate a variety of patterns within a passage. How do you know what the predominant pattern is? Look at the underlined words in this example:

> To those who have not experienced racial profiling or do not know someone who has, it may seem to be nothing more than a mere inconvenience. <u>However</u>, racial profiling is much more than a hassle or an annoyance. It has real and direct <u>consequences</u>. Those who experience profiling pay the price emotionally, psychologically, mentally and in some cases even financially and physically.*

In this example, the words indicate both contrast and effect. Given that both thought patterns are reflected, which is the predominant or main pattern of organization? The

---

* Ontario Human Rights Commission. "The Effects of Racial Profiling." *Paying the Price: The Human Cost of Racial Profiling.* Inquiry Report, 21 Oct. 2003, www.ohrc.on.ca/en/paying-price-human-cost-racial-profiling/effects-racial-profiling/. © Queen's Printer for Ontario, 2003. Reproduced with permission.

main pattern of organization is always reflected in the main idea. Ask yourself these two questions: What is the topic? What is the author's most important point about the topic?

The topic is racial profiling. The main idea is that racial profiling is more than an annoyance and has significant consequences. So, what is the main pattern of organization? It is cause and effect—specifically effect. You can see that the pattern of organization can help you determine the main point just as the main point can help you determine the pattern of organization. Since both are paramount, seeing the relationship between the two is instructive.

▶ Apply the Skill

Recognizing Patterns of Organization

For the following passages, underline transition words (and words or phrases that indicate the relationship between ideas) and determine the pattern of organization. Share your answers with a group, in class, or in writing.

1. It is widely acknowledged that employee morale is inextricably linked to customer satisfaction and organizational performance. Thus, through this link to the morale of the individual, the Commission concludes that racial profiling may well have an effect on the performance of both public and private sector organizations.

Source: Ontario Human Rights Commission. "The Effects of Racial Profiling." *Paying the Price: The Human Cost of Racial Profiling.* Inquiry Report, 21 Oct. 2003, www.ohrc.on.ca/en/paying-price-human-cost-racial-profiling/effects-racial-profiling/. © Queen's Printer for Ontario, 2003. Reproduced with permission.

2. While many of the existing definitions of racial profiling, primarily originating in the United States, focus on law enforcement, the Ontario Human Rights Commission's Terms of Reference define racial profiling more broadly to include any action undertaken for reasons of safety, security or public protection that relies on stereotypes about race, colour, ethnicity, ancestry, religion, or place of origin rather than on reasonable suspicion, to single out an individual for greater scrutiny or different treatment. The Commission has noted that profiling can occur because of a combination of the above factors and that age and/or gender can influence the experience of profiling.

Source: Ontario Human Rights Commission. "What Is Profiling?" *Paying the Price: The Human Cost of Racial Profiling.* Inquiry Report, 21 Oct. 2003, www.ohrc.on.ca/en/paying-price-human-cost-racial-profiling/what-racial-profiling/. © Queen's Printer for Ontario, 2003. Reproduced with permission.

3. In fact, many participants in our process discussed the difficult job that those in a position of authority, especially the police, have. They nevertheless emphasized that racial profiling can occur because of the challenges of the job. Similarly, many acknowledged that many persons in an organization may be doing their job admirably but that others, who are stereotyping, are having a significant impact on the community and its perception of the organization as a whole.

Source: Ontario Human Rights Commission. "What Is Profiling?" *Paying the Price: The Human Cost of Racial Profiling.* Inquiry Report, 21 Oct. 2003, www.ohrc.on.ca/en/paying-pricehuman-cost-racial-profiling/what-racial-profiling/. © Queen's Printer for Ontario, 2003. Reproduced with permission.

4. Stephen Lewis' 1992 *Report to the Premier on Racism in Ontario* on the issue of police/visible minority relations concluded that visible minorities, particularly African Canadians, experienced discrimination in policing and the criminal justice system. Stephen Lewis recommended that the Task Force on Race Relations and Policing be reconstituted owing to perceived inadequacies with the implementation of the 57 recommendations in its 1989 report. A second report of the Task Force was published in November 1992 which examined the status of the implementation of the recommendations from the 1989 report and offered additional recommendations.

Source: Ontario Human Rights Commission. "The Existence of Racial Profiling." *Paying the Price: The Human Cost of Racial Profiling.* Inquiry Report, 21 Oct. 2003, www.ohrc.on.ca/en/paying-price-human-cost-racial-profiling/existence-racial-profiling/. © Queen's Printer for Ontario, 2003. Reproduced with permission.

5. At the outset, the Commission set out what its inquiry does and does not do.

   What the inquiry does:

   • responds to community concerns about the impact of profiling;

   • looks at the effects of profiling;

   • measures the human impact of this practice on individuals, families, communities and society as a whole;

   • considers profiling in a number of contexts including housing, services, education and private security;

   • takes measures to ensure that participants do not reveal names or other information that could identify specific individuals during any public hearing process; and

   • respects the privacy of all individuals.

   What the inquiry does not do:

   • does not investigate individual allegations of racial profiling;

   • does not focus on one type of profiling or target a particular system in society, e.g. police;

   • is not about numbers or statistics;

   • is not another study and does not set out to prove or disprove the existence of profiling; and did not accept anonymous submissions.

Source: Ontario Human Rights Commission. "Inquiry Scope and Objectives." *Paying the Price: The Human Cost of Racial Profiling.* Inquiry Report, 21 Oct. 2003, www.ohrc.on.ca/en/paying-price-human-cost-racial-profiling/inquiry-scope-and-objectives. © Queen's Printer for Ontario, 2003. Reproduced with permission.

6. "Family status" is defined as "the status of being in a parent and child relationship." This can also mean a parent and child "type" of relationship, embracing a range of circumstances without blood or adoptive ties but with similar relationships of care, responsibility and commitment.

Source: Ontario Human Rights Commission, Code Grounds, "Family and Maritlal Status," http://www.ohrc.on.ca/en/code_grounds/family_marital_status. © Queen's Printer for Ontario, 2018. Reproduced with permission.

7. In housing, the Code protects tenants against discrimination based on receipt of public assistance. "Public assistance"—more commonly referred to as social assistance—includes Ontario Works, OSAP, ODSP, Old Age Security, Employment Insurance, etc.

Some housing providers have negative attitudes towards people who are poor. They may take several steps that could contravene the Code, such as:

- screen out prospective tenants based on stereotypes about poverty and poor people

- impose illegal rental criteria (such as security deposits)

- provide substandard housing-related services

- harass tenants

- be more quick to try to evict.

Source: Ontario Human Rights Commission, Code Grounds, "Receipt of public assistance," http://www.ohrc.on.ca/en/code_grounds/receipt_public_assistance. © Queen's Printer for Ontario, 2018. Reproduced with permission.

8. "Sexual orientation" is a personal characteristic that forms part of who you are. It covers the range of human sexuality from lesbian and gay, to bisexual and heterosexual. The Code makes it against the law to discriminate against someone or to harass them because of their sexual orientation.

Source: Ontario Human Rights Commission, Code Grounds, "Sexual Orientation," http://www.ohrc.on.ca/en/code_grounds/sexual_orientation. © Queen's Printer for Ontario, 2018. Reproduced with permission.

9. The Ontario Human Rights System is made up of three separate agencies:

- The Ontario Human Rights Commission (that's us) works to promote, protect and advance human rights through research, education, targeted legal action and policy development.

- The Human Rights Legal Support Centre gives legal help to people who have experienced discrimination under the Code.

- The Human Rights Tribunal is where human rights applications are filed and decided.

Source: Ontario Human Rights Commission, Human Rights in Ontario, http://www.ohrc.on.ca/en. © Queen's Printer for Ontario, 2018. Reproduced with permission.

10. You have the right to be free from discrimination when you receive goods or services, or use facilities. For example, this right applies to:

- stores, restaurants and bars

- hospitals and health services

- schools, universities and colleges

- public places, amenities and utilities such as recreation centres, public washrooms, malls and parks

- services and programs provided by municipal and provincial governments, including social assistance and benefits, and public transit

- services provided by insurance companies

- classified advertisement space in a newspaper.

Source: Ontario Human Rights Commission, Social Areas, "Goods, services and facilities," http://www.ohrc.on.ca/en/social_areas/goods_services_facilities. © Queen's Printer for Ontario, 2018. Reproduced with permission.

Finding Key Points in a Reading

Now that you have experience determining the pattern of organization in paragraphs, apply what you have learned to a longer reading. Answer the following questions about the reading "How Americans and Canadians Differ on Right and Wrong" from the beginning of this chapter. Then, read the explanations that follow.

Determine the following to fully understand the reading:

1. What is the topic?
2. What is the author's most important point about the topic?
3. Is the most important point about the topic directly stated? If so, underline the thesis. If it is implied, what method for finding an implied main idea did you use?
4. Based on this information—reflected in the topic and the main point—what pattern of organization does the author use?
5. What transition words indicate this pattern?
6. Now, go back and determine the topic, the main idea, and the pattern of organization of each of the two body paragraphs. Also, list the major supporting details that back up the main idea.

After you think about this, read the explanation below.

Paragraph 2:

Topic:
Main Idea (underline if directly stated):
Pattern of Organization:
Major Details:

Paragraph 3:

Topic:
Main Idea (underline if directly stated):
Pattern of Organization:
Major Details:

You have now mapped out the key elements of the text. In Chapter 4, you will see that this approach will yield an effective summary of the key points in the reading.

- The topic of the passage is Americans and Canadians and perceptions of right and wrong.
- The thesis is directly stated in the last sentence of the introduction: *But there's at least one thing Canadians and Americans don't share: our view of what is morally acceptable.* The pattern of organization is compare and contrast and this pattern is reflected in the word "but" in the thesis statement as well as the word "differ" in the title.

In Paragraph 2, the topic is the Canadian versus the American moral compass. Again, the pattern is compare and contrast and the word *comparing* in the first sentence—the topic sentence—reflects the pattern of organization. Key supporting points reflect contrast:

- Canadians are significantly more likely to find doctor-assisted death, abortion, and gay and lesbian relationships "morally acceptable."
- Americans are more comfortable with medical testing on animals, wearing fur, and cloning animals.

In Paragraph 3, the topic is Canadians, Americans, and the death penalty. Again, the pattern is compare-contrast, and the word *differentiation* in the first sentence reflects the pattern of organization. In this case, words need to be added to the first sentence, so the main idea makes sense by itself: A particularly interesting find was the lack of differentiation *between Canadians and Americans* on the question of the death penalty. So, this is an example of an implied main idea—using Method 1 from Chapter 2, add a word or phrase to an existing sentence. The supporting points are given below:

- Fifty-nine per cent of Americans find the death penalty morally acceptable.
- Whereas, 58 per cent of Canadians find the death penalty morally acceptable.

Later in the chapter, you will practise decoding the key points of a graphic by focusing on the pattern of organization and supporting details in visual aids.

▶ Apply the Skill

Finding Key Points in a Reading

Determine the answers to the following questions to fully understand the reading "Canada's Race Problem? It's Even Worse than America's."

1. What is the topic?

2. What is the author's most important point about the topic?

3. Is the most important point about the topic directly stated? If so, underline the thesis. If it is implied, what method for finding an implied main idea did you use?

4. Based on this information—reflected in the topic and the main point—what pattern of organization does the author use?

5. What transition words indicate this pattern?

6. Now, go back and determine the topic, the main idea, and the pattern of organization of each of the body paragraphs. Also, enumerate the major supporting details that back up the main idea.

CANADA'S RACE PROBLEM? IT'S EVEN WORSE THAN AMERICA'S

For a country so self-satisfied with its image of progressive tolerance, how is this not a national crisis?

By Scott Gilmore

1 The racial mess in the United States looks pretty grim and is painful to watch. We can be forgiven for being quietly thankful for Canada's more inclusive society, which has avoided dramas like that in Ferguson, Mo. We are not the only ones to think this. In the recently released Social Progress Index, Canada is ranked second amongst all nations for its tolerance and inclusion.

2 Unfortunately, the truth is we have a far worse race problem than the United States. We just can't see it very easily.

3 Terry Glavin, recently writing in the Ottawa Citizen, mocked the idea that the United States could learn from Canada's example when it comes to racial

harmony. To illustrate his point, he compared the conditions of the African-American community to Canada's First Nations. If you judge a society by how it treats its most disadvantaged, Glavin found us wanting. Consider the accompanying table. By almost every measurable indicator, the Aboriginal population in Canada is treated worse and lives with more hardship than the African-American population. All these facts tell us one thing: Canada has a race problem, too.

4   How are we not choking on these numbers? For a country so self-satisfied with its image of progressive tolerance, how is this not a national crisis? Why are governments not falling on this issue?

5   Possibly it is because our Fergusons are hidden deep in the bush, accessible only by chartered float plane: 49 per cent of First Nations members live on remote reserves. Those who do live in urban centres are mostly confined to a few cities in the Prairies. Fewer than 40,000 live in Toronto, not even one per cent of the total population of the Greater Toronto Area. Our racial problems are literally over the horizon, out of sight and out of mind.

6   Or it could be because we simply do not see the forest for trees. We are distracted by the stories of corrupt band councils, or flooded reserves, or another missing Aboriginal woman. Some of us wring our hands, and a handful of activists protest. There are a couple of unread op-eds, and maybe a Twitter hashtag will skip around for a few days. But nothing changes. Yes, we admit there is a governance problem on the reserves. We might agree that "something" should be done about the missing and murdered women. In Ottawa a few policy wonks write fretful memos on land claims and pipelines. But collectively, we don't say it out loud: "Canada has a race problem."

7   If we don't have a race problem then what do we blame? Our justice system, unable to even convene Aboriginal juries? Band administrators, like those in Attawapiskat, who defraud their own people? Our health care system that fails to provide Aboriginal communities with health outcomes on par with El Salvador? Politicians too craven to admit the reserve system has failed? Elders like Chief Ava Hill, cynically willing to let a child die this week from treatable cancer in order to promote Aboriginal rights? Aboriginal people themselves for not throwing out the leaders who serve them so poorly? Police forces too timid to grasp the nettle and confront unbridled criminality like the organized drug-smuggling gangs in Akwesasne? Federal bureaucrats for constructing a $7-billion welfare system that doesn't work? The school system for only graduating 42 per cent of reserve students? Aboriginal men, who have pushed their community's murder rate past Somalia's? The media for not sufficiently or persistently reporting on these facts?

8   Or: us? For not paying attention. For believing our own hype about inclusion. For looking down our noses at America and ignorantly thinking, "That would never happen here." For not acknowledging Canada has a race problem.

9   We do and it is bad. And it is not just with the Aboriginal peoples. For new immigrants and the black community the numbers are not as stark, but they tell a depressingly similar story.

10   If we want to fix this, the first step is to admit something is wrong. Start by saying it to yourself, but say it out loud: "Canada has a race problem."

A NATIONAL DISGRACE

	ABORIGINAL CANADIANS	AFRICAN-AMERICANS
Unemployment rate	14%	11%
Unemployment rate vs. the national rate	2.1 times	1.9 times
Median income	$22,344	$23,738
Median income vs. the national average	60%	74%
Incarceration rate (per 100,000 population)	1,400	2,207
Incarceration rate vs. the national rate	10 times	3 times
Homicide rate (per 100,000 population)	8.8	17.3
Homicide rate vs. the national rate	6.1 times	3.7 times
Infant mortality rate (per 1,000 live births)	11.7	12.4
Infant mortality rate vs. the national rate	2.3 times	2 times
Life expectancy (in years)	72.8	74.9
Life expectancy vs. the national average	91%	95%
Dropout rate*	23%	8%
Dropout rate vs. the national average	2.7 times	1.1 times

*20- to 24-year-olds without a high school diploma, and not in school

Source: Gilmore, Scott. "Canada's Racism Problem? It's Even Worse than America's." *Macleans.ca,* 16 Mar. 2017, www.macleans.ca/news/canada/out-of-sight-out-of-mind-2/. Accessed 13 July 2016. Used with permission of Rogers Media Inc. All rights reserved.

Review

Patterns of Organization

Discuss your response to the following questions in a small group or in a class discussion. Alternatively, write a paragraph response to one or more of these questions. Make sure to clearly explain your ideas.

1. Describe the benefits of patterns of organization in reading.

2. Describe the benefits of patterns of organization in writing.

3. Explain the characteristics of patterns that list: time/chronologicial, process order or steps, order of importance, and random or simple list.

4. Explain the characteristics of patterns that explain: definition, clarification, and description.

5. Explain the characteristics of patterns that analyze: classification, cause–effect, and compare–contrast.

Writing Structure

You were introduced to the concepts of purpose, topic, thesis, and audience in Chapter 1 and know how important they are when first considering a reading or when writing. Which structure you choose to use in your writing or can find in a reading depends on a few factors (see Figure 3.3).

- **Purpose:** The structure will be influenced by the purpose you have for writing (see Figure 3.3) or, when you are a reader, that the writer had in mind. For example, if a writer's purpose is to persuade, then reasons or causes may be the predominant focus of the paper. Similarly, if you aim to instruct in a paper, then perhaps sequence of steps in a process will be appropriate.
- **Topic:** The topic of a passage can be recognized in three ways as you learned in Chapter 1: from the title or heading; from boldfaced, italicized words; from words repeated throughout the passage or used and then replaced by pronouns. The topic can strongly suggest the pattern of organization. For example, if a title uses language that suggests contrast, then this gives you a clue as to how to structure your essay response or interact with the key points.
- **Thesis:** The pattern of organization you choose will be reflected in your thesis statement. Since a thesis is made up of your topic plus your assertion, the point you convey needs to be supported by details arranged in a logical order that reflects your thesis. As a reader, notice that the pattern of organization should be indicated in the wording of the thesis—this will help you focus on targeting key supporting points as you read.
- **Audience:** Just as purpose, topic, and thesis influence your decisions about how to structure a writing assignment, to whom you are aiming to write influences your choice. If you are writing to someone who may have little prior knowledge about your topic, you might choose a pattern that explains the idea for the reader like definition or clarification. If the audience has background knowledge on the topic then your details might be arranged to show intricacies of classification. Who is reading is an important consideration when planning your writing and crafting your prose. Similarly, the writer's intended audience can give you as a reader insight into how the writer may present information and what structure best suits that audience.

As you know, choosing the pattern of organization for your own writing stems from your purpose, topic, thesis and audience. To enable a logical decision, use a step-by-step approach to choose the best structure for your product.

FIGURE 3.3
PURPOSE, TOPIC, THESIS, AND AUDIENCE INFLUENCE ORGANIZATION

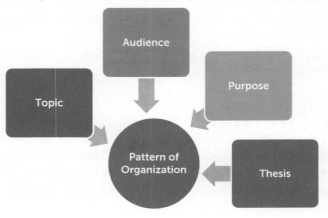

Steps to Determine an Organizational Pattern for Your Writing

1. When determining the structural pattern in your writing, ask yourself, what am I trying to do: list, explain, or analyze?
2. If your answer to Question 1 is list, do you intend to list
   - items in a random order so that the details would make sense in any order?
   - items arranged according to importance?
   - events organized by time?
   - steps in a process?
3. If your answer to Question 1 is that you intend the passage to explain something, do you intend to
   - make a general point with examples to make it clearer?
   - give a definition along with examples?
   - describe a topic using sensory details?
4. If your answer to Question 1 is that you want to analyze something, do you intend to
   - break a big concept into different parts, classifications, or categories?
   - show causes or effects?
   - show comparison and/or contrast?

Answering these questions will result in the best organization of your writing.

Different Structures for Compare–Contrast Essays

As you learned in Chapter 2, an essay contains an introduction, body paragraphs, and a conclusion. Not all essays follow the same structure as you saw in the introductions and conclusions "Apply the Skill" exercises in Chapter 2. Some essays have a one-word introduction or conclusion, for example, instead of a paragraph. A writer may choose a method or methods for the introductions and conclusions as well as the body paragraphs that he feels is most appropriate to convey the overall point to the audience. Remember that thinking about what you are writing and how best to write it is metacognition. You were introduced to the concept of metacognition or metacomprehension in Chapter 1.

When writing a compare–contrast essay the essay structure is a bit more challenging. The reason is that, in a compare–contrast type of essay, you are juggling more than one task: you are showing similarities between two or more things or showing differences between two or more things. So, being mindful of this challenge, there are two primary methods for structuring your supporting evidence.

POINT-BY-POINT METHOD

In this structure, a writer uses the body paragraphs to compare two things on several points. For example, you may compare property crime rates in the United States and Canada. In the point-by-point structure, your body paragraphs may look like this:

Body paragraph 1: Property Crime
Topic sentence: Overall statement about property crime rates in the United States versus Canada.
Subtopic or point 1: Car theft rates in the United States versus Canada
    Supporting example about US car theft rates
    Supporting example about Canadian car theft rates

Subtopic or point 2: Burglary rates in the United States versus Canada
Supporting example about US burglary rates
Supporting example about Canadian burglary rates
Subtopic or point 3: Arson rates in the United States versus Canada
Supporting example about US arson rates
Supporting example about Canadian arson rates
Concluding sentence: Summative sentence about property crime rates in the United States vs. Canada

This format is called point-by-point because each point of comparison or contrast is debated in each body paragraph. In this model, the next body paragraph would go on to discuss another category of crime rate, comparing the two countries' rates as it proceeds, point-by-point or feature-by-feature.

BLOCK METHOD

Another structure for a compare–contrast essay is to use the block method. This is called the block method because, continuing with our example on Canadian and American crime rates above, each country would be discussed in its own block or body paragraph with regard to the points of comparison. Look at this example:

Body paragraph 1: US property crime rates
Topic sentence: Overall statement about property crime rates in the United States
Subtopic 1: Car theft rates in the United States
Supporting example about US car theft rates
Subtopic 2: Burglary rates in the United States
Supporting example about US burglary rates
Subtopic 3: Arson rates in the United States
Supporting example about US arson rates
Concluding sentence: Summative sentence about property crime rates in the United States
Body paragraph 2: Canadian crime rates
Topic sentence: Transition word, phrase, or clause indicating shift from discussing the United States to discussing Canada, as well as an overall statement about property crime rates in Canada
Subtopic 1: Car theft rates in Canada
Supporting example about Canadian car theft rates
Subtopic 2: Burglary rates in Canada
Supporting example about Canadian burglary rates
Subtopic 3: Arson rates in Canada
Supporting example about Canadian arson rates
Concluding sentence: Summative sentence about property crime rates in Canada.

In the block method, interweaving the two countries' rates of crime most likely would be done in the introduction or conclusion. Whether you choose point-by-point or block method, you would decide based on your purpose, topic, main idea, and audience. For example, if you want to emphasize the contrast because your purpose is to persuade your reader of a point, perhaps the point-by-point method would do that best; whereas, if you are doing a research paper and your purpose is to inform, the block method may be your best choice.

Reading Graphic Material

Graphics such as charts, graphs, webs, or clusters are key methods to organize information in a prewriting strategy as you learned in Chapter 1. However, you can use a method for probing the key points in graphic materials similar to the method you have learned for understanding key points in a reading. The steps are as follows:

1. Determine the topic of the graphic.
2. Determine the pattern of organization of the graphic.
3. Determine the supporting points in the graphic.
4. Given the above, what do you think is the author's overall main idea?

Consider the graphic from "How Americans and Canadians Differ on Right and Wrong," from the beginning of the chapter.

FIGURE 3.4

RIGHT OR WRONG: HOW DO CANADA AND AMERICA COMPARE?

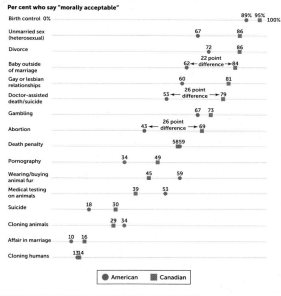

Source: Shendruk, 2016.

Topic: How Canadians and Americans compare on moral issues by percentage who say the issue is morally agreeable.

Pattern of organization: Compare–contrast.

Supporting details: The views on moral issues between the two countries are compared.

Main idea: While Canadians and Americans tend to agree generally on most moral issues, they differ on three key issues: parenthood outside marriage, doctor-assisted suicide, and abortion.

What is implied by the data? Looking more closely at the data, notice that while there is a differential in responses on parenthood outside marriage and doctor-assisted suicide, in these categories the majority of respondents do find these issues morally acceptable, with Canadian respondents being in greater support. However, the big difference between Canadian and American views is on the subject of abortion; a minority of Americans find abortion morally acceptable (43%), whereas the majority of Canadians find abortion morally acceptable (69%).

Graphic material can reveal a great deal of information in a concise manner. Using your skills for reading text and applying it to graphic material can ensure you get the most out of the information. You may have to create your own graphics for a research paper or report. Use your skills for effective writing and organization to present graphics that help your reader process information smoothly since well-organized graphics function to clearly communicate key ideas to your reader. Be alert to using this method in upcoming graphic material in later chapters, research assignments, or readings for your other classes.

▶ Apply the Skill

Reading Graphics

Apply this method of reading graphic material to the visual "A National Disgrace," following the reading "Canada's Race Problem? It's Even Worse than America's" earlier in this chapter. Determine the topic, pattern of organization, supporting details, and main idea of the graphic. Discuss the implications of the graphic in a short paper, in a small group, or in a class discussion.

Review

Writing Structure and Reading Graphics

Discuss your response to the following questions in a small group or in a class discussion. Alternatively, write a paragraph response to one or more of these questions. Be sure to clearly explain your ideas.

1. How do purpose, topic, thesis, and audience affect a writer's choice of pattern of organization?
2. What are some tips for selecting a pattern of organization for your writing?
3. Explain the differences and similarities between the block and point-by-point structure.
4. What might help you determine the best structure to use for a compare-contrast writing assignment?
5. Explain the application of reading skills to "reading" graphic material.

▶ Did You Know?

COMBINING CLAUSES

In Chapter 2 you learned about clauses, which are the largest building blocks of sentences. You learned that a clause must contain a subject and its corresponding verb, and that there are two categories of clauses: an independent clause (IC), which expresses a complete thought, and a dependent clause (DC), which expresses an incomplete thought and therefore needs to be attached to an independent clause in order to be fully understood. Most importantly, you learned that every sentence comprises one or more clauses.

There are only four different types of sentences in English, all of which are defined by their combinations of independent and dependent clauses.

TABLE 3.3
FOUR SENTENCE TYPES

SENTENCE TYPE	CLAUSE COMBINATION
Simple Sentence	One independent clause
Compound Sentence	Two independent clauses
Complex Sentence	One independent clause and one *or more* dependent clauses
Compound-Complex Sentence	Two independent clauses and one *or more* dependent clauses

▶ Apply the Skill

Types of Sentences

The following sentences are taken from Paragraph 3 of "Canada's Race Problem? It's Even Worse than America's." Label each sentence as a simple sentence (SS), compound sentence (CS), complex sentence (CX), or compound-complex sentence (CCX). The first one has been done for you.

__CX__ 1. Terry Glavin, recently writing in the *Ottawa Citizen*, mocked the idea that the United States could learn from Canada's example when it comes to racial harmony.

_____ 2. To illustrate his point, he compared the conditions of the African-American community to Canada's First Nations.

_____ 3. If you judge a society by how it treats its most disadvantaged, Glavin found us wanting.

_____ 4. Consider the accompanying table.

_____ 5. By almost every measurable indicator, the Aboriginal population in Canada is treated worse and lives with more hardship than the African-American population.

_____ 6. All these facts tell us one thing: Canada has a race problem, too.

_____ 7. How are we not choking on these numbers?

_____ 8. For a country so self-satisfied with its image of progressive tolerance, how is this not a national crisis?

_____ 9. Why are governments not falling on this issue?

Source: Source: Gilmore, 2017.

Knowing the sentence types in Table 3.3 will help you both as a reader and as a writer. As a reader, knowing these sentence types helps you effectively process a writer's ideas, just as patterns of organization do. When writers write in repetitive, predictable, yet varied sentence types, we can follow their ideas easily. As a writer, knowing these types will allow you to communicate your own ideas clearly. Because of this connection between sentence types and reading comprehension, it is imperative that you know how to construct these sentence types correctly, following the rules for combining clauses. If you do not combine clauses correctly, your reader may have difficulty understanding what you are trying to communicate.

Compound Sentences

Simple sentences obviously don't require any clause combinations. Compound sentences, however, do involve the process of combining clauses. Three methods can be used to combine two independent clauses into a compound sentence.

TABLE 3.4

THREE METHODS FOR COMBINING INDEPENDENT CLAUSES TO FORM A COMPOUND SENTENCE

METHOD	FORMULA	EXAMPLE SENTENCE FROM THIS CHAPTER
Comma and coordinating conjunction (cc)	IC + , + cc + IC	Both causes and effects can be discussed, but usually the focus is on causes or effects.
Semicolon and conjunctive adverb (ca)	IC + ; + ca + , + IC	Recognizing the main idea of a reading passage or constructing your own main idea in writing is your primary focus;however, that main idea is only as good as its support.
Semicolon by itself (used only if the connection between the two independent clauses is self-evident)	IC + ; + IC	This list is a solution list; this is how the Ontario Human Rights Commission seeks to solve the problem of discrimination and promoting human rights.

Coordinating Conjunctions and Conjunctive Adverbs

Because coordinating conjunctions and conjunctive adverbs are important for combining independent clauses, you need to be familiar with both.

Coordinating conjunctions are words that connect two equal parts: two words, two phrases, two clauses, or two sentences. There are just seven coordinating conjunctions: *for, and, nor, but, or, yet, so.* Many people use the acronym FANBOYS to remember these seven conjunctions. It should be noted that the word *for* is rarely used as a coordinating conjunction. As a conjunction, the word *for* indicates cause and effect, as in this example: *I am tired, for I did not get enough sleep last night.* More often, *for* is used as a preposition, as in *I have a gift for you.*

Conjunctive adverbs are often called transition words or connectors. Many conjunctive adverbs are clue words for the patterns of organization described in this chapter. Table 3.5 lists some, but not all, conjunctive adverbs:

Whether you use a coordinating conjunction or a conjunctive adverb, be aware that these conjunctions are *not* actually part of the independent clauses they connect.

TABLE 3.5

LIST OF COMMON CONJUNCTIVE ADVERBS CLASSIFIED BY PATTERNS OF ORGANIZATION

Listing	*then, next, furthermore, in addition, also*
Explaining	*in other words, for example, for instance, that is*
Analyzing: cause–effect	*therefore, as a result, thus, consequently*
Analyzing: comparison–contrast	*similarly, likewise, on the other hand, in contrast, however, nevertheless, conversely, meanwhile*

Compound Sentences

The following groups of sentences are simple sentences that could be combined into compound or compound-complex sentences. Combine the sentences in two different ways: (1) using a coordinating conjunction and (2) using a conjunctive adverb. Be sure to choose a coordinating conjunction and conjunctive adverb that provide a logical connection between the two sentences.

As well, be sure to punctuate appropriately.

1. Canada and the United States have many differences.

   They also share many similarities because of their proximity to each other.

2. Just because *many* Canadians feel a certain way about controversial issues does not mean that *all* Canadians feel that way.

   Not all Americans necessarily feel the same way on controversial issues.

3. Educational institutions provide us with the tools to make informed decisions on controversial issues.

   We need to make sure these institutions do not force us to follow only one specific point of view.

4. Every day, we interact with people who have opposing viewpoints from our own.

   We need to acknowledge the merits of these viewpoints rather than allowing them to cause divisions or conflicts in our relationships.

5. You can choose to cause conflict.

   You can choose to engage in meaningful debate to resolve conflict.

Complex Sentences

We have seen that many compound sentences require conjunctions to combine their clauses. The same is true for complex sentences that involve adverb clauses. You will remember from Chapter 2 that adverb clauses are just one of three types of dependent clauses, but they are unique in the way in which they are combined with independent clauses. There is essentially one rule when it comes to attaching an adverb clause to an independent clause, as demonstrated in Table 3.6: if the adverb clause comes *before* the independent clause, use a comma to separate the two clauses; however, if the adverb clause comes *after* the independent clause, do *not* use any punctuation to separate the two clauses.

You can identify an adverb clause from its first word, which is known as a subordinating conjunction. These conjunctions are called subordinators because they can transform a complete sentence into an incomplete sentence. Here is an example:

Complete sentence: Racial tensions exist in both Canada and the United States.

Incomplete sentence: Because racial tensions exist in both Canada and the United States

Note how the incomplete sentence, which begins with the subordinating conjunction *because*, begs the question, "What is the result?" What happens because racial tensions exist in both Canada and the United States?

TABLE 3.6

COMBINING AN ADVERB CLAUSE WITH AN INDEPENDENT CLAUSE

PATTERN	EXAMPLE
DC + comma + IC	Because they are vital for following an author's train of thought, transition words were mentioned in the first chapter.
IC + DC	Transition words were mentioned in the first chapter because they are vital for following an author's train of thought.

Table 3.7 provides some of the most common subordinating conjunctions, organized by the relationships they indicate between clauses:

TABLE 3.7

LIST OF COMMON SUBORDINATING CONJUNCTIONS ORGANIZED BY RELATIONSHIP

CONTRAST OR CONCESSION	CAUSE AND EFFECT	CONDITION	TIME
though	because	if	since
although	since	unless	when
even though	so that	as long as	until
even if	as	in the event that	while
despite the fact that			after
whereas			whenever
while			as
			before
			once
			as soon as

▶ **Apply the Skill**

Complex Sentences

1. Go back to the sentences from the previous exercise. This time, however, try combining the two sentences by transforming one of the sentences into a dependent clause and attaching it to the other sentence. In other words, create complex sentences instead of compound or compound-complex sentences. Make sure you choose a subordinating conjunction that logically connects the clauses and be sure to punctuate correctly.

2. Select one paragraph from one of the readings in this chapter. Then, do the following:

   a. Identify the sentence type of each sentence (simple, complex, compound, compound-complex).

   b. Write a paragraph of your own, on a topic of your own choosing, that mimics the sentence types in the paragraph from the reading.

c. Write a paragraph using the exact same content as you did in 2b, but this time, use different sentence types.

d. Determine which paragraph, 2b or 2c, you think is best. Justify your response, being sure to include an explanation about how sentence types and the ways in which clauses are combined influence your perception of your own writing.

▶ Questions for Writing and Discussion

1. The reading "What Canadian Police Are Doing So Ferguson Doesn't Happen Here," has five subsections: the introductory paragraphs, the subsections entitled *Implicit biases: Not your racist grandpa, How to combat biases when you don't know you're biased, Contact theory and getting into high-crime neighbourhoods*, and *Why it comes down to trust*. First, determine the topic, the pattern of organization, and the thesis of the whole reading. If the thesis is implied, write your own statement; if it is directly stated, underline it. Next, for each of the five subsections, determine the topic, the pattern of organization, and the main idea. If the main idea is implied, write your own statement; if it is directly stated, underline it.

2. Each of the readings in this chapter concerns cultural issues that contrast American and Canadian perspectives. Choose a topic of comparison and/or contrast as the focus of your response—some possibilities are race, morality, policing, community engagement, or community protest. Summarize the differences and/or similarities between the two cultures as they pertain to your chosen topic, making sure to have a thoughtful and clear thesis for your writing or discussion. Then, support your thesis with direct references to each of the three readings. Clearly plan a pattern of organization to structure your response.

3. *Canada's race problem is even worse than America's.* Defend or refute this statement, drawing on specific evidence from the readings, particularly the article, "Canada's Race Problem? It's Even Worse than America's."

4. Why do you think Canadians and Americans differ on specific social issues as explored in the reading "How Americans and Canadians Differ on Right and Wrong"? How do you think these differences transfer to or influence views on criminal justice and policing?

5. Is it possible to attain a post racial society in Canada? In the United States? What specific steps would each country need to take to realize this? Support your answer with your own ideas and those of the authors of the readings in this chapter.

6. Choose another culture with which you are familiar outside of the United States or Canada. Compare or contrast the Canadian perspective with your chosen culture regarding one of the following topics: criminal justice, racialized groups, social morality, social justice, the impact of media on advancing or minimizing news events, or the power of media to amplify or reduce social change.

By Erika Tucker

1 TORONTO—The fatal shooting of teenager Michael Brown by a police officer in Ferguson, Missouri happened 1,000 kilometres from, and a year after, teenager Sammy Yatim was fatally shot by an officer in Toronto.

2 Both victims were 18 years old and both were shot multiple times but their deaths came after very different circumstances—Yatim was wielding a knife on a streetcar and Brown was unarmed and walking on the street.

3 While there were anti-police protests in Toronto following Yatim's death, there was none of the rioting and looting witnessed in Ferguson, where the black majority population is policed by mostly white officers.

4 Toronto police chief Bill Blair has said his force will likely never have to deal with the same kind of racial tension.

5 "We work really closely with the minority communities here in Toronto," said Blair at an Aug. 14 press conference. "I think those relationships that we worked for so many years on building, and that the trust that exists between us would help us through such a crisis."

Implicit biases: Not your racist grandpa

6 Toronto police training was significantly impacted by 2013's Police and Community Engagement Review (the PACER report)—which came out three months after Yatim's death. The report made 31 recommendations, including many related to bias, prejudices, racial profiling, and public trust—and recommended a review of training protocols and the introduction of new training.

7 One new program is being conducted by the "pre-eminent trainer in the United States on implicit bias," said Deputy Chief Peter Sloly.

8 That trainer is Dr. Lorie Fridell, a social scientist who teaches at the University of South Florida, and founded the Fair and Impartial Policing program. The Toronto Police Service is the first law enforcement agency she's worked with in Canada, but she plans to train the Vancouver Transit Authority in January.

9 Fridell said bias has changed in our society: When it manifested "in our grandparents' time" it was most likely to look like what we now call explicit bias—people who consciously linked others to stereotypes. "A racist would be an example," she said.

10 But implicit bias is different—and that's what the Fair and Impartial Policing program aims to tackle.

11 "[Implicit bias] can operate outside of our conscious awareness, it can impact our perceptions, it can impact our behaviour and this occurs even in people who—at the conscious level—reject stereotypes," said Fridell. "So even well-intentioned people, and therefore well-intentioned officers who want to be fair and impartial have implicit biases."

12 Social science research suggests these biases come from entertainment media, news media, as well as individual upbringing and environment, said Fridell.

13 "Stereotypes are based, in part, in fact. And we have to recognize that demographic groups are not all equally represented amongst the people who commit street crimes," she said. "But we go on to say: Even if stereotypes are based in part on fact, we cannot—police or any of us—make decisions treating an individual as if they are the stereotype.

14   "That's where we go wrong: Treating all people of colour as if they're criminals, treating all women as if they're not."

15   It's a lesson Sloly says is particularly important for police.

16   "When you're a human being in general society, you're not necessarily held to that account—when you're a police officer, and you're sworn to uphold the law and be compliant with the Charter and the Human Rights Code, you can't allow that thinking to impact your decisions."

How to combat biases when you don't know you're biased

17   Fridell gives police two tactics to combat these biases: one is recognizing your own biases and actively choosing to implement unbiased behaviour.

18   "For me, as a professor, I might have a blink response depending on who darkens my doorway," said Fridell. "Maybe it's an Asian female versus a Hispanic in a football jersey. And as you might imagine, I have very different academic stereotypes associated with those groups—and I'm sorry I have them, but I do—but the key here is that I recognize them and make sure that my behaviour is bias-free."

19   Sloly said another new training tool that comes on the heels of the Fair and Impartial Policing program is intercultural competence development training, brought in by another American company—Intercultural Developmental Inventory (IDI). Though the IDI assessment has been used in educational institutions, non-profit organizations and companies in the country, the Toronto Police Service is the first law enforcement agency to use it for organization-wide assessment and training in Canada, according to IDI owner and president Mitch Hammer.

20   The deputy chief described it as a survey diagnostic that allows officers to recognize how their own cultural/racial/religious background will come into play with the background of other people with whom they interact.

21   "The part of me that is a Jamaican-born, black person can be a more dominant factor in certain circumstances. The part of me that's a 25-year police officer at the rank of a deputy chief, can in other cases become a more dominant factor. And the part of me that's the dad of a young family in a mixed marriage can also be a different factor—and . . . most times all three are at play. So how do you recognize that, how do you decode that, and how do you manage that better, more consistently—both at home and at work?"

Contact theory and getting into high-crime neighbourhoods

22   The second tactic Fridell uses to combat implicit biases has to do with contact theory, which says if we interact in a positive way with people different from us, that interaction will reduce both our conscious and implicit biases. Fridell's personal example was volunteering at a homeless shelter—watching movies, having conversations—to reduce her own bias that homeless people were a threat.

23   She acknowledged that police work inevitably involves a number of negative interactions, but suggested there's an increasing emphasis in policing to make positive contacts with the "good people" in various neighbourhoods.

24   It's a shift Toronto Police seems to have embraced.

25   "We have consultative committees with demographic groups: Aboriginal First Nations, the black community, the Asian community, the South Asian community, the LGBTQ community as examples, and those are all high-level, chief

command-level consultative communities that meet on a monthly basis and have done so over the last two decades," Sloly said.

26   He added there are additional consultative committees at the divisional level—"if it's an area with a high Chinese population, there might be a Chinese consultative committee like there is in 42 Division"—and at the neighbourhood level where there are high levels of victimization and crime.

27   "Because we are the most diverse city in the world, and because crime and disorder doesn't happen equally in a city like ours, we have to be highly focused on relationship-building with victimized communities, with marginalized communities; in the world's most diverse city, with racialized communities, or new immigrant communities," said Sloly.

28   "If you don't have a trusting relationship with broad members of your community, then you can't really get to a level of safety that's acceptable."

Why it comes down to trust

29   The issue of trust is at the centre of Fridell's analysis of the death of Brown: "what we're seeing in Ferguson is a great deal of mistrust between the African-American community and the police."

30   "In every community there's a great deal of concern about this, and they want answers and they want investigations–but in some other communities they have enough trust to say, 'Okay, I think this is going to get investigated and, as necessary, people are going to be held to account.'"

31   Sloly called the relationship between police and minority communities "the number one public trust issue that we struggle with."

32   "That's what the whole Police and Community Engagement Review is about—acknowledging it, recognizing it, and putting in place systemic level programs and individual supports to help our people be the best they can be . . .

33   "I'm not sure that we can eliminate racism or bias out of a public institution any more than we can eliminate it out of society, but we're going to do our best to get as close to that goal as we possibly can."

Source: Tucker, Erica. "What Canadian Police Are Doing So Ferguson Doesn't Happen Here." *Global News*, 21 Aug. 2014, www.globalnews.ca/news/1520068/what-canadian-police-are-doing-so-ferguson-doesnt-happen-here/. Accessed 22 July 2016. Courtesy of Global News.

Lightspring/Shutterstock.com

SUMMARIZING A READING

BY THE END OF THIS CHAPTER, YOU WILL BE ABLE TO

- Use active reading strategies to comprehend the content and organization of a text.
- Select relevant content for a summary of a text by distinguishing among main ideas, major supporting details, and minor supporting details.
- Paraphrase a text by applying strategies such as chunking and analyzing patterns of organization.
- Write a coherent summary of a text using graphic organizers as part of the process.

▶ WHY IS THIS INFORMATION IMPORTANT?

Summarizing information is a fundamental skill in any postsecondary learning environment. Your ability to learn and remember information depends, in large part, on your ability to summarize information. Writing a summary of the information you are reading is one way to help ensure you comprehend the reading. In Chapter 2, you learned about clarifying key points—both explicit and implicit main ideas. In Chapter 3, you learned to focus on structure and use these organizational patterns to clarify both major and minor details. It is main ideas and major details that coalesce, or come together, into a summary. In addition to serving as a learning tool, summarizing also helps you

- ensure you fully understand what you are reading;
- synthesize ideas from multiple sources to enhance your understanding of a topic that you may need to write about on your own;
- situate your own writing in the writing of others, allowing you to enter into a conversation with other writers;
- provide a preview of your own academic research paper to other researchers;
- provide a preview of recommendations in a business report or proposal; and
- communicate important ideas to somebody else: your employer, your colleagues, your friends, your family.

As you can see, the ability to summarize has significant positive effects for both you and the people you interact with every day.

▶ Think about It!

In this chapter, you will think, read, and write about the trust we put into technologies and those who operate them, knowing that safety is never guaranteed. Here are some questions to consider as you move through this chapter and as you read the following essay.

1. Is there a point at which we must draw the line when it comes to trusting automation?

2. How do you establish trust in someone whom you have never met, but in whose hands you put your life, such as an airline pilot, a doctor, or a police officer?

3. When it comes to life-and-death scenarios, are we more trusting of automation, or do we trust humans more?

Now, read this essay and consider these questions:

1. What is the author's central idea or thesis?

2. Why, according to the author, is it difficult "to trust a self-driving car"?

3. Are there other technologies that we have difficulty trusting because they have virtually eliminated the human element? If so, what are these technologies and why are they difficult to trust? If not, why is the self-driving car particularly difficult to trust?

4. What are your own views regarding self-driving cars? Are they paving the way for safer roadways, or are they simply another complication for drivers and pedestrians?

5. What responsibility do automakers have in ensuring vehicle innovations promote safety and avoid danger?

LEARNING TO TRUST A SELF-DRIVING CAR

By Simon Parkin

1   On a clear morning in early May, Brian Lathrop, a senior engineer for Volkswagen's Electronics Research Laboratory, was in the driver's seat of a Tesla Model S as it travelled along a stretch of road near Blacksburg, Virginia, when the car began to drift from its lane. Lathrop had his hands on the wheel but was not in control of the vehicle. The Tesla was in Autopilot mode, a highly evolved version of cruise control that, via an array of sensors, allows the car to change lanes, steer through corners, and match the lurching of traffic unaided. As the vehicle—one of a fleet belonging to Virginia Tech's Transportation Institute, which Lathrop was visiting that day—lost track of the road markings, he shook the wheel to disengage Autopilot. "If I hadn't been aware of what was happening, it could have been a completely different outcome," Lathrop told me recently.

2   The same week, six hundred miles south of Blacksburg, in Florida, a forty-year-old Tesla driver named Joshua Brown experienced that different outcome. His Model S, driving on Autopilot along Route 27, crunched into the side of an eighteen-wheeler, passing beneath the vehicle's trailer, which sheared off the Tesla's roof and windshield. Brown was killed. The crash is the subject of an ongoing inquiry—on Tuesday, the U.S. National Highway Traffic Safety Administration, which investigates defects, publicly released a series of questions that it sent Tesla earlier this month—but the company was quick to issue an explanation. In a blog post published on June 30th, the day that the accident was first announced, Tesla stated, "Neither Autopilot nor the driver noticed the white side of the tractor trailer against a brightly lit sky, so the brake was not applied." The company further noted the "extremely rare circumstances of the impact."

3   Journalists, engineers, science-fiction authors, ethicists, car manufacturers, and, naturally, lawyers, had long anticipated this moment. In testimony before the Senate Committee on Commerce, Science, and Transportation in mid-March, Mary Cummings, the director of Duke University's Humans and Autonomy Laboratory, called for a "significantly accelerated self-driving testing program" in order to avoid the first fatality of semi-autonomous driving. That time is now past, and the challenge of persuading customers of the trustworthiness of these vehicles has become even more salient.

4   As Tesla pointed out in its blog post, Brown's is the only death so far in more than a hundred and thirty million miles of Autopilot driving. Google's fleet of similar vehicles has, according to the company, driven more than 1.5 million miles with only one minor collision, a fender bender involving a self-driving Lexus S.U.V. and a bus. Uber, a company for which self-driving taxis may become the full and final act of putting cabbies out of work, has a test car on the road in Pittsburgh that it hopes will make "transportation as reliable as running water." Indeed, so far, autonomous vehicles have had an exemplary safety record. Tesla's data demonstrates a slight improvement over humans, who, according to a 2015 report by the nonprofit U.S. National Safety Council, account for 1.3 deaths per hundred million vehicle miles—nearly thirty-three thousand people a year. But it is a flawed comparison. Autopilot is designed for use only on freeways, where human drivers, too, have far fewer accidents. And even if travelling by autonomous vehicle is shown to be statistically safer, car designers will need to find ways

to reassure people beyond mere numbers. According to a recent survey from AAA, only one in four U.S. drivers would place their trust in an autonomous vehicle.

5   "The real hurdle to the widespread adoption of autonomous vehicles is psychology," Chris Rockwell, the C.E.O. of Lextant, a research consultancy that focusses on user experience, told me. "People will forgive other humans much more quickly than they will technologies when they fail." At Volkswagen, Lathrop is currently working on the problem with Traffic Jam Pilot, which is expected to feature in the next Audi D-Class. The system can control the car and issue a warning should a human be seen by its cameras to fall asleep at the wheel—a provision similar to Tesla's requirement that drivers keep their hands on the wheel, even when in Autopilot. "There are three key ways to make the occupants of a self-driving car feel safe," Lathrop said. "It must be clear when the vehicle is operating in autonomous mode. Occupants must know that the car is sensing its environment—other vehicles and pedestrians and so on. Finally, the vehicle must prime people before it makes a maneuver. There's nothing more disconcerting for passengers than when a driver makes abrupt lane changes or swerves." According to a paper published in 2014 in the *Journal of Experimental Social Psychology*, the more humanlike the car's alert features—name, voice, gender—the more people trust it to operate competently, as a human driver would. The Model S indicates visually whether Autopilot is engaged, but some users have complained about the absence of a voice prompt.

6   The problem of trust faces outward as well as inward. How do pedestrians and other drivers distinguish a vehicle that is driving autonomously from one that is not? A recent memorable YouTube clip shows a group of men in suits at a car dealership testing a Volvo that they believed to be equipped with sensors to prevent the car from hitting pedestrians. The crash-test-dummy volunteer tosses a smile at the camera as the engine starts. He instinctively braces for impact. The treacherous car knocks him onto its hood. (Volvo later claimed that the vehicle in the clip was not equipped with the appropriate sensors, which cost extra.) The same day that the video, which has been viewed more than five million times, was uploaded, Google was awarded a patent for an adhesive hood, designed to stick a human to the front of a self-driving car, preventing secondary injuries caused by tumbling into the windshield or rebounding onto the asphalt. Volkswagen's solution to instilling pedestrian trust is rather more mundane. The company has tested an autonomous Audi A7 that features a strip of L.E.D.s facing out of the front windshield. The lights blink and follow pedestrians at a crosswalk to signal that the car sees them—the equivalent, perhaps, of a friendly wave of the hand.

7   While one's first time behind the wheel of an autonomous car (or in front of it) may feel perilous, Volkswagen's research has shown that trust between human and vehicle blossoms rapidly and, in many cases, completely. A decade ago, according to Lathrop, the company ran a series of internal studies in which it put people in the driver's seat of a car that they were informed was fully autonomous. Behind them, behind a curtain, sat a driver, who controlled the car using a camera feed of the road ahead, as if playing a video game. "We found that people get comfortable very quickly—almost too quickly, in fact—in letting the car drive itself," Lathrop said. Unyoked from the activity of driving, most people experience what researchers refer to as passive fatigue, a state in which awareness is dulled. It can set in after as little as ten minutes. While wearied by inactivity, a car's occupants typically look for distractions. Frank Baressi, the sixty-two-year-old driver

of the truck that killed Brown, claims that when he approached the wrecked Tesla he heard one of the Harry Potter films playing inside the car. Investigators found both a portable DVD player and a laptop inside.

8   Tesla strenuously warns consumers to pay attention while their car is in autonomous mode, but the caveat may not be strong enough. On Thursday, Laura MacCleery, the vice-president of consumer policy and mobilization for *Consumer Reports*, said that the very name of Tesla's self-driving feature—Autopilot—"gives consumers a false sense of security." Lathrop is working with his colleagues at Virginia Tech on using drivers' phones or tablets to pass along alerts while they're at the wheel, to make them harder to ignore. But whether or not Brown was distracted at the time of the collision, Lathrop said that, as autonomous systems improve and trust in them increases, the temptation for occupants to do other things will grow stronger. "We are not naïve," he said. "But ultimately the operator of the vehicle is responsible for having some degree of situational awareness. When it comes to autonomous cars, it's a system. It's a machine. It's not making decisions. It's not aware of everything. It's simply sensing its environment and responding as it has been trained." This is the paradox facing auto engineers: how to design self-driving cars that feel trustworthy while simultaneously reminding their occupants that, no matter how pristine a given model's safety record, no driver—human or artificial—is perfect. How, in other words, to free drivers from the onus of driving, while burdening them with the worry that, at any moment, they will need to take back control.

Source: Parkin, Simon. "Learning to Trust a Self-Driving Car." *The New Yorker*, 15 July 2016, www.newyorker.com/tech/annals-of-technology/learning-to-trust-a-self-driving-car. Simon Parkin/The New Yorker © Conde Nast.

Reading with the Intention to Summarize

You will remember from Chapter 1 that just as a writer has a purpose for writing, so too does a reader have a purpose for reading. When you know your purpose for reading is to write a summary of a text, you need to take a very deliberate, systematic approach to reading.

In a summary, your goal is to explain a writer's main ideas to your audience. Because you are working at the level of a whole reading, this involves identifying the writer's thesis as well as the main ideas in each of the subsections and/or paragraphs of the reading that support the thesis. You will also need to identify the major supporting details necessary to understand the main ideas of the subsections and/or paragraphs. Minor supporting details are generally not included in a summary, but it is important for you to be able to identify these minor supporting details, so that you can assess whether or not they provide an integral, or necessary, piece of information that helps to unlock a main idea or major supporting detail. In addition, you need to understand the pattern of organization in the reading you aim to summarize since this structure will be also used in your summary.

In short, any summary you write should clearly explain to someone who is not familiar with the reading what the writer's central or most important point is and how the writer goes about supporting that point or coming to that conclusion. A summary should be self-sustaining, which means that you should not rely on your reader to have read the original text.

Due to the intense focus required to read a text with the intention of summarizing it, you must employ an active reading approach. The first step is to preview, just as you learned in Chapter 1. Taking a look at the source of the reading, researching the writer of the reading, and skimming the overall organization of the reading will help you begin to understand the topic, purpose and audience of the material you are summarizing. Reading the title, the introductory paragraph, the concluding paragraph, and the first sentence of all other paragraphs will help give you an overall understanding of what the writer is trying to express and how she is expressing it. When you are ready to dive into the text after previewing, you should employ all the strategies from Chapters 2 and 3: how to find main ideas, major supporting details, minor supporting details, and patterns of organization.

Explicit and Implicit Main Ideas

In Chapter 2, you learned the strategies for finding explicit and implicit main ideas. Explicit main ideas are found in the form of topic sentences. In other words, an explicit main idea is expressed in one sentence in a paragraph. Implicit main ideas, on the other hand, can be determined only by combining words, phrases, or ideas from multiple sentences. That is why making a note of repeated words, phrases, or ideas, including synonyms, is an important step when reading for summarizing.

▶ Apply the Skill

Analyzing a Reading to Summarize

Take a look at Paragraph 5 of "Learning to Trust a Self-Driving Car." Determine the main idea of this paragraph by answering the following questions:

1. What is the purpose of this particular paragraph? Is the author trying to inform, instruct, entertain, or persuade you?

2. What key words, phrases, or ideas are repeated in the paragraph that reveal the topic?

3. What is the organizational pattern of the paragraph? What signal words indicate this pattern of organization?

4. Is the main idea of this paragraph explicit or implicit? How do you know?

5. Using your answers to all of the above questions, can you state the main idea of this paragraph in your own words?

Major and Minor Supporting Details

When writing a summary it is vital to distinguishing major supporting details from minor supporting details. The major supporting details of a paragraph are essential to understanding the main idea of that paragraph. The minor supporting details usually provide an example or instance of the major supporting details, to explain or support the major supporting details. Generally, major supporting details are included in a summary whereas minor supporting details are excluded from a summary. To help you with distinguishing between the two, you should analyze the text for *hierarchies*. Major supporting details are higher in the hierarchy of ideas. They are more specific than a main idea, but they are not at the level of concrete examples. Minor supporting details, on the other hand, are specific and concrete. Such ideas are considered to be at the bottom of the hierarchy because they are the most concrete or specific.

If a major supporting detail can be understood without the help of a minor supporting detail, then you would not include the minor supporting detail in your summary. This is the case with the example from Figure 4.1. Volume of pedestrians at school crossings can be understood without exact times of days and exact numbers of students since most people understand that schools contain lots of people. If, however, a major supporting detail would not make sense on its own to a reader who has not read the reading you are summarizing, then you may need to include the minor supporting detail in your summary. This would definitely be the case if the major supporting detail is actually an implicit one that can be arrived at only by synthesizing, or combining, the minor supporting details. Either way, the key point to remember is that your goal is to get your reader to understand the most important point made in the reading and how the writer has arrived at that most important point.

FIGURE 4.1

HIERARCHY OF IDEAS WITH EXAMPLE

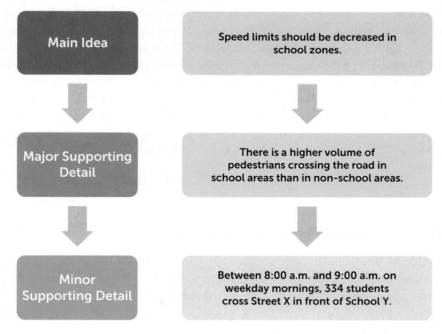

▶ **Apply the Skill**

Focusing on Supporting Details with the Goal of Summarizing

Go back to Paragraph 5 of "Learning to Trust a Self-Driving Car." You know the main idea and the organizational pattern of the paragraph, so you should be able to find the major supporting details. The major supporting details will explain the main idea.

In other words, they will explain the solution to the problem of occupants not having a safety mindset when it comes to self-driving cars. Answer the following questions to help you determine the major supporting ideas:

1. Is there a key phrase that signals when the solution to the problem will be listed?

2. How many solutions to the problem are presented?

3. Are there any stylistic features that help you identify the solutions? For example, has the author used a repeated sentence structure or a repeated word when providing all of the solutions?

4. Are there any minor supporting details within these solutions that you would need to mention in a summary in order for the reader to fully understand the solution?

5. Can you state the solutions to the problem, which are actually the major supporting details of the paragraph, in your own words?

TEXT ANNOTATION WITH THE GOAL OF SUMMARIZING

Annotating a text and text marking are important strategies for summarizing a text. In Chapter 1, you read about active reading as a reading comprehension strategy. Annotating is part of active reading. When you annotate, you write notes directly on the text or in the margins to ensure you can comprehend ideas in the first place and retrieve those ideas if you need them after reading. When you are summarizing a text, your annotations should focus on main ideas and supporting details. Because main ideas and supporting details are tied to the patterns of organization of a text, you should make notes about the patterns of organization as well. Figure 4.2 provides an example of a possible annotation of the first paragraph of "Learning to Trust a Self-Driving Car." Before looking at the example, complete the Apply the Skill activity below.

▶ Apply the Skill

Text Annotation with the Goal of Summarizing

Annotate the title, author, and first paragraph of the reading "Learning to Trust a Self-Driving Car." Use the following questions to guide your annotations. When you are done, compare your annotations with the example provided in Figure 4.2.

- Does the title hint at the topic of the reading?
- Who is the author? What is his occupation? What can his occupation tell you about his knowledge of the topic?
- The source of the reading is the *New Yorker*. Write notes that address the journalistic questions: Who? What? Why? When? Where? How?
- Can you determine an overall pattern of organization in the reading? If so, what is it?

FIGURE 4.2

EXAMPLE OF ANNOTATING AN INTRODUCTION

On a clear morning in early May, Brian Lathrop, a senior engineer for Volkswagen's Electronics Research Laboratory, was in the driver's seat of a Tesla Model S as it travelled along a stretch of road near Blacksburg, Virginia, when the car began to drift from its lane. Lathrop had his hands on the wheel but was not in control of the vehicle. The Tesla was in Auto-pilot mode, a highly evolved version of cruise control that, via an array of sensors, allows the car to change lanes, steer through corners, and match the lurching of traffic unaided. As the vehicle—one of a fleet belonging to Virginia Tech's Transportation Institute, which Lathrop was visiting that day—lost track of the road markings, he shook the wheel to disengage Auto-pilot. "If I hadn't been aware of what was happening, it could have been a completely different outcome," Lathrop told me recently.

← Story of an electronics engineer experiencing a problem with a self-driving car

← Definition of autopilot for self-driving cars

← Human interference needed to avoid danger

Source: Parkin, 2016.

From Figure 4.2, you see that when you put the annotations of the introduction paragraph together, you get an overall sense of what the author is trying to do in the introduction. The annotations provide the story of an electronic engineer's experience with a self-driving car, which resulted in his having to use human interference when the car steered off-course. It also provides a definition of *autopilot* to help the reader get a sense of what a self-driving car actually does. Therefore, this introductory paragraph seems to provide a bit of background information and hints that there is a problem with self-driving cars. The introductory paragraph, then, is a narrative, anecdote or short story about an individual's frightening experience driving an automated car. The main idea is implied: Brian Lathrop's experience driving an automated car was frightening. The rest of the paragraph serves to underscore this point.

The author doesn't seem to have made his overall main point about self-driving cars in the introductory paragraph, but on the basis of the title, "Learning to Trust a Self-Driving Car," and the end of the story he tells, you can infer that the organization of the reading is problem and solution or cause and effect. The cause is that there is distrust with self-driving cars; the solution is not yet clear from the opening paragraph. The introduction, then, grabs the reader's attention by describing an experience driving an automated car—an experience that could have ended badly. Using this technique, the author sets the scene for the discussion of problems and possible solutions with automated vehicles. Beginning with an anecdote is a common introductory technique, as you learned in Chapter 2.

You would then proceed to annotate the rest of the reading, ensuring that you take notes particularly on the problems and solutions presented in the reading.

Text Annotation with the Goal of Summarizing

Annotate the remainder of "Learning to Trust a Self-Driving Car." When annotating, keep in mind the title of the text, the topic, the pattern of organization, and the genre and purpose of the reading. When you are done, see if you can use your annotations to identify the thesis of the reading, the main ideas that support the thesis, and the major supporting details that support the main ideas.

OUTLINES

Creating an outline is a good strategy to use before writing. You are likely used to creating outlines for your own essays as you learned in Chapter 1. These essay outlines help you organize your ideas, and when you create an outline, you begin to predict the structure and the content of your own essay. For writing a summary, the task of constructing an outline is a bit different. Rather than creating an outline that *predicts* your own writing, you are instead crafting an outline that *describes* a piece of writing that already exists. That being said, you still end up using the outline to plan a new piece of writing, just as you do with an essay outline. However, your new piece of writing, the summary, will not provide too much expansion on the ideas in your summary outline. It will simply glue these ideas together, keeping intact the relationship among main ideas and major supporting details.

You will notice from Table 4.1 that the key similarity between a summary outline and an essay outline is that they both capture the main ideas and major supporting details and show how they are all related. The key differences are the stage in the process at which the outlines are written, the exclusion of minor supporting details in the summary outline, and how the outlines are actually developed into pieces of writing.

TABLE 4.1

WRITING AN OUTLINE FOR A SUMMARY VERSUS WRITING AN OUTLINE FOR AN ESSAY

	OUTLINE FOR A SUMMARY	OUTLINE FOR AN ESSAY
Purpose	Organize your reading comprehension.	Organize your writing.
Sequence	Read the essay first; then, create the outline; then, write the summary.	Create the outline first; write the essay after.
Content	Capture the main ideas and major supporting details (minor supporting details are usually not included), as well as the relationships among them.	Capture the main ideas, major supporting details, and minor supporting details, as well as the relationships among them.
Use	Craft a paragraph that captures the content of the reading, ensuring unity, coherence, and brevity.	Craft an essay that captures your content, ensuring the ideas are developed in great depth.

Figure 4.3 provides a partial outline for the "Learning to Trust a Self-Driving Car" reading. This outline provides the main idea, major supporting details, and minor supporting details of the fifth paragraph.

FIGURE 4.3

PARTIAL OUTLINE OF A READING FOR THE PURPOSE OF WRITING A SUMMARY

Main idea: Automotive engineers of self-driving cars need to put people in the mindset that self-driving cars are safe.

Major supporting detail: Vehicle occupants need to know when the vehicle is in self-driving mode.

Major supporting detail: Vehicle occupants need to know that the vehicle is actually responding to its surroundings when in self-driving mode.

Major supporting detail: Vehicle occupants need to know when the vehicle is about to make a maneuver based on the sensing of its surroundings.

When creating an outline for a summary, it is best to paraphrase the writer's thesis, main ideas, and major supporting details rather than stating them word for word. Paraphrasing at the outline stage will help to ensure that you (1) understand the writer's ideas and details and (2) avoid plagiarism in your summary. You will learn more about paraphrasing later in this chapter.

▶ Apply the Skill

Outlining a Reading

The following is an outline for the reading "Learning to Trust a Self-Driving Car." Complete the outline by filling in the missing main ideas and major supporting details. Try to paraphrase these ideas and details rather than quoting them directly. Paraphrasing requires that you use your own word choices and sentence structures rather than using the same ones that the author used in the reading. If you want more information on paraphrasing before you begin this task, review the "Writing a Summary" section of this chapter.

OUTLINE FOR "LEARNING TO TRUST A SELF-DRIVING CAR"

Thesis: Automotive engineers have a difficult time convincing drivers to be onboard with self-driving cars because of the paradox that drivers need to trust the vehicle's ability to drive itself while at the same time being aware that they may need to interfere if the self-driving feature fails.

Main idea 1: Self-driving cars have an excellent safety record, but there have still been accidents.
   Major supporting detail: Death of Joshua Brown
   Major supporting detail: Better safety record than humans when measured against number of vehicle miles (U.S. National Safety Council report)
   Major supporting detail:

Main idea 2:
    Major supporting detail:
    Major supporting detail: Vehicle occupants need to know that the vehicle is actually responding to its surroundings when in self-driving mode.
    Major supporting detail: Vehicle occupants need to know when the vehicle is about to make a maneuver based on the sensing of its surroundings.

Main idea 3:
    Major supporting detail:
    Minor supporting detail: Google is using an adhesive hood to prevent further injuries if a pedestrian is struck.
    Minor supporting detail: Volkswagen is using blinking LED lights on the front windshield that follow pedestrians while they are walking in front of the vehicle.

Main idea 4: Once drivers are convinced to try a self-driving car, their trust in the vehicle grows quickly.
    Major supporting detail:
    Minor supporting detail: In some cases, it takes only 10 minutes.
    Major supporting detail:

Main idea 5:
    Major supporting detail: Automotive engineers need to keep in mind that people may stop paying attention when in a self-driving car.
    Major supporting detail: Drivers still need to take responsibility in a self-driving car because they can make decisions a self-driving car cannot (it is a system designed to respond to stimuli, not to make its own decisions).

Once you have created the outline of the reading, you essentially have a summary in point form. You then just need to massage the main ideas and supporting details into a paragraph that provides a unified, coherent structure to deliver the ideas to your audience in a comprehensible way. You learned about unity and coherence in Chapter 2; you will examine strategies for unity and coherence in a summary later in this chapter.

GRAPHIC ORGANIZERS

Graphic organizers visually represent main ideas and supporting details. You learned about graphic organizers in Chapter 1 as a means to organize ideas for writing or represent key points in a reading. In Chapter 3 you also learned a method to "read" graphic material. Keep in mind that in the context of summarizing another writer's text, a graphic organizer has two functions:

1. To help you comprehend how the writer's ideas are organized in the text by visualizing these ideas in a meaningful way
2. To act as a guide as you write your summary of the text, which will communicate the text's organization to your own audience

You are using the organizer as both a reading aid and a writing aid. Because the purpose of the organizer is to help you, as the summary writer, you should create an organizer that is meaningful to *you*: you are the audience for your graphic organizer.

► **Apply the Skill**

Graphic Organizers

Create a graphic organizer that would help you summarize "Learning to Trust a Self-Driving Car." Use the work you've done in the other Apply the Skill features in this chapter to help you. When you are done, compare your graphic organizer with one of your peers. Describe the similarities and differences and explain to your peer why your particular graphic organizer is helpful to you.

TABLES

As you learned in Chapter 1, tables are a simple way to help you sort and classify information into the categories of main ideas, major supporting details, and minor supporting details. Table 4.2 provides an example of how one reader has used a table to clarify the organization of ideas in Paragraph 5 of "Learning to Trust a Self-Driving Car."

TABLE 4.2

ORGANIZING THE IDEAS OF PARAGRAPH 5 OF "LEARNING TO TRUST A SELF-DRIVING CAR"

MAIN IDEA	MAJOR SUPPORTING DETAIL	MINOR SUPPORTING DETAIL
Automotive engineers of self-driving cars need to put people in the mindset that self-driving cars are safe.	Vehicle occupants need to know when the vehicle is in self-driving mode. Vehicle occupants need to know that the vehicle is actually responding to its surroundings when in self-driving mode. Vehicle occupants need to know when the vehicle is about to make a maneuver based on the sensing of its surroundings.	Vehicle needs to sense pedestrians and other vehicles.

Note how this table provides the same information that an outline or graphic organizer would. It is just another way to help you organize the ideas of the reading before you write a summary in paragraph form. When trying to choose among outlines, graphic organizers, and tables, think carefully about how you process information best as well as which method would best reflect the pattern of organization. Remember that these organizing mechanisms are intended for you and you alone, unless your instructor specifically requests to see them as proof of the prewriting process. If that is the case, be sure to ask if there is a preferred organizing mechanism. If there is, be sure to use that mechanism. If that particular mechanism is not the one that is most meaningful to you, simply start with the mechanism that is most meaningful and then translate it into the required one.

► **Apply the Skill**

Tables

Create a table that would help you summarize "Learning to Trust a Self-Driving Car." Then, compare this table with the graphic organizer and outline you completed in earlier Apply the Skill activities. Which mechanism for organizing and classifying the information for the reading do you find most helpful? Why?

Writing a Summary

If you are diligent in the reading and prewriting phases of summary writing, the actual writing of the summary should be an exercise in paraphrasing the main ideas and major supporting details and massaging them into a paragraph. *Paraphrasing* is capturing the ideas and details of a writer using your own words and sentence structure. Massaging ideas and details into a paragraph involves piecing together the paraphrased ideas and details into a paragraph that demonstrates unity and coherence.

Writing Effective Paraphrases

Paraphrasing is one part of summary writing that many writers find difficult because it involves strong reading comprehension, a wide vocabulary, and a good grasp of various sentence structures. You have been learning strategies for developing reading comprehension skills and sentence structure skills in the previous chapters of this book. You will need to review these strategies and employ them often in order to develop strong paraphrasing skills. These steps are then explained and demonstrated following the figure, using this sentence from Paragraph 5 of "Learning to Trust a Self-Driving Car."

STEP 1: ENSURE YOU FULLY COMPREHEND THE TEXT

Step 1 requires you to engage in the reading process described in Chapter 1 to ensure you understand exactly what the writer is communicating. Be alert to any comprehension problems: If you did not know what the word *prime* meant in the source text, for example, you could read the other sentences surrounding it that reveal the importance of a self-driving car *making people aware* of what it is doing.

FIGURE 4.4
SEVEN STEPS FOR PARAPHRASING

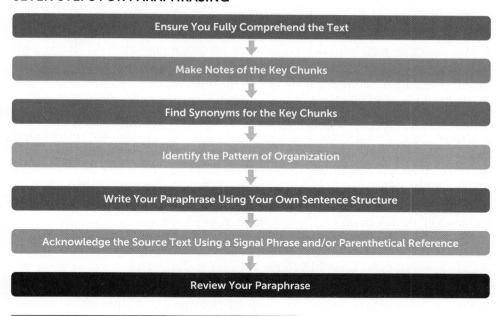

Ensure You Fully Comprehend the Text

Make Notes of the Key Chunks

Find Synonyms for the Key Chunks

Identify the Pattern of Organization

Write Your Paraphrase Using Your Own Sentence Structure

Acknowledge the Source Text Using a Signal Phrase and/or Parenthetical Reference

Review Your Paraphrase

Source: Finally, the vehicle must prime people before it makes a maneuver.

STEP 2: MAKE NOTES OF THE KEY CHUNKS

Chunking gets you to see the *ideas* of the sentence rather than just the words in isolation. The key chunks of a passage are the words and phrases that carry the essential meaning of the passage. Without these key words and phrases, the passage would lose its meaning, or the meaning would be misconstrued. If you have difficulty trying to determine what the key chunks are, try to read the source text and then look away and explain the point to someone else. The ideas that you include in your explanation point to the main chunks. Any other information from the source text that you did not use is likely additional wording that does not contain the essential meaning of the passage.

You can also find key chunks with the help of the journalistic questions: *who, what, when, where, why, and how.* Table 4.3 analyzes the source text using journalistic questions as a way to identify key chunks of information.

TABLE 4.3
CHUNKING A SOURCE TEXT BY ANSWERING JOURNALISTIC QUESTIONS

QUESTION	ANSWER
What is this sentence about?	"the vehicle" (an autonomous one, specifically)
What does the sentence say about the vehicle?	It "must prime people"
When must the vehicle prime people?	"before it makes a maneuver"

As you can see, for this passage, three questions cover the full meaning of the sentence. Two of the questions are "what" questions because the question "what?" applies to both the subject of the sentence and what the sentence is actually saying about the subject. Keep in mind that most sentences will answer some of the journalistic questions, not all of them.

You will note that the journalistic questioning method has chunked the information into three parts. It has also omitted the adverb *finally*, which is really a transition word linking this major supporting detail to the other two major supporting details that come before it. If you are paraphrasing this sentence in isolation, then you can ignore this *finally*. If you are paraphrasing it along with the other major supporting details, then you will need to consider it.

No matter which method you choose—the look-away-and-explain method or the journalistic questioning method—the information is still chunked into smaller ideas that you can find synonyms for in the next step. In fact, if you use the look-away-and-explain method, you may already be engaging in finding synonyms for the key chunks. You should take advantage of whichever method you are most comfortable with. Both methods help reinforce your comprehension of the passage and ensure that you are including all the key chunks of the sentence in your paraphrase.

STEP 3: FIND SYNONYMS FOR THE KEY CHUNKS

Now that you know the key pieces of information in the source text, it is time to put these pieces of information into your own words. You need to select different words from what the writer used in her text, while still maintaining the meanings of those words. In other words, you need to find synonyms for the words the writer has used.

When deciding on synonyms for your paraphrases, keep in mind each of the following ideas:

- **Not all synonyms work in the same context.** A thesaurus is a good place to find synonyms for key words and phrases. When you use a thesaurus, however, you need to keep in mind that even though two different words are synonyms, one may work in a particular sentence but the other may not work in that same sentence. Always consider the context in which you want to use a word and double-check that your chosen word is appropriate within that context.
- **A phrase may be a synonym for a single word and vice versa.** You may not always be able to rely on a thesaurus because it does not address the issue of single-word synonyms for phrases or phrasal synonyms for single words. This is where your own usage of English comes in, as well as your own experience with reading and writing texts. Understanding that phrases can replace words and words can replace phrases is crucial for paraphrasing, as you will come across many instances where you just won't be able to do a word-for-word substitution.
- **Not all words have synonyms.** Some words do not have an appropriate synonym. Examples of such words are proper nouns—specific names or titles—that have no replacement, a term that has a very precise meaning or context that would change if a synonym were used, or a technical term used in a specific field. When you write a paraphrase with these kinds of words, you can use the exact same word.

► **Apply the Skill**

Finding Synonyms for a Paraphrase

The table below lists the key chunks of the source text. Add synonyms for each of these chunks. Keep context in mind and remember that your synonym does not have to be the same number of words as the key chunk. If a key chunk or part of it does not have an appropriate synonym, explain why. The last chunk has been done for you as an example.

KEY CHUNKS	SYNONYMS
The vehicle (an autonomous one, specifically)	
must prime	
people	
before it makes a maneuver	prior to conducting a maneuver (*maneuver* is a specialized term indicating a skillful movement and is often associated with vehicle movements, specifically; therefore, you can leave it as it is)

STEP 4: IDENTIFY THE PATTERN OF ORGANIZATION

To identify the pattern of organization for the text you are paraphrasing, you need to look for signal words that indicate that pattern. If you need help, consult Table 3.2 in Chapter 3 to review a list of common signal words for various patterns.

The source text, "Finally, the vehicle must prime people before it makes a maneuver," seems to best fit the listing pattern of *time order*. The word "before" is a subordinating conjunction that indicates this particular organizational pattern. Therefore, in your paraphrase, you need to make sure that the time order pattern remains intact.

STEP 5: WRITE YOUR PARAPHRASE USING YOUR OWN SENTENCE STRUCTURE

Step 5 now requires that you piece all previous steps together, with the added condition that the sentence structure must be different from the one that the writer used. Here again, the grammar presented in the first three chapters of this book is crucial to understand. In order to use your own sentence structure, you need to be aware of the parts of sentences, of different types of clauses, and of modifiers (adjectives and adverbs). Manipulating the structure and order of these grammatical elements will produce a sentence structure that differs from the one used by the writer of the original text.

After you have decided on your own sentence structure for the paraphrase, you are now ready to combine it with your synonyms from Step 3 and your pattern of organization from Step 4 to write an effective paraphrase. See some examples in Figure 4.5.

FIGURE 4.5
PARAPHRASING EXAMPLES

Original passage: The vehicle must prime people before it makes a maneuver.

- Paraphrase example 1: Prior to maneuvering, a self-driving car needs to send a signal to its occupants.
- Paraphrase example 2: A self-driving car can maneuver itself only after it has prepared its occupants for the maneuver.
- Paraphrase example 3: When a self-driving car wants to conduct a maneuver, it needs to send a signal to its occupants prior to doing so.

STEP 6: ACKNOWLEDGE THE SOURCE TEXT USING A SIGNAL PHRASE AND/OR PARENTHETICAL REFERENCE

Your paraphrase will often require a signal phrase and/or parenthetical reference to let your reader know where the paraphrase has come from. A *signal phrase* is a group of words that tells the reader that you are about to state someone else's idea rather than provide your own. Most signal phrases are formed using the author's last name and a reporting verb; for example, *Parkin argues*, *Parkin claims*, and *Parkin says*. Other signal phrases do not include a reporting verb; for example, *According to Parkin* and *It is the opinion of Parkin that*. If you do not use a signal phrase because you want to de-emphasize the author or because the signal phrase disrupts your own writing style, then you can also put the author's name inside a parenthetical reference directly after the paraphrase.

Here are some examples of how to acknowledge the author for the first paraphrased sentence from Step 5:

Signal phrase: Parkin claims that prior to maneuvering, a self-driving car needs to send a signal to its occupants (par. 5).

No signal phrase: Prior to maneuvering, a self-driving car needs to send a signal to its occupants (Parkin par. 5).

The two examples above use the Modern Language Association (MLA) style of referencing to acknowledge the source. Different disciplines use different style guides. The important thing is that you remember to acknowledge the original source of your paraphrase and that you do so in a way that allows your writing to flow, while using whatever documentation guidelines you have been asked to follow. More information on referencing and documentation is provided in Chapter 5 and the appendix on documentation.

If your writing task is a one-paragraph summary of a single text, you likely will not need to provide a signal phrase or parenthetical reference for every paraphrased sentence. Verify your instructor's preference.

STEP 7: REVIEW YOUR PARAPHRASE

When you think you are done writing your paraphrase, be sure to review it. Ensure your paraphrase accurately and precisely captures the writer's idea, double-check that you have used your own word choices and your own sentence structure, and confirm that you have provided a signal phrase and/or parenthetical reference where required. Table 4.4 indicates what you should do when reviewing your paraphrase for accuracy, precision, unique vocabulary, and unique sentence structure.

TABLE 4.4

REVIEWING THE ACCURACY, PRECISION, UNIQUE VOCABULARY, AND UNIQUE SENTENCE STRUCTURE OF A PARAPHRASE

WHEN CHECKING FOR . . .	DO THE FOLLOWING . . .
Accuracy	Ask the journalistic questions for both the source text and your paraphrase of it. If your answers are the same, then you know the paraphrase is accurate.
Precision	Compare each synonym in the paraphrase to the original language used in the source text. Ensure the synonym captures the same meaning in the same context. Find the transition word that indicates the organizational pattern in each of the sentences. Ensure that the transition words in both sentences indicate the same relationship.
Unique Vocabulary	Ensure no words are repeated between the source text and the paraphrase. If there are repeated words, make sure you can justify the repetition (for example, a technical term, a term with a unique meaning, a proper noun).
Unique Sentence Structure	Analyze the source text and the paraphrase in two ways: 1. by sentence parts (subjects, verbs, objects, complements) and 2. by clauses (independent, dependent). Compare the analysis, ensuring that the two sentences are different in both types of analysis.

If your review indicates that there is a problem with your paraphrase, you will need to go back to the step at which you think the problem began. For example, a problem with accuracy may have taken place in Step 1 when you were trying to fully comprehend the text, whereas a problem with unique vocabulary may have been a result of an oversight in Step 3 when you were finding synonyms for the key chunks. The earlier in the process that the problem presents itself, the more work you will need to do to correct the problem.

Putting Paraphrased Content into a Summary Paragraph

With your prewriting and paraphrasing complete, the last step for writing a summary involves the construction of the summary paragraph. Just like any other paragraph, a summary paragraph presents a main idea in a topic sentence, which is then supported with major supporting details. While minor supporting details are not typically included, they may be part of the summary paragraph as well if they are needed for your reader to comprehend one of the major supporting details.

In the case of a summary paragraph, the topic sentence should provide the paraphrased thesis of the text being summarized. In addition, it should provide the bibliographic information for the text so that the reader knows what text is being summarized.

Example of a first sentence for a summary:

> In "Learning to Trust a Self-Driving Car," Simon Parker explains that automotive engineers have a difficult time convincing drivers to be onboard with self-driving cars because of the paradox that drivers need to trust the vehicle's ability to drive itself while at the same time be aware that they may need to interfere if the self-driving feature fails.

At minimum, the first sentence of the summary needs to include the title of the reading and the writer's full name (you should refer to writer by last name or by pronoun during the rest of the summary). Depending on the documentation style you are using, other information—such as the date of publication—may be required. The amount of information provided here also depends on whether or not an end-of-text bibliography will be included. End-of-text bibliographies provide all of the publication information for the text (usually author, title of article, date of publication, title of newspaper/magazine/journal/book, name of publisher). If you are not including such a page, then you should include all of that information directly in the summary itself. If you are including such a page, then the title of the article and author's name should be sufficient. Always check with your instructor to determine the specific requirements for your course.

The rest of the summary presents all of the author's major supporting details, and, only if necessary, some minor supporting details. These details need to be logically connected to one another with carefully chosen transition words that indicate the relationships between them. You should revisit the patterns of organization from the previous chapter to remind yourself of key words that can help indicate relationships between ideas. Keep in mind that showing your reader the relationships between the writer's ideas is just as important as the ideas themselves. A good summary writer assumes his reader has not read the original text, and therefore provides the reader with all the information necessary to fully comprehend it.

To remind your reader that you are summarizing a text, you should also acknowledge the writer throughout the summary. While you need not mention the writer's name in every sentence, it should appear at least a few times during the summary to continuously remind your reader—and yourself—that you are summarizing rather than providing your own argument.

Using the writer's name will also help you remain objective in the summary. Remember that the point of a summary is to restate, in your own words, the writer's main ideas. You should not articulate your own opinion of the ideas, and you should not bring to the summary any information external to the writer's work. To enhance objectivity, you should also write the summary in third-person point of view. In other words, avoid pronouns such as *I, me, we, us,* and *you.* A summary does not speak directly to your reader. Review the key features of a summary in Figure 4.6.

FIGURE 4.6
KEY FEATURES OF A SUMMARY PARAGRAPH

Topic sentence that includes bibliographic information and a paraphrase of the author's thesis	Supporting sentences that provide paraphrases of the author's major supporting details, and possibly some minor supporting details	Signal words/transitions that accurately indicate the relationships between the author's ideas
Repeated instances of the author's name (last name or pronoun)	Objective style, using third-person point of view	Omits unnecessariy details and avoids adding details external to the text

When you are finished writing your summary, you will want to review it carefully to ensure it contains all the key features above. If it does not satisfy one or more of the key features, you will need to revise it. For example, if the summary paragraph of a 1,500-word article is going beyond 300 words, you would likely want to shorten it by getting rid of unnecessary details or wordiness. You will also want to check the accuracy, precision, vocabulary, and sentence structure of your paraphrasing.

▶ Apply the Skill

Evaluating a Summary

The following paragraph is a summary of "Learning to Trust a Self-Driving Car." Read the paragraph, and then answer the questions that follow it.

> In "Learning to Trust a Self-Driving Car," Simon Parkin explains how automotive engineers have a difficult time convincing drivers to be onboard with self-driving cars because of a paradox: drivers need to trust the vehicle's ability to drive itself while at the same time be aware that the self-driving feature may fail. He begins by discussing how self-driving cars have an excellent safety record, but people still lack trust in them because there have been accidents, such as that of Joshua Brown who died in a self-driving car when it collided with a large transport truck. Statistics, according to Parkin, are not enough to convince people of the safety of self-driving cars. Instead, as senior Volkswagen electronics engineer Brian Lathrop says, people need to actually feel safe inside the cars. Lathrop says that self-driving cars need to perform three functions to make people feel safe: clarify when the vehicle is driving on its own; make occupants aware that the car is actually responding to pedestrians and other traffic; and, prior to maneuvering, send a signal to prepare the vehicle's occupants. In addition to getting occupants to trust self-driving vehicles, Parkin also mentions that those outside the vehicle—other drivers and pedestrians—also need to trust in the safety of these vehicles. Parkin says Google is addressing this particular concern with an adhesive hood to prevent struck pedestrians from receiving further injuries, while Volkswagen is using blinking LED lights on the front windshield that follow pedestrians when they are walking in front of the vehicle. Near the end of the article, Parkin explains how despite these challenges of getting people to trust a self-driving car initially, once the drivers are actually in one, their trust in the vehicle grows quickly. Volkswagen's research indicates many people stop paying attention to the vehicle and look for other things to do because they are bored. Parkin concludes by re-emphasizing the key challenge with self-driving cars: they encourage passivity while requiring awareness at the same time. (Word count: 331 words)

Questions

1. What bibliographic information has the summary writer provided?

2. How many times is Parkin's name mentioned or referred to in the summary? Do you think it is mentioned the right number of times, too few times, or too many times?

3. Why has the summary writer included Brian Lathrop's name in the summary?

4. The summary writer provides a number of transition/signal words or phrases to indicate the relationships among Parkin's main ideas. Underline these transition/signal words or phrases in the summary and discuss whether or not they are effective.

5. Evaluate the quality of paraphrasing in the summary. Has the writer ensured that the paraphrasing demonstrates accuracy, precision, unique vocabulary, and unique sentence structure?

6. Has the summary writer included any minor supporting details? If so, are these details necessary for understanding a major supporting detail, or could they have been omitted?

7. Is the summary written in the third-person point of view?

8. Is the summary objective? In other words, has the summary writer avoided giving her opinion on the issue of self-driving cars?

9. The summary is 331 words. Do you think this length is reasonable? Can you see any parts of the summary that could be omitted or described more concisely?

10. If you were to write a summary of the article, would you have done anything differently from the sample summary? If so, what would you have done differently and why?

Review

Paraphrasing

Answer the following review questions in paragraph form or generate ideas to contribute to a group or class discussion.

1. What is paraphrasing and why is it important?
2. What are the seven steps for paraphrasing and why is each step important?
3. Describe what is meant by the following terms and why they are important for a well-crafted summary: *accuracy, precision, unique vocabulary* and *unique sentence structure*.

▶ Did You Know?

PROOFREADING FOR CORRECT SENTENCE BOUNDARIES

In the previous chapter, you learned how to combine clauses into compound, complex, and compound-complex sentences. Sometimes when writers are trying to get nuanced, or subtle, ideas down on paper, however, they may not be paying careful attention to the way they are combining or separating clauses. As a result, the writing may contain run-ons or fragments. Run-ons occur when independent clauses have not been properly joined or separated. Fragments, on the other hand, occur when the subject or verb (or both) of an independent clause is missing or when a dependent clause is punctuated as its own sentence. Both run-ons and fragments cause confusion for readers because they prevent the reader from understanding the logical connections between the writer's ideas. Good writers employ careful proofreading strategies after they are done writing to ensure they do not make these types of sentence boundary errors.

Run-Ons

Run-ons can be broken down into two different types: fused sentences and comma splices. Fused sentences happen when a writer combines two independent clauses without any punctuation to separate them.

> Example of fused sentence: People have difficulty trusting machines they also have difficulty trusting other people.

A comma splice is when a writer combines two independent clauses with just a comma to separate them.

> Example of a comma splice: People have difficulty trusting machines, they also have difficulty trusting other people.

Both of these run-on sentences neglect the rules for combining independent clauses that you learned in the previous chapter. To fix them, you can use any of the strategies for combining independent clauses into compound sentences that you learned in Chapter 3.

▶ **Apply the Skill**

Run-On Sentences

Using the techniques provided, correct this run-on sentence:

> People have difficulty trusting machines, they also have difficulty trusting other people.

The first one has been done as an example.

1. converting the compound sentence into a simple sentence

   People have difficulty trusting machines and other people.

2. independent clause + comma + coordinating conjunction + independent clause

3. independent clause + semicolon + conjunctive adverb + comma + independent clause

4. independent clause + semicolon on its own + independent clause

Fragments

Just like run-ons, fragments can be broken down into different types: (1) fragments that are not clauses at all and (2) dependent clause fragments. To avoid fragments that are not clauses at all, simply analyze your sentences for subjects and verbs. If either a subject or a verb is missing in your sentence, then your sentence is a fragment. Remember that all sentences are made up of clauses and every clause must have a subject and a verb. Therefore, if you are missing a subject or a verb, then you do not have a clause, so you do not have a sentence.

When analyzing sentences for subjects and verbs to verify that they are, in fact, sentences, do not be fooled by nouns that look like verbs. Gerunds, which are nouns ending with –*ing*, look like verbs but actually function as nouns. An -*ing* word is a verb only if it has a form of the verb *be* in front of it—for example, *is driving, was driving, are driving, will be driving*. Infinitives, which are the word *to* plus the base form of the verb (to run, to write), also look like verbs but actually function as nouns. If you see a base form of a verb (the form without any ending on it) preceded by the word *to*, remember that it is an infinitive functioning as a subject, object, or complement—it is *not* a verb.

Examples of fragment with missing subject and verb:

1. The trick to getting people to trust in a self-driving car
2. In order to make people feel secure in a self-driving car

The way to correct these fragments is to form a subject-verb combination. Therefore, information should be added to the sentences:

1. The trick to getting people to trust in a self-driving car is providing them with easy-to-use features.
2. In order to make people feel secure in a self-driving car, they need to be provided with easy-to-use features.

Unlike fragments missing a subject and/or verb, dependent clause fragments do have both a subject and a verb, which is why they are sometimes more difficult to detect. However, dependent clauses have a specific identifier: a subordinating conjunction at the beginning of the dependent clause. If you see one of these dependent clauses punctuated as its own sentence, you know it is a fragment. You know this because in the previous chapter you learned that a dependent clause must be attached to an independent clause. It cannot be its own sentence.

Example of a dependent clause fragment: Automotive engineers of self-driving cars need to be clever. Because people have difficulty trusting these vehicles.

The dependent clause, highlighted in yellow, is a fragment because it is punctuated as its own sentence: there is a period before it and a period at the end of it. To fix the dependent clause fragment, you need to attach it to an independent clause using the rules for combining clauses into complex sentences, or you need to eliminate the subordinating conjunction at the beginning of the clause to convert it into an independent clause.

Attach the dependent clause to the independent clause:

Automotive engineers of self-driving cars need to be clever because people have difficulty trusting these vehicles.

Eliminate the subordinating conjunction at the beginning of the clause:

Automotive engineers of self-driving cars need to be clever. People have difficulty trusting these vehicles.

Figure 4.7 summarizes strategies to fix run-on sentences and sentence fragments.

FIGURE 4.7
PROOFREADING STRATEGIES TO AVOID RUN-ONS AND FRAGMENTS

- Analyze your sentences for subjects and verbs, keeping in mind that gerunds and infinitives function as nouns, not verbs. Ensure each verb has a corresponding subject.
- Label the clauses in your sentences, distinguishing independent clauses from dependent clauses.
- Ensure each dependent clause is attached to an independent clause.
- Identify your compound and compound-complex sentences to ensure that two independent clauses have been joined according to the rules from the previous chapter.
- Analyze the commas you have used in your sentences. If there is an independent clause before the comma and an independent clause after the comma, ensure you have a coordinating conjunction directly after the comma.
- Proofread your writing in reverse. Begin at your last sentence, move to the second-last sentence, and so on until you get to the first sentence. Doing so will slow your reading pace and help you examine the sentences in isolation. Examining sentences in isolation helps identify sentence-level errors such as fragments and run-ons.

▶ Apply the Skill

Proofreading for Sentence Boundaries

Write a paragraph that responds to the first question posed in the Think about It section near the beginning of the chapter: Is there a point at which we must draw the line when it comes to automation? Then, make the following markings on your paragraph:

1. Draw a line under any gerunds and infinitives in the paragraph.

2. Label the subjects and verbs in the paragraph.

3. Circle the subordinating conjunctions in the paragraph.

When you are done annotating your paragraph, use the annotations to ensure you do not have any fragments. If you find any fragments, correct them.

Read the article below from *Maclean's* magazine about the debate surrounding mentally ill employees—those suffering from depression or anxiety—being permitted to work in careers in which they are accountable for people's lives. This topic has been in the news, ever since the March 2015 Germanwings jet crash in the Alps that was concluded to be purposefully caused by a mentally ill co-pilot. When you are done reading, consider the following questions:

1. Determine the purpose, audience, and overall pattern of organization of the article. Use the author's purpose, audience, and overall pattern of organization to determine the thesis, the main ideas of each section, and the major supporting details of those main ideas. Organize these ideas as they are related to one another in an outline, graphic organizer, or table.

2. Using the work you have done in Question 1, summarize the article. Write a one-paragraph summary of the article that includes all the key features from Figure 4.4, Seven Steps for Paraphrasing.

3. In Paragraph 12, the author references Claude Thibault, an aviation medical adviser, who says that the Germanwings tragedy of March 2015 "speaks in favour of systems that encourage people suffering from mental illness to come forward." What do you think needs to be done so that people feel safe and empowered to reveal their mental illness? Is it just employers who need to do something? Or is the issue bigger than employment?

4. In Paragraph 18, the author addresses the dilemma that authorities face. On the one hand, they need to ensure that those who suffer from depression and anxiety have equal access to jobs even if those jobs involve, as the author puts it, "life-and-death responsibilities." On the other hand, "public perception looms large, as authorities worry about the fallout should someone known to have psychological troubles break down in a way that costs lives." Explain the specific factors that need to be taken into consideration when trying to resolve this tension. What are the risks and liabilities involved in the various solutions to this problem?

5. Take a position on the debate presented in Gillis's article: do you believe that people who have depression or anxiety should be permitted to work in careers in which they are accountable for people's lives? Provide specific reasons and concrete evidence to support your point of view.

6. Both readings in this chapter examine the theme of trust as it applies to potentially life-and-death situations. In "One Man's Fight to Help Jets Fly—Despite Mental Illness," Gillis articulates the problems people have with trusting other people, whereas in "Learning to Trust a Self-Driving Car," Parkin articulates the problems people have with trusting automation. What factors do people consider when deciding whom or what to trust? What can others do to help instill people's trust in them or the machines they have created? Support your answer with your own ideas, as well as with the ideas and details provided in both of this chapter's readings.

ONE MAN'S FIGHT TO HELP JETS FLY—DESPITE MENTAL ILLNESS

A debate rages: Should people with depression be allowed in jobs with life-or-death responsibilities?

By Charlie Gillis

1   Becoming an air traffic controller is one of the country's most gruelling career paths: an ordeal of interviews, personality assessments, math exams and pattern-recognition tests that take place over months. So Jade Bethune was understandably proud when he reached the final stage of Nav Canada's recruitment process, qualifying as a trainee at the company's Pacific area control centre on B.C.'s Lower Mainland. If successful, the 34-year-old would be queuing up jumbo jets to land at Vancouver International Airport from his seat in a space-age setting of dimmed lights and flickering consoles.

2   It was, in his words, "about the coolest job you could imagine," but there was a hitch. Bethune has suffered in the past from anxiety and depression, for which he takes medication. He disclosed the information as part of a medical fitness assessment, sending along a letter from his psychiatrist showing he'd been symptom-free for years. But Transport Canada had final say, and doctors advising the department were unmoved. "This man has been under treatment since 2005 . . . for what is said to be a single past episode," observed an internal medical review board. "It seems highly unlikely that he's had [only] a single past episode when in fact he has been in treatment for nine years."

3   Final verdict: rejected.

4   Bethune was devastated. Both his parents were pilots, he says, and it was motion sickness, not depression, that prevented him from following them to a career in the skies. He'd spent his twenties obtaining a science degree, teaching abroad and working office jobs. But a chance visit to the control tower in Kelowna, B.C., where his mother had worked as a flight instructor, had revived his appetite for a career in aviation. "That planted the seed," he says. "I thought, this is a job that I can do."

5   What's more, Transport Canada's policies seemed to open the door to candidates who, like him, take a selective seratonin reuptake inhibitor (SSRI) commonly prescribed for depression. Bethune takes a second drug called lamotrigine, which he and his doctor found worked perfectly with his SSRI, citalopram. Guidelines published on the department's website suggested candidates taking more than one psychotropic drug may be ineligible. But they also note that combination drug therapies are increasingly the norm, stressing that exceptions should be considered on a case-by-case basis.

6   So Bethune fought back. Last May, he won a decision from an internal appeal panel of Transport Canada that the government must consider the last five years of Bethune's psychiatric records, and prove why lamotrigine usage prevents him from safely guiding air crews. Ottawa appealed to federal court, but Bethune won again, striking a blow for people with mental health problems trying to gain entry to aviation and other high-stakes professions, from medicine to law enforcement. While the public fixates on alarming cases like last year's Germanwings crash caused by a suicidal pilot, people medicated for depression have been showing they can handle increasingly sensitive jobs when stabilized by innovative new therapies. Now, they're challenging long-standing barriers that keep them out of the high-pressure, yet prestigious positions that carry life-and-death

responsibility. If they're qualified, and can prove they're in good mental health, they ask, why not put the safety of the public in their hands?

7   To a degree, we already do. The same officials blocking Bethune's career path boast that Canada has been ahead of the curve, opening the door in 1992 to pilots and controllers using SSRIs, and expanding accommodations since. Under current guidelines, updated in 2010, applicants are to be considered if they can show they've been on stable dosages for four months with no symptoms and side effects, while providing a detailed report of their psychiatric histories. Once on the job, they must undergo a psychiatric evaluation every six months, and if their mental condition takes a turn for the worse, their licence is temporarily suspended while they seek help. They can return to work once they've shown they've been stable for four months. "Canada is a leader, I would say *the* leader in the world, on this issue," Dietmar Raudzus, Transport Canada's aviation medical officer for the Pacific region, wrote in a letter filed at Bethune's appeal hearing in 2015.

8   That's the aspiration, at least. How often Transport Canada fulfills it is less clear. The department can't say how many aviation applicants using psychotropic drugs have been approved or rejected, a spokeswoman says, because the medical reports containing that information are protected by doctor-patient confidentiality. Nor do they know how many pilots and air traffic controllers are currently using SSRIs—though it's hard to imagine mental disorders are unheard of on the flight deck. According to statistics cited on Transport Canada's website, one in 17 air crew suffer from depression, a rate close to that of the general population.

9   The fear this idea evokes among air travellers has a power all its own. The archetype of the crazed air traffic controller is a mainstay of popular culture, from the stricken father who causes a midair collision in *Breaking Bad* to John Candy's stressed-out character in the '80s comedy *Summer Rental*. In aviation circles, the assumption was that the high-pressure environment surrounding flight was bound to trigger mental or emotional problems, says Scott Shappell, a neuroscientist at the Embry-Riddle Aeronautical University in Daytona Beach, Fla. "Until about a decade ago, if you were taking any medications for any kind of mental disorder," he says, "that was considered disqualifying."

10   That changed with the advent of SSRIs, notes Shappell, which can stabilize sufferers of depression and anxiety without dangerous side effects like fatigue. Human rights law, meanwhile, evolved in many jurisdictions to define mental illness as a disability, preventing employers from using it as a basis to disqualify candidates.

11   Still, most countries have left a great deal of discretion in the hands of aviation authorities, who are as sensitive as anyone to horrors like the March 2015 downing of Germanwings Flight 9525. Co-pilot Andreas Lubitz deliberately crashed the airliner, killing all 150 on board; investigators found he'd been declared unfit to fly after being treated for suicidal tendencies, but withheld the information from Germanwings and showed up for work. Consensus among aviation experts was that blanket prohibitions on the mentally ill would not prevent such a disaster: you need to know they're ill in the first place. But media coverage of the crash also led anyone who has buckled up to wonder about the mental state of their air crews, and authorities felt compelled to respond. "This is a very sad story," says Claude Thibault, medical adviser of the Montreal-based International Air Transport Association (IATA). "But proportionally speaking, this kind of event is extremely rare."

12   To Thibault, the Germanwings tragedy speaks in favour of systems that encourage people suffering from mental illness to come forward. In previous decades, he notes, fear of losing one's professional licence (or not get it in the first place) led pilots and controllers to keep their problems to themselves—in some cases pressuring sympathetic doctors to understate their conditions in medical reports. "It's better to have someone who's properly medicated and under close surveillance flying," he concludes, "than someone whose condition is not known, who is flying depressed or is on medication that is not acceptable."

13   Aviation isn't the only sector coming to grips with Thibault's way of thinking. In a widely cited case from 2010, the Human Rights Tribunal of Ontario ordered Toronto's city police board to reinstate a probationary officer who'd been fired after an apparently pointless scuffle with a drunk man in a McDonald's. The officer had been suffering post-traumatic stress stemming from a previous gun incident, the tribunal heard; he was suspended and received successful psychiatric treatment while off duty, but was fired before he could return to work. In refusing to consider medical evidence that the officer was fit for duty, the tribunal ruled, the police board had discriminated on the basis of disability.

14   This legal nudge resonated throughout Canadian law enforcement, and when a similar case arose two years later in Halton, Ont., the regional police force bent over backwards to help the officer. In that instance, a constable suffering from severe obsessive compulsive disorder was deemed unable to do patrol work: he was consumed by fear of contracting disease from exposure to bodily fluids of suspects. The force scrambled to find positions he could manage (though even handling documents triggered his compulsion to wear gloves or wash his hands) and eventually gave him a civilian position as a clerk. The human rights tribunal ruled that was a fair attempt at accommodation.

15   That cops deserve extra consideration makes intuitive sense—few occupations test one's mental health so severely. Less understood has been the plight of doctors suffering from mental disorders, in part because stability seems a prerequisite for the job. These are the people, after all, on whom we unload our own problems.

16   By the 1970s, however, concern arose over the number of troubled physicians medicating themselves with alcohol, or the drugs in their office cabinets. The result was a patchwork of addiction resources offered by medical associations, which in some provinces has evolved into a kind of separate intake system for doctors with psychiatric or medical problems. In Ontario, for instance, a physician in crisis can dial up the Ontario Medical Association's "Physician Health Program" (PHP), where he or she will receive confidential advice, referrals for treatment and if needed, ongoing monitoring.

17   The response depends on the severity of the problem, says Derek Puddester, the program's associate medical director. Some are directed to the PHP by the College of Physicians and Surgeons of Ontario, after informing the provincial regulator they have a problem. Others have not, but are advised to stop treating patients while they seek help, and to inform the college of their diagnosis, as required by law. A few are already facing complaints or discipline. "If we can prevent issues," says Puddester, "or we can help people access care so they don't become identified by the regulator, then great." The OMA receives about 50 calls per week from doctors, he adds, but doesn't track the number with mental health problems.

18   Still, for all the talk of attitudinal shift, concern about public perception looms large, as authorities worry about the fallout should someone known to have psychological troubles break down in a way that costs lives. That's especially true in aviation, where the travelling public keenly feels its dependence on those in the tower and cockpit. Pilots, Transport Canada notes in its policy on SSRIs, are "in a position where the safety of the fare-paying public is front and centre and expectations about [their] medical competency and stability are high."

19   That leaves little room for case-by-case exceptions, if Bethune's experience is any guide. His psychiatrist, Paul Latimer, could hardly have given a stronger endorsement, telling Transport Canada that his patient was in full remission, adding, "in my opinion, his prognosis is excellent." But in an emailed response to *Maclean's*, a Transport Canada spokeswoman said use of a second medication still raises flags, because it points to "a more complicated medical file." For now, wrote Natasha Gauthier, "there is insufficient information on the combination and interaction of more than one medication for the department to determine how these can be used safely in the aviation environment." (As for Nav Canada, the private company that provides air navigation service across the country, it was aware of Bethune's condition and medications, and was ready to take him on as a trainee if he got the all-clear from Ottawa.)

20   Bethune hasn't given up hope. The feds have advised him they won't appeal the federal court ruling, and has requested the five years of medical records Justice Michael Phelan ordered it to examine. There's no guarantee that will tip the balance in Bethune's favour—the decision requires little more of Transport Canada than a closer look at facts and documentation. Still, Bethune quickly had his doctor send them off, telling *Maclean's* he remains in excellent spirits despite the setback, and would gladly apply all over again. "In the best case scenario," he told his hearing, "I would pass the training and I would become the poster child: a stellar air-traffic controller, someone who has a mental illness but has not let it prevent him from succeeding in life."

Source: Gillis, Charlie. "One Man's Fight to Help Jets Fly—Despite Mental Illness." *Maclean.ca*, 18 July 2016, www.macleans.ca/news/canada/one-mans-fight-to-help-jets-fly-despite-mental-illness/. Used with permission of Rogers Media Inc. All rights reserved.

Lightspring/Shutterstock.com

RESEARCH AND EXPOSITORY WRITING

BY THE END OF THIS CHAPTER, YOU WILL BE ABLE TO

- Distinguish between primary-source and secondary-source research.
- Employ concrete strategies for conducting research.
- Synthesize research into your own writing.
- Create a variety of expository documents.

▶ WHY IS THIS INFORMATION IMPORTANT?

In Chapter 1, you learned about four purposes for writing: to inform, instruct, entertain, or persuade. Expository writing aims to inform. It helps you learn about a topic and communicate what you have learned to others. While you may often see the goal of writing as communicating ideas to someone else, expository writing necessitates that you inform or educate yourself on a topic before you are able to pass on that information and knowledge. This is why expository writing is referred to as *writing to learn*. Through doing expository writing, you learn more about the topics you are interested in, and you learn more about your own position in relation to those topics.

Because the heart of expository writing is to communicate information rather than to persuade someone to accept a particular point of view, you need to ensure that the writing is as neutral or objective as possible. This means that you should not take sides when writing an expository piece, just as you do not insert your opinion when summarizing a reading. Your goal is to present all the information in an unbiased manner to allow your reader to make up her own mind about the topic. Trying to remain neutral can be difficult, but if you follow good research practices when gathering, evaluating, and communicating information, you will be able to present a balanced piece of writing. This chapter will help you do just that by introducing you to the concepts of primary and secondary sources for research and walking you through how to find quality sources, evaluate sources, and incorporate them into your writing.

▶ Think about It!

In this chapter, you will read and write about the impact humans have on their environment. Here are some questions to consider as you move through this chapter and as you read the following essay:

1. Who is responsible for waste management when it comes to food and water? Think about all of the stakeholders and the degree to which they influence waste.

2. What strategies can individual citizens employ to reduce food and water waste? What are the pros and cons of these strategies?

3. What are the potential consequences of ignoring food and water waste or implementing unsuccessful solutions to food and water waste?

Now, read the essay below and consider these questions:

1. What is the topic, thesis, and overall pattern of organization of the essay?

2. Why does the author believe that "conflating and confusing" hunger and food waste is problematic?

3. To what extent do your own food practices prevent or contribute to food waste? If you prevent it, what strategies do you use? If you contribute to it, what strategies could reduce your contribution?

4. Do you agree with the author that "hunger isn't about a lack of food" but is instead "about a lack of income"?

5. What can individual citizens do to solve the hunger problem in Canada? Can these same solutions be applied to other countries?

STOP TRYING TO SOLVE HUNGER WITH CORPORATE FOOD WASTE

By Nick Saul

1   It seems like a marriage made in heaven. Eliminate the vast amount of food waste in our society by giving it to the poor and hungry. No more hunger. No more waste. At least that's what advocates for food-waste-to-the-poor schemes will have

us believe. Here at home, MP Ruth-Ellen Brosseau's private member's bill, C-231, Fight Against Food Waste Act, will continue being debated in the House of Commons in the coming weeks.[1]

2   But this is a relationship doomed before it even begins. That's because this bill and other initiatives like it fail to address the real root causes of hunger and food waste. In fact, by conflating and confusing these issues, it makes it harder to develop meaningful and effective strategies to address both of these growing problems.

3   Simply put, food waste will never be able to address hunger because hunger isn't about a lack of food. It's about a lack of income. People are food insecure because they can't afford to eat.

4   Food waste diversion strategies aimed at the poor don't fix the food waste problem, either.

5   Waste isn't about not having enough mouths to feed. It's about inefficiencies and bureaucracy in the food system that see crops tilled under and lost in the production process; other crops that are overproduced as a result of antiquated agricultural policy and incentive programs; a retail system that has overabundance built into its operation model; and individual consumers who buy food with the best intentions, only to have it spoil in the back of the fridge.

6   There's a lot of work to be done on all these fronts. But if we're going to make any progress on any of these issues, we need to think upstream.

7   If we want to stop millions of Canadians from going to bed hungry every night, we need to ensure that they have the ability to access food. That means shaking up our outdated notions of who is going hungry in this country.

8   We have a growing population of working poor in Canada whose wages do not cover basic necessities. The most recent findings from the University of Toronto's PROOF Food Insecurity Policy Research program show that the majority of food insecure households in Canada rely on wages or salaries from employment. Inadequate wages, shrinking social assistance rates, meagre pensions, illness and disability are at the heart of food insecurity in this country. All of this has nothing to do with the fact that we throw away 30 to 40 per cent of the food we produce.

9   Which is not to say that food waste isn't a problem. In fact, it's a massive issue that requires our attention. The food that we throw out unnecessarily gobbles up resources, including energy, water, land and labour to the tune of $100 billion each year. And the food that ends up rotting in landfills fuels climate change by generating 20 per cent of Canada's methane gas emissions.

10   But this waste isn't concentrated at the retail level, where food waste plans are focused. Waste happens across the chain from field to fridge: 34 per cent of it is generated before food reaches the store, and a whopping 47 per cent of it happens in our homes. That means that only 10 per cent of all food waste in Canada is created at the retail level, and another nine per cent by restaurants.

11   If we want to tackle this monumental problem, we need a whole-system approach—from taxing waste to public education on reducing waste in our own kitchens.

12   But let's not conflate a food waste strategy with a poverty reduction strategy. It's destructive to do so. Are we saying that the poor among us are only

worthy of the castoffs of the industrial food system—the majority of which is unhealthy food, laden with fat, sugar, and salt, which increases the risk of diet-related illnesses? There's no question we can and must do better than this as a society.

13   When food banks were first established in Canada 40 years ago, they were intended to act as a stopgap. But the problem of food insecurity in Canada didn't stop, and the gap has only grown bigger. Since food banks opened their doors in 1970s, hunger has only gone in one direction: up.

14   Today more than four million people in this country are unsure about when they'll eat next or skip meals so their kids can eat. Diverting food waste to fill the shelves of a growing number of food banks can't and won't stop the problem of hunger in Canada. It makes for good PR for the companies that donate, but does little for the people it's intended to help.

15   Similarly, the new schemes about food waste—such as National Zero Waste Council's push to create tax incentives for companies who donate their waste to non-profits working with the poor—benefit the companies first and foremost. They do little to encourage real change and actually hijack productive discussions about how to tackle poverty.

16   Instead of incentivizing waste by dangling corporate tax credits, we ought to support employees fighting for fair, livable wages. And let's put those same tax dollars into building the social infrastructure required to ensure no one will ever again need to rely on someone else's leftovers for sustenance. It's time that politicians, backed by citizen voices, talk about justice and equity. It's time to create real, long lasting solutions to poverty and hunger, policies that bring us together, rather than divide us as citizens.

---

[1] This bill was defeated on October 5, 2016 (www.openparliament.ca/bills/42-1/C-231/).

Source: Saul, Nick. "Stop Trying to Solve Hunger with Corporate Food Waste." *The Huffington Post,* 7 June 2016, www.huffingtonpost.ca/nick-saul/food-waste-poverty_b_10327320.html. Reproduced with permission of the author.

Conducting Research

To become knowledgeable about a topic for a paper, you must conduct research. Research will help you communicate information to others, and you will often synthesize researched information with your own ideas. This chapter focuses on research from its beginning phases to its ultimate inclusion in a written document.

Primary Sources versus Secondary Sources

When conducting research, you will analyze a number of different sources of information, which may include newspaper articles, journals, books, images, people, music, and government documents. All of these sources of information can be defined as either primary sources or secondary sources (see Figure 5.1).

FIGURE 5.1
PRIMARY VS. SECONDARY SOURCES

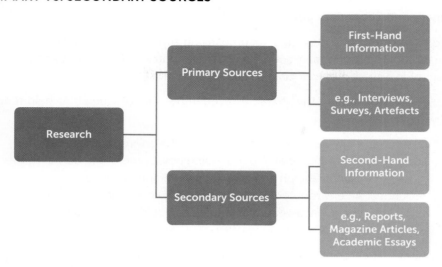

PRIMARY SOURCES

A primary source is often defined as first-hand information. There are essentially two types of primary sources: people and artefacts.

You may have heard the expression "straight from the source"—this refers to primary source material that has come from someone who has experienced what you are researching. For example, if you were conducting research on the wildfire that swept through Fort McMurray, Alberta, in 2016, then testimonies from any of the residents or first responders who were actually at the scene would be considered primary sources of information. Interviews and surveys are common primary sources that researchers use to collect data and information from those directly involved in an event.

An *artefact* is considered a primary source when it is a direct product of a certain time, place, or event. Artefacts can be pieces of writing, art, music, or other oral or written documents. If you were researching the history of changes to environmental laws in your city, then a document of environmental bylaws would be an example of an artefact functioning as a primary source for your research.

SECONDARY SOURCES

A secondary source is often defined as second-hand information. It is often information other people have written or said about a primary source. For example, if politicians who had not travelled to Fort McMurray during the wildfires engaged in a recorded debate responding to the event, you could use this debate as a secondary source in your research on the wildfires. Rather than getting information from those directly involved, you are getting the information second-hand from politicians who may have spoken with individuals affected by the fire or are simply commenting on the incident. In the context of researching the history of changes to environmental laws in your city, a secondary source might be a newspaper article someone else has written about the environmental laws.

Depending on your research task, what constitute primary sources and secondary sources will differ. The reason for this difference is that primary and secondary sources are defined *in relation* to each other; what may be a secondary source in one context may be a primary source in another context, and vice versa.

► **Apply the Skill**

Primary and Secondary Sources

Read each research context and accompanying sources. Identify each source as a primary source or secondary source within that context. Discuss your answers with a peer or in a small group or class discussion.

1. You are researching the *strategies* used in the City of Guelph to help reduce water waste.

   Source 1: A city councillor responsible for the environmental portfolio
   Source 2: A newspaper article describing how some of the homes in the City of Guelph are using greywater and rainwater
   Source 3: An environmental specialist who is knowledgeable about water waste reduction strategies but is not familiar with the City of Guelph, in particular

2. You are researching *reactions* to the newest water restriction bylaw in your city.

   Source 1: Interviews with homeowners
   Source 2: A letter to the editor in the local newspaper
   Source 3: A survey that you conduct yourself to gauge people's responses to the bylaw
   Source 4: Survey data that you've obtained from an online source that has collected people's responses to the bylaw

3. You are researching *how to format* a report for your Environmental Studies class.

   Source 1: Reports that have been written by experts in environmental science
   Source 2: A style guide produced by an environmental company that indicates how reports need to be formatted for that particular company
   Source 3: A one-on-one meeting with your instructor for recommendations on how to best format your report

Locating Sources: Overview

Finding sources when conducting research can be a difficult and time-consuming task. The Internet alone contains millions of sources of information, so it can be difficult to determine where to actually find the most appropriate source for your specific research project. In fact, the discipline of Information Science is the study of locating, evaluating, and synthesizing information effectively. You do not need to be a research expert in order to conduct good research, however. Instead, you need to be aware of common strategies and guidelines to help you research effectively, and you need to know when to consult experts to help you. To get started on the path toward good research, use the following three strategies summarized in Figure 5.2.

FIGURE 5.2

STRATEGIES FOR CONDUCTING EFFECTIVE RESEARCH

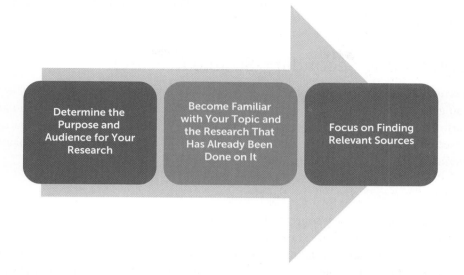

Determine the Purpose and Audience for Your Research

Become Familiar with Your Topic and the Research That Has Already Been Done on It

Focus on Finding Relevant Sources

STRATEGY 1: DETERMINE THE PURPOSE AND AUDIENCE FOR YOUR RESEARCH

Finding the best sources for your research largely depends on purpose and audience. Think about why and for whom you are doing the research. What research does your audience expect or need? For example, if you are doing research to help your employer make decisions on ways to reduce water waste, then you need to research water conservation *in the workplace* instead of water conservation at home. You would also need to focus on budgeting in your research, as cost will impact your employer's decision as to which water reduction strategy is best.

STRATEGY 2: BECOME FAMILIAR WITH YOUR TOPIC AND THE PRE-EXISTING RESEARCH

One of the best places to start research is by going to sources that provide an overview on the topic. Textbooks, encyclopedias, famous research studies, and experts are just some of the sources that will provide you with a broad understanding of the topic and help you become familiar with the topic's multiple perspectives. These sources can also direct you to other valuable sources that have explored the topic in greater depth. Moreover, they help you to become familiar with the research that has already been done in the topic area so that you can avoid repeating available research.

STRATEGY 3: FOCUS ON FINDING RELEVANT SOURCES

Once you have started conducting research, you may find that you read about tangential, or indirectly related, information. You need to make sure you keep focused on your particular research question rather than get distracted by related, but irrelevant, information. Pay attention to the amount of time you are spending on your research and the particular focus of the sources you are analyzing. While it is important to put a substantial amount of time into research, you want to avoid the trap of spending too much time on research and not enough time on other parts of the writing process, such as drafting and revision. Keep in mind, as well, that research is a process: you will do some as part of your prewriting work, but you will come back to it as you draft and revise.

Conducting Secondary-Source Research

It is usually good practice to begin your research with secondary sources. Doing so helps you gain a good grounding in the topic before approaching human subjects who are part of your primary-source research. In the field of research itself, this investigation of secondary sources before moving on to primary-source research is referred to as a *literature review*.

FINDING SECONDARY SOURCES

The search for secondary sources often begins online. However, we have become so accustomed to using online search engines that we often enter search terms without much thought. When conducting research, be mindful of the information you put into a search engine. Your goal is to find specific, relevant, informative, and trustworthy sources. You want to weed out unhelpful or untrustworthy ones. Select your search terms carefully. Use jargon—words specific to a certain field of study—if you are searching for work written by knowledgeable experts from that specific field. Another strategy is to put quotation marks around word groups that you want to appear in that particular order within the sources you are searching for. For further tips and tricks for finding useful online information, check with your school's librarian or instructional resource staff; in particular, they can help you navigate advanced search features that help you find sources by date, publication type, and word count, for example. They can also help you find peer-reviewed sources. *Peer-reviewed* sources are those that have been vetted by other experts within the discipline. Library databases, unlike most search engines that produce results based on popularity, prioritize *your* research goals and purpose. Databases can be difficult to navigate, but your librarian will have strategies you can use to help narrow your search.

▶ Apply the Skill

Investigating Library Resources

Visit a librarian at your institution and have the librarian show you how to do research in your field using one of the library's databases. Then, write a short essay that explains what database you used, the strategies for using it, and the type of information you were able to retrieve. Reflect on the effectiveness or ineffectiveness of the particular database.

EVALUATING SECONDARY SOURCES

Because of the quantity of information accessible to you as a writer, you must be diligent in assessing the validity and reliability of your sources. How do you know if the information you seek is authentic, unbiased, and fair?

FIGURE 5.3

CHARACTERISTICS OF A VALID AND RELIABLE SECONDARY SOURCE

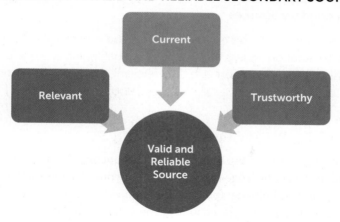

Here are three basic criteria (illustrated in Figure 5.3) that you can use as a checklist to confirm the validity and reliability of a secondary source:

- **Criterion 1: Relevance.** Always keep in mind the purpose and audience for your research. If the secondary source does not directly address this purpose and/or audience, then you should not use it.
- **Criterion 2: Currency.** Currency refers to the date the source was published. You want to ensure that you find sources that are up to date, reflecting the current research being done in the field. That does not mean that all older resources should be ignored: there is value in finding older sources as well, particularly when those sources have laid the foundation for the field in which you are conducting your research. You want to avoid using older sources that contain information that is irrelevant or has been disproven or discredited within the field by later studies.
- **Criterion 3: Trustworthiness.** You can determine trustworthiness using a number of strategies.

  - First, investigate the writer. Ensure her credentials indicate experience with the topic area, and check to see if any other respected writers in the field have cited the work of this writer. You will learn more about analyzing a writer's credentials and motives in the following chapter.
  - Second, investigate the publication. Determine whether the publication is respected in the field you are researching by checking which writers have written for the publication and analyzing references to the publication in other works or publications from the field. You will learn more about analyzing publications in the following chapter.
  - Third, check to ensure that factual information in the sources is consistent with other sources that provide the same facts.
  - Finally, analyze the source to ensure it takes an unbiased approach. An unbiased approach is one in which the writer acknowledges other perspectives and uses language that focuses on *logic* and the quality of information rather than language intended to persuade someone by influencing his or her *emotions*. You will learn more about bias in the following chapter.

Assessing Secondary Sources

Imagine you are writing a report on reducing food and water waste at your workplace or educational institution. Assess the articles at the beginning and end of this chapter in terms of their fit for your report. Are they relevant, current, and trustworthy?

TAKING NOTES ON SECONDARY SOURCES

Whenever you are incorporating information that someone else has written or spoken, you are required to acknowledge that individual in your piece of writing. That is why it is important to record bibliographic information as you conduct your research (see Table 5.1). Depending on the type of source, you will need to take note of one or more of the following pieces of bibliographic information:

- author of the source
- year of publication
- title of the source
- genre of the source (e.g., journal article, proposal, website)
- web addresses
- volume and issue number (for magazines and journals, if applicable)
- date the information was accessed

TABLE 5.1

EXAMPLES OF SOURCES AND THE BIBLIOGRAPHIC INFORMATION THAT SHOULD BE RECORDED

SOURCE	INFORMATION TO RECORD
Webpage	Author (whether an individual, organization, company, etc.)
	Publication date of the material
	Title of webpage
	Address of webpage
	Date you accessed the information
	Paragraph number of cited material, if possible
Article from a Peer-Reviewed Journal	Author of article
	Title of article
	Title of journal
	Page numbers on which the article appears in the journal
	Volume and issue number of journal, as applicable
	Web address of homepage of journal (if accessed online)
	Page number of any cited material
Newspaper Article	Author of article
	Title of article
	Title of newspaper
	Page number on which the article appeared in the newspaper
	Page number of any cited material
	Web address for the specific article, if the newspaper is online

- paragraph number of quoted or paraphrased material
- page number of quoted or paraphrased material
- page numbers of an article within a larger text

Noting this information will help you keep track of your sources, re-consult them with ease, and present them with integrity in the writing that communicates your research.

NOTE-TAKING STRATEGIES

It is important to be mindful of key strategies when taking notes for secondary research as summarized in Figure 5.4. When taking notes during your research, be sure to carefully distinguish quotations from paraphrases. You are responsible for representing your sources honestly and accurately, so you need to indicate when you are copying exact phrases and sentences from them versus when you are restating their ideas in your own words. In your piece of writing, quotations will require quotation marks around them to let your reader know that you've used the writer's exact phrasing. Paraphrases, on the other hand, will not require quotation marks. However, even with paraphrased ideas, if the ideas come from someone else, you need to acknowledge that source. Not acknowledging others' ideas is an ethical infringement called *plagiarism*. *Plagiarism* is representing ideas as your own when they actually came from someone else.

FIGURE 5.4

STRATEGIES FOR TAKING EFFECTIVE NOTES DURING SECONDARY RESEARCH

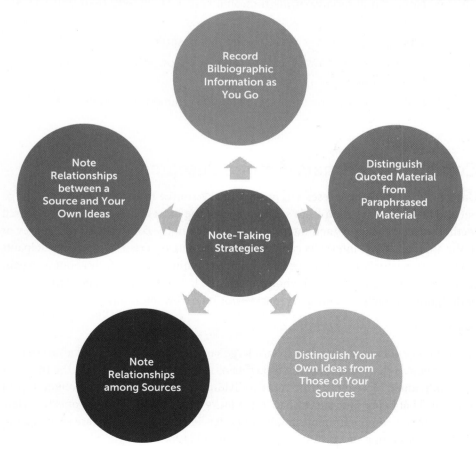

It is also important that you take very clear notes to distinguish a writer's ideas from your own ideas. When you are doing research, you will be annotating your sources by asking questions and responding to the information you are reading. Be sure that you do not inadvertently mix up your ideas with those of your sources. Academic integrity insists that you clearly distinguish yourself from other researchers so that people receive proper acknowledgments for their intellectual property.

Finally, be strategic when taking notes. If you notice relationships among the sources you find, be sure to indicate these relationships in your notes. Use charts, cluster diagrams, or other visual representations that will help you remember how the sources connect with one another and with your own knowledge of the topic. Use the reading and summary skills strategies you learned about in the previous chapters of this book to keep your research clear, organized, and accessible.

Review

Finding Secondary Sources

Answer the following review questions in paragraph form or generate ideas to contribute to a group or class discussion.

1. What are primary and secondary sources?
2. Explain the three strategies for locating secondary sources.
3. How can librarians or instructional resource experts help you focus your research?
4. What are criteria for evaluating secondary sources?
5. What information should you take note of when researching secondary sources?
6. Outline the key strategies for taking notes during secondary research.

Conducting Primary-Source Research

Unlike secondary-source research, most primary-source research requires you to go out and collect information from scratch. Two of the most common primary research methods used are surveys and interviews. A misstep in the construction of a survey or in the approach to an interview can result in faulty data or a refusal of key participants to take part in your research. Therefore, you need to think very carefully about who your survey participants should be or whom you should interview. You also need to take care in designing and implementing your survey or interview questions.

SURVEYS

Surveys are good for gaining data from a large sample size. The benefit of a survey over an interview is that it captures the thoughts of many people rather than the thoughts of an individual. More input from more individuals adds credibility and weight to your research. That being said, survey data often lacks the depth of a one-on-one interview, which is why a combination of surveys and interviews is ideal. There are several strategies for conducting successful surveys as seen in Figure 5.5.

FIGURE 5.5
STRATEGIES FOR CONDUCTING SUCCESSFUL SURVEYS

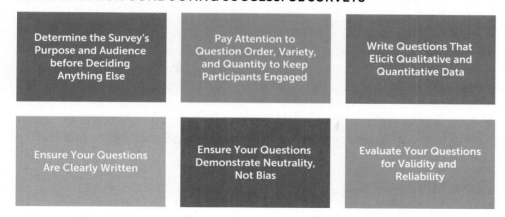

The first step when conducting a survey is determining the survey's purpose: what do you hope to achieve with it? Keeping the audience of your research front and centre will help you narrow down the survey's purpose, select the appropriate sample group and sample size to survey, and hone in on the questions you really want to ask. You want to design questions that will get the answers you and your audience need.

When writing your questions, keep your participants engaged. Put the most intriguing questions at the beginning to help direct your respondents through the survey, and keep the survey focused on a limited number of questions. People will spend about five to ten minutes of their time on a particular survey. Surveys that are much longer than 10 minutes may be ignored or only partially completed.

OPEN-ENDED AND CLOSED-ENDED QUESTIONS: QUALITATIVE VERSUS QUANTITATIVE DATA

The questions you write should be a combination of open-ended and closed-ended questions. An *open-ended* question allows participants to write their own, unique response. These responses provide you with in-depth, qualitative information that can later be quoted in the presentation of your research. *Qualitative information* is a person's opinion, whereas *quantitative information* refers to numbers or statistics. The downfall of too many open-ended questions is that participants can become overwhelmed or even bored by them. That is why closed-ended questions are useful in keeping respondents engaged. *Closed-ended* questions require participants to respond in a limited manner, often in the form of multiple choice or ranking. These questions provide you with the opportunity to obtain aggregate, or combined, data. Many organizations make decisions based on numerical, or quantitative, data, which can be derived from the responses to closed-ended questions. In addition, many research publications insist on statistically significant data, and closed-ended research responses are a means to this end.

You should always consider the clarity and neutrality of your questions. If survey participants do not understand the question you are asking, then they may provide you with inaccurate responses that can muddy the data you collect. If they sense any bias in your questions, they may refuse to participate, or if they do still choose to participate, you will get information that you personally hope to get rather than information that paints an accurate, objective picture.

VALID AND RELIABLE QUESTIONS

When you think you have the questions "right," be sure to assess their validity and reliability. A *valid* question prompts a response that is useful to you as a researcher and provides you with the specific information you are seeking. A *reliable* survey question leads all respondents to the same type of answer. This does not mean that the question should elicit identical responses; instead, it means that the *type* of information each respondent provides is the same. Your survey questions need to be both valid and reliable: they need to elicit the type of information you are looking for from every person that you interview. To ensure validity and reliability, it is always good to test your survey questions on a very small sample size before administering a large-scale survey.

▶ Apply the Skill

Surveys

With a peer or in a small group, write one open-ended and one closed-ended question regarding recycling plastics in a community for each of the following scenarios. Do your questions fit the criteria for validity and reliability?

1. You are surveying members of your community to determine their current household recycling practices.

2. You are surveying business owners in your community to determine their daily waste production.

3. You are surveying school boards to determine the green education programs they are using with their students.

INTERVIEWS

There are several strategies for conducting successful interviews as outlined in Figure 5.6. When conducting interviews for your primary research, select a person who not only has the ability to give you the information you need, but also has a good reputation in his or her field or discipline. When selecting this person, think about his or her relationship to the target audience for your research. Keep in mind your audience and consider the following criteria: who would be of interest as an interviewee? Should this be a familiar or unfamiliar source? Is it desirable to cultivate a particular experience or one that challenges audience perceptions?

You also need to think carefully about your interview questions. Again, think about the questions that you and your audience need answered. Try to focus on open-ended questions: that is the whole point of doing an interview rather than a survey. You want detailed, expert testimonial that will add depth to your research.

Take your interviewee's preferences, comfort, and understanding into consideration when planning and conducting the interview. Be specific about why you are interviewing her, how you plan on interviewing her, and how you will use the information she gives you. Being respectful to interviewees and acknowledging their important role

FIGURE 5.6
STRATEGIES FOR CONDUCTING SUCCESSFUL INTERVIEWS

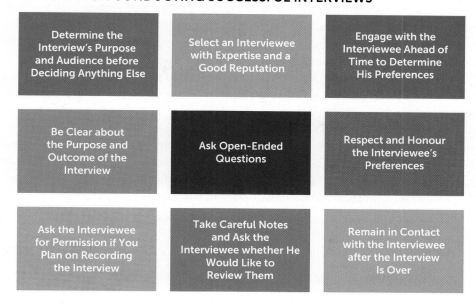

Determine the Interview's Purpose and Audience before Deciding Anything Else

Select an Interviewee with Expertise and a Good Reputation

Engage with the Interviewee Ahead of Time to Determine His Preferences

Be Clear about the Purpose and Outcome of the Interview

Ask Open-Ended Questions

Respect and Honour the Interviewee's Preferences

Ask the Interviewee for Permission if You Plan on Recording the Interview

Take Careful Notes and Ask the Interviewee whether He Would Like to Review Them

Remain in Contact with the Interviewee after the Interview Is Over

in your research is good practice that will help you build a rapport that may have long-lasting benefits.

As with secondary-source research, interview research requires careful, accurate note-taking. Be sure to distinguish your own thoughts on what the interviewee has said from the interviewee's ideas. Review your notes as you progress through the interview and review them once more at the end. If anything seems unclear, request clarification at an appropriate time (wait for an opening rather than interrupt your interviewee). You do not want to leave an interview with any doubts about your notes because you may not get another chance to clarify the details with your interviewee. It is also an excellent idea to show your interviewee your notes. Doing so helps her be assured that she is being represented accurately, and it helps you ensure your information is correct.

▶ Apply the Skill

Interview

With a peer or in a small group, write two interview questions eliciting qualitative responses for each of the following scenarios:

1. You are interviewing a member of your community to determine her current household recycling practices.

2. You are interviewing a business owner in your community to determine the daily waste production.

3. You are interviewing the director of education for one of your local school boards to determine the green education programs being offered to students.

Integrating and Citing Sources in Your Writing

The purpose of conducting research for an expository piece of writing is to not only present the research of others, but also integrate that research into your own knowledge base and to adapt it for your unique purpose. Therefore, you need to be skillful in the way in which you present your research and integrate it with your own writing.

There are two ways information can be incorporated into your writing: quotations and paraphrases. Quotations involve copying a writer's wording exactly as it appears in the original source and using quotation marks around it. Paraphrasing, as you learned in the previous chapter, involves using another writer's ideas but putting them into wording that is completely your own. Generally, paraphrases are preferable because they allow you to maintain your own voice in a piece of writing, and they demonstrate that you have clearly grasped another writer's ideas and the implications of those ideas. That being said, quotations do have their place in writing.

A quotation should be used if

- The purpose of citing the writer is to analyze the specific language the writer has used.
- You do not think the writer's idea can be stated any better than how the writer has stated it.
- Changing the writer's language would change the subtleties of the idea, such as the idea's tone (emotional resonance) or implications.

No matter which method you use, quotation or paraphrase, you need to be careful that you integrate the information into the logic and grammar of your own writing. For quotations, doing so can be particularly difficult, which is why you should follow these two guidelines:

Guideline 1: Contextualize and explicate the quotation. Make sure your reader understands where the quotation has come from and what it is actually communicating. Keep in mind that your reader may not be familiar with the source you are quoting from, so you may need to provide background knowledge about some of the content within the quotation, particularly if there are pronouns or references to other parts of the source that are not actually mentioned within the quoted material. Assume your reader has no knowledge of the source beyond the information you are quoting.

Here is an example of a quotation that has *not* been contextualized:

Nick Saul indicates that we are doing a poor job of addressing the issue of food waste. "By conflating and confusing these issues, it makes it harder to develop meaningful and effective strategies to address both of these growing problems."

Imagine that your audience has not read Saul's article. Would your audience understand what issues are being "conflated" and "confused"? Would your audience know what the two "growing problems" are and who is responsible for bringing these two unrelated issues together? The answer to all three questions is *no* since there has been no indication of the second problem he addresses, which is hunger, and there is no indication that he has been discussing government responses to the issue. Compare this lack of context to the following contextualized quotation integration:

Nick Saul indicates that governments are making a mistake by addressing the issues of food waste and hunger at the same time: "By conflating and confusing these issues, it makes it harder to develop meaningful and effective strategies to address both of these growing problems."

The writer has now clearly indicated the two issues at hand, as well as clarified who is responsible for making the error of merging these two issues together.

The key to remember is that quotations cannot speak for themselves: you must help them provide meaning for your reader. You must be clear about why you have incorporated a specific quotation by analyzing it and explaining how it connects with your own ideas.

Guideline 2: Incorporate the quotation into your own sentence. Don't let the quotation be a sentence on its own. The purpose of your writing is to provide your own perspective on a topic, and the quotations you integrate are meant to serve *your* purpose. As such, they need to be integrated into the grammar of your sentences, and they should not be left as sentences on their own. In the example of the decontextualized quotation in Guideline 1 above, you saw what can happen with a quotation written as a sentence on its own: it can leave the reader confused. In the corrected, contextualized example, the quotation became embedded in the writer's sentence with the help of a colon, and its connection with the writer's words became much clearer. Table 5.2 shows three common ways in which writers integrate quotations into the grammar of their own sentences.

TABLE 5.2

STRATEGIES FOR INTEGRATING QUOTATIONS INTO YOUR SENTENCES

STRATEGY	EXAMPLE
Use an independent clause followed by a colon.	Nick Saul indicates that governments are making a mistake by addressing the issues of food waste and hunger at the same time: "By conflating and confusing these issues, it makes it harder to develop meaningful and effective strategies to address both of these growing problems."
Use the writer's name and a reporting verb followed by a comma.	Nick Saul indicates that governments are making a mistake by addressing the issues of food waste and hunger at the same time. He claims, "By conflating and confusing these issues, it makes it harder to develop meaningful and effective strategies to address both of these growing problems."
Embed the quotation within one of your independent or dependent clauses; use the grammar of your own sentence to determine what, if any, punctuation is required.	Nick Saul makes it clear that food waste and hunger will be difficult to overcome if governments continue "conflating and confusing these issues."

In addition to ensuring that quotations and paraphrases are integrated with the logic and grammar of your own writing, you must be absolutely clear in distinguishing the source's ideas from your own. For quotations, this is done by putting quotation marks around the writer's wording and acknowledging the writer in an in-text citation. For paraphrases, this is done by virtue of the in-text citation alone.

An *in-text citation* refers to brief bibliographic information that you put in the body of your writing. It can be a signal phrase, a parenthetical reference, or a combination of both. You will remember from the previous chapter that a signal phrase indicates a writer's name and the fact that the writer has stated, claimed, or informed a reader about something. "According to Saul," "Saul claims," or "Saul says" are all examples of signal phrases. These signal phrases actually form a part of your sentence. A parenthetical reference, on the other hand, provides the source information in parentheses at the end of a sentence rather than being a grammatical part of the sentence itself.

Example of in-text citation with only a parenthetical reference:

> Governments are making a mistake by addressing the issues of food waste and hunger at the same time: "By conflating and confusing these issues, it makes it harder to develop meaningful and effective strategies to address both of these growing problems" (Saul par. 2).

Example of an in-text citation with a signal phrase plus parenthetical reference:

> Saul indicates that governments are making a mistake by addressing the issues of food waste and hunger at the same time: "By conflating and confusing these issues, it makes it harder to develop meaningful and effective strategies to address both of these growing problems" (par. 2).

It should be noted that each discipline has its own preferred method of referencing. While all disciplines insist on distinguishing your own ideas from those of other writers, the details by which this is done differs. Consult the style and referencing guide that your particular discipline or workplace follows to ensure appropriate citation practices. Do this before you begin your research so that you record appropriate bibliographic information as you go along. Be aware, as well, that most style guides insist on some form of bibliography for secondary sources (usually in the form of a references page, footnotes, or end notes), while many may differ in terms of what is appropriate for citing primary source material gained through a survey or interview. See the appendix on documentation for more information about citations and standard methodology.

▶ Apply the Skill

Integrating and Citing Sources in Your Writing

These sentences come from "Stop Trying to Solve Hunger with Corporate Food Waste" by Nick Saul, from the beginning of this chapter.

  a. If we want to stop millions of Canadians from going to bed hungry every night, we need to ensure that they have the ability to access food.

  b. We have a growing population of working poor in Canada whose wages do not cover basic necessities.

Choose one of these sentences and practise the following skills:

  a. Paraphrase the point and cite it correctly in a paragraph.

  b. Use the sentence as a quotation in a paragraph, using correct citation protocol.

  Next, compare your work with a small group.

Incorporating Visuals into Your Writing

In Chapter 3, you learned a method of decoding the key points in visuals included in a reading. You can also incorporate visuals into your writing. When you incorporate visuals into a report, you need to carefully integrate them with your textual information to ensure the reader understands the visuals' purposes. Placement of a visual on a page is very important. Generally, visuals should be placed as close as possible to the text that refers to them. The text should also explicitly reference the visual so that the audience understands when they should be consulting the visual. Therefore, the visual needs to be clearly titled, usually with the words *Table* or *Figure* plus a number (e.g., Table 1 or Figure 2.2). Tables provide information using rows and columns. Figures are often used to refer to any other type of visual, from a graph to an image to a photograph. Visuals should be easy for your audience to read, and, if they contain any information that is not your own, they must be cited. Your citation should clearly indicate whether you have reproduced the visual from another source or whether you have created the visual on your own using information from another source. Figure 5.7 provides a list of questions to ask yourself when you incorporate visuals into a report.

FIGURE 5.7

QUESTIONS TO ASK WHEN INCORPORATING VISUALS INTO A REPORT

☑ Does the visual have a specific purpose, and is that specific purpose evident to the audience?

☑ Is the chosen visual the best way to communicate the information?

☑ Is the visual appropriately labelled with an identifier (*Table* or *Figure*) and title (words that summarize the purpose of and information in the visual)?

☑ Has the visual been referenced in the text?

☑ Has the visual been placed as closely as possible to the text that refers to it?

☑ Is the visual easy for the audience to read?

☑ Has the visual been cited appropriately?

▶ Apply the Skill

Using Visuals

Examine the excerpt and visual in the following figure taken from the City of Calgary's website. Evaluate the use of the visual by answering the questions from Figure 5.7. Be sure to justify your answers with clear and detailed explanations.

How Is Water Used Indoors?

In Calgary, the average person uses about 7,000 litres of water a month. This amount includes water used for irrigation. A home's indoor water consumption will usually remain about the same throughout the year unless you have house guests or you go on vacation.

The chart below shows typical water use for common household fixtures and appliances. Actual water use can vary depending on your water-use habits and efficiency of your fixtures.

CITY OF CALGARY: WATER USE IN THE HOME

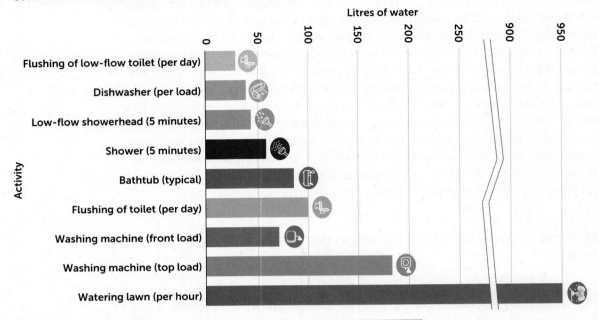

Source: City of Calgary. "How Is Water Used Indoors?" *Water Use in the Home*, www.calgary.ca/UEP/Water/Pages/Water-conservation/Indoor-water-conservation/Water-Use-in-the-Home.aspx/. Image courtesy of The City of Calgary—not for further reproduction.

Translating Your Own Survey Data into a Visual

You can also capture data from your own surveys through the use of a table or graph. No matter what visual representation you use, make sure you have a clear title that indicates the topic of the graphic, and label the headings, partitions, or axes of your tables or graphs clearly for the reader. It is imperative that your reader be able to read your table or graph with ease. Because you have sought the survey information on your own, you become your own source. Some style guides or companies do not require a citation for such data, while others prefer that the company name or official name of the survey be included in the data in case other researchers incorporate your visual representation into their own work.

Regardless of the citation practice, when incorporating survey data into your writing, you need to clearly explain your methodology and the demographic of your respondents. It is also good practice to attach a copy of the survey questions as an appendix to your document and to mention the existence of the appendix within the body of your piece of writing. Finally, just as with quoted or paraphrased information, you should provide explications of your data for the reader: help the reader understand the information he is looking at and how it relates to your writing. See Figure 5.8 for an example of how to integrate survey data into a report.

FIGURE 5.8
EXAMPLE OF SURVEY DATA INTEGRATED INTO A REPORT

Food Insecurity by Household Type

Previous research has also shown a strong relationship between food insecurity and household type. Whether individuals live alone, with a significant other, or with children are all factors related to household food insecurity. Household food insecurity was examined by various household types and sources of income. In every type of household, rates of food insecurity were higher in households where the main source of income was government benefits [see figure below].

Description for Figure

In 2011–2012, lone-parent families with children under 18 reported the highest rate of household food insecurity at 22.6%. In addition, 11.9% of unattached individuals and 7.1% of couples living with children under 18 experienced household food insecurity. Couples with no children reported the lowest rate of household food insecurity at 3.5%.

FOOD INSECURITY BY MAIN SOURCE OF HOUSEHOLD INCOME AND HOUSEHOLD TYPE, CANADA, 2011–2012

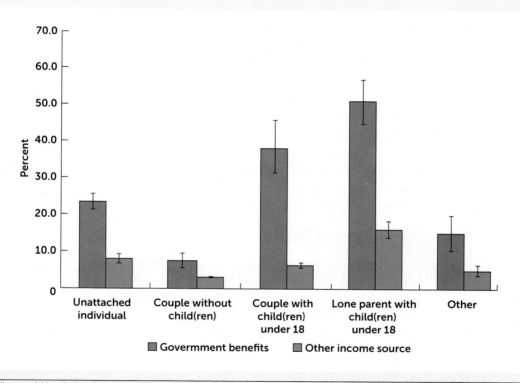

Note: The lines overlaid on the bars indicate the 95% confidence interval. They enable comparison of statistical differences between estimates.

Source: Roshanasfshar, Shirin and Emma Hawkins. "Food Insecurity in Canada." *Health at a Glance*, Statistics Canada, Catalogue No. 82-624-X, 25 March 2015, www.statcan.gc.ca/pub/82-624-x/2015001/article/14138-eng.htm/.

Review

Finding and Integrating Research

Answer the following review questions in paragraph form or generate ideas to contribute to a group or class discussion.

1. What are fundamental differences of finding primary- and secondary-source material?
2. Explain the key strategies for interviews and surveys to gather primary-source data.
3. What are the benefits and drawbacks of closed-ended and open-ended questions?
4. When should quotations be used?
5. When should paraphrasing be used?
6. Explain the two guidelines for integrating quotations into your writing.
7. What are some considerations when incorporating visuals into a written report?

Writing to Learn

Earlier in this chapter, you read about how expository writing can be defined as writing to learn. Expository writing not only benefits the reader but also the writer who is able to learn more about the topic by investigating questions about it.

Expository writing comes in many forms, some of which are discipline-specific and some of which reach across many disciplines. Now that you have some background, you will learn how to write a number of cross-disciplinary types of expository pieces: an exploratory paper (sometimes referred to as a problem-centred paper), an annotated bibliography, a research report, and a reflection.

Exploratory Paper

As its name suggests, an exploratory paper investigates one or more questions about a particular topic. The goal is to become more informed about the topic, rather than arriving at a final, definitive answer to the question(s) posed (see Figure 5.9). The article at the end of this chapter, "Canadians Rank among World's Top Water Hogs," is a type of exploratory paper. While it is not academic in tone or style, it still demonstrates an exploratory paper's key characteristics. These characteristics are listed in Figure 5.9.

FIGURE 5.9
KEY CHARACTERISTICS OF EXPLORATORY PAPERS

- Provide a description of an issue and an explanation of the issue's importance.
- Ask one or more specific questions about the issue.
- Provide multiple, thoroughly researched answers to the question(s) rather than focusing on a single, definitive answer.

Exploratory Paper

Carefully read "Canadians Rank among World's Top Water Hogs," and then answer the questions below.

1. What is the issue or problem being explored?

2. According to the author, why is this issue or problem important?

3. What specific questions does the author ask about the issue or problem? Are these questions explicitly stated, implicitly stated, or a combination of both?

4. What are some of the answers the author provides? Does he use research to arrive at these answers?

Annotated Bibliography

An annotated bibliography is a helpful tool for research but also an expository piece of writing in its own right. As the term *bibliography* suggests, an annotated bibliography is a list of sources that a writer plans on using as part of her research. However, as the adjective *annotated* suggests, this type of bibliography includes notes about each source. A typical annotated bibliography will include, at minimum, a brief summary of each source and an evaluation of each source's usefulness within the context of the larger research project. In order to write a good annotated bibliography, you need to have strong summary, assessment, and documentation skills.

Figure 5.10 provides an example of an entry for an annotated bibliography. It is formatted according to the style guide of the American Psychological Association (APA).

FIGURE 5.10
EXAMPLE OF AN ANNOTATED BIBLIOGRAPHY ENTRY

Saul, N. (2016, June 7). Stop trying to solve hunger with corporate food waste. *The Huffington Post*. Retrieved from www.huffingtonpost.ca/nick-saul/food-wastepoverty_b_10327320.html

In this newspaper article from the *Huffington Post*, Nick Saul argues that hunger and food waste are not related problems, so they should not be dealt with simultaneously. He claims that hunger is the result of low income, not the result of a food shortage (par. 3); meanwhile, food waste is the result of "inefficiencies and bureaucracy" within the food industry, not the result of a lack of "mouths to feed" (par. 5). Based on these reasons for hunger and food waste, Saul recommends a different solution than those currently being discussed. He argues that hunger needs to be addressed by lobbying for wages that adequately cover the costs of food (par. 16). On the other hand, he says food waste needs to be addressed through "taxing waste" and "public education on reducing waste in our own kitchens" (par. 9).

This article is relevant to my research report project of recommending two effective strategies for reducing food waste in my community. I originally planned to investigate what Saul calls a few "food-waste-to-the-poor schemes" (par. 1), but I now believe it may be problematic to do so because of Saul's compelling claims and evidence. His article is recent, which means his data and references are up to date, and he is the president and CEO of Community Food Centres Canada, which demonstrates he has a depth of knowledge on the subject. This article has convinced me to look beyond issues of hunger when trying to determine how to combat food waste. I will take his suggestion of looking into possible waste taxing alternatives, and I will also begin to search for education programs that have proven successful in reducing at-home food waste.

Keep in mind that annotated bibliographies can differ in terms of scope and expectations, so it is always important to follow your instructor's directions for these types of assignments. The example given above is just *one* approach to an annotated bibliography entry.

▶ **Apply the Skill**

Annotated Bibliography

Imagine that you have been asked by your college or university to write a recommendation report identifying a cost-effective mechanism for reducing water waste at your campus. As part of this recommendation process, you have been asked to research strategies that have proven successful both within Canada and internationally. Write an annotated bibliography for "Canadians Rank among World's Top Water Hogs" by Randy Shore that includes a summary of the article and an evaluation of its effectiveness in the context of your water waste reduction report. Then, research two more articles on water waste reduction and write annotated bibliography entries for them. In the end, you should have one annotated bibliography containing three different entries. Be sure to ask your instructor if she has specific requirements or guidelines.

Research Reports

Research reports are common in both academic and workplace settings. As their name suggests, they involve careful research that is then reported or delivered to a specific audience, often to help that audience make a decision. For example, a report on water usage may be used to help government officials make decisions about how to conserve water. Sometimes research reports come in the form of guides or white papers. While these other types of reports may have slightly different purposes or formatting, they all aim to provide research-based information intended to help decision makers.

▶ Apply the Skill

Research Reports

Use the skills you've learned in this chapter to find a research report on water conservation. Once you've found one, answer the following questions:

1. How do you know that the document you have found is a research report? In other words, where is there evidence of research? Where is there evidence of a recommendation? Who is the audience, and how do you know? What decision does the audience have to make?

2. Does the research report make use of visuals? If so, have these visuals been incorporated effectively? Use the questions in Figure 5.7 to help respond to this question.

3. Longer research reports contain front matter and end matter. Front matter refers to a title page, table of contents, and summary of the report placed in front of the report itself. End matter refers to references pages, in addition to appendices of additional information that is important to the report but too detailed to place in the report itself (such as policies related to the report). Does your chosen research report contain front matter or end matter? If so, what type of matter is included? How does it help guide the reader through the report and through making a decision?

4. Write your own research report on reducing water waste at your campus. Alternatively, write a research report on a topic of your own choosing or on a topic assigned by your instructor. Be sure to identify your purpose and audience before you write, as well as the decision your audience needs to make based on the information you provide. If suitable, use your annotated bibliography from the previous Apply the Skill exercise to help you write your report.

Reflections

One of the most valuable forms of expository writing is a reflection (see Figure 5.11). In a reflection, you take time to think about yourself in relation to whatever it is that you are thinking about, writing about, or doing. For example, it is often useful to write a reflection on your writing process. This metacognitive strategy helps you think carefully about the steps you have taken or forgotten to take, the struggles you have had, the successes you have achieved, and your overall opinion of the outcome of your writing. These kinds of reflections can help make you aware of the gaps in your writing and the sources of those gaps, thus helping you to fill them in a constructive, meaningful way. You can also reflect on other things beyond writing: a TV show you have seen, an experience you had at school or work, or even a story you read in the newspaper. Whatever you reflect on, you need to be clear and honest, and you need to focus on *you*. Doing so will help you make sense of your experiences and respond to those experiences in an informed, targeted, and critically thought-out manner.

FIGURE 5.11
THE PROCESS OF REFLECTION

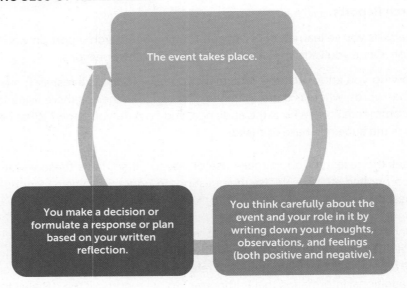

The event takes place.

You think carefully about the event and your role in it by writing down your thoughts, observations, and feelings (both positive and negative).

You make a decision or formulate a response or plan based on your written reflection.

▶ Apply the Skill

Reflection

Think about the last writing assignment you submitted and received feedback on. Answer the following questions in either point form or complete sentences. Then, use those answers to develop a plan or strategy to ensure you are successful on your next writing assignment. Put this plan into writing. Use Figure 5.12 as a guide.

1. According to your instructor's feedback, what was your greatest strength on the assignment? What area do you need most improvement on?

2. How much time did you spend on the writing assignment? How was this time spent? Were you focused or distracted?

3. Did you seek feedback from your instructor or your peers before submitting the assignment?

4. Did you follow the reading and writing processes that you learned about in Chapter 1? If you did, which ones, specifically? If you did not, why not?

5. How did you feel while you were writing the assignment? Were you in good health or poor health? Did you have a positive state of mind or a negative one?

6. What are some of the challenges you experienced with the writing assignment? Can you identify the sources of these challenges?

FIGURE 5.12

EXAMPLE OF REFLECTION: STRENGTHS AND WEAKNESSES OF A SUMMARY

Today I received my summary writing assignment back from my instructor. I received a grade of 65%, which I think means I'm on the right track but still have a ways to go. According to my instructor, the greatest strength of my summary is my ability to paraphrase the writer's ideas rather than copying them word for word. Therefore, for my next summary assignment, I will continue with strong paraphrasing, ensuring that the word choices and sentence structures are my own. The greatest weakness of my summary is distinguishing between a writer's main ideas and supporting details. I'm still not sure how to do this, so I think I will ask my instructor for help, and I will reread the parts of the textbook that describe how to put information into a hierarchy. Perhaps I can also get help from the Writing Centre in terms of learning key vocabulary that will help me distinguish main ideas from supporting details. I can also practise writing summaries that are not being graded for class and get feedback from the Writing Centre. I never learned how to write a summary in high school, so I think the reason I'm struggling so much right now is that I'm trying to perform the task for the first time. Continued practice, both in class and outside class, will help me become a better summary writer.

Review

Writing to Learn

1. What are the different forms of writing to learn?
2. Why are annotated bibliographies helpful in the research process?
3. What are the key considerations for an effective research report?
4. What are the benefits of writing a reflection? How does reflection writing help you learn?

Did You Know?

PROOFREADING FOR CORRECT MODIFIER USAGE

In the previous chapters, you learned about the role modifiers have in sentences as either adjectives or adverbs, and you are aware that these modifiers can often shift positions within a sentence. While the placement of modifiers is flexible, however, it does not mean they can appear *anywhere* in a sentence. Two common pitfalls to avoid with modifier usage are *misplaced modifiers* and *dangling modifiers*.

A *misplaced modifier* happens when a modifier is placed too far away from the part of the sentence it is supposed to be modifying. This misplacement can sometimes make it seem as though the modifier is actually modifying a part of the sentence other than the part it is intended to modify.

Example of a misplaced modifier: We need to stop giving food to food banks that is unhealthy.

In this sentence, the modifier, "that is unhealthy," is intended to describe the *food*, not *food banks*. Based on its position in the sentence, however, the modifier is actually describing food banks.

To avoid writing a misplaced modifier, always place the modifier as close as possible to the part of the sentence it is intended to modify.

Example of corrected modifier: We need to stop giving food that is unhealthy to food banks.

▶ Apply the Skill

Misplaced Modifiers

In each sentence below, identify the misplaced modifier and explain the confusion or inaccuracy it causes. Then, rewrite the sentence to fix the problem. The first one has been done as an example.

1. You can only solve the hunger problem by looking at employment.

   Explanation: *Only* should describe the solution to the problem, not the verb *solve*. It sounds as though you can't discuss, debate, or question the hunger problem—you can only *solve* it. This likely isn't the author's intention.
   Correction: You can solve the hunger problem only by looking at employment.

2. We cannot stop hunger focused on corporations.

   Explanation:
   Correction:

3. In Canada, citizens nearly contribute to half of the total food waste.

   Explanation:
   Correction:

4. Statistics indicate most food is wasted in the home by Nick Saul.

   Explanation:
   Correction:

A *dangling* modifier happens when a modifier phrase is not actually modifying anything in the sentence. In other words, the part of the sentence being modified is not in the sentence at all.

Example of dangling modifier:

When searching for ways to reduce water consumption, our solutions often focus on using less water instead of different water.

In this sentence, the modifier, "when searching for answers to reduce water consumption," is *intended* to describe what *we* are doing. *We* are the ones searching for solutions to water waste. However, *we* does not actually appear anywhere in the sentence, so the modifier is dangling. Dangling modifiers occur most often at the beginning of a sentence.

If you are proofreading and come across a dangling modifier, you have two options to correct it: (1) change the modifier from a phrase to a dependent clause by adding in a subject and verb, or (2) rewrite the main clause so that it contains the subject that the modifier is intended to modify.

Corrected Modifier: Option 1

When we are searching for ways to reduce water consumption, our solutions often focus on using less water instead of different water.

Corrected Modifier: Option 2

When searching for ways to reduce water consumption, we often focus our solutions on using less water instead of different water.

In both corrections, the subject *we* has now been added. This change makes it clear that *we* are the ones searching for solutions.

▶ Apply the Skill

Dangling Modifiers

Rewrite each of the following sentences so that the dangling modifier is eliminated. Use either one of the two methods described in this chapter. The first one has been done as an example.

1. Having exhausted all other options, greywater toilets were installed to save money on the monthly water bill.

   Correction: Having exhausted all other options, the homeowners installed greywater toilets to save money on the monthly water bill.

2. Not realizing how much water would be saved, their final decision was to forego dual flush toilets because of the higher initial cost.

   Correction:

3. Worried about the rising prices of water consumption, your gardening practices are a good place to implement some changes.

   Correction:

4. After considering all of the benefits of rainwater, the eventual payoff of installing an efficient rainwater system is well worth the upfront cost.

   Correction:

Misplaced and dangling modifiers can be difficult to detect, but if you use the recommended proofreading strategy from the previous chapter, whereby you proofread your writing from the last sentence to the first, you should be able to spot and correct them. Watch for introductory phrases containing gerunds and infinitives, which you also learned about in the previous chapter, as these phrase types are where dangling modifiers most often occur. You want to ensure your writing is free of misplaced and dangling modifiers as they not only create confusion for your reader but also potentially have more serious consequences, as you will discover in the Apply the Skill activity below.

▶ **Apply the Skill**

Dangling and Misplaced Modifiers

Find an example of a dangling or misplaced modifier and write a paragraph describing its impact or significance. Does the error result in confusion or humour? Does the error reflect negatively on the writer? Could the error result in a loss of readership? In the context of a company, could the error result in a loss of customers or funding? Could the error lead to a lawsuit? Possible sources to examine include advertisements, newspaper articles, company websites, blogs, and social media.

▶ **Questions for Writing and Discussion**

Read the article below from *The Vancouver Sun* about water usage in Canada compared to other places in the world and possible solutions for lowering daily water use. Then, consider the following questions.

1. What kind of research does the author use in his article—primary, secondary, or a combination of both? Is the author's research relevant, current, and trustworthy? How do you know?

2. What is Randy Shore's background? How does this background impact the purpose, audience, and subject matter of the article? Are the purpose and audience for Randy Shore's article similar to or different from the purpose and audience for Nick Saul's article, "Stop Trying to Solve Hunger with Corporate Food Waste"? How do you know?

3. Compose a three-entry annotated bibliography for an exploratory paper on the topic of water metering that explores the following two questions: (a) Does water metering have a significant impact on water waste reduction? (b) Is water metering a cost-effective option for homeowners?

4. Write the exploratory paper that corresponds with the annotated bibliography you wrote in Question 3.

5. Write a reflection essay on your own use of water. Consider the following questions to help you: In what ways do you use water and why? How much do you think you use? Can you think of more strategic ways to use water? What water reduction strategies from Shore's article do you currently use? What strategies might you consider using in the future?

6. Choose one of the following writing projects based on what you have learned in this chapter.

a. Randy Shore references the POLIS Project in the article. Use the research strategies from this chapter to learn about the POLIS Project. Present the findings to your instructor in a short informational report that explains what POLIS is, when it started, what it has done so far, what it is currently working on, and what its ultimate goal is. Use headings and visuals to help present your information effectively.

b. What measures are taken in Australia to make it a leader in water conservation? Can the same measures be taken in your own city or town? Write a research report that explores three different water conservation approaches used in Australia that could potentially be used in your own city or town. Be sure to include front matter, end matter, and visuals in your report. To turn your report into a recommendation report, create criteria by which to select the best of the three approaches and measure each approach against these criteria. You will use the criteria to justify the approach you select.

c. Write a research report about either food waste or water waste in your own community. In your report, be sure to outline the causes of the problem, the consequences of the problem, and the possible solutions for the problem. Use at least five secondary sources in your report and at least two primary sources. Address the report to an appropriate leader in your community and keep this leader in mind as you go about collecting your research and presenting your findings. Use headings and visuals to enhance the readability of your report.

CANADIANS RANK AMONG WORLD'S TOP WATER HOGS

By Randy Shore

1   While public education and water restrictions help to conserve water, dramatic reductions can be achieved through water pricing and government incentives to upgrade wasteful appliances.

2   A study by researchers at University of California Davis found that the Golden State was able to trim per capita water consumption by 10 per cent over a decade with a combination of watering restrictions and public policy, which required people to install water-saving toilets in new construction.

3   Efforts in Metro Vancouver which have included toilet bylaws, rain barrel rebates, sprinkler bans and public education have brought down per capita water consumption by 20 per cent in the past 10 years, a worthy achievement.

4   However, Australia was able to reduce water use by 35 per cent over roughly the same period, according to the UC Davis study.

5   "In the water conservation world, Australia is the furthest ahead of any jurisdiction," said Troy Vassos, a professor of engineering at the University of British Columbia.

6   New South Wales requires all new homes to incorporate water-saving features such as dual-flush toilets, rainwater collection, surface stormwater collection, and on-site treatment of greywater recovered from baths, showers and laundry.

7   Greywater is untreated waste water that contains relatively few pathogens compared with so-called black water, which comes from kitchen sinks and toilets. Greywater can be used for landscape irrigation and toilet flushing, which represents 30 to 40 per cent of indoor water use.

8   In NSW, the builder must select a suite of conservation measures that meet the state's sustainability goals before construction permits are issued. Plus, state and federal governments offer rebates on the purchase of rainwater and greywater systems.

9   "You get 100-per-cent uptake on conservation technology in this way," said Vassos.

10 As a result, 46 per cent of Australian homes have rainwater collection and 86 per cent have dual-flush, ultra low-flow toilets, which use 50- to 75-per-cent less water than conventional toilets.

11 Despite passing a requirement for ultra low-flow toilets in 1978, the uptake in California is only 26 per cent.

12 The City of Melbourne—among the stingiest water consumers in Australia—adopted permanent year-round watering restrictions in 2012.

13 Melbourne also recovered and treated about 50 million litres of water from its sewage, equal to about one-eighth of its total drinking water supply. The water is used mainly for irrigation.

Water metering

14 Metering and water pricing in Australia have also served to drive consumption down. Australians pay about 62-per-cent more for water and sewage services than Canadians and 100-per-cent more than Americans, according to the Organization for Economic Co-operation and Development.

15 Water pricing—which goes hand in glove with household water metering—is by far the most effective way to curb residential water use and a handful of European nations have used it to drive per capita water use down to levels that make North Americans look positively profligate.

16 In the global pantheon of water hogs, Metro Vancouverites are among the biggest consumers, according to the POLIS Project, a collaboration between governments, foundations and universities. We use less than Los Angelinos, but so does nearly everyone.

17 We use twice as much water per capita as Germany, where metering is universal for single-family homes. To achieve such gains, Germans pay five times more by volume than Canadians, according to POLIS.

18 Even without punitive pricing for water, metering and the opportunity to pay only for what you use can generate modest reductions in water consumption.

19 Nowhere is it easier to see the impact of metering than Surrey, where 56,000 homes are metered and 27,000 are not.

20 Water use in single family homes equipped with meters is about 40-per-cent lower than that of homes without meters in Surrey, according to the city's water planning manager KK Li.

21 "We have had a full-scale voluntary metering program since 2003 and all new construction is mandated to have meters since 1999," he said.

22 The city's total water consumption has been flat for more than 10 years, despite welcoming 1,000 new residents each month.

23   Surrey's extraordinary success at curbing water use is driven in part by people who have self-selected for metering, who likely did so on the assumption they would pay less than the 2014 flat rate of about $1,360 a year, said Li.

24   The annual savings for a household of two is estimated to be as much as $900, while a family of four could pay up to $527 less.

25   In 2009, UBC dean of forestry John Innes decided to walk the sustainability talk and installed a variety of water-saving technologies in order to certify his West Vancouver home to LEED Gold standard, the first of its kind in Canada.

26   Innes installed dual-flush toilets and a rainwater collection system that stores 15,000 litres of water, which he is now using to irrigate his garden.

27   The problem is that drinking water in Canada is cheap by international standards, "so you have to do quite a lot to realize any significant savings," he said.

28   Innes would have installed a greywater system, too, had regulations existed at the time. Even now the regulation of greywater systems is spread across several government departments so few municipalities have adopted it into building code.

29   Vancouver allows residential greywater systems, but only for flushing toilets, while Guelph, Ont., offers $1,000 rebates on the purchase of the equipment, which can run up to $5,000. But greywater represents up to 50 per cent of indoor water use and offers great potential as a conservation strategy.

Turning off the taps

30   When metering is universal—as it is in Nanaimo, Sidney and Victoria—the water savings are significant.

31   Nanaimo residents use about 17-per-cent less water than Metro Vancouver residents, the result of a metering program that started more than 35 years ago because of consistent droughty conditions on southern Vancouver Island. Nanaimo water resources manager Bill Sims expects that gap to widen in 2015.

32   "It's dropping this year with the drought," he said. "Our daily flows are 15-per-cent below normal."

33   The city also employs water pricing that places the entire cost of water delivery on users without any subsidy from property tax.

34   "That has had a huge impact," said Sims. "As (capital) costs have gone up, we've turned the water rates up and people have responded by turning their hoses off."

35   Nanaimo overhauled its water conservation strategy last year and plans to promote greywater use at the residential level, as well as [expand] its toilet rebate program. And, just to keep the message positive, Nanaimo promotes awareness with "water hero" promotions that encourage people to report their neighbours for extraordinary conservation.

Time to transition

36   So, should we bite the bullet and install meters on every home in the region? Not so fast, said Vassos. There is an argument to be made for the gradual approach.

37   A rush to save water on a large scale will come with consequences, such as dramatically lower sewage flows that lead to blocked pipes and confounding disruptions in the way we fund water systems.

38   In Germany, sewage flows dropped so much in some cities that drinking water has to be used to flush the pipes just to move solid waste through the system.

39   "One of the things the Australians discovered when radical water savings are achieved is that as water use dropped, so did revenue to the water utilities," he said.

40   Water conservation technologies were meant to be incorporated into new home construction, allowing a long, smooth transition. Instead, homeowners flocked to the program and began to retrofit their homes en masse, causing a deep drop in water use and cash flow.

41   Many Metro Vancouver municipalities require meters on newly constructed homes, meaning total conversion will likely take decades.

42   The City of Vancouver began to require meters in new and substantially renovated homes and duplexes in 2012 and has 1,200 metered homes. The Greenest City Action Plan lists metering and greywater capture as goals, but sets no time frame for implementation.

43   Uptake of water-saving technology in commercial and office buildings remains stubbornly slow, with just a handful of developers opting to harvest rainwater, according to Alberto Cayuela, director of UBC's Centre for Interactive Research on Sustainability.

44   Buildings seeking LEED sustainability certification can easily collect and use rainwater for irrigation and with a larger investment, for flushing toilets. about 90 per cent of the water used by an office building is for flushing toilets.

45   "The problem is that water is so cheap that the amortization period on that investment is very long," said Cayuela.

46   The potential, however, is enormous. He estimates that five billion litres of rain falls on UBC's campus each year, while the university buys four billion litres of water annually from Metro.

Source: Shore, Randy. "Canadians Rank among World's Top Water Hogs." *Vancouver Sun,* 8 Aug. 2015, p. A8. www.vancouversun.com/Canadians rank among world water hogs/11274891/story.html/. Material republished with the express permission of Edmonton Sun, a division of Postmedia Network Inc.

Lightspring/Shutterstock.com

INTRODUCTION TO CRITICAL READING AND WRITING: ANALYZING LANGUAGE, TONE, AUTHOR, AND PUBLICATION

BY THE END OF THIS CHAPTER, YOU WILL BE ABLE TO

- Describe the relationship among language, tone, audience, and purpose.
- Explain the importance of analyzing authors and publications as part of the critical reading and writing process.
- Write an analysis of a text's language, tone, author, and publication.
- Compose your own text using language and tone appropriate to your purpose and audience.

▶ WHY IS THIS INFORMATION IMPORTANT?

In this chapter, you will take a nuanced, careful approach to reading and writing by learning how to analyze the specific language used by other writers and in your own writing. You will also look beyond a text at the publication and author in order to understand how these elements relate to the text's content. This insight, in turn, helps you examine your own authority as a writer and the best forum for sharing your own writing. This chapter encourages you to cross the line from reading for comprehension to reading for critical relationships among the various components of a text. In so doing, you move toward effective writing by learning how to synthesize language, tone, authorship, and publication strategically.

▶ Think about It!

In this chapter, you will read and write about crime and what affects crime rates. Here are some questions to consider as you move through this chapter and as you read the following essay.

1. What might account for the drop in Canadian (and American) crime rates over the past 20 years?

2. To what extent do social media, entertainment, or communication channels play a role in crime rates?

3. Are younger generations less violent, or are there other explanations for lower crime rates?

In the reading below, the author reflects on violence as it relates to video game use—do violent video games increase violent crime? This topic has been in the news, with public opinion and research swaying from one side of the debate to the other. At the start of this reading, the author is referencing the mass shooting in an Orlando, Florida nightclub on June 12, 2016, by a gunman who purportedly played violent video games.

Read this essay and consider these questions:

1. What is the author's main idea or thesis?

2. Is the publication reputable? How do you know?

3. Do you trust the author? Analyze and evaluate his tone and do some research to determine his experience with the topic.

4. Determine the main idea of the three graphics in this article. Is this support convincing?

5. What are your views on our preoccupation with violent video games?

6. After reading this essay, have you changed your views about violent video games and crime?

TEN-COUNTRY COMPARISON SUGGESTS THERE'S LITTLE OR NO LINK BETWEEN VIDEO GAMES AND GUN MURDERS

By Max Fisher
The Washington Post

1   The search for meaning is a natural response to any tragedy, and the latest U.S. mass shooting is eliciting questions about, among other things, the potential role of violent video games. After all, with kids and increasingly teenagers spending so much time hammering away at simulated shooters, is it any wonder when they pick up actual guns? Obama campaign adviser David Axelrod lamented on

Twitter, "In NFL post-game: an ad for shoot 'em up video game. All for curbing weapons of war. But shouldn't we also quit marketing murder as a game?"

2   But it turns out that the data just doesn't support this connection. Looking at the world's 10 largest video game markets yields no evident, statistical correlation between video game consumption and gun-related killings.

3   It's true that Americans spend billions of dollars on video games every year and that the United States has the highest firearm murder rate in the developed world. But other countries where video games are popular have much lower firearm-related murder rates. In fact, countries where video game consumption is highest tend to be some of the safest countries in the world, likely a product of the fact that developed or rich countries, where consumers can afford expensive games, have on average much less violent crime.

4   Here's the data for video game spending per capita and gun-related homicides in the world's 10 largest video game markets. The United States, as it so often does on gun-related statistics, really stands out:

GUN-RELATED MURDERS AND VIDEO GAME CONSUMPTION

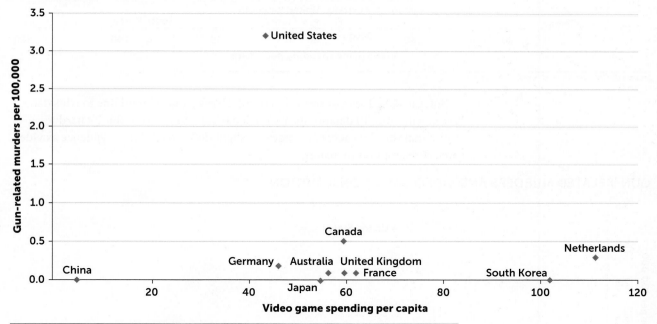

Source: UNODC, others. (Max Fisher/*Washington Post*)

5   Of course, these comparisons assume that national video game markets are largely uniform, with Dutch, Korean and American consumers playing the same spectrum of games. With the possible exception of Japan, video game markets are quite global, so this is an imperfect but generally safe assumption.

6   Now, if there were in fact a close correlation between video game consumption and gun violence, then we would expect the data to trend upward. That is, we would expect that the countries that spend the most on video games per person

would also be the most violent, by virtue of the effects of the games. Here's what the data should look like, in that case:

GUN-RELATED MURDERS AND VIDEO GAME CONSUMPTION

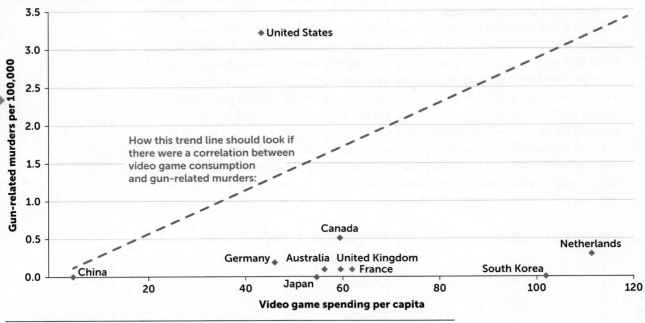

Source: UNODC, others. (Max Fisher/*Washington Post*)

7   But, the data does not show this trend. Here's a linear trend line for this data. Again, with only 10 datapoints, it's not a perfect comparison. But it's hard to ignore that this data actually suggests a slight downward shift in violence as video game consumption increases.

GUN-RELATED MURDERS AND VIDEO GAME CONSUMPTION

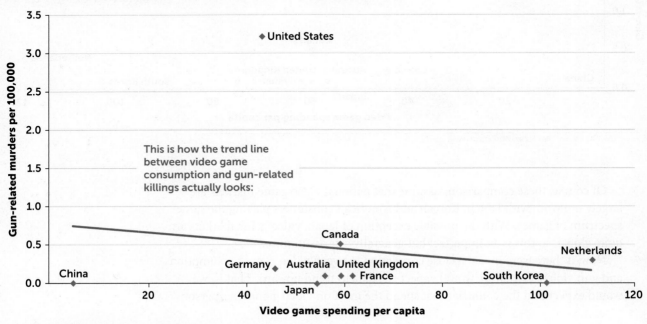

Source: UNODC, others. (Max Fisher/*Washington Post*)

8   So, what have we learned? That video game consumption, based on international data, does not seem to correlate at all with an increase in gun violence. That countries where video games are popular also tend to be some of the world's safest (probably because these countries are stable and developed, not because they have video games). And we also have learned, once again, that America's rate of firearm-related homicides is extremely high for the developed world.

What Is Critical Reading and Writing?

Critical reading and critical writing involve going beyond the basic or literal message of a text as indicated in Figure 6.1. *Critical reading* means reading deeply by using the following three skills:

- Analysis: taking a text apart to examine how the pieces work together to produce meaning;
- Evaluation: assessing the strengths and weaknesses of a text, author, and publication; and
- Synthesis: bringing together different texts, different parts of a single text, and/or your own knowledge and opinions.

FIGURE 6.1

COMPONENTS OF CRITICAL READING AND WRITING

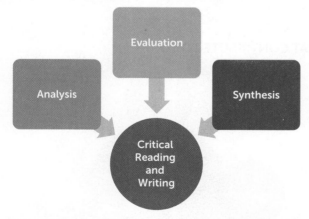

The components of a text that you will analyze, evaluate, and synthesize include the following:

- language
- author
- publication
- arguments (argument = claim plus support for the claim)

Critical writing involves both critical reading and critical thinking as you draw on the writings of others to formulate your own point of view. When writing critically, you must

- analyze and evaluate your sources (language, author, publication, arguments) before synthesizing them with your own ideas;
- analyze and evaluate your own writing after integrating your sources with your own ideas; and
- acknowledge the strengths and limitations of your sources and your own material.

In this chapter and Chapter 7, you will focus on the skill of analysis. This chapter will help you analyze language, author, and publication, while Chapter 7 will help you analyze a text's arguments. In Chapters 8 and 9, you will focus on the skill of evaluation, and in Chapter 10 you will focus on the skill of synthesis.

Analyzing Language

In both reading and writing, the vehicle for communication is language. Examining language often reveals a writer's tone—or underlying attitude—toward the subject matter. It can also give an indication of the intended audience. Being aware of your own language when writing is important. You want to make sure you get your message across clearly for your audience, and you want to make sure you use language that will appeal to them.

Language and Tone

Tone refers to the underlying attitude or emotion the writer conveys in writing. Tone is influenced by a writer's topic, purpose, language, and audience as seen in Figure 6.2. Writers use specific language to communicate this tone. You can describe a writer's tone using any adjective such as *serious, neutral, sarcastic, humorous, angry,* or *frustrated.*

FIGURE 6.2
ELEMENTS THAT CONTRIBUTE TO TONE

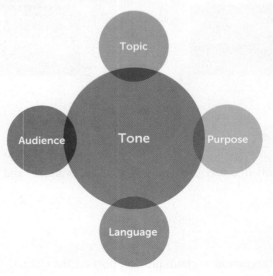

Take a look at the following two examples. Both express the same idea about how weekend trips to the country can relieve stress for people who live in an urban centre, but they do so using a different tone:

> Example 1: For many people who live in an urban centre, weekend travel to the country can reduce stress.

> Example 2: People who submit themselves to the excessive stresses of cramped, frenetic city life must flood into the country at week's end to recuperate and decompress until the grind begins again.

Writers choose their tone based on their topic, purpose, and audience. You learned about how the concepts of topic, purpose, and audience intersect in Chapter 1. As a result of this intersection, a writer will convey a tone based on his use of language and sentence structure. In both examples above, the topic is weekend trips to the country. In the first example, the purpose is informational, letting the audience know about the potential benefits of travelling to the country on weekends; therefore, the writer uses a neutral tone. In the second example, the purpose is to *persuade* the audience that urban life is stressful and a trip to the country is essential to combat that stress; therefore, the writer uses a stressed, frustrated tone. Specific words such as *excessive stresses, cramped, must,* and *grind* indicate this tone.

▶ Apply the Skill

Connecting Tone, Language, Purpose, and Audience

1. For each of the tones in the first column, think of five words that would communicate that tone. Then, consider the purpose a writer may have in using those words and that tone. The first example is done for you.

TONE	WORDS THAT COMMUNICATE EMOTION	POTENTIAL PURPOSE AND AUDIENCE
Angry	Outrageous, intolerable, ridiculous, unbearable, unbelievable, absurd	To persuade residents that installing a wind turbine will have a negative impact on their community
Suspicious		
Confused		
Hopeful		
Fearful		
Contemptuous		
Disgusted		
Embarrassed		
Surprised		
Impatient		
Superior		
Objective		
Factual		

2. Identify the author's tone in these examples from the reading at the beginning of this chapter, "Ten-Country Comparison Suggests There's Little or No Link between Video Games and Gun Murders" by Max Fisher. Remember that tone can be described by any adjective. Underline the words that suggest the tone. When you are done going through all examples, decide on the overall tone of the article. Compare your answers in a small group or in a class discussion.

   a. "After all, with kids and increasingly teenagers spending so much time hammering away at simulated shooters, is it any wonder when they pick up actual guns?"

   b. "Obama campaign adviser David Axelrod lamented on Twitter, 'In NFL post-game: an ad for shoot 'em up video game. All for curbing weapons of war. But shouldn't we also quit marketing murder as a game?'"

   c. "With the possible exception of Japan, video game markets are quite global, so this is an imperfect but generally safe assumption."

   d. "So, what have we learned? That video game consumption, based on international data, does not seem to correlate at all with an increase in gun violence."

   e. "And we also have learned, once again, that America's rate of firearm-related homicides is extremely high for the developed world."

Language and Bias

Strong emotional words show bias. *Bias* is taking a side on an issue. Being biased isn't necessarily a bad thing; however, you need to be aware of writers' biases to make sound judgments about what they are communicating. In addition, you need to be aware of your own biases to ensure your own audience makes judgments that align with your purpose and specific goal for writing. A writer is biased if the choice of words suggests a point of view and a tone that is not objective.

Take a look at the following two statements. Which one reveals bias? How do you know?

   1. What is disturbing about video games is that some studies have shown that youth who play violent games act in a violent manner.
   2. Studies show that there is a link between violent video games and violent actions.

While both sentences concern the same topic, sentence one contains biased language while sentence two does not. The use of the word *disturbing* suggests that the author is taking a position on the controversy rather than reporting the information objectively.

▶ Apply the Skill

Analyzing Biased Language

   1. Reread Max Fisher's "Ten-Country Comparison Suggests There's Little or No Link between Video Games and Gun Murders" from the beginning of this chapter. Underline any words that indicate a bias in the debate of video games and gun violence.

2. Write a paragraph in which you agree or disagree with Max Fisher's thesis. When you are done, underline the words in your own writing that indicate your agreement or disagreement. Have you chosen words that sound biased or objective? How will these word choices impact your audience's reaction to your point of view? How might changing the words change the reaction?

3. Sometimes writers believe they need to use strong, biased language to be persuasive. Others believe calmer, neutral language is more effective in some cases. Can you think of an example when strong emotional language is more persuasive than neutral language? Can you think of an example when neutral language can actually make you more convincing than using biased language? What role do topic, purpose, and audience play in your examples?

Language: Denotation and Connotation

To gain a better understanding of how certain words indicate a particular tone and/or bias, you need to be aware of both the denotative and connotative meaning of words as indicated in Figure 6.3. *Denotation* refers to the non-symbolic, dictionary definition of a word—its literal meaning. *Connotation* refers to the suggested or implied emotional load of a word—its symbolic meaning. Tone and connotation are closely linked. You understand the tone due to the word's connotations. To understand connotation, you must make an inference or "read between the lines," drawing on your understanding of how certain words are used in certain contexts. Consider these pairs of words:

1. smirk/smile
2. cackle/giggle

FIGURE 6.3
DENOTATION AND CONNOTATION

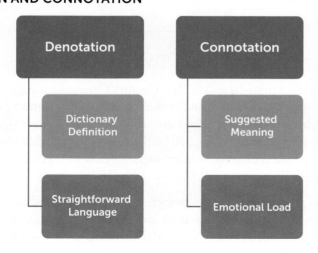

One word in each pair has a more positive connotation, yet the denotative meanings are the same. *Smirk* implies disrespect or making fun of something, whereas *smile* indicates friendliness. *Smile* has a positive connotation whereas *smirk* has a negative connotation. However, denotatively, both words mean a facial expression where there is an upward curving of the mouth.

Consider the second example: *giggle* has a positive connotation, suggesting light-heartedness, whereas *cackle* is a laugh usually attributed to a witch. A *cackle* is more sinister and therefore has a negative connotation. Denotatively, both words mean audible expression of amusement.

▶ Apply the Skill

Identifying Connotative Meanings of Words

1. Which word in each pair has a positive connotation? What are the subtle differences in meaning between each word? Be prepared to defend your answer.

   a. slim/thin

   b. chubby/fat

   c. house/home

   d. execute/slaughter

   e. war/dispute

2. For the following neutral words, find a word with a positive connotation and one with a negative connotation that means the same thing denotatively. The first example is completed as a guide.

NEUTRAL WORD	POSITIVE CONNOTATION	NEGATIVE CONNOTATION
1. Joke	Amuse	Ridicule
2. Speak		
3. Dislike		
4. Advise		
5. Disagree		
6. Avoid		

Analyzing Language and Tone

Consider Paragraph 8 from the article "Ten-Country Comparison Suggests There's Little or No Link between Video Games and Gun Murders" at the beginning of this chapter. In this paragraph, the author carefully chooses his wording to convey tone and communicate his point of view. What is implied by the passages highlighted in yellow below? After you consider the connotations of the highlighted words, how would you describe the author's tone?

> So, what have we learned? That video game consumption, based on international data, does not seem to correlate at all with an increase in gun violence. That countries where video games are popular also tend to be some of the world's safest (probably because these countries are stable and developed, not because they have video games). And we also have learned, once again, that America's rate of firearm-related homicides is extremely high for the developed world.*

*Fisher, 2012.

The author's tone is critical and condescending, revealed in his use of specific language. To begin the paragraph with "So what have we learned?" implies that he is talking down to those who hold the alternative point of view that violent video games do affect violent crime. Furthermore, he notes that countries with high levels of video gaming have low crime rates. He says these countries are "*stable* and developed." This in and of itself may be straightforward enough. However, Fisher goes on to criticize the United States by stating that gun violence rates are "*extremely* high for the developed world." Notice that he did not use the word *stable* as he does in describing high-video gaming/low-crime nations. It is the juxtaposition here that shows Fisher's attitude to the United States. Furthermore, he inserts the words *once again* in the last sentence. The use of this phrase suggests frustration and, again, a condescending tone.

Now consider the second paragraph from the article "The Real Reason Crime Is Falling So Fast" by Zoe McKnight later in the chapter. In this paragraph, the author carefully chooses her wording to convey a particular tone and communicate her point of view. What is implied by the words highlighted in yellow? Think about the connotative meaning of each highlighted word. What do these connotations say about the author's tone?

> The crime, which became known as the "cellphone slaying," left the nation stunned. A group of young men had allegedly killed another young man over a mobile phone. For those who believe that crime is out of control in this country, who harbour suspicions that growing numbers of youth are prone to violence, and who are upset by what they see as society's dangerous addiction to technology, Cook's tragic death confirmed their worst fears. "A cellphone!" one man exclaimed in the *London Free Press*. "Society is changing." The warnings from police at the time that phone robberies were rampant, and could lead to tragedy, only served to heighten the panic.*

Compare your perceptions of the words to these suggested connotative meetings.

- *Stunned* implies strong shock.
- *Addiction* speaks to the compulsive overuse of technology.
- *Rampant* suggests widespread to the point of losing control.
- *Tragedy* implies a catastrophe that may have been avoided.
- *Panic* implies desperate fear.

Just viewing these words in a list conveys the tone of fear and alarm. The author is communicating fear and desperation, and her choice of words cements this tone.

▶ Apply the Skill

Conveying Tone in Your Own Writing

1. Read the article "The Real Reason Crime Is Falling So Fast" by Zoe McKnight. Then, identify the topic, purpose, and audience. What is the thesis? What is the tone of the reading?

2. Identify the connotative (suggested) meaning of each highlighted word or passage.

---

*McKnight, 2015.

3. Write a multi-paragraph response to this reading in which you agree or disagree with McKnight's thesis. When you are done, highlight two to three words in each paragraph that have specific connotative meanings to convey a specific tone. Write down the connotative meaning of each word and describe the tone it is intended to convey.

4. Rewrite your response from 3 using the same point of view but a different tone. Again, highlight two to three words in each paragraph that have connotative meanings to convey the tone. Write down the connotative meaning of each word and describe the tone it is intended to convey.

5. Write a paragraph that describes which tone, the one from 3 or 4, does a better job of expressing your point of view. You will need to identify a specific purpose and audience for your response in order to determine which tone is more effective.

THE REAL REASON CRIME IS FALLING SO FAST
By Zoe McKnight

1 Jeremy Cook was just 18 when he was murdered, a crime that made national headlines. Last month, while on a trip to London, Ont., the Brampton teen forgot his iPhone in a taxi. Using the phone's built-in tracking feature, he later traced the device to a parking lot, where he confronted three men in a car. When he tried to stop the vehicle from driving away by grabbing the driver's side door, it's alleged that one of the occupants of the car gunned Cook down. His body was found behind a strip mall. The phone was found abandoned, along with the car. One suspect, a 23-year-old Calgary man, later drowned in Ottawa after being pursued by police, while a second suspect, 24, turned himself in after being named in a Canada-wide arrest warrant for the charge of second-degree murder. A third suspect has been identified but is not co-operating with police.

2 The crime, which became known as the "cellphone slaying," left the nation stunned. A group of young men had allegedly killed another young man over a mobile phone. For those who believe that crime is out of control in this country, who harbour suspicions that growing numbers of youth are prone to violence, and who are upset by what they see as society's dangerous addiction to technology, Cook's tragic death confirmed their worst fears. "A cellphone!" one man exclaimed in the *London Free Press*. "Society is changing." The warnings from police at the time that phone robberies were rampant, and could lead to tragedy, only served to heighten the panic.

3 But away from the headlines and breaking-news hits, it turns out there's another side to the story of youth and crime and technology, and it's one that's becoming increasingly apparent to some who study the world of crime. It's already well-established that the story of crime in Canada does not align with our darkest fears. Indeed, since 1991, both violent and non-violent Criminal Code offences have been falling. Just last week, Statistics Canada released figures showing that crime rates continued their decades-long decline. Last year, the overall crime rate, as measured by the number of incidents reported to police per 100,000 people, hit a low not seen since 1969.

4 Most of the focus is on the top line number. But it's only when the statistics are broken down by age group that the most powerful and dramatic

underlying trend becomes apparent: Canada is fast becoming a safer place, largely because huge numbers of those aged 18 to 24, the slice of the population historically responsible for the largest share of crimes in the country, are staying on the right side of the law.

5   Consider the following, drawn from data that StatsCan provided to *Maclean's* about police charges for a selection of criminal violations. Over the five-year period between 2009 and 2013, the latest year for which numbers are available, charges laid for robbery, motor vehicle theft, aggravated assault and breaking and entering among those aged 18 to 24 dropped by between 23 and 31 per cent, while the charges stemming from the most serious crime, homicide, were down 29 per cent. (Because charges are more specific than incidents and reflect varying response rates across the country, only the last five years of StatsCan data is comparable.) There were declines among other demographic groups, as well as some increases but consistently, the biggest drop in crime was among 18- to 24-year-olds—which, as the group that commits the most crimes in Canada, goes a long way to explaining why the country's overall crime rate is falling so precipitously.

6   The overall crime drop has been described as the most important criminological phenomenon of modern times and, in North America, Europe, Australia and other developed countries, many common street crimes have fallen by half since the early 1990s. What's behind the phenomenon? Theories abound, including better security—from improved locks, closed-circuit television and the widespread adoption of home alarm systems—as well as the sheer number of police on the street and bodies in prison. But a growing number of criminologists are also considering another factor they argue has not been given its due—namely, our obsession with technology. "Frankly, there are more interesting things to do indoors now than going out and nicking things," says leading British criminologist Ken Pease.

7   Pease, a visiting professor at several British universities who has published hundreds of academic papers on crime and was once head of the police research group at the U.K. government's Home Office, is a firm believer that improved security has helped to drive down crime levels. But he argues that the staggering reach of the online world—whether through video games, social media, access to instant and unlimited video and texting, always within arm's reach on our smartphones—is reshaping the modern world to such an extent that it may even be affecting crime rates. "Cyberspace becomes more interesting than meatspace," he says, referring to a term for the physical world first coined by American-Canadian science-fiction author William Gibson. "As our lives move from meatspace to cyberspace, the opportunity for violent crime and acquisitive crime change and reduce in the aggregate, and that's what I think has happened."

8   Pease is not alone. Other researchers, as well as those working in law enforcement, including the president of the Canadian Police Association and those on the front lines with at-risk youth, are observing fundamental changes taking place among the most digitally connected generation the world has ever known. It's a realm of criminology research that may only be in its infancy, but in future, it may show that our chronic technology habit, long criticized for its corroding influence on society, is actually keeping us safe.

9   The harmful effects of technology have been well-catalogued: It's been blamed for obesity, dwindling attention spans and sedentary lifestyles.

Texting and walking is hazardous, while texting and driving can be fatal. Meanwhile, medical experts regularly warn us that Internet addiction is breaking up families, that the glowing screens of our devices are making us sleep-deprived, and that social media are making us depressed. And that's just the cat-loving Internet. Anxieties about video games are even more entrenched, with the horrors of the 1999 Columbine High School massacre in Colorado—when two students, avid players of the violent video game *Doom*, killed 13 teachers and classmates—still echoing in the debate over whether virtual violence can spill over into the real world.

10   Yet for all the warnings, headlines and medical advice, our infatuation with technology continues to grow, particularly among the young. One survey of 5,000 Canadian students found 99 per cent have access to the Internet outside of school, while 45 per cent use a smartphone to go online. It's a similar story among young adults. Another study, by the Pew Research Center, found a quarter of American teens reported that they're online "almost constantly," with the typical teen sending 30 texts a day. And when people aren't updating their Facebook status, they're playing games. According to the Entertainment Software Association of Canada, nearly two-thirds of adults aged 18 to 34 play video games, while among children and teens, that figure reaches 80 per cent.

11   This digital preoccupation has been the focus of a multitude of studies, by neurologists, sociologists and psychologists. A few years ago in the U.K., criminologist Mike Sutton and psychologist Mark Griffiths, who studies gaming and addiction, first realized the extent to which their fields overlap. So together, they came up with what they call the crime substitution hypothesis, which suggests that the overwhelming preoccupation with our devices may have contributed to the crime drop.

12   Though Griffiths admits their theory is "speculative and correlational," and still requires much research to confirm, it does have what he calls "good faith validity"—it rings true. People his age and his children's age have an almost pathological need to look at their phones when the devices buzz with an incoming text, Facebook message or email. "The bottom line is, if teen-agers are so engaged in social networking or playing their computer games, they can't physically do two activities at one time," Griffiths says. "If you've got great millions of children in whatever jurisdiction playing online, particularly during their leisure time, this is a time they can't possibly be engaged in crime, as well."

13   There is growing support for this idea. Harvard economist Lawrence Katz has suggested that "video games and websites" may have provided such an effective distraction during the 2008 financial collapse that the crime wave predicted by conventional wisdom during hard economic times did not materialize. Meanwhile, a 2013 study published by the American Psychological Association found that violent crime actually went down, even as video game sales went up. The authors chalk this up to either catharsis through simulated violence, or the simple fact that if violent people are drawn to violent video games, they keep the streets safer by staying—and playing—at home.

14   And it's not only crime; rising rates of technology use also correlate with a drop in other undesirable behaviours. Research has suggested that the same forces have helped to discourage young people from risky sex, drug use and aggression. The post-Millennial demographic known as Generation Z,

defined loosely as those born after 1995, is known to be better-behaved than their older peers. As they enter their late teens, the most likely age of criminal inclination, Gen Z youths are smoking less, graduating more, having fewer pregnancies, and committing fewer robberies, car thefts and murders.

15   One might assume that the president of the Canadian Police Association would attribute the drop in crime to, above all, ace policing. But when Tom Stamatakis, a former police constable in Vancouver for 19 years, is asked for his theory, one of the first things he talks about is technology. "Perhaps, generations ago, when [young people] weren't as engaged with technology as they are now, you'd have to go out to find entertainment, as opposed to staying in your home and getting into Xbox or being engaged with your friends through social media," he says. "Technology definitely plays some role in influencing youth and the kind of activities they're involved in. If you go back to a time before cellphones and social media and game consoles, there would be boredom and you would leave your home, be out and about in the community with friends, looking for activities to engage in."

16   Not everyone is convinced that chronic use of technology is helping to bring down crime. The crime substitution theory put forth by Griffiths and Sutton, for one, has faced detractors. University of Toronto criminologist Anthony Doob considers such theories "a dime a dozen," because there have been countless changes to society since 1991. Likewise, Simon Fraser University criminology professor Graham Farrell isn't convinced. He's a former graduate student of Pease's in the U.K. and a childhood friend of Sutton's. Farrell attributes most of the crime drop to an increase in security. Since "debut crimes" such as car thefts and shoplifting have become more difficult, young people may be less likely to start a criminal career in the first place, he says. "That might be the stepping stone to why some violent crimes have gone down," Farrell says. He's also skeptical that video games, social media and smartphones contributed to the crime drop, which began in 1991, before Google and texting and before Gen Z was even born. But while he's quick to point out that correlation is not causation, he's not totally against further investigation to finally prove or disprove the hypothesis.

17   Even if the proof isn't absolute, investment in technology has worked its way into social programs in Canada and the U.S. Programs providing at-risk youths with access to mobile phones have popped up in Vancouver, Edmonton and Toronto, funded by phone companies. Taylor-Rae Foster, a program coordinator at the Youth Restorative Action Project in Edmonton, which has distributed phones to 30 teens aged 17 and under, acknowledges that the devices could facilitate drug deals or gang activity. Instead, she says they've been used by youth to find safe places to sleep and to keep in touch with friends.

18   The Internet, especially Facebook, is often the only way at-risk youths can stay in touch with their families, says Kelly Holmes, executive director of Resource Assistance for Youth in Winnipeg, an agency that deals with street-involved youth up to age 29. The agency's 15 computers are used by roughly 20 young people a day. "The demand is so much more, and there's so much more for them to do in making contact, Facebooking, applying for jobs and checking out vacancies for housing," she says. "It's a pretty important tool."

19   But while it's easy to worry about kids these days being attached to their devices, and the hand-wringing about video games and Facebook is likely

to continue, it's clear the digital revolution has brought enormous positive changes, often in unexpected ways. Society will continue to grapple with social ills such as crime and addiction, but, with access to new information, ideas and distractions, it's possible our very dependence on technology has actually made the world a little safer.

This is the author's biography from her website www.zoemcknight.com:

I'm a *Toronto Star* reporter.

I've also written for *Maclean's, Vice Canada, Vancouver Sun, National Post, Financial Post, J-Source, Canadian Running* magazine and others.

Source: Edited from McKnight, Zoe. "The Real Reason Crime Is Falling So Fast." *Maclean's*, 21 July 2015, www.macleans.ca/society/the-real-reason-crime-is-falling-so-fast/. Used with permission of Rogers Media Inc. All rights reserved.

Writing an Analysis of Language and Tone

One of the best ways of ensuring you fully understand the impact of a writer's language and the resulting tone is by writing out a formal analysis of these two elements. Likewise, the best way of ensuring you are communicating the intended tone in your own writing is to reflect upon, in writing, the impact your language use will have on your audience.

You have already seen how to write a language and tone analysis in the context of "Ten-Country Comparison Suggests There's Little or No Link between Video Games and Gun Murders." To refresh your memory, here is the paragraph that analyzed the language and tone of Paragraph 8:

> The author's tone is critical and condescending, revealed in his use of specific language. To begin the paragraph with "So what have we learned?" implies that he is talking down to those who hold the alternative point of view that violent video games do affect violent crime. Furthermore, he notes that countries with high levels of video gaming have low crime rates. He says these countries are "*stable* and developed." This in and of itself may be straightforward enough. However, Fisher goes on to criticize the United States by stating that gun violence rates are "*extremely* high for the developed world." Notice that he did not use the word *stable* as he does in describing high-video gaming/low-crime nations. It is the juxtaposition here that shows Fisher's attitude to the United States. Furthermore, he inserts the words *once again* in the last sentence. The use of this phrase suggests frustration and, again, a condescending tone.*

The above paragraph demonstrates a number of elements that need to be included in an analysis of language and tone as depicted in Figure 6.4:

- A topic sentence (or thesis) that defines the tone;
- Specific examples of word choices (diction) used by the author that indicate the tone; and
- Explanations of the connotative meanings of the author's word choices to show how those words reveal the tone.

---

*Fisher, 2012.

FIGURE 6.4

WRITING AN ANALYSIS OF LANGUAGE AND TONE

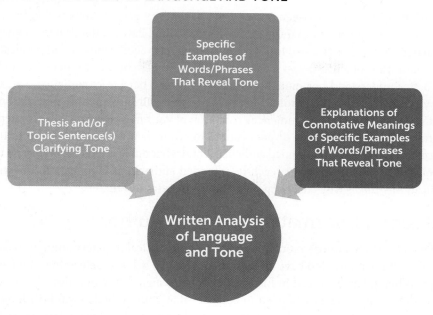

When you include the above elements in your analysis of the author's tone, both you and anyone reading your analysis get a clear sense of the author's word choices and the tone he implies. Similarly, after writing a reflection on your own language and tone, you will have a better idea of how your message will be perceived by your audience. Perception is extremely important in a persuasive piece of writing, as it will influence your audience's decision to agree or disagree with you. That is why analyzing your own language and tone is so important in persuasive writing: you may need to revise your language and tone to help get your audience on your side. In Chapter 8, you will take an even closer look at how tone and language impact how persuasive a writer is. You will learn strategies to evaluate how effective a writer's language and tone are in achieving the author's writing goals.

Review

Analyzing Language

Answer the following review questions in paragraph form or generate ideas to contribute to a group or class discussion.

1. What is involved in critical reading and writing?
2. Define and explain tone.
3. Describe how tone is related to topic, audience, and purpose.
4. Define and explain bias.
5. Explain the difference between connotation and denotation.

Analyzing Author and Publication

One of the differences between pre-and postsecondary expectations is the degree to which you are expected to analyze what you are reading. Paying attention to language is a vital part of that analysis—so too is paying attention to a text's author and publication. Who the author of a text is and what publication a writer chooses for her text can help you better understand her motivation for writing and her target audience. Similarly, as a writer, your own background and experiences will inform your motivation for writing and will shape your audience's reception of your message. You will also need to carefully consider the venue, or publication, for your own writing. You need to think critically about who your intended audience is and what publications they typically read. A well-written text may never reach its intended audience if it appears in the wrong publication—this is why analyzing publications is so important.

Gathering Information about an Author

Understanding an author's motivation for writing is critical in determining the effect a specific text is supposed to have on its audience. It also helps to determine whether the author is being fair or biased in his writing. It helps answer the question, "Can I trust this author?" As a writer, you need to consider that your audience will be asking this question of you. Therefore, it is important to build trust by helping readers understand your background and motivation for writing.

Motivation for writing can be clarified by asking a number of questions about the author and then seeking answers as seen in Figure 6.5. Remember that you should be asking these questions of your own writing, as well.

FIGURE 6.5
HOW TO DETERMINE AN AUTHOR'S MOTIVATION

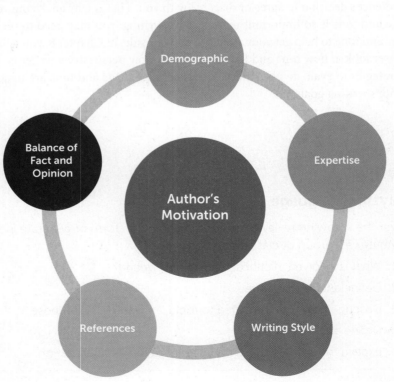

1. What are the author's demographics? Consider age, country of residence, culture, etc.
2. What is the author's area of expertise? Consider the author's educational background, research, and other publications.
3. What is the author's writing style in the specific text you are examining? Consider level of formality (formal vs. informal), level of vocabulary (sophisticated vs. plain language), level of detail (very detailed vs. brief), and sentence variety (well varied vs. all long vs. all short).
4. Who does the author cite in the text you are examining? Consider primary and secondary sources, experts vs. non-experts, those who agree with the author vs. those who disagree with the author, reputation of those being cited, and number of citations.
5. What is the balance of fact and opinion in the text you are examining?

Consider Max Fisher's motivation for writing "Ten-Country Comparison Suggests There's Little or No Link between Video Games and Gun Murders." To help determine this motivation, ask and provide answers to the five questions above.

1. What are Fisher's demographics?
   - Age—approximately early 30s based on university graduation date (www.facebook.com/max.fisher.3760)
   - Residence—formerly United States; currently England (www.facebook.com/max.fisher.3760)

2. What is Fisher's expertise?
   - Educational background: Master of Arts in Global Security (www.facebook.com/max.fisher.3760)
   - Other publications: Writes and edits a column in *The New York Times*, "exploring the ideas and context behind major world events" (twitter.com/Max_Fisher?ref_src=twsrc%5Egoogle%7Ctwcamp%5Eserp%7Ctwgr%5Eauthor)

3. What is Fisher's writing style in this article (formality, vocabulary, detail, sentence variety)?
   - Writing is mainly informal as there is evidence of
     - contractions (e.g., "here's" instead of "here is" in par. 4)
     - sentences beginning with a coordinating conjunction (e.g., "But it turns out that the data just doesn't support this connection" in par. 2)
     - language that talks down to those who hold the opposing viewpoint (e.g., "So, what have we learned?" in par. 6)
     - plural first-person point-of-view (use of "we" throughout).
   - Vocabulary is common (no jargon or specialized language).
   - Details are present, but they come from a single source (United Nations Office on Drugs and Crime).
   - Sentence length varies, mimicking a conversational style.

4. Who does Fisher cite?
   - Citations are few and come from politically focused sources (David Axelrod, United Nations Office on Drugs and Crime).

5. What is the balance of facts and opinions?
   - The article is fact-based, but there is only one source for these facts (United Nations Office on Drugs and Crime).

So what can you conclude regarding Fisher's motivation for writing? Well, Fisher grew up in the United States but now lives in England, which explains why he is writing about gun violence in the United States versus other developed countries. His age, approximately 30, indicates he was of a generation who grew up playing video games, which could indicate why he is interested in their impact on gun violence. He is writing about trends that have a direct impact on his life and those who share a similar demographic background.

Fisher's education in global security matches the content of his article very well: he is exploring gun violence and video games from a global perspective. The fact that he is also a journalist helps us understand that he is writing both to inform and to persuade. He has conducted research to obtain facts that he wants to use to persuade Americans that gun violence is not related to violent video game consumption.

The generally informal approach to his writing, in addition to his use of plain language, tells us he is trying to engage all adult citizens in a conversation about video games and gun violence. His focus on just a few details, presented in a visual form, also help us understand that he is trying to present his information for quick and easy consumption by the audience. His choice of using just one source for his factual evidence also indicates he wants to persuade his audience quickly without having to acknowledge other evidence that may be contradictory to his point of view.

In short, his motivation is to persuade Americans that discussions of gun violence need to be focused elsewhere, not on video games.

Now that you know how to analyze an author's motivation, you will be better positioned to assess an author's trustworthiness and reliability. You will learn how to make the connection among motivation and trustworthiness and reliability in Chapter 8.

▶ Apply the Skill

Analyzing an Author's Motives

1. Consider the other two readings in this chapter, "The Real Reason Crime Is Falling So Fast" and "Our Secret Love Affair with Assault Rifles." For each reading, answer the following questions, which will help you analyze the authors' motives.

   a. How do the author's demographics relate to the topic area of the reading?

   b. Does the author have an educational or employment background in the topic area of the reading? How do you know? Is there evidence of the background—or lack thereof—in the article itself? Do you have to do additional research?

   c. How would you describe the author's writing style? Is it formal or informal? Is the vocabulary generic or specialized? How much detail does the author provide? Does the author use short sentences, long sentences, or a balance of both?

   d. What sources does the author cite? Do these sources represent differing points of view? Who are the authors of these sources?

   e. What is the balance of fact and opinion in the article? Is it more fact based or more opinion based?

   f. What do your answers to the five questions above tell you about the author's motivation for writing?

2. Consider the last piece of writing that you wrote. What was your motivation? How did this motivation relate to your demographics and education? How did it influence the formality, vocabulary, level of detail, and sentence variety in your writing? What sources did you cite and why? How balanced were the facts and opinions, and why?

Gathering Information about Publications

Publications—the formal places where writing appears—often feature the same authors repeatedly, and the writing within the publications is often directed toward the same audience. For example, a local newspaper will have the same columnists writing week after week, and this newspaper will be read by citizens on a weekly basis. Knowing the typical authors and target audience of a publication is helpful to you as both a reader and a writer as seen in Figure 6.6. As a reader, publication knowledge helps you find readings of interest with ease, navigate repetitive patterns in the readings, and determine the purpose and audience of the readings. As a writer, publication knowledge helps you determine topics of interest for your audience, the writing style you should adopt, and what purposes you can fulfill with your writing.

FIGURE 6.6
PUBLICATIONS, READERS, AND WRITERS

Max Fisher's article from the beginning of this chapter was published in *The Washington Post*. If you go to the *Washington Post* website (www.washingtonpost.com), you will notice that the newspaper's tagline is "Democracy Dies in Darkness." What does that tell you about the writing that will appear in this newspaper? Darkness refers to ignoring or not seeing what's going on around us. So, if this is the place where democracy dies, then the place where democracy lives must be the light—the ability to see or pay attention to what's going on around us. In other words, the tagline indicates that the newspaper brings controversial issues into the light. It explores what's going on around us so that we can ensure democracy lives on. Because democracy means that the public needs to have a voice in the government of a society, you can determine that this news publication intends to give a voice to the public.

Upon further examination of the *Washington Post* website, you will see the sections that comprise the newspaper: Politics, Opinion, Sports, Local, National, World, Business, Tech, Lifestyle, and Entertainment. From these categories, you can see that this is a politically charged newspaper, since politics and opinion appear first. You can also see the newspaper covers a broad scope of events—local, national, and world. Lifestyle and Entertainment are last in the list, likely indicating their relatively low importance within the publication.

If you dig deeper into the site, you will notice that the opinion section includes a list of opinion writers, indicating that these writers contribute often to the newspaper. You can also imagine, again from the tagline of the newspaper, that the audience is typically the same week after week: those who want to engage in democracy and are open to questioning and critiquing the government.

▶ Apply the Skill

Analyzing a Publication

Complete each of the following tasks individually or in a small group.

1. Describe how Max Fisher and his article "Ten-Country Comparison Suggests There's Little or No Link between Video Games and Gun Murders" is a good fit for *The Washington Post*.

2. Find a local online newspaper and answer the following questions:

   a. Does the newspaper have a tagline? If so, what is it? What does it mean?

   b. What are the sections of the newspaper? What do these sections tell you about the types of writing that will appear?

   c. Does the newspaper have particular columnists who write regularly for the newspaper? If so, research one of these columnists and articulate her or his motivation for writing.

   d. Write an analysis of the newspaper, similar to the analysis of *The Washington Post* presented above. Use your answers from (a) to (c) to help you.

   e. If you were to write an article for the newspaper, what would be your topic, purpose, and audience? What style would you need to adopt? Justify your answers by describing how these choices align with the publication and the expectations of the publication's audience.

3. Select a publication of your own choosing. Then, write an analysis of the publication from the perspective of a reader. What types of writing would you expect to find in the publication? Are you the publication's target audience? Will you find a topic of interest? Explain what it is about the publication that helps you determine the answers to these questions. (Hint: Look at the above analysis of *The Washington Post*.)

4. Select a publication of your own choosing. Write an article for inclusion in the publication. Describe how your article aligns with the publication and the expectations of its audience.

Review

Analyzing an Author and Publication

Answer the following review questions in paragraph form or generate ideas to contribute to a group or class discussion.

1. Why is it important to understand an author's motivation for writing?
2. What factors contribute to an author's motivation for writing?
3. Why is publication knowledge important for both readers and writers?
4. How do you gain knowledge about a publication?

> ### Did You Know?

USING COMMAS

It's a common misperception that commas are tied to a "pause" in reading. In fact, comma usage depends on phrases, clauses, and individual words. Here are five common instances in which commas are required.

1. Dependent clause followed by independent clause (DC, IC)

   When you put a dependent adverb clause (DC) in front of an independent clause (IC), use a comma to separate the two clauses, just as in this sentence from "The Real Reason Crime Is Falling So Fast":

   Since "debut crimes" such as car thefts and shoplifting have become more difficult, young people may be less likely to start a criminal career in the first place …

2. Two independent clauses joined by a coordinating conjunction (IC, cc IC)

   When you combine two independent clauses with a coordinating conjunction (cc)—for, and, nor, but, yet, or, so—a comma must go in front of the coordinating conjunction, as in this sentence from "The Real Reason Crime Is Falling So Fast":

   It's a realm of criminology research that may only be in its infancy, but in future, it may show that our chronic technology habit, long criticized for its corroding influence on society, is actually keeping us safe.

3. List of three or more items

   When you list a series of three or more items, use commas to separate the items, as in this sentence from "The Real Reason Crime Is Falling So Fast":

   As they enter their late teens, the most likely age of criminal inclination, Gen Z youths are smoking less, graduating more, having fewer pregnancies, and committing fewer robberies, car thefts and murders.

4. Introductory phrases

> When you place a phrase before an independent clause, use a comma to separate the phrase from the independent clause. Here is an example from "The Real Reason Crime Is Falling So Fast":

Last year, the overall crime rate, as measured by the number of incidents reported to police per 100,000 people, hit a low not seen since 1969.

5. Non-essential clauses

> When you place a non-essential clause in the middle of an independent clause, put a comma before *and* after the non-essential clause. A clause is considered non-essential when it provides additional, but not necessary, information. Take a look at this example from "The Real Reason Crime Is Falling So Fast":

A few years ago in the U.K., criminologist Mike Sutton and psychologist Mark Griffiths, who studies gaming and addiction, first realized the extent to which their fields overlap.

> The green clause is not essential to the meaning of the sentence. If you were to remove the green clause from the sentence, none of the meaning of the sentence would be lost.

▶ Apply the Skill

Analyzing and Using Commas

1. Select one paragraph from the final reading in this chapter, A. J. Somerset's "Our Secret Love Affair with Assault Rifles." Then, do the following:

   a. Number each comma in the paragraph. The first comma will be number one, the second comma will be number two, and so forth.

   b. On a separate piece of paper, explain why each comma is required. Keep in mind that some of the commas may be working together as part of a list or non-essential clause, for example.

2. Write a one- or two-paragraph response to one of the claims Somerset makes in "Our Secret Love Affair with Assault Rifles." In your response, include at least one instance of each of the following, making sure each one is properly punctuated:

   a. a sentence that begins with a dependent clause followed by an independent clause

   b. a sentence that joins two independent clauses with the word *and, but,* or *so*

   c. a sentence with a list of three or more items

   d. a sentence with an introductory phrase

   e. a sentence with a non-essential clause

   f. a sentence without any commas required

▶ Questions for Writing and Discussion

1. Read the article "Our Secret Love Affair with Assault Rifles." First, determine the purpose, topic, audience, and the thesis of the reading. Then determine the tone of the reading. Catalogue specific words or specifics about the writing style to support your decision.

2. Both "Our Secret Love Affair with Assault Rifles" and "Ten-Country Comparison Suggests There's Little or No Link between Video Games and Gun Murders" refer to the Orlando nightclub shooting in June 2016. Why do both authors refer to this horrific event in order to initiate their essays? How do their respective theses link to this event or events like it? Is there anything in the authors' backgrounds or in their source material that relates to this reference?

3. Which of the three readings in this chapter do you think is the strongest in explaining crime rates? Which of the three readings do you think is the least convincing? Are there other factors that you believe are important to explain crime rates? Support your answers with specific, credible information and/or sound external source material.

4. In the reading at the beginning of this chapter, "Ten-Country Comparison Suggests There's Little or No Link between Video Games and Gun Murders," the author says, "countries where video game consumption is highest tend to be some of the safest countries in the world." How does the author support this claim? Come up with other explanations aside from those of the author to explain this phenomenon. Use credible sources.

5. Zoe McKnight and A. J. Somerset are the authors of two readings in this chapter. Explain how each author is connected to her/his writing and to the source in which the writing appears. In other words, how do the author, her/his article, and the article's sources all connect?

6. In the reading "The Real Reason Crime Is Falling So Fast," the author says, "Yet for all the warnings, headlines and medical advice, our infatuation with technology continues to grow, particularly among the young." Write an essay drawing information from this reading and "Ten-Country Comparison Suggests There's Little or No Link between Video Games and Gun Murders," contrasting positive and negative possible consequences of technology use. Take a position and find other credible sources to support your point of view. Make sure to shape your language and tone to your topic, purpose, and audience.

OUR SECRET LOVE AFFAIR WITH ASSAULT RIFLES

Canada's lax gun regulations means an Orlando-style shooting could happen here.

By A. J. Somerset

1   As the holder of a firearms licence, I can go down to my local Ontario gun shop and buy an assault weapon. Of course, the gun shop won't call it that, and I'd be ill-advised to do so. "Assault weapon," a term often applied to the AR-15, the mass shooter's rifle of choice, is a controversial label, as is "assault rifle." At the

gun shop, it might be called a black rifle (because most models are all black), or a "modern sporting rifle"—the name approved by an industry determined to rebrand military weapons as ordinary hunting rifles.

2   In Canada, we're not just confused over what to call these guns. We're also confused over how to regulate them: some are classified as restricted firearms, and tightly controlled. Others are not. The ongoing uncertainty over how such guns should be classified means that Canadians have easy access to weapons that are functionally the same as the restricted AR-15. The Tavor, for example, is a semi-automatic rifle that fires the same ammunition as the AR-15 with the same nato-standard magazines. The VZ-58 is a Czech-made semi-automatic rifle that, while externally similar to the prohibited AK-47, has a different mechanism; it fires AK-47 ammunition from a thirty-round magazine. Both guns are non-restricted. Both can be purchased over the counter.

3   As non-restricted guns, the Tavor and the VZ-58 don't need be registered, and require no special transportation rules. I can resell them to anyone, without telling anyone, provided the buyer is licensed. And if the buyer is a lifelong criminal, prohibited from owning weapons, I could still get away with selling him the gun. The lack of a long gun registry and mandatory sales records means that, as long as the buyer keeps his mouth shut, the weapon is unlikely to be traced back to me. Canadian gun shops are filled with similar examples.

4   Black rifle enthusiasts argue that semi-automatic rifles aren't a public safety risk. Tony Bernardo, the head of the Canadian Shooting Sports Association—Canada's most effective gun lobby—went so far as to tell the *Washington Post* that "we have never had a single crime committed in Canada by an AR-15." But Louise Russo might be surprised to hear that. In 2004, she found herself in a North York sandwich shop when two gunmen opened fire in an attempted mob hit. A bullet fragment hit her spine, leaving her paralyzed. One of the weapons involved was a Colt AR-15.

5   One shooting does not make a trend. But we regulate weapons based on the risk they pose, not on how many people they've killed. And the problem posed by black rifles is that, while they are rarely involved in crime, the crimes they feature in tend to be particularly serious. It's precisely because they may face such weapons (military rifles were involved in the RCMP deaths at Mayerthorpe and in Moncton) that police now arm themselves with the C8 "patrol carbine"—an assault weapon by yet another name.

6   Why are these guns so poorly regulated? In 1995, when Canada's criteria for restricted and prohibited weapons were last changed, the market for them was non-existent. And so Allan Rock's new gun control law essentially ignored semi-automatic rifles. But when the Clinton-era assault weapon ban expired in 2004, the lucrative American gun market was soon flooded with black rifles. In Canada, Stephen Harper's government faced a problem: a hard pro-gun stance might alienate softer Conservative support in Ontario, but the Conservatives had pandered to gun owners by promising to eliminate the Firearms Act, and gun owners were impatient. Many felt they had been betrayed by a Conservative Party that claimed to be their ally but was taking no action. The last thing the Conservatives wanted was to alienate a dissatisfied voting bloc. And so, for almost a decade, the Canadian government did nothing at all about a proliferation of black rifles.

7   Just how many black rifles Canadians now own is a mystery. But we know that over the course of Harper's tenure as prime minister, the number of *restricted* firearms licences in Canada rose by 82 percent. So it's no surprise that a petition to reclassify the AR-15 as non-restricted—presented to the House of Commons just one month before the Orlando massacre—bore more than 25,000 names.

8   The petition to deregulate the AR-15 is the gun lobby's blinkered response to our confused classification system: surely if the Tavor is non-restricted, the AR-15 should be, too. And the petition, which appeals to the government to make the AR-15 legal for hunting, reflects a larger attempt to rebrand the AR-15 as a modern sporting rifle and market it to hunters. But few hunters seem to want one, and many of the signatures likely come from non-hunters hoping to get their rifles moved to non-restricted status—which has the side effect of taking them out of the gun registry, which still exists for restricted firearms.

9   An AR-15 is not easy to get in Canada. You need a restricted firearms licence, called an RPAL, which requires a training course, written and practical tests, an extensive background check, and a waiting period. After you get a RPAL, and purchase your AR-15, you'll need to register the gun. The weapon can only be loaded and fired on a police-approved range, and must be transported to and from that range by the most direct route, in a locked case, with a trigger lock, and unloaded. At home, your AR-15 must be kept in a locked safe.

10   Clearly, owning an AR-15 in Canada offers not much scope for fun—which helps to explain why so many Canadian gun owners want to deregulate it. But there remains one additional rule that reduces your fun still further: your thirty-round AR-15 magazines must be altered so that they can hold no more than five rounds. Canada chooses not to ban semi-automatic firearms. Instead, we regulate magazines.

11   Regulating magazines is a good idea. The fundamental design feature of black rifles is not their semi-automatic action, or their military appearance. It's a thirty-round detachable box magazine, released at the press of a button. To reload your AR-15, you simply press the magazine release button with the tip of your trigger finger, push in a new magazine, smack the bolt release with your free hand, and fire. You do all this without taking your trigger hand off the pistol grip, and without taking the rifle off your shoulder. More than any other, this is the feature that enables mass shootings.

12   But a law restricting magazine capacity imagines a world where gun owners don't import thirty-round nato-standard magazines *altered* to hold only five rounds. These magazines can easily be altered back. Nor does it imagine a world in which those magazines—and rifles that accept them—are easily resold onto the criminal black market, as backup firepower for gangs. If we still had a long gun registry, or if all such rifles were restricted, we wouldn't have to worry about that. And if the US had meaningful laws to restrict magazine capacity, then the supply of these magazines would dry up, to be replaced by smaller five- or ten-round mags. It's another case where a failure to put meaningful regulations in place in the US weakens the effect of our own laws.

13   Semi-automatic firearms are not the problem. Not all semi-automatics ought to be considered assault weapons. Two thirds of duck hunters, for example, use semi-auto shotguns. These are limited to a three-round magazine and are inconvenient to reload; they're a poor choice for armed mayhem and there is no special

reason to regulate them. But centrefire, semi-auto rifles like the AR-15 are a different story. This is the standard military and police rifle, and it is designed for easy, quick reloading for a reason: so that you can shoot as many bullets in as little time as possible. All rifles originate from military designs, but modern military rifles have evolved beyond any civilian application.

14   As long as these rifles exist in Canada, a massacre like Orlando is not simply a US nightmare on the news; it's a shadow falling over us, a possibility we can't ignore.

A. J. Somerset (@ajsomerset) is the author of *Arms: The Culture and Credo of the Gun*.

Source: Somerset, A.J. "Our Secret Love Affair with Assault Rifles." *The Walrus*, 24 June, 2016, www.thewalrus.ca/dont-be-smug-we-love-assault-weapons-too/. Accessed 19 July 2016. Reproduced by permission of the author.

INTRODUCTION TO CRITICAL READING AND WRITING: ANALYZING ARGUMENTS

BY THE END OF THIS CHAPTER, YOU WILL BE ABLE TO

- Describe the components of an argument.
- Classify types of support for an argument.
- Distinguish between inductive and deductive arguments.
- Determine whether an argument is sound.
- Identify hidden assumptions in arguments.
- Use logic, credibility, and emotion to persuade.

▶ WHY IS THIS INFORMATION IMPORTANT?

In Chapter 6, you learned how to analyze language to determine tone, and you learned how to ask questions about writers and publications to help better understand writing intentions and motivations. In other words, you examined some of the formal elements of a piece of writing to see how they work together to produce meaning. Now you will move from examining the form a writer chooses to examining the content. Specifically, you will learn to analyze a writer's argumentation strategies, pulling apart the various components of an argument to see how these components work together to persuade the audience to accept the writer's ideas.

▶ Think about It!

In this chapter, you will read and write about the pros and cons of two controversial issues. The first is whether there is a gender gap in video gaming. Some people and agencies are concerned with misogyny (hatred toward women) in what some call a male gaming world. Yet, the number of women involved in gaming is on the rise. The second issue is whether virtual reality should be more regulated than video games. Virtual reality is computer technology using display screens, headsets, projectors, or other devices to generate experiences and sensory simulations. The simulation can be so realistic that users may not be able to decipher it from the real thing. Along with virtual reality technology that pushes the boundaries of what we know comes possible ethical concerns; how to rein in potential problems with emerging technologies becomes an issue. Here are some questions to consider as you move through this chapter and as you read the following essay.

1. Is gaming a male domain?

2. What is the status of women in gaming in general and its online gaming space specifically? What influences gender status?

3. "Gamergate," as mentioned in the reading, was an online gaming controversy that erupted in 2014 and spread with the hashtag #gamergate. The controversy mainly concerned the ethics in video game journalism and the treatment of women in the gaming industry. Why do you think online gaming would fuel such controversy?

4. Should we regulate gaming, especially regarding virtual reality gaming?

In this reading, the author argues that video gaming does not have a gender gap. As you read, think about the evidence the author presents to support her point of view.

1. What is the author's main idea or thesis?

2. Is the author authoritative and reputable in the field about which she writes?

3. Is the argument convincing?

4. What type of support does the author use to back up her perspective? Is this support convincing?

5. What are your views on gender and video games?

6. After reading this essay, have you changed your views about gender representation or bias in video gaming?

DOES VIDEO GAMING HAVE A GENDER GAP?

By Kishonna Gray
Director, Critical Gaming Lab, and Assistant Professor,
School of Justice Studies, Eastern Kentucky University

1 A gender gap does not exist in gaming. According to the Pew Research Center, women and men play video games at about the same rate. Fifty percent of men and 48 percent of women say they play video games on a console, personal computer or handheld device. This directly counters what 60 percent of Americans told Pew: that men play video games more. Even women who play video games had that belief.

2   Partly because game company marketing pushed a very masculine product with masculine advertising, the constructed identity of a gamer was long associated with men and boys. When more women began playing games, the narrative began to shift, redefining what it meant to be a gamer.

3   Even so, when women are viewed as part of gaming culture, they are assumed to be interested in the "casual" gaming market—games that are simpler and easy to learn—while men are assumed to favor immersive, violent games. Games such as "Candy Crush" and "Just Dance" have been cited as casual games popular among women. Additionally, many gamers suggest that women are not hardcore gamers, leading to further divides along gender lines. But one should ask: Why don't women play hardcore games at higher rates compared to the casual ones. The answer may point to a different kind of gap in gaming.

4   While there is no numerical gender gap in gaming, an inclusivity gap does exist, in which the presence of women in games, gaming communities and gaming culture in general sometimes leads to disparate treatment. As researchers have long noted, women gamers experience hostile environments.

5   Much of the recent debate around the reality of women in gaming emerged with the "Gamergate" controversy, in which several women in the industry were subjected to prolonged harassment from men. It started as a conversation about ethics in game journalism but ended with a largely male gaming community marginalizing women who spoke out about their antagonistic treatment.

6   While public perception may not view women as gamers, numbers reveal the truth. Women are playing and have been playing all along. We need to move beyond these simple constructions and improve marketing, advertising and representations of women in games; increase the numbers of women in game development; ensure inclusive gaming environments and increase the value of women within gaming.

Source: Ault, Alicia. "Video Games and Learning" *The CQ Researcher*, 12 February 2016, http://library.cqpress.com.ezproxy.stlcc.edu/. Accessed 21 July 2016. Republished with permission of CQ Press Researcher, from Alicia Ault, "Video Games and Learning: Do games help students in the classroom?" CQ Researcher, vol. 26(7), February 12, 2016, pp. 145–168; permission conveyed through Copyright Clearance Center, Inc.

Components of an Argument

When writers make arguments, they are presenting their position on a controversial topic and defending that position with various types of support. Arguments in some form or another are very common in postsecondary writing—think of all the assignments that require you to make a point or a claim and then back up your assertion with supporting information.

Writing an argument is quite complex because arguments are iterative in nature. In other words, a larger argument is built up from smaller arguments, which are also built up from even smaller arguments. This pattern is potentially endless, but writers must obviously define a point at which the foundation of an argument is either a fact or at the very least a claim that need not be defended because most people would easily agree with it. Within each of these arguments are two key components: claims and support. The claim of a smaller argument becomes some of the support for a larger argument.

Claims

A *claim* is a position on an issue. An *issue* is a topic that invites more than one position or point of view. Consider the issue of whether online video gaming should be more regulated. There are two possible positions, or claims, for this issue: (1) Yes, online video gaming should be more regulated, or (2) No, online video gaming should not be more regulated.

You can think of a claim as the main idea of an argument. When you think about claims this way, you should recall that you have already learned to identify claims in the writing of others and write claims of your own: you learned how to do this in Chapter 1 with a thesis and also Chapter 2, which used the language of "main idea" instead of claim. A claim is a special type of main idea—a main idea that is debatable. If the statement is not debatable, then there is no claim and no argument.

When reading the claims of others, be on the lookout for general versus focused claims. General claims are usually ineffective, and they may indicate a weakness on the part of the writer. Keeping that in mind, you should always take care with crafting focused claims in your own writing. Doing so will help make your claim seem relatable, worth reading about, and trustworthy.

Take a look at the following claim:

Some video games are bad for society.

Like you learned in earlier chapters about focused and limited thesis statements and topic sentences, a statement of claim also needs to be focused since it is a thesis of an essay or a main idea of a body paragraph. The claim above is too broad and therefore would not make the foundation of a good argument. "Some video games" is vague, the adjective "bad" is vague, and the term "society" is vague. Nothing in this claim is relatable, worthwhile, or credible. Now, consider this claim:

The game "Grand Theft Auto" promotes misogyny due to the stereotyped characterization of women in the first five minutes of play.

This claim is much more focused. It identifies a specific game (Grand Theft Auto), so the topic is limited. In addition, it has a specific way in which it is bad (it promotes misogyny), and it addresses a specific societal issue (stereotypes); therefore, the point about the topic is focused. The audience can enter into this discussion much more easily than the "Some video games are bad for society" discussion because of the concrete areas to focus on.

▶ Apply the Skill

Analyzing and Writing Claims

1. For the following statements, put a checkmark in the "debatable" box if the statement is debatable, and put a checkmark in the "limited and focused" box if the statement is appropriately limited and focused.

STATEMENT	DEBATABLE?	LIMITED AND FOCUSED?
Social media promotes community.		
Online gaming should be monitored in teenagers.		

(Continued)

STATEMENT	DEBATABLE?	LIMITED AND FOCUSED?
"Grand Theft Auto" is controversial.		
Mental health is improved by positive thinking.		
Social media has good and bad qualities.		
Virtual reality games should be regulated more than conventional games.		
Twitter is right to take steps to regulate online bullying.		
Virtual reality games should not be more regulated than conventional games.		
Twitter's regulation of online bullying is ineffective.		

2. Identify the main idea—claim—in each of the following paragraphs from "Does Video Gaming Have a Gender Gap?" by Kishonna Gray. Then, write your own limited and focused claim that indicates whether you agree or disagree with Gray's claim. When you're finished, review the author's claims and your own claims to ensure they are debatable, limited, and focused. Next, compare your answers with a peer or in a small group.

Paragraph 3

Even so, when women are viewed as part of gaming culture, they are assumed to be interested in the "casual" gaming market—games that are simpler and easy to learn—while men are assumed to favor immersive, violent games. Games such as "Candy Crush" and "Just Dance" have been cited as casual games popular among women. Additionally, many gamers suggest that women are not hardcore gamers, leading to further divides along gender lines. But one should ask: Why don't women play hardcore games at higher rates compared to the casual ones. The answer may point to a different kind of gap in gaming.

    Author's Claim:
    Your Claim:
    Are both claims debatable, limited, and focused?

Paragraph 4

While there is no numerical gender gap in gaming, an inclusivity gap does exist, in which the presence of women in games, gaming communities and gaming culture in general sometimes leads to disparate treatment. As researchers have long noted, women gamers experience hostile environments.

    Author's Claim:
    Your Claim:
    Are both claims debatable, limited, and focused?

Paragraph 6

While public perception may not view women as gamers, numbers reveal the truth. Women are playing and have been playing all along. We need to move beyond these simple constructions and improve marketing, advertising and representations of women in games; increase the numbers of women in game development; ensure inclusive gaming environments and increase the value of women within gaming.

> Author's Claim:
> Your Claim:
> Are both claims debatable, limited, and focused?

Source: Ault, 2016.

Support

Support refers to everything a writer uses to justify his claim. Generally, support is divided into two categories: evidence and explanations (see Figure 7.1). *Evidence* refers to the facts, examples, and testimony used to support or clarify a claim. An *explanation* is what the writer uses to connect the evidence to the claim; it is the writer's reasoning as to how the evidence proves the claim. Writers of arguments often consider three subcategories of evidence: facts, examples, and testimony. Similarly, there are two subcategories of explanations: *reasons* (also known as *subclaims*) and *counterargument* and *refutation*. You need to be familiar with this categorization of support so that you can analyze the arguments of others and build well-developed arguments of your own.

FIGURE 7.1
ARGUMENT STRUCTURE

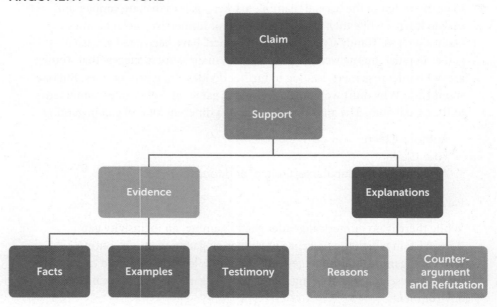

TYPES OF EVIDENCE

To be a critical writer as well as a critical reader, you need to recognize the relative merits and strengths of different types of evidential support. Remember that *evidence* is proof in support of a claim. It typically comes as one of three types: facts, examples, and testimony.

FACTS

A *fact* is something that cannot be debated. In other words, a fact can be proven beyond a doubt. For example, it is a fact that the title of this textbook is *Interchange*. A fact can also be defined as a contrast to an *opinion*. While a fact is not debatable, an opinion is debatable. An *opinion* is a person's belief, and this belief cannot be proven beyond a reasonable doubt. Others can disagree with it. For example, it is an opinion that violent video games lead to violent behaviours in those who play them. A writer can use facts to try to help strengthen this opinion and get others to believe it, but he cannot claim beyond a doubt that video games lead to violent behaviours in everyone who plays them.

At first glance, the distinction between fact and opinion may seem obvious, but fact and opinion can be complex. For example, statistics (which are facts in numeric form) are factual—in other words, these numbers actually exist in a research study. However, the interpretation of the statistics—of what the numbers mean—is opinion. Take a look at this example:

> A researcher conducts a study examining how effective hypnosis is in helping people quit smoking. In this study, 6 out of the 10 participants were able to quit smoking after receiving the hypnosis.

Is there a fact here? Yes, the statistic is factual. We can prove that the number is accurate. We could observe the study taking place, and we can observe the smoking behaviours of the study participants afterward. The interpretation, however, is up for debate. Some may argue that the 6 out of 10 statistic indicates the hypnosis is an effective treatment to help smokers quit smoking. Others may argue that 6 out of 10 is not a high enough percentage to indicate that the treatment is effective. Others still may state that the sample size—10 participants—is not large enough to come to any reasonable conclusion. Table 7.1 speaks to the complex relationship between facts and opinions.

TABLE 7.1
COMPARING AND CONTRASTING FACTS AND OPINIONS

FACTS (= PROVABLE)	OPINIONS (= UP FOR DEBATE)
Statistics	Interpretation of statistics (e.g., What do the numbers mean?)
An event took place	Interpretation of the event (e.g., Was it successful? did you enjoy it?)
Observation	Interpretation of the observation (e.g., Did you like what you saw?)
A statement some-one made	Interpretation of the statement (e.g., Can you trust what was said?)

For our purposes, then, facts are straightforward, provable, and documented pieces of information—facts exist, are known to exist, or can be verified or proven to exist. Opinions, on the other hand, are an *interpretation* of facts. Opinion statements cannot be verified or proven. An opinion is a claim—it can be debated since an opinion is a value judgment. A *value judgment* means that another person could counterargue and also be considered "right."

Often, a statement contains elements of both fact and opinion. Consider this example from "Does Video Gaming Have a Gender Gap?"

A Pew study shows that 60 percent of respondents believe that video gaming is a male-dominated world, yet I don't believe those figures are accurate.

In this example, it is a fact that 60 percent of respondents reported that video gaming is male-dominated; that the author doesn't believe the figure is an opinion. So, this statement is both fact and opinion.

▶ Apply the Skill

Distinguishing between Fact and Opinion

Which of the following statements are fact and which are opinion? Put an "F" by a statement of fact, an "O" by a statement of opinion, and "F/O" by a statement of both fact and opinion. These passages come from "Does Video Gaming Have a Gender Gap?" by Kishonna Gray at the beginning of this chapter.

_____ 1. A gender gap does not exist in gaming.

_____ 2. According to the Pew Research Center, women and men play video games at about the same rate.

_____ 3. Fifty percent of men and 48 percent of women say they play video games on a console, personal computer or handheld device.

_____ 4. Partly because game company marketing pushed a very masculine product with masculine advertising, the constructed identity of a gamer was long associated with men and boys.

_____ 5. Even so, when women are viewed as part of gaming culture, they are assumed to be interested in the "casual" gaming market—games that are simpler and easy to learn—while men are assumed to favor immersive, violent games.

_____ 6. When more women began playing games, the narrative began to shift, redefining what it meant to be a gamer.

_____ 7. While there is no numerical gender gap in gaming, an inclusivity gap does exist, in which the presence of women in games, gaming communities and gaming culture in general sometimes leads to disparate treatment.

_____ 8. Much of the recent debate around the reality of women in gaming emerged with the "Gamergate" controversy, in which several women in the industry were subjected to prolonged harassment from men.

EXAMPLES

Examples are specific instances that support a point of view. There are four types of examples (see Figure 7.2). While some examples can be factual, keep in mind that the broader point the example is supposed to prove will actually be an opinion. In the reading at the end of this chapter, "Should Virtual Reality Be More Regulated than Video Games?" by Doug Bierend, the following example is used: "Consider that Facebook spent $2 billion on a small headset startup called Oculus" (par. 1). This example is a fact.

FIGURE 7.2

TYPES OF EXAMPLES

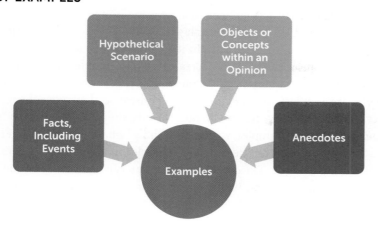

You can do some research to verify that Facebook made such an investment. The point this example is trying to prove, however, is an opinion—a claim. The opinion is that "virtual reality may be unusually dramatic" in comparison to "television, video games or the Internet" (par. 1).

Examples are not always facts, however. In some cases, examples themselves may be hypothetical scenarios. Imagine, for example, that you are arguing in favour of more online course options at your school. To support this point of view about needing more online courses, you may provide a hypothetical scenario about a parent with a full-time job who wants to attend school to upgrade his skills but cannot find a class schedule that accommodates his personal life and work schedule. While this scenario is possible, it does not refer to a specific, real person. As such, it is not factual. It is, however, a specific instance—an example—that demonstrates why more online courses may be beneficial. While factual examples may be considered more persuasive than hypothetical scenarios, these factual examples are not always accessible to a writer. Moreover, hypothetical scenarios could provide greater critical thinking and ingenuity than facts can provide. They can help readers think about examples that don't yet exist but could exist for the benefit of many.

Examples could also just be objects or concepts used as part of a claim. In the reading "Should Virtual Reality Be More Regulated than Video Games?" by Kate Edwards, which you can find at the end of this chapter, Paragraph 4 provides a claim with this type of example embedded within it: "A quantitative scale for the 'impact' of games and virtual reality is just as useless a concept as measuring the impact of a short story versus a novel, film or television program."

The use of objects—short story, novel, film, TV program—helps the writer make her point that just as you cannot compare the impacts of short stories, novels, films, and TV shows, so too can you not compare the impact of video games to the impact of virtual reality. Here, the examples are not facts or opinions in and of themselves. In this case, the examples are simply objects that are part of a comparison strategy the author uses to convince the reader to accept her point of view.

Finally, examples can come in the form of anecdotes, which are also known as narratives or stories. Anecdotes can be particularly compelling because people can relate to them, and they often provide a more complete picture than other types of examples. Writers can use nonfiction anecdotes, which means the stories are true, or fictional anecdotes, which means the stories are make-believe but realistic. You may recall this narrative strategy as a frame for writing introductory paragraphs from Chapter 2. In Chapter 6, Zoe McKnight's article, "The Real Reason Crime Is Falling So Fast," begins with an anecdote about the "cell phone slaying." This anecdote allows McKnight to provide an example of how certain cases in the media make it appear as though crime is on the rise, when in reality, crime is decreasing. This example is part of her counter-argument and refutation strategy, which you will learn about later in this chapter.

Examples are a critical component of any argument, as they move the reader from an abstract concept to a concrete one. In other words, they allow readers to "see" what a writer means. Through examples, writers can "show" what they mean rather than just "tell." As a writer, you need to select strong examples that will help readers visualize what you are trying to argue. The clearer a picture you can paint for your audience, the better your chances of connecting with them and convincing them of your point of view.

▶ Apply the Skill

Analyzing and Constructing Examples

1. Using one reading from this textbook or another source, do the following:

   a. Identify each example provided in the reading.

   b. Classify the example as fact, hypothetical scenario, object/concept within an opinion, or anecdote.

   c. Paraphrase the claim the example is intended to clarify or support.

   d. Comment on the effectiveness of the example.

   Use a chart, similar to the following, to record your answer. This chart also includes a model as an example.

EXAMPLE	CLASSIFICATION	PARAPHRASED CLAIM	EFFECTIVENESS
"Consider that Facebook spent $2 billion on a small headset startup called Oculus" (Bierand par. 1).	Fact	Virtual reality will have a signifi-cant impact on its users, possibly even surpassing the impact of other pervasive technology such as the Internet.	This is fairly effective. Facebook is a large, well-known, and powerful company, so if it is investing a large sum of money in virtual reality, it must be a life-changing technology. There isn't mention, however, of any other high-tech companies investing in virtual reality.

2. For each of the claims listed below, provide an example to help support that claim. You can use "for example" or "for instance" to start your example sentence(s). Classify your example as a fact, hypothetical scenario, object/concept, or anecdote.

   a. Men are more likely to become addicted to videogames than women are.

   b. Virtual reality will have a negative effect on the way people socialize in real-world, everyday settings.

c. Video games depicting fantasy are more engaging than video games depicting reality.

d. TV screens are no longer the best option for an immersive video game experience.

e. Too much time spent on video games results in lower academic performance for postsecondary students.

TESTIMONY

Testimony refers to a statement someone has provided. So, it has a factual component insofar as it is true that the person said that particular statement. You could go back to a recording of the statement and verify the words the person spoke. Whether the person is being truthful or accurate, on the other hand, is a matter of opinion. Yes, the person said something, but is this something true or factual? Every testimony has this dual element of being factual but questionable at the same time. Three types of testimony are common: eyewitness accounts, self-reporting statements, or expert opinions (see Figure 7.3).

FIGURE 7.3
TYPES OF TESTIMONY

In an *eyewitness account*, a witness reports a perspective on a series of events. Think, for example, of someone who has witnessed a theft. This report should be factual insofar as it should reveal what actually took place, what really happened. However, just because a person perceives that an event unfolded in a certain way does not mean that perception is correct or verifiable. The person may have misremembered, or perhaps the person thought he saw one thing, but it was really another. An eyewitness account, then, is both factual and debatable. The words the eyewitness speaks are real, verifiable words, but the events these words refer to may not have unfolded exactly as the eyewitness says.

Self-reporting statements are also factual in that the statements were uttered, but the statements themselves are opinions. An example of self-reporting statements can be found in Paragraph 1 of "Does Video Gaming Have a Gender Gap?" by Kishonna Gray:

> According to the Pew Research Center, women and men play video games at about the same rate. Fifty percent of men and 48 percent of women say they play video games on a console, personal computer or handheld device. This directly counters what 60 percent of Americans told Pew: that men play video games more. Even women who play video games had that belief.*

The highlighted statements indicate what the participants said about their own video game habits versus their perceptions of which gender plays more video games. These side-by-side statements demonstrate the factual-debatable nature of testimony. It's a fact that both men and women said video games are mostly played by men, but in this case, it's not actually a verifiable fact that men play these games significantly more often, as evidenced by the people who self-reported as video game players.

Expert testimony refers to statements provided by authorities in a particular subject area or field of study. When it comes to expert testimony, it almost seems as though what the expert claims is a fact because the expert is usually trusted and well informed. However, what the expert says is still an opinion. It's true that she made the particular utterance, but the utterance itself is debatable. Again, the line between fact and opinion is blurred.

In Chapter 6, you read "The Real Reason Crime Is Falling So Fast" by Zoe McKnight. In Paragraph 7, McKnight uses expert testimony to support her claim that crime is declining because we are spending more time online. The paragraph has been reproduced below, with the expert testimony highlighted in green.

> Pease, a visiting professor at several British universities who has published hundreds of academic papers on crime and was once head of the police research group at the U.K. government's Home Office, is a firm believer that improved security has helped to drive down crime levels. But he argues that the staggering reach of the online world—whether through video games, social media, access to instant and unlimited video and texting, always within arm's reach on our smartphones—is reshaping the modern world to such an extent that it may even be affecting crime rates. "Cyberspace becomes more interesting than meatspace," he says, referring to a term for the physical world first coined by American-Canadian science-fiction author William Gibson. "As our lives move from meatspace to cyberspace, the opportunity for violent crime and acquisitive crime change and reduce in the aggregate, and that's what I think has happened."**

Note how McKnight specifically mentions that Pease is a prolific writer about crime and was part of the U.K. government's crime research team. These details help make Pease sound more believable—more factual—even though what he says is actually an opinion, not a fact.

▶ **Apply the Skill**

Analyzing and Constructing Testimony

1. Select one reading from this book or another source. Then, do the following:

   a. Identify each instance of testimony provided in the reading.

---

*Ault, 2016.
**McKnight, 2015.

b. Classify the testimony as eyewitness, self reporting, or expert.

c. Paraphrase the claim the testimony is intended to clarify or support.

d. Comment on the effectiveness of the testimony.

Use a chart, similar to the following, to record your answer. This chart also includes an example to follow.

QUOTED TESTIMONY	CLASSIFICATION	PARAPHRASED CLAIM	EFFECTIVENESS
"As our lives move from meatspace to cyberspace, the opportunity for violent crime and acquisitive crime change and reduce in the aggregate, and that's what I think has happened." (Ken Pease, as qtd. in McKnight par. 7)	Expert	Crime is declining because we are spending more time online.	This is very effective since Pease is a prolific research writer on crime.

2. For each of the claims listed below, invent testimony to help support that claim. (Note: these are the same claims from the previous Apply the Skill activity. Ensure the testimony is significantly different from the examples you wrote in that activity.) Classify your testimony as eyewitness, self reporting, or expert.

a. Men are more likely to become addicted to videogames than women are.

b. Virtual reality will have a negative effect on the way people socialize in real-world, everyday settings.

c. Video games depicting fantasy are more engaging than video games depicting reality.

d. TV screens are no longer the best option for an immersive video game experience.

e. Too much time spent on video games results in lower academic performance for postsecondary students.

TYPES OF EXPLANATIONS

Evidence is a crucial component for supporting your claim. However, even the best evidence will not be convincing without a clear explanation connecting that evidence to the claim it is intended to support. Explanations help clarify and justify your claim. Some explanations link evidence to your claim. Other explanations provide their own justification without concrete evidence, particularly when evidence may not be readily available. You can think of explanations as answering the question *how so?* There are two subcategories of explanations: (1) reasons and (2) counterargument and refutation.

REASONS

Reasons are logical arguments a writer uses to convince readers to accept her claims as true. Often, reasons are based on facts or at the very least opinions that most readers would agree with, but they are not facts themselves. Because facts are not always available, sound reasoning is a key persuasive technique for any writer. The latter half of this chapter, as well as the remaining chapters of this textbook, focus on reasoning in great depth.

COUNTERARGUMENT AND REFUTATION

A *counterargument* is providing an outline of another side's point of view on an issue. A *refutation* is explaining why this other side's point of view is incorrect using credible evidence to prove your point. Max Fisher uses the counterargument and refutation strategy in the article "Ten-Country Comparison Suggests There's Little or No Link between Video Games and Gun Murders" that you read in Chapter 6.

> Obama campaign adviser David Axelrod lamented on Twitter, "In NFL post-game: an ad for shoot 'em up video game. All for curbing weapons of war. But shouldn't we also quit marketing murder as a game?" (par. 1)
> But it turns out that the data just doesn't support this connection. Looking at the world's 10 largest video game markets yields no evident, statistical correlation between video game consumption and gun-related killings. (par. 2)*

In the example above, the yellow highlighted sentences are the counterargument. They present a viewpoint opposite to Fisher's viewpoint. The green sentences are the refutation. These sentences explain why the counterargument made by David Axelrod is wrong.

Counterargument and refutation is an effective explanation strategy, as it demonstrates the author is thinking critically about the issue. Counterargument and refutation lets the reader know the author has thought about all sides of an issue, which builds up the author's credibility and reduces perceptions of bias. Moreover, the strategy allows the author to demonstrate the superiority of her position on an issue by dismantling the positions of others.

▶ Apply the Skill

Analyzing and Constructing Counterarguments and Refutations

1. Select one reading from this book or another source. Then, do the following:

   a. Identify each instance of counterargument and refutation provided in the reading.

   b. Paraphrase the claim the counterargument and refutation are intended to clarify or support.

   c. Comment on the effectiveness of the counterargument and refutation strategy in the reading.

   Use a chart, similar to the following, to record your answer. This chart also includes a model for you to draw from for your own chart.

---

*Fisher, 2012.

COUNTERARGUMENT AND REFUTATION	PARAPHRASED CLAIM	EFFECTIVENESS
Obama campaign adviser David Axelrod lamented on Twitter, "In NFL post-game: an ad for shoot 'em up video game. All for curbing weapons of war. But shouldn't we also quit marketing murder as a game?" (Fisher par. 1) But it turns out that the data just doesn't support this connection. Looking at the world's 10 largest video game markets yields no evident, statistical correlation between video game consumption and gun-related killings. (Fisher par. 2)	Violent video games do not contribute to an increase in gun violence.	This is quite effective. Statistics are being used to prove that someone's testimony is incorrect. Statistics are more reliable than testimony.

2. For each of the claims listed below, provide a counterargument and a refutation to support the claim.

   a. Men are more likely to become addicted to videogames than women are.

   b. Virtual reality will have a negative effect on the way people socialize in real-world, everyday settings.

   c. Video games depicting fantasy are more engaging than video games depicting reality.

   d. TV screens are no longer the best option for an immersive video game experience.

   e. Too much time spent on video games results in lower academic performance for postsecondary students.

Now that you are aware of the different types of support, it is important that you look out for this support as a reader and make use of the various support types as a writer. Analyzing support as a reader will help you understand why you are or are not convinced of a writer's argument. It will also help ensure you don't fall prey to faulty or ill-supported claims. As a writer, selecting appropriate support is crucial in ensuring your audience gets on board with your claims. In fact, you need to think about your purpose and audience when determining what support to include in your arguments. Think about whether your audience prefers facts to reasons or real examples to hypothetical examples. Include the support you know your audience will need in order to agree with you.

▶ Apply the Skill

Recognizing Types of Support

Write "F" for fact, "R" for reason, "E" for example, "T" for testimony, "CA" for counter-argument, and "Ref" for refutation. These passages come from "Does Video Gaming Have a Gender Gap?" by Kishonna Gray at the beginning of this chapter. The issue and claim are listed below. Determine the type of support for the argument.

Issue: Whether a gender gap exists in gaming
Claim: A gender gap does not exist in gaming.

_____ 1. According to the Pew Research Center, women and men play video games at about the same rate.

_____ 2. Fifty percent of men and 48 percent of women say they play video games on a console, personal computer or handheld device.

_____ 3. This directly counters what 60 percent of Americans told Pew: that men play video games more.
_____

4. Even women who play video games had that belief.

_____ 5. Misperception is because marketing promoted that the identity of a gamer was men and boys.

_____ 6. When more women began playing games, the narrative began to shift, redefining what it meant to be a gamer.

7. Women are assumed to be interested in the "casual" gaming market—
_____ games that are simpler and easy to learn—while men are assumed to favor immersive, violent games.

_____ 8. Games such as "Candy Crush" and "Just Dance" have been cited as casual games popular among women.

_____ 9. Additionally, many gamers suggest that women are not hardcore gamers, leading to further divides along gender lines.

_____ 10. While there is no numerical gender gap in gaming, an inclusivity gap does exist, in which the presence of women in games, gaming communities and gaming culture in general sometimes leads to disparate treatment.

_____ 11. As researchers have long noted, women gamers experience hostile environments.

_____ 12. Much of the recent debate around the reality of women in gaming emerged with the "Gamergate" controversy, in which several women in the industry were subjected to prolonged harassment from men.

_____ 13. It started as a conversation about ethics in game journalism but ended with a largely male gaming community marginalizing women who spoke out about their antagonistic treatment.

_____ 14. While public perception may not view women as gamers, numbers reveal the truth.

_____ 15. Women are playing and have been playing all along.

Mapping Arguments

To enhance your ability to read arguments critically and write arguments effectively, you should learn how to map an argument. Mapping an argument is like creating an outline of the main idea, major supporting details, and minor supporting details. This means that you need to be clear on the issue, the point of view or primary claim, and the supporting arguments that back up the primary claim. Furthermore, you need to differentiate between major and minor supporting details. Refer to Chapters 2 and 3 to review major and minor details and how they relate to patterns of organization.

Figure 7.4 provides the steps you need to follow to map out an argument. Note how the first step is to determine the claim at the heart of the argument. Then, you should analyze the type of support before providing a full map—or outline—of the argument. Knowing the types of support will help with mapping the major and minor supporting ideas.

FIGURE 7.4
HOW TO MAP ARGUMENTS

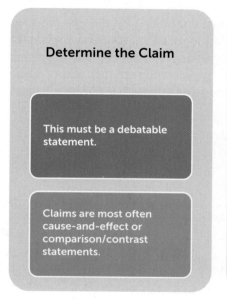

Determine the Claim

This must be a debatable statement.

Claims are most often cause-and-effect or comparison/contrast statements.

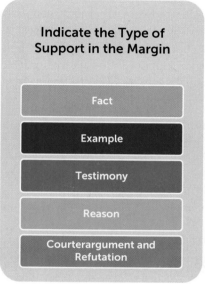

Indicate the Type of Support in the Margin

Fact

Example

Testimony

Reason

Counterargument and Refutation

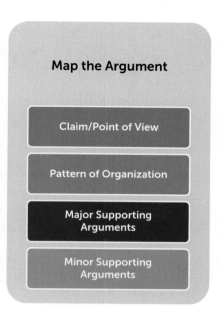

Map the Argument

Claim/Point of View

Pattern of Organization

Major Supporting Arguments

Minor Supporting Arguments

Here is what an argument map may look like:

1. Issue: Whether or not . . . [summarize the topic of the argument]
2. Author's point of view/claim: The author's conclusion(s) about the issue.

Major Support 1:
    Minor Support:
    Minor Support:

Major Support 2:
    Minor Support:

Major Support 3:
    Minor Support:

Major Support 4:
    Minor Support:
    Minor Support:

Major Support 5:

There may or may not be five supporting points to back up a writer's point of view or your own point of view. In addition, each major supporting point may have any number of minor supporting points. It is up to the author to determine how many major and minor supporting arguments he needs to substantiate his point of view.

▶ Apply the Skill

Mapping an Argument and Recognizing Support

Reread "Does Video Gaming Have a Gender Gap?" by Kishonna Gray. As you are reading, ensure you make notes that will provide you with the material necessary to construct an argument map. In other words, pay careful attention to the reading's claims, type of support, major supporting details, and minor supporting details. When you are ready, construct an argument map, using an outline format similar to the template above. After you've constructed your argument map, compare your map with the one provided below. Note how the example below uses a chart format and includes a column for the type of support. In the chart, the numbers indicate major support and the letters indicate minor support. It doesn't matter which style of argument map you use: you are the audience for your own argument map, so use one that you find most effective.

Issue: Whether or not there is a gender gap in gaming
Claim/point of view: A gender gap does not exist in gaming.

Fact	1. According to the Pew Research Center, women and men play video games at about the same rate.
Fact/Refutation	A. Fifty percent of men and 48 percent of women say they play video games on a console, personal computer or handheld device.
Fact/ Counterargument	B. This directly counters what 60 percent of Americans told Pew: that men play video games more.
Reason	C. Even women who play video games had that belief.
Reason	2. Misperception is because marketing promoted that the identity of a gamer was men and boys.
Reason	A. When more women began playing games, the narrative began to shift, redefining what it meant to be a gamer.
Reason	3. Women are assumed to be interested in the "casual" gaming market—games that are simpler and easy to learn—while men are assumed to favor immersive, violent games.
Fact/Example	A. Games such as "Candy Crush" and "Just Dance" have been cited as casual games popular among women.
Reason	B. Additionally, many gamers suggest that women are not hardcore gamers, leading to further divides along gender lines.
Reason	4. While there is no numerical gender gap in gaming, an inclusivity gap does exist, in which the presence of women in games, gaming communities and gaming culture in general sometimes leads to disparate treatment.
Fact	A. As researchers have long noted, women gamers experience hostile environments.
Reason/Fact	B. Much of the recent debate around the reality of women in gaming emerged with the "Gamergate" controversy, in which several women in the industry were subjected to prolonged harassment from men.
Fact	C. It started as a conversation about ethics in game journalism but ended with a largely male gaming community marginalizing women who spoke out about their antagonistic treatment.
Counterargument	5. While public perception may not view women as gamers, numbers reveal the truth.
Refutation	A. Women are playing and have been playing all along.
Prescription/ Solution	We need to move beyond these simple constructions and improve marketing, advertising and representations of women in games; increase the numbers of women in game development; ensure inclusive gaming environments and increase the value of women within gaming.

Reasoning in Arguments

Now that you are familiar with the components of an argument and are able to map out the arguments of others and of your own, you are ready to carefully examine and apply reasoning within an argument. Strong reasoning is the key to getting an audience to accept a claim or point of view.

There are two ways of constructing an argument: inductive and deductive. The difference between inductive and deductive arguments has to do with the strength of the support—that is, the strength of the reasoning—to back up the claim or point of view. In an *inductive* argument, the supporting details lead to a *likely* conclusion. In a *deductive* argument, the supporting details lead to a *definite* conclusion.

Inductive Arguments

Inductive arguments are designed so that if the supporting details are true or reasonable, the conclusion is *likely* to be correct. Take a look at the following example of inductive reasoning:

Eyewitnesses saw Lori download the video game illegally, so Lori broke the law.

In this example, the conclusion is that Lori broke the law. The support for that conclusion is that the eyewitness saw Lori download the video game illegally. If the supporting detail is true—that there was an eyewitness to her crime—then the conclusion that Lori broke the law is likely, but not guaranteed, to be true.

Now take a look at this example:

Eyewitnesses said that Lori did not illegally download the video game. Lori wasn't near a computer at the time of the theft. Lori doesn't even play video games, so Lori didn't commit the crime.

In this example, the conclusion is that Lori isn't guilty of illegally downloading the video game. The support for this conclusion is that eyewitnesses say Lori did not download the game. Second, Lori doesn't even play video games. So, if these supporting details are true, then the conclusion that Lori is not guilty is likely to be true.

The second example is a stronger inductive argument than the first example. In the second example, more supporting details make the conclusion more likely.

Deductive Arguments

An argument that is deductive is designed so that if the supporting details are true or reasonable, the conclusion is automatically correct. Think about this common deductive argument in math:

$$\text{If } A = B \text{ and } B = C, \text{ then } A = C.$$

In this example, the supporting details are that $A = B$ and $B = C$. If these supporting details are true, then A must necessarily be equal to C.

▶ **Apply the Skill**

Inductive and Deductive Reasoning

Write an "I" beside examples of inductive reasoning and a "D" beside examples of deductive reasoning. In addition, indicate whether or not there is a flaw with the reasoning. If there is a flaw, explain what the flaw is.

_____ 1. Jerry is a gamer. All men are gamers. Therefore, Jerry is a man.

_____ 2. Amina played competitively but lost every time. So, the next time Amina plays she will lose.

_____ 3. Our neighbour's cat ran away. He has run away before and has always come back. So, the cat will come back.

_____ 4. All *zebras* are *cats*, and all *bears* are *cats*; therefore, all *zebras* are *bears*.

_____ 5. Four and six are composite numbers, so all composite numbers are even numbers.

Soundness in Arguments

An argument—whether inductive or deductive—is sound if its supporting details are (a) reasonable or true, (b) relevant to the claim they are supporting, (c) compatible with one another and with the claim, and (d) representative of the bigger picture (that is, they are the norm rather than the exception) as seen in Figure 7.5. Because arguments are defined by their subjectivity, what you deem sound may not be what someone else deems sound. The important thing to remember as a reader is to question the soundness of a writer's arguments. The important thing to remember as a writer is to always think of your audience. What would they deem to be sound? What support do you need in order to appeal to their sense of reasonability?

FIGURE 7.5

QUALITIES OF SOUND ARGUMENTS

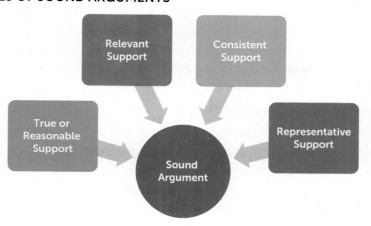

Take a look at this argument:

Claim: Video games can be bad for your health.

Supporting Detail 1: Obesity is bad for your health.

Supporting Detail 2: Video games can cause obesity.

In this example, the first supporting detail is true. Medical studies have proven that obesity is bad for your health. The second supporting detail, on the other hand, is not necessarily true. Yes, video games can cause obesity, but is it reasonable to blame obesity on video games alone without considering other issues like food intake and genetics? Because this second detail is questionable, you would likely deem this detail unsound. If this detail is unsound, then the whole argument is unsound.

Now take a look at this argument, which has the same claim, but is more sound:

Claim: Video games can be bad for your health.

Supporting Detail 1: Too much time staring at a screen can strain your eyes.

Supporting Detail 2: The more you play video games, the less you are participating in physical activity.

Both of these details are reasonable. Still, though, you may have some readers who doubt the accuracy of the second supporting detail. They may argue that some video games are quite active and therefore encourage *more* physical activity rather than *less*. This example demonstrates the subjectivity involved in determining the soundness of an argument.

Even if the supporting details pass the reasonability test, you still need to verify that they are relevant to the claim—that is, on topic. Observe this argument in which the supporting details all appear reasonable, but the third supporting detail is irrelevant or off topic:

Claim: Video games can be bad for your health.

Supporting Detail 1: Too much time staring at a screen can strain your eyes.

Supporting Detail 2: The more you play video games, the less you are participating in physical activity.

Supporting Detail 3: Eating more vegetables and fewer sugary treats will help you to become healthier.

This argument would be considered unsound because of the irrelevant final detail. All details are reasonable, but they are not all relevant to the claim. If you were to use the terminology from Chapter 2, you would say the argument lacks unity.

In addition to reasonability and relevance, you need to ensure the supporting details are compatible with one another, which means they work together to support the claim and do not contradict one another. Observe this argument in which the third supporting detail is not compatible with the first supporting detail.

Claim: Video games can be bad for your health.

Supporting Detail 1: Too much time staring at a screen can strain your eyes.

Supporting Detail 2: The more you play video games, the less you are participating in physical activity.

Supporting Detail 3: The health of your eyes is one of the lesser health concerns when it comes to excessive video game playing.

The first supporting detail focuses on the negative effects of too much screen time on your eyes, but the third supporting detail undermines the importance of eye health. It is problematic to focus on eye health as a health concern and then mention that eye health isn't actually that important. Because of the incompatibility between the first and third details, this argument is unsound. If you were to use the terminology from Chapter 2, you would say the argument lacks coherence.

Last but not least, in the context of presenting specific evidence, it is important to ensure the evidence is representative of the bigger picture. It should be the rule rather than the exception to the rule, unless, of course, the whole point is to demonstrate there is an exception.

Consider this claim and its support:

Claim: Video games are dangerous.

Supporting Detail: Last week, a child in Ottawa sustained a head injury when his friend accidentally lost the grip on his video game controller.

The example provided in the supporting detail is exceptional. Most of the time, when friends play video games, they don't sustain head injuries from video game controllers. This incident is not representative of what happens most of the time. As a result, the argument becomes weakened and may be deemed unsound. As a reader, be on the lookout for these types of supporting details, as they are often intended to trick you into thinking less critically about the claim being supported. As a writer, make sure you select representative examples, not exceptional ones, to prove your claims,. Exceptional examples should be included only when you specifically want to emphasize the exception. Avoid making the exception seem like the norm.

▶ Apply the Skill

Sound Arguments

For each argument in "Does Video Gaming Have a Gender Gap?" by Kishonna Gray, write a paragraph that describes how sound the argument is. Use the argument map in the section "Mapping Arguments" to help you. Be sure to consider the reasonability, relevance, compatibility, and representativeness of the supporting details.

ASSUMPTIONS

When people make arguments, sometimes certain assumptions are left implicit or unstated. In some cases, these assumptions, which are always opinions, are fair or logical. In other cases, these assumptions are flawed. By identifying hidden assumptions, you can see potential flaws in the reasonability of a writer's argument. Take a look at this example:

Playing video games is wrong because it is unproductive.

The part of the reasoning that is missing is the hidden assumption that anything that is unproductive is wrong. It is only when this assumption is added that the argument becomes reasonable.

Playing video games is unproductive.

Anything that is unproductive is wrong.

Therefore, playing video games is wrong.

Once you can see a hidden assumption in an argument, you can target the argument's weakness and refute it. For example, is it true that anything that is unproductive is wrong? Sleep is unproductive, dining is unproductive, watching television is unproductive, and so on. We don't consider all of these actions wrong, so there is a flaw in this argument. To refute the argument, you would need to state that not everything that is unproductive is wrong, and you can provide specific examples to support your refutation. In your own writing, thinking about hidden assumptions in an argument can help you write a stronger argument. It can help you detect potential flaws and prevent them from infiltrating your writing.

Read the following argument statements, and then think about the hidden assumptions stated below the statement. Could you come up with a refutation for the hidden assumption to discredit the argument? In other words, can you explain why the hidden assumption is incorrect or untrue, thus making the argument unsound?

1. Failing students will erode their self-confidence. Therefore, we should not fail students.
   → We should not erode students' self-confidence.

2. We should increase the penalty for online bullying to deter people from doing it.
   → Bullying is bad.
   → Increasing penalties deters people from doing bad things.

3. There is nothing wrong with online bullying. People do it all the time.
   → If people do something all the time, then there is nothing wrong with it.

4. It should not be illegal for children to play violent video games. It does not harm anyone.
   → Anything that does not cause harm should be legal.

▶ Apply the Skill

Hidden Assumptions

Find the hidden assumptions in the arguments below and assess their reasonability. Then, discuss in a small group or in a class discussion how you could refute the author's reasoning.

1. Don't listen to Fotoula. She doesn't play video games.

2. Kobe gets straight A's in all classes because he is a good listener.

3. Kandace is a gamer, so she can't swim.

4. Virtual reality is new technology, so it's no good.

5. Cam must be a good player. He is always eager.

Review

Soundness and Assumptions

Answer the following review questions in paragraph form or generate ideas to contribute to a group or class discussion.

1. What is the difference between an inductive and deductive argument?
2. How do you know if an argument is sound?
3. What are assumptions?
4. Why is it important to identify assumptions in both your own writing and the writing of others?

Moving beyond Logic: Other Types of Reasoning

Throughout this chapter, the focus has been on reasoning through the use of logic. In other words, you have been examining the ways in which writers support their claims by establishing sound arguments. Similarly, you have been introduced to strategies that help you develop your own sound arguments. While this logical type of reasoning is a key component of argumentation, it is not the only type of reasoning available to you.

The Greek philosopher Aristotle coined three types of rhetorical approaches—reasoning strategies—in crafting an argument. Logic, or *logos*, is one of them. The other two are known as *ethos* and *pathos*.

Ethos refers to writer credibility and the relationship writers develop with their readers. Writers can achieve credibility by

- referencing trustworthy sources,
- citing respected publications,
- demonstrating a command of the subject matter,
- developing a reputation for unbiased writing, and
- connecting with their audience through empathy and things they have in common.

In essence, most of what you learned about in Chapter 6 around analyzing writers and sources plays a role in establishing credibility and using it as a persuasive device.

Pathos refers to emotion. Depending on the discipline and intended audience, you can use emotion as a persuasive device. You can convince audiences by making them feel emotions—excitement, fear, and sadness, for example. However, you need to use this persuasive device appropriately and with discretion. You do not want your readers to think you are manipulating their emotions to get them on board with your argument. Similarly, you want to be on the lookout for writers who have unsound arguments and so resort to *pathos* as a way to make you overlook problematic claims. *Pathos* needs to be done in concert with establishing logic and credibility.

Remember, the goal of writing an argument is to convince your reader. A well-balanced combination of *ethos*, *pathos* and *logos* will help you achieve that goal. Just make sure to choose the predominant approach in harmony with your assignment.

▶ Apply the Skill

Arguing with Logos, Ethos, and Pathos

1. Select one of the readings from this textbook and analyze the balance of *logos, ethos,* and *pathos*. Which of these rhetorical appeals is most dominant in the reading? Does the author use the rhetorical appeals effectively? How do you know?

2. Take a position on a topic related to technology or cyberspace. Craft a focused claim. Then, write three short arguments. In each, focus on one of the following rhetorical approaches: *logos, ethos* or *pathos*. Which of the three arguments is the most effective and why?

▶ Did You Know?

THE NUANCES OF MODALS

The English language has modal verbs and verb phrases that serve to define or qualify the main verb of a clause. Writers of arguments select modals very carefully to make nuances—small but important distinctions—in their arguments. Consider the difference between the following two claims:

> Parents *must* monitor their children when the children are playing video games.

> Parents *could* monitor their children when the children are playing video games.

In the first claim, the author says it is *mandatory* for parents to monitor their children when the children are playing video games. In the second claim, the author merely suggests that monitoring children when the children are playing video games *may be* a good idea.

Table 7.2 provides a list of modal verbs in English, along with their popular usage. Periphrastic synonyms (modals that are phrases instead of a single word) are also provided.

TABLE 7.2
MODALS AND THEIR MEANINGS

MODAL	USED TO INDICATE	EXAMPLE
Can (present or future) Able to (past, present, future, hypothetical)	Possibility, capability, or ability	They can ban violent video games. They are able to ban violent video games. They were able to ban violent video games.
Could (past, present, future, or hypothetical)	Possibility	They could ban violent video games. They could have banned violent video games.
Shall Will Going to	Definitely happening in the future	I/we shall ban violent video games. They will ban violent video games. They are going to ban violent video games.
Should	Strong suggestion or recommendation	They should ban violent video games. They should have banned violent video games.
May Might	Possibility, uncertainty	They may ban violent video games. They might ban video games.
Must Need to	Mandatory, not optional; Likely occurred (past)	They must ban violent video games. They need to ban violent video games. They must have banned violent video games.
Would	Possibility under certain conditions	They would ban violent video games if these games were proven to incite violence among teenagers. They would have banned violent games if these games were proven to incite violence among teenagers.

Note that all modals are followed by the base form of the main verb (i.e., the verb form without any endings).

▶ Apply the Skill

Modals

1. Describe the meaning of the italicized modals in each of the following sentences from the two readings at the end of this chapter entitled "Should Virtual Reality Be More Regulated than Video Games?"

   a. What's in store for virtual reality *may* be unusually dramatic.

   b. This is what makes virtual reality such a wonderful technology, one that *must* be respected and, to the extent that it can do harm, regulated.

   c. We actively encourage research into all aspects of virtual reality, but any research *needs to* be objective, with all preconceived biases disclosed and with thorough peer review.

   d. It's possible that over-regulating this technology [virtual reality] *could* prevent the best it has to offer from reaching people.

   e. In the probably-sooner-than-we-think future, virtual reality *will* become a profound bridge between digital and physical realms, connecting people in powerful new ways while making possible unprecedented experiences of significant psychological and even physiological heft.

2. Rewrite each of the sentences from Question 1 but change the modal to one with a different meaning. Explain the difference between the original sentence's meaning and the rewritten sentence's meaning.

3. Discuss, in a group, the impact that modals can have on the soundness of an argument.

4. Analyze and evaluate the use of modals in "Should Virtual Reality Be More Regulated than Video Games?" What are the most common modals used? How does this impact the arguments being made? Have the authors chosen the most effective modals to present their points of view?

5. Write your own argument on an issue of your own choosing. When you are done, circle all the modals you have used and evaluate their appropriateness and effectiveness. Do they enhance your credibility as a writer? Do they ensure your arguments are sound?

▶ Questions for Writing and Discussion

1. Preview the articles "Should Virtual Reality Be More Regulated than Video Games?" by Doug Bierend and "Should Virtual Reality Be More Regulated than Video Games?" by Kate Edwards. Identifying the issue and each author's point of view or claim. Then, read the articles through, identifying the supporting arguments and noting them in the margins. Next, identify the type of support for each argument. Then, determine whether the reasoning in the arguments is inductive or deductive and whether the arguments are sound. Last, identify any of the authors' assumptions that may weaken their arguments.

2. Which of the readings at the end of this chapter presents the strongest argument: the reading by Doug Bierend or Kate Edwards? In your assessment, take into account the types of support each author uses to support his or her claim. In addition, pay attention to the authors' credentials when making your assessment. Clearly defend your perspective.

3. In "Does Video Gaming Have a Gender Gap?" Kishonna Gray says the gap in inclusivity between males and females in the world of gaming is primarily due to marketing. She says that advertising or marketing promotes typical gamers as men and boys instead of girls and women. Do you agree or disagree with this idea? If you agree, how do marketing companies target the audience of video games? How is sexism reinforced? If you disagree, state clear reasons for your opposition and cite examples of marketing that does not promote a gender bias. Try to use specific examples of media to back up your claim.

4. If video games have a gender gap, what other domains, such as sports, leisure activities, or pastimes, also are gendered? Use testimony, facts, examples, or reasons as you construct an essay on this topic. Include both a counterargument and a refutation in your paper.

5. Do you agree with Doug Bierend that virtual reality ought to be more regulated than video games? Support your perspective with original ideas. If you disagree with his perspective, refute his arguments with evidence and explanations in a well-structured response.

6. Conduct some research—both primary and secondary if possible—on virtual reality technology and its emergent uses. In what field—medicine, national defense and policing, leisure, or another domain—do you think this technology has most power for good? In which domain do you feel that virtual reality technology may be misused? Support your answers with sound reasoning to support your claim.

SHOULD VIRTUAL REALITY BE MORE REGULATED THAN VIDEO GAMES?

By Doug Bierend
Technology Journalist

Pro

1   Virtual reality appears poised to become at least as widespread, sophisticated, powerful and subversive as any other form of transformative media—television, video games or the Internet. What's in store for virtual reality may be unusually dramatic. Consider that Facebook spent $2 billion on a small headset startup called Oculus and that Magic Leap, a Google-backed outfit engaged in "augmented reality"—a species of virtual reality—describes its upcoming product as "a user interface for reality."

2   In the probably-sooner-than-we-think future, virtual reality will become a profound bridge between digital and physical realms, connecting people in powerful new ways while making possible unprecedented experiences of significant psychological and even physiological heft. This is what makes virtual reality such a wonderful technology, one that must be respected and, to the extent that it can do harm, regulated.

3   Effective virtual reality doesn't just create the impression of 3-D images and places. Its goal, as stated by those leading the charge in the field, is to achieve "immersion," the tipping point past which our senses forget they're being "shown" something and instead interpret the stimulus just as they would any other experience. The bar for immersion is surprisingly low and already within reach. This is why virtual-reality technology already has been applied effectively to therapies for such problems as phobias and post-traumatic stress disorder, and why even crudely rendered experiences are enough to create intense and deep psychosomatic effects.

4   Of course, most people aren't going to use virtual reality to get over a fear of heights, but rather to be entertained, to connect with one another, to have experiences that wouldn't otherwise be possible. As the technology advances, assuming its developers meet their aims, experiences with virtual-reality goggles will become as powerful as those without. The purpose of Entertainment Software Rating Board ratings, to which the video game industry voluntarily submits, is to allow parents to determine if a game's contents are inappropriate. But those ratings simply don't approach the import of virtual reality.

5   It's easy to imagine regulatory overreach, and any system for virtual reality must be crafted carefully. It's possible that over-regulating this technology could prevent the best it has to offer from reaching people. An acknowledgement of virtual reality's incredible power must be baked into any regulation without standing in the way of its development toward positive ends.

SHOULD VIRTUAL REALITY BE MORE REGULATED THAN VIDEO GAMES?

By Kate Edwards

Executive Director, International Game Developers Association

Con

1   Every new media technology has experienced a certain level of caution and critical examination upon its introduction. This has been the case for the printed book, film, radio, television and video games, and now it's the case for virtual reality.

2   After the initial interest and scrutiny of a new technological medium, society eventually acclimates, and some people opt to consume the medium while some don't. As a society, we now understand that the impact of a medium depends on the artistry of those making it, not on the technology itself. After all, we all will eventually become familiar with this new technology.

3   Just as we are no longer shocked at the spectacle of television, moving pictures or video games, the same will happen with virtual reality. Once we are as familiar and comfortable with it as we are with film, the real impact of a virtual-reality experience will depend solely on the artistry of those creating it.

4   A quantitative scale for the "impact" of games and virtual reality is just as useless a concept as measuring the impact of a short story versus a novel, film or television program. A theatrical film can have a very strong impact due to the size of the image (e.g., IMAX) and the proximity of strangers in the audience sharing the experience. But smaller images can be equally impactful when viewed alone at home on TV. Both forms of media can leave a strong impression, but the impacts often are felt quite differently.

5   The newer artistic mediums of games and virtual reality are no different; they are both impactful, but in different ways.

6   Every new idea brings risk—not merely of increased liability but of opportunists seeking to capitalize on public perceptions of liabilities that do not exist. We actively encourage research into all aspects of virtual reality, but any research needs to be objective, with all preconceived biases disclosed and with thorough peer review.

7   It's important to remind ourselves that virtual-reality experiences are products of artistry that the U.S. Supreme Court considers speech protected by the First Amendment—just as clearly as video games, movies and books are protected speech. Thus, any discussion of the regulation of virtual reality as a technology is at best grossly premature and at worst dangerously presumptuous.

Source: Marshall, Patrick. "Virtual Reality." *CQ Researcher*, 26 February 2016, www.library.cqpress.com.ezproxy.stlcc.edu. Accessed 21 July 2016. Republished with permission of CQ Press Researcher, from Patrick Marshall, "Virtual Reality: Will consumers embrace the emerging technology?" CQ Researcher, vol. 26(9), February 26, 2016, pp. 193–216; permission conveyed through Copyright Clearance Center, Inc.

WRITING TO EVALUATE A TEXT

BY THE END OF THIS CHAPTER, YOU WILL BE ABLE TO

- Distinguish among various levels of critical analysis.
- Write a claim that evaluates how well a writer has crafted a text.
- Develop support for an evaluative claim by critically analyzing a variety of textual components.
- Create a coherent, unified essay that evaluates a text.

▶ WHY IS THIS INFORMATION IMPORTANT?

In Chapters 6 and 7, you learned how to analyze a number of textual elements. In this chapter, you will move beyond analysis to evaluation—also known as *critical analysis*—which is an important task for both academic study and everyday citizenship. In academic settings, writing a critical analysis can help you navigate information and decide which information is valuable to your own research. You did a bit of critical analysis in Chapter 5 when you learned about assessing sources. Analysis determines how a writer puts a text together, while evaluation or *critical* analysis

Lightspring/Shutterstock.com

comments on the *effectiveness* of how a writer puts a text together. In other words, analysis answers the question "how," while evaluation answers the question "how *well*?" In the final chapter of this textbook, you will use critical analysis as you write your own argument. In fact, you will critically analyze your own essay to ensure it is sound and well supported.

For everyday citizenship, being able to explain the strengths and weaknesses of an argument can help you participate in democracy. You need to be keenly aware of the information that you consume every day—information you receive through social media, through the conversations you have, through advertisements, and so on. You need to be able to communicate the soundness—or lack of soundness—of these messages because critical thinking depends on communicating ideas with others. Without the ability to articulate your own thinking and your own assessment of key issues, you will not be able to contribute to key decisions that impact your community.

▶ Think about It!

In this chapter, you will read and write about the business and politics of sports. Here are some questions to consider as you move through this chapter and as you read the following essay.

1. What roles *do* and *should* sports play in society?

2. What influence do marketing and advertising have on sports? Think of the influence at all levels, from local recreational leagues to professional competitive leagues.

3. Is the sporting world currently in crisis?

In the following reading, the author describes changes he has seen to sports now that they are becoming more privatized and professionalized. He remembers the lessons he learned through sports—"sportsmanship, healthy body development, teamwork and co-operation" (par. 16)—and explains how privatization and professionalization have "devalued" these lessons in the name of "tangible outcomes" such as "goals, assists and competitive achievement" (par. 16). Read this essay and consider these questions:

1. What is the author's main idea or thesis?

2. What is the author's tone in this essay? How do you know?

3. What kinds of evidence (e.g., facts, statistics, expert testimony, anecdote) does the author use to support his point of view? Do you find this evidence convincing? Why or why not?

4. Do you think the author has missed any evidence that could make his argument stronger?

5. Overall, would you consider this persuasive essay to be strong or weak? Justify your answer.

CORPORATE HOCKEY'S HOME-ICE ADVANTAGE

How Privatization and Professionalization Are Remaking the Sport I Love

By Stefan Decosse

1   The local public ice rink and the non-profit minor hockey association are fast becoming relics. Neither is likely to survive the juggernaut of a new culture of privatized minor sport administration.

2   The concept of the hockey "season" is also becoming antiquated. The word implies a distinct beginning and an end. But in the all-consuming world of elite minor hockey, the "season" now often runs from August to August. Even the term "athlete" will soon be consigned to the dustbin of history. Its longstanding association with well roundedness and an amateur ethic bears little relation to the hyper-specialized professionalization that today defines the training of youth hockey players and other minor sport participants.

3   What are we to make of these transformations?

Frozen Assets

4   In British Columbia, where I grew up and played competitive hockey, municipalities and regional districts owned all but four ice rinks until 1990. For decades, minor hockey seasons were decided in and across a vast network of publicly owned arenas and civic recreation centres in communities throughout the province. Non-profit minor hockey associations were often their primary winter tenants.

5   Public facilities have a mandate to serve their communities. The local recreation centre is where my friends and I learned to shoot and skate, to be sure, but it's also where we attended pre-school and kicked our first soccer balls. For years, the traditional hockey season would begin in late August and wrap up by late March. In the warmer months, the ice would be removed to make room for other activities, maybe summer day camps or lacrosse.

6   But the old single ice-sheet public recreation centre is ill equipped to deal with the demands of today's privatized minor hockey environment. Increasingly, the sport is played in purpose built for-profit rinks that serve their clientele on a year-round basis.

7   In the last 25 years, 13 of the 30 new ice rinks in British Columbia were built by or operated by private interests. As minor hockey training has transformed from seasonal youth recreation to a year-round youth vocation, new opportunities for profitable accumulation have opened themselves to corporate actors who have the wherewithal to capitalize.

8   The transformation of a rink in suburban Vancouver exemplifies minor hockey's shifting environments. The Burnaby 8, now owned and operated by Canlan Ice Sports Corporation, was recently retrofitted from an aging four-sheet barn into a state-of-the-art facility. Today it's outfitted with six NHL-sized rinks, a figure skating sheet, an indoor soccer field, a restaurant complex and cutting-edge gym facilities that include a skating treadmill.

9   Canlan is no mom-and-pop shop. The corporation's assets include 18 facilities and 68 sheets of ice across North America. In the 2014 fiscal year, it generated more than $56.7 million from its rink and field activities. Twenty-eight per cent of its revenues came from third-party ice rentals (including minor hockey associations) and another 18 per cent from in-house minor hockey leagues.

10   Companies like Canlan not only feed on a public appetite for year-round hockey, they actively encourage and depend upon it. Their facilities are blanketed in advertisements for equipment retailers and posters promoting high-performance training companies that sell opportunities to "train like the pros."

Year-round Players vs All-round Athletes

11   Indeed, services that offer to professionalize youth training are the stock-in-trade of private ice rinks requiring year-round occupants. Today, it is entirely likely that large chunks of family hockey budgets will go directly to for-profit training companies that offer a host of services in for-profit facilities. The market for supplementary instruction has exploded and sports entrepreneurs now offer tutelage in everything from offensive and defensive skating to tactical stickhandling to on-ice cognitive functioning and shooting.

12   In short, sport specialization has become the norm in minor athletics. Hockey culture is animated today by popular idioms and ideologies that tell us that the world of sport is flat. We're told that any kid who is willing to dedicate significant time to improving their game can attain athletic expertise—and maybe even make it to the pros. Malcolm Gladwell's popularization of the "10,000-hour rule" has only reinforced such fantasies. Today, youth sport is often less about recreation or healthy activity than about the attainment of expertise. Multi-sport athletes are rapidly being replaced by single-sport specialists.

13   I became a specialist myself at the age of 16. But today kids are encouraged to commit themselves much earlier. One parent of a current professional hockey player told me that, by the time his son was 12 years old, coaches were advising that he fully commit himself to a life on the ice.

14   The professionalization of youth hockey training has even spawned year-round academies where kids commit to their athletic development with a single-minded zeal. The Canadian Sports Hockey League (CSHL) was founded in 2009 with the promise of "enabling like-minded players increased levels of competition and exposure."

15   Beyond hockey, players are enrolled in local high schools where the curriculum includes a mix of academics and on- and off-ice training. The success of these institutions is measured not in academic achievement but in the number of players that they manage to place in major junior leagues, college hockey and, most importantly, the NHL. Parents who see this as a desirable path for their children shoulder a heavy burden. CSHL academies have an average annual tuition of $20,000, nearly a third of the median family income in Canada.

16   Professionalization fundamentally alters the meaning of youth athletics, distorting the value of sport and competition. Rather than life lessons learned, goals, assists and competitive achievement become the indicators of money well spent. Success in the world of professionalized youth hockey is wholly oriented and defined in terms of tangible outcomes. Winning is what matters. More and more, positive lessons about sportsmanship, healthy body development, teamwork and co-operation are devalued.

17   To be clear, I am not a hockey dinosaur. Evolution is inevitable and I don't long nostalgically for a fast-disappearing past. As a mentor and a coach, I am

motivated by a desire to be part of reforming the game that I love, for the benefit of players themselves. At the very least, the privatization and professionalization of our sport has made us lose sight of what matters.

Source: Decosse, Stefan. "Corporate Hockey's Home-Ice Advantage: How Privatization and Professionalization Are Remaking the Sport I Love." *Canadian Dimension*, vol. 50, no. 2, Spring 2016. *Academic OneFile*, https://canadiandimension.com/magazine/issue/spring-2016. Accessed 2 Jan. 2017. Reproduced by permission.

Macro versus Claim-by-Claim Critical Analysis

In the previous two chapters, you learned about how to approach a writer's writing analytically. In other words, you learned how to examine a writer's writing for language, tone, and argumentation strategies (this is called *analysis*). Now, you will use this analysis in order to assess the strengths and weaknesses of the writer's writing rather than accepting it at face value (this is called *critical analysis* or *evaluation*). When you want to communicate this critical analysis in writing, you have two options as seen in Table 8.1: a macro critical analysis of the article as a whole or a claim-by-claim critical analysis that provides a detailed assessment of specific claims and their support.

TABLE 8.1

MACRO VERSUS CLAIM-BY-CLAIM CRITICAL ANALYSIS

MACRO CRITICAL ANALYSIS	CLAIM-BY-CLAIM CRITICAL ANALYSIS
Examines and evaluates the overall quality of a writer's writing	Examines and evaluates specific arguments in a writer's writing
Uses multiple types of textual evidence from across the entire article to justify the evaluation	Uses evidence applicable to the specific claims being examined; evidence is from a subsection of the article
Subsections or paragraphs of the critical analysis essay are organized by areas of focus (e.g., credibility, tone, reasoning, evidence)	Subsections or paragraphs of the critical analysis essay are organized by claim

In a *macro critical analysis*, you make a claim about the overall quality of the writer's writing, and you proceed to defend or justify your claim by providing evidence from *many* parts of the article. You should organize your analysis according to the components you choose to examine and evaluate. For example, you could have one section of your analysis that evaluates the credibility of the writer and of the publication, a second section that evaluates the writer's claims, a third section that evaluates the writer's use of evidence, and a fourth section that evaluates the writer's tone.

In a *claim-by-claim critical analysis*, on the other hand, you provide an in-depth evaluation of specific arguments in the article. As you learned in the previous chapter, an argument is a claim plus its support. You evaluate the strengths and weaknesses of the evidence and explanations for the claim, focusing on qualities such as relevance, credibility, and currency. In other words, it is a much more in-depth analysis of a subsection of an article rather than a broad-strokes analysis of the article as a whole. Such an analysis assumes that the portion being analyzed is representative of the entire article.

No matter which method you choose for approaching your critical analysis, you need to make sure that you clearly state your evaluation and that you fully justify your evaluation with evidence and explanations. Moreover, you need to remain focused on the strengths and weaknesses of the article. Your goal is *not* to present your opinion on the issue the writer is discussing; instead, your goal is to present your opinion on *how the writer addresses the issue*.

Critical analysis = how well a writer argues
Critical analysis ≠ whether you agree or disagree with the writer's position on the issue.

▶ Apply the Skill

Matching Claims to Essay Types

Each of the following statements is a claim about the article "Corporate Hockey's Home-Ice Advantage: How Privatization and Professionalization Are Remaking the Sport I Love" by Stefan Decosse. Identify whether the claim indicates a macro critical analysis essay (M), a claim-by-claim critical analysis essay (C), or a response essay (R) that focuses on the issue rather than on the author's argumentation strategies. The first one has been done for you.

__M__ 1. Stefan Decosse presents a strong argument by using hyperbolic diction.

_____ 2. Through a combination of defining terminology, presenting statistics, and articulating his own experience with sports, Stefan Decosse makes a convincing, well-supported argument about how sport has changed for the worse.

_____ 3. I agree with Decosse that "the privatization and professionalization of our sport has made us lose sight of what matters" (par. 17).

_____ 4. While most of what Decosse says is supported with solid evidence, his claim that "multi-sport athletes are rapidly being replaced by single-sport specialists" (par. 12) is unfounded.

Writing an Evaluative Claim

An *evaluative claim* is your main idea about the quality of the writer's writing. It requires two parts: a comment on *how* the writer argues and a comment on *how well* the writer argues. If you do not explain the focus of your analysis—the *how*—then your reader will not understand the basis for your evaluation. If you do not explain your assessment of the writer's argumentative strategies—the *how well*—then you have only an analysis, not a *critical* analysis. Remember that the whole point of evaluating a writer's work—of critically analyzing it—is to explain its strengths and weaknesses.

Because an evaluative claim requires the *how* element, you need to be familiar with the terminology used to analyze various components of a writer's text. While such terminology may differ from discipline to discipline or institution to institution, many core terms are understood across multiple contexts. You have learned these terms in previous chapters. Table 8.2 provides a list of such terminology along with definitions.

TABLE 8.2
TERMINOLOGY USED TO ANALYZE COMPONENTS OF AN AUTHOR'S TEXT

COMPONENT	DEFINITION
Author	The person(s) who wrote the article
Publication	The source that the article appears in (e.g., *The Toronto Star*, *Canadian Dimension*)
Argument	A claim and its support Claim = a debatable statement; an opinion on an issue Support = evidence and reasoning to justify a claim Evidence = concrete proof to show a claim is sound (e.g., facts, statistics, expert testimony, anecdote) Reasoning = explanation of how the evidence demonstrates that the claim is sound
Language or diction	The specific words the author uses
Tone	The underlying attitude the author conveys (e.g., positive, negative, serious, comical)

An evaluative claim also requires that you have an arsenal of vocabulary that refers to the strengths and weaknesses of a text—the *how well* element. While you can use commonplace vocabulary—e.g., *effective, ineffective, strong, weak, logical, illogical, reasonable, unreasonable*—specialized evaluative vocabulary will add greater specificity to your evaluations. Table 8.3 provides a list of such terminology along with definitions.

TABLE 8.3
EVALUATIVE TERMINOLOGY

TERM	DESCRIPTION
Reliable versus unreliable	An author and publication are reliable if they are credible, consistent with other sources, and unbiased. • Credible: author is experienced with the subject matter; publication is peer reviewed or well reputed • Consistent: facts are verifiable in other sources • Unbiased: author and source consider opposing viewpoints rather than ignoring them
Sound versus unsound	A supporting detail is sound if it is reasonable, relevant to the claim it's supporting, compatible with other supporting details, and representative. For more information on all of these qualities, refer to "Soundness in Arguments" in Chapter 7.

If you use the terminology from Table 8.2 and Table 8.3, you will be able to write an effective, precise evaluative claim. Take a look at how the following evaluative claims take advantage of this terminology:

Decosse uses *relevant* Canadian *examples* to *prove* his *claim* that the privatization of sport is becoming more common in Canada.

Decosse's *anecdote* about his own hockey experience makes him a *credible source* on the topic of the privatization of hockey.

▶ Apply the Skill

Evaluative Terminology

Referring to Tables 8.2 and 8.3, underline the components for analysis and circle the evaluative terminology for each of the evaluative claims below. With a peer, discuss whether the evaluative term is effective or whether it could be replaced with a more precise term.

1. Stefan Decosse presents a strong argument by using hyperbolic diction.

2. Through a combination of defining terminology, presenting statistics, and articulating his own experience with sports, Stefan Decosse makes a convincing, well-supported argument about how sport has changed for the worse.

3. While most of what Decosse says is supported with solid evidence, his claim that "multi-sport athletes are rapidly being replaced by single-sport specialists" (par. 12) is unfounded.

Writing a Critical Analysis

When you write a critical analysis, you need to state your evaluative claim and then present the evidence and explanations that support this claim (see Figure 8.1). While the evaluative claim is often stated before its support in a critical analysis essay, the actual process of arriving at that evaluative claim begins with gathering and analyzing evidence. You should write your evaluative claim *after* you have gathered and explained the evidence that led you to that claim. After all, you cannot make an effective claim without having a strong basis for it.

FIGURE 8.1
SUPPORTING AN EVALUATIVE CLAIM

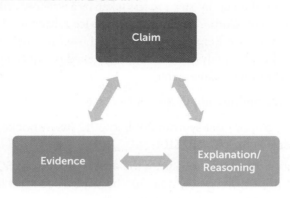

Even though the claim is commonly placed before the evidence and explanation/reasoning, that is not always the case. You need to think about the best way to present your evaluation to your reader, so the order of these elements will depend on purpose and audience. The specific content will also depend on the components you choose to analyze:

- author and publication
- claims, evidence, and reasoning
- language and tone

Evaluating Author and Publication

If you choose this specific component to evaluate, your goal is to justify whether or not the author and publication are *reliable* in relation to the subject matter of the text. This justification requires you to use and explain evidence that illustrates the author's experience with the subject matter, or lack thereof. You can include evidence from the article itself since many authors discuss their experience overtly to gain your trust, while others demonstrate it through terminology, concepts, and examples specific to the subject area. You should also do research so that you can present additional evidence. For example, you should present research that proves or disproves the facts the author presents or that verifies or discredits the author's reputation with the subject matter.

You also need to present research to prove or disprove the credibility of the publication. Remember that a publication's credibility depends on its reputation, its contributors, its audience, and its use in other sources. Provide as much of this information to your reader as possible in order to justify your assessment of the source's publication.

Objectivity—the degree to which a source is unbiased or biased—is another area you should write about when critically analyzing an author and publication. If you want to convince your reader that an author is unbiased, you need to provide evidence that indicates the author considers multiple viewpoints and evidence and fairly refutes or concedes them. On the other hand, if you want to convince your reader that an author is biased, you need to explain how the author is purposefully ignoring opposing viewpoints and evidence or refusing to give them fair consideration. Explaining bias requires you to focus on not only what the author *does* say but also what the author *does not* say.

WRITING A CRITICAL ANALYSIS OF AN AUTHOR AND PUBLICATION

The following explains the step-by-step process taken by a writer to critically analyze the author and publication of "Corporate Hockey's Home-Ice Advantage: How Privatization and Professionalization Are Remaking the Sport I Love." It provides one paragraph of critical analysis, but the analysis could be lengthened or shortened depending on purpose, audience, or other requirements.

STEP 1: Gather information about Stefan Decosse.

- born 1987; played hockey from 2005 to 2012 (www.hockeydb.com/ihdb/stats/pdisplay.php?pid=102310)
- The following information is from the article: He is from BC (par. 3); "played competitive hockey" (par. 4); "became a specialist in hockey" at 16 (par. 13); "a mentor and a coach" (par. 17)

STEP 2: Gather information about the publication, *Canadian Dimension*.

- It has been around for 53 years; left-wing publication; based in Winnipeg with contributors from across Canada; writers are well educated from different fields (canadiandimension.com/about)

- Peer reviewed; pays attention to licensing; website is current (canadiandimension.com/about)

STEP 3: Explain whether or not the information gathered (i.e., the evidence) indicates the author and source are reliable (credible, consistent with other sources, and/or unbiased).

- Decosse has experience with hockey as both a player and coach but does not seem to have experience with for-profit business (credibility is questionable).
- He provides only drawbacks to privatization and professionalization—no benefits (bias detected).
- *Canadian Dimension* is a left-wing publication and so likely opposes big corporations and private interests; however, it is reputable as evidenced by its longevity, the peer review process, and currency of its website (politically biased, but a reputable publication).

STEP 4: Write an evaluative claim based on your evidence and explanations.

Stefan Decosse is a credible author and *Canadian Dimension* is a credible source, but when it comes to the topic of privatization and professionalization of hockey, both indicate bias.

STEP 5: Write a critical analysis of the author and source. Include the evaluative claim and your support for it.

Stefan Decosse's experience as a competitive hockey player (par. 4) and coach (par. 17) make him a credible voice for the sport of hockey. His choice of publication, *Canadian Dimension,* also enhances his credibility since it is a magazine that has been around for 53 years (*About Us*) and has a built-in peer review process (*Writer's Guidelines*). On the specific topic of privatization and professionalization of hockey, however, both Decosse and *Canadian Dimension* demonstrate bias. Most of Decosse's article is based on his own experience, and he does not provide the points of view of those involved in the privatization or professionalization of hockey. He talks about how much money some of these companies, such as Canlan, make (par. 9), but he does not actually explain their point of view on the matter. Furthermore, he puts a negative spin on everything to do with privatization and professionalization, even considering "supplementary instruction" to be a bad thing just because it helps companies make money (par. 11). Decosse's publication choice also demonstrates bias. Because *Canadian Dimension* is a self-proclaimed left-wing publication (*About Us*), it is evident that there would be a bias against corporatization.

▶ Apply the Skill

Critical Analysis of Author and Publication

1. Analyze the critical analysis example above by doing the following:

   a. Underline the evaluative claim and circle the terms that indicate the components being analyzed *and* the terms that indicate the writer's evaluation of the components.

b. Draw a box around the evidence that supports the evaluative claim.

c. Draw a wavy line under any sentence that explains the evidence and its connection to the evaluative claim.

2. Select another reading from this textbook and write a critical analysis of its author and publication. When you are done, complete Question 1 again, but this time mark up your own critical analysis to ensure your analysis is complete and effective.

Evaluating Claims, Evidence, and Reasoning

A critical analysis of claims, evidence, and reasoning can be done at either a macro or claim-by-claim level. At the macro level, you can comment on the overall quality of the claims the author makes. Alternatively, you could comment on the overall quality of the evidence the author presents: its diversity, appropriateness, and reliability. At the claim-by-claim level, you can examine the relationships between specific claims and evidence, assessing how well the author's evidence supports the particular claims. This type of critical analysis is an assessment of the writer's reasoning skills. A writer's reasoning skills refer to the ability of the writer to find good evidence to support a claim and explain the evidence's fitness for that claim.

WRITING A MACRO CRITICAL ANALYSIS OF AN AUTHOR'S CLAIMS

If you want to write a macro critical analysis of an author's claims, you need to present a number of these claims and describe the degree to which they are sound (see Figure 8.2). If your overall assessment is that the author's claims are sound, you need to prove that your selected claims are reasonable, relevant, compatible, and representative. If your overall assessment is that the author's claims are unsound, you need to prove that your selected claims are unreasonable, irrelevant, incompatible, or non-representative.

FIGURE 8.2
EVALUATING THE SOUNDNESS OF AN AUTHOR'S CLAIMS

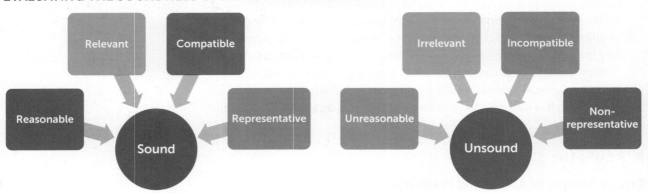

CRITICAL ANALYSIS OF SOUNDNESS IN AN AUTHOR'S CLAIM

The following explains the step-by-step process taken by a writer to critically analyze the soundness of one of Decosse's claims in "Corporate Hockey's Home-Ice Advantage: How Privatization and Professionalization Are Remaking the Sport I Love."

STEP 1: Determine the author's thesis.

Privatization and professionalization of youth hockey has had a negative impact on the values of the sport.

STEP 2: Select a claim from the article.

"The concept of the hockey 'season' is also becoming antiquated" (par. 2).

STEP 3: Explain whether the claim is reasonable, relevant to the thesis, compatible with other supporting details, and representative.

Is it reasonable? **No.**

- Most people are familiar with the term *off-season*, which, by definition, means not in season. If there is an off-season, then there must be a season as well.

- Many people still use the term *hockey season* and understand that it refers to the part of the year in which competitive hockey is actually played, so it is not becoming antiquated.

Is it relevant to the thesis? **No.**

- A hockey season can definitely be impacted by privatization and professionalization, so the claim seems to be on topic. However, there is no indication that a hockey season and the value of the sport have any connection, let alone a cause-and-effect relationship whereby the length of the hockey season negatively impacts the value of the sport.

Is it compatible with other supporting details? **Yes.**

- The claim does not contradict other supporting details. It works with them to help prove the author's thesis.

Is the claim representative of most people's experiences? **No.**

- The NHL, which is the most popular hockey league in the world, runs from October to May/June—not year round; therefore, this claim is not representative of all hockey leagues.

STEP 4: Make an evaluative claim based on your evidence and your critical thinking/reasoning surrounding it.

Decosse's claim that "[t]he concept of the hockey 'season' is also becoming antiquated" (par. 2) is unsound.

STEP 5: Write your critical analysis of the soundness of the author's claim. Make sure you include your evaluative claim and your reasons and evidence for it.

Decosse's claim that "[t]he concept of the hockey 'season' is also becoming antiquated" (par. 2) is unsound. This claim is unreasonable, as the term "hockey season" is very much still commonplace among the hockey community, and so too is the term "off-season." While he may be right that hockey is now a year-round activity, that does not mean it is played competitively year round. The term "season" refers specifically to the time at which competitive games are played, not the time at which players train to play in these games. There is still a distinct hockey season, and hockey players know exactly when that season is. For example, the NHL has a distinct season that runs from October to May/June—not year round;

therefore, this claim is not even representative of the world's most popular hockey league. There is also no indication that "[t]he concept of the hockey 'season'" (par. 2) and the value of hockey have any connection, let alone a cause-and-effect relationship whereby the length of the hockey season negatively impacts the value of the sport. Therefore, this claim does not relate to Decosse's thesis about the negative impact of privatization and professionalization on youth hockey values.

▶ Apply the Skill

Critical Analysis of Soundness in an Author's Claim

1. Mark up the above critical analysis paragraph by doing the following:

   a. Underline the evaluative claim and circle the term that indicates the writer's evaluation.

   b. Draw a box around the evidence that supports the evaluative claim.

   c. Draw a wavy line under any sentence that explains the evidence and its connection to the evaluative claim.

2. Write a paragraph that critically analyzes the soundness of another claim from Decosse's article.

3. Complete Question 1 again, but this time mark up your own critical analysis paragraph to ensure your analysis is complete and effective.

WRITING A MACRO CRITICAL ANALYSIS OF AN AUTHOR'S EVIDENCE

If you want to write a macro critical analysis of an author's evidence, then you need to present a number of pieces of evidence and describe the degree to which the evidence is varied, appropriate, and reliable (see Figure 8.3).

Evidence is *varied* if it is both opinion based and fact based. Opinion-based evidence is strong only if the opinion is informed—backed up by sound reasoning or credibility. Examples of strong opinion-based evidence are expert testimony or a well-developed and reasonable hypothetical scenario. You learned about these types of opinion-based evidence in Chapter 7. Fact-based evidence is often considered stronger than opinion-based evidence because it is grounded in truth. Statistics, events, and real-life anecdotes all provide different levels of fact-based information, as you learned in Chapter 7.

Evidence is *appropriate* if it is current and relevant to the claim it is trying to support. It should also be useful for the author's intended audience.

Evidence is *reliable* if it has been fact-checked against other sources, ensuring it is accurate and consistent. It also needs to be appropriately referenced unless it represents common knowledge.

FIGURE 8.3
EVALUATING AN AUTHOR'S EVIDENCE

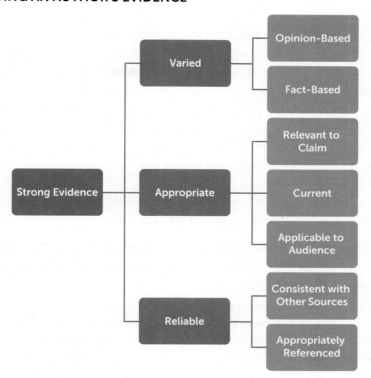

WRITING A CRITICAL ANALYSIS OF AN AUTHOR'S EVIDENCE

The following explains the step-by-step process taken by a writer to critically analyze the evidence in "Corporate Hockey's Home-Ice Advantage: How Privatization and Professionalization Are Remaking the Sport I Love."

STEP 1: Determine the author's thesis or main claim.

Privatization and professionalization of youth hockey has had a negative impact on the values of the sport.

STEP 2: Gather evidence from each major section or paragraph of the article. Identify the evidence type (e.g., expert testimony, hypothetical scenario, example, statistic, anecdote, observation).

In the last 25 years, 13 of the 30 new ice rinks in British Columbia were built by or operated by private interests (par. 7).—*statistics/historical data*

The transformation of a rink in suburban Vancouver exemplifies minor hockey's shifting environments. The Burnaby 8, now owned and operated by Canlan Ice Sports Corporation, was recently retrofitted from an aging four-sheet barn into a state-of-the-art facility. Today it's outfitted with six NHL-sized rinks, a figure skating sheet, an indoor soccer field, a restaurant complex and cutting-edge gym facilities that include a skating treadmill (par. 8).—*example*

The corporation's [Canlan's] assets include 18 facilities and 68 sheets of ice across North America. In the 2014 fiscal year, it generated more than $56.7 million from its rink and field activities. Twenty-eight per cent of its revenues came from third-party ice rentals (including minor hockey associations) and another 18 per cent from in-house minor hockey leagues (par. 9).—*example/ statistics*

I became a specialist myself at the age of 16 (par. 13).—*anecdote*

One parent of a current professional hockey player told me that, by the time his son was 12 years old, coaches were advising that he fully commit himself to a life on the ice (par. 13).—*anecdote/expert testimony*

[The success of] local high schools where the curriculum includes a mix of academics and on- and off-ice training . . . is measured not in academic achievement but in the number of players that they manage to place in major junior leagues, college hockey and, most importantly, the NHL (par. 15).—*observation*

CSHL academies have an average annual tuition of $20,000, nearly a third of the median family income in Canada (par. 15).—*example/statistics*

STEP 3: Explain whether the evidence is varied, appropriate, and reliable.

- The evidence is varied, including both claim-based and fact-based evidence types.
- It is appropriate in terms of its currency (e.g., 2014 fiscal year of Canlan) and its appropriateness for the audience, which is those who are interested in youth hockey, most likely parents and coaches (the evidence is accessible and straightforward; it is directly related to hockey).
- It seems to be inappropriate in terms of its relevance, though. None of it indicates why the values of hockey are negatively impacted by privatization and professionalization. Why does it matter that Canlan made a lot of money in 2014? Why does it matter that hockey is being played in large sports complexes rather than local arenas? The only negative impact I can see is in the evidence about the costs of CSHL academies (if they are too expensive, then some players won't be able to access them).
- The evidence seems to lack appropriate referencing, so it may not be reliable. Where has the data about Canlan's earnings come from? How do we know for sure that the success of CSHL academies does not take academic achievement into consideration? How has the author arrived at "an average annual tuition of $20,000" for the CSHL academies (par. 15)?

STEP 4: Make an evaluative claim based on your evidence and your critical thinking/reasoning surrounding it.

While the evidence Decosse provides is current, varied, and appropriate for his audience, it seems to lack relevance.

STEP 5: Write your critical analysis of the author's evidence. Make sure you include your evaluative claim and your reasons and evidence for it.

While the evidence Decosse provides is current, varied, and appropriate for his audience, it seems to lack relevance. He claims that privatization and professionalization have "made us lose sight of what matters" when it comes to hockey (par. 17), but none of the evidence demonstrates this loss of sight. He provides an example of how The Burnaby 8 was transformed by Canlan Ice Sports Corporation into a complex that now has "an indoor soccer field, a restaurant complex and cutting edge gym facilities" in addition to its "six HNL-sized rinks" (par. 8); this does not, however, prove that privatization makes us lose sight of the values hockey can provide. He also provides details about Canlan's earnings in 2014 (par. 9), which again does not prove that the company has negatively impacted the value of hockey. The only thing the evidence seems to prove is that hockey is becoming more expensive, and cost is not relevant to his argument. Yes, rising prices are a negative consequence of privatization, but this consequence is not related to the attainment of "sportsmanship, healthy body development, teamwork and cooperation" in hockey—the values that Decosse argues are being destroyed (par. 16). It is related only to accessing the sport.

▶ Apply the Skill

Critical Analysis of an Author's Evidence

1. Mark up the above critical analysis paragraph by doing the following:

   a. Underline the evaluative claim and circle the term that indicates the component being analyzed *and* the terms that indicate the writer's overall evaluation of the component.

   b. Draw a box around the evidence that supports the evaluative claim.

   c. Draw a wavy line under any sentence that explains the evidence and its connection to the evaluative claim.

2. The critical analysis paragraph above explains the irrelevance of the evidence, but it does not explain the problems with its reliability. Write a critical analysis paragraph that evaluates the reliability of the author's evidence. Be sure to begin with a topic sentence that states your evaluative claim.

3. Complete Question 1 again, but this time mark up your own critical analysis paragraph to ensure your analysis is complete and effective.

WRITING A CLAIM-BY-CLAIM CRITICAL ANALYSIS OF AN AUTHOR'S CLAIM AND SUPPORT

If you want to write a claim-by-claim critical analysis of some of the author's sub-arguments—that is, specific claims and their accompanying support (evidence and explanations)—then you need to focus on the relationship between the author's claims and the evidence for those claims. You already did this in Chapter 7 when you learned how to investigate the soundness of an author's argument.

Evidence for a claim is effective only if it is relevant to the claim it is supporting, reasonable, credible, current, and representative of the bigger picture. Its connection to the claim must also be clearly explained by the author in order for the argument to be considered effective. Readers should not have to do too much work to understand how the evidence actually proves the author's claim.

WRITING A CRITICAL ANALYSIS OF AN AUTHOR'S ARGUMENT

The following explains the step-by-step process taken by a writer to critically analyze an argument in "Corporate Hockey's Home-Ice Advantage: How Privatization and Professionalization Are Remaking the Sport I Love."

STEP 1: Determine the author's thesis or main claim.

> Privatization and professionalization of youth hockey has had a negative impact on the values of the sport.

STEP 2: Focus on one argument (claim plus support) at a time. Write down the claim and its accompanying evidence.

> Claim: "Multi-sport athletes are rapidly being replaced by single-sport specialists" (par. 12).

> **Evidence:**

> [Privately owned rinks] are blanketed in . . . posters promoting high-performance training companies that sell opportunities to "train like the pros" (par. 10).

> The market for supplementary instruction has exploded and sports entrepreneurs now offer tutelage in everything from offensive and defensive skating to tactical stickhandling to on-ice cognitive functioning and shooting (par. 11).

> We're told that any kid who is willing to dedicate significant time to improving their game can attain athletic expertise—and maybe even make it to the pros. Malcom Gladwell's popularization of the "10,000-hour rule" has only reinforced such fantasies (par. 12).

> I became specialist myself at the age of 16 (par. 13).

> One parent of a current professional hockey player told me that, by the time his son was 12 years old, coaches were advising that he fully commit himself to a life on the ice (par. 13).

> The Canadian Sports Hockey League (CSHL) was founded in 2009 with the promise of "enabling like-minded players increased levels of competition and exposure" (par. 14).

STEP 3: Explain whether the evidence is well connected to the claim, reasonable, credible, current, and representative.

- The evidence concerning "supplementary instruction" and "professionalize[d] youth training" (par. 11) definitely relates to becoming specialists in a sport. It is reasonable to think that if extra time is being poured into one sport, then less time will be spent on others.

- Some of the evidence is credible as it is based on popular and respected organizations (CSHL) and authors (Malcolm Gladwell). Other evidence lacks credibility; for example, Decosse does not provide the name of the "current professional hockey player" who was advised to "fully commit himself to a life on the ice" at the age of "12 years old" (par. 13).

- The currency of the evidence is questionable. The Malcolm Gladwell evidence refers to his 2008 book *Outliers: The Story of Success,* which was published eight years prior to Decosse's article. Decosse's own example of how he was specialized "at the age of 16" actually demonstrates that specialization was happening a long time ago rather than being a new phenomenon.

- His own experience and the experience "of a current professional hockey player" is not sufficient evidence to indicate single-sport specialists are now the norm. Moreover, his evidence focuses only on hockey, yet the claim is generalized to all sports.

STEP 4: Make an evaluative claim based on the connection between the claim and the author's support.

Decosse claims that "[m]ulti-sport athletes are rapidly being replaced by single-sport specialists" (par. 12). While his reasoning for supporting this claim is quite strong, his evidence for the claim is quite weak.

STEP 5: Write your critical analysis of the author's argument. Make sure you include your evaluative claim and your reasons and evidence for it.

Decosse claims that "[m]ulti-sport athletes are rapidly being replaced by single-sport specialists" (par. 12). His reasoning for supporting this claim is quite strong. He provides a clear, logical explanation as to how single-sport specialization is being encouraged: "We're told that any kid who is willing to dedicate significant time to improving their game can attain athletic expertise—and maybe even make it to the pros" (par. 12). It makes sense that if someone is dedicating lots of time to a single sport, then he or she is likely to have less time to play other sports.

The evidence Decosse provides for his claim, however, is weak. One thing his evidence lacks is credibility. He does mention some credible sources such as the CSHL (par. 14) and Malcolm Gladwell (par. 12), but other evidence is vague, such as the "current professional hockey player" who was advised to "fully commit himself to a life on the ice" at the age of "12 years old" (par. 13) and the privately owned rinks that "are blanketed in . . . posters promoting high-performance training companies that sell opportunities to 'train like the pros'" (par. 10). He does not explain who the hockey player is, nor does he give any examples of training companies that advertise at rinks.

The currency of his evidence is also questionable. His Malcolm Gladwell reference is from 2008, eight years before Decosse wrote this article, and Decosse's own experience with specialization is from when he was 16 years old, which, according to hockeydb.com, was back in 2003. Moreover, his own experience and the experience "of a current professional hockey player" are not sufficient evidence to indicate that single-sport specialists are now the norm. Two examples are not representative of the bigger picture. It is also problematic that his evidence focuses only on hockey, yet the claim is generalized to all sports.

▶ Apply the Skill

Critical Analysis of an Author's Argument

1. Mark up the above critical analysis paragraphs by doing the following:

   a. Underline the evaluative claims and circle the terms that indicate the components being analyzed *and* that indicate the writer's overall evaluation of the components. Note that the evaluative claim is not presented as a single sentence in this example.

     b. Draw a box around the evidence that supports the evaluative claims.

     c. Draw a wavy line under any sentence that explains the evidence and its connection to the evaluative claims.

2. Write one or two critical analysis paragraphs that evaluate a different argument (claim + support) from Decosse's article. Be sure to begin with a topic sentence that states your evaluative claim. Keep in mind that your evaluation can point out both strengths and weaknesses, as demonstrated in the previous critical analysis paragraphs.

3. Complete Question 1 again, but this time mark up your own critical analysis paragraph(s) to ensure your analysis is complete and effective.

WRITING A MACRO CRITICAL ANALYSIS OF AN AUTHOR'S LANGUAGE AND TONE

A critical analysis of language and tone is typically done at a macro level. This type of analysis requires that you analyze the word choices and tone of the author, just as you did in Chapter 6, paying careful attention to how these two elements contribute to the persuasiveness of the article. In particular, you should look at whether the vocabulary differs when an author is describing her own viewpoint versus an opposing viewpoint. In order to write such an analysis, you will need to keep in mind the connotations of words, which you learned about in Chapter 6. You will then need to determine whether the language and tone strengthen or weaken the author's argument, a decision that will largely depend on your analysis of the author's purpose and audience. Your ultimate goal is to describe the fitness of the language and tone with the author's purpose and audience. You can also comment on bias if the author uses language that indicates a bias.

When writing a macro critical analysis of an author's language and tone, you need to provide specific examples of diction (word choices) from across the entire article, and you need to explain their connotative meanings, their degree of difficulty, and persuasive merit (see Figure 8.4).

FIGURE 8.4
EVALUATING AN AUTHOR'S LANGUAGE AND TONE

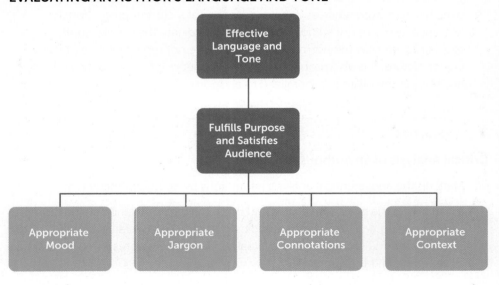

WRITING A CRITICAL ANALYSIS OF AN AUTHOR'S LANGUAGE AND TONE

The following explains the step-by-step process taken by a writer to critically analyze the language and tone in "Corporate Hockey's Home-Ice Advantage: How Privatization and Professionalization Are Remaking the Sport I Love."

STEP 1: Determine the author's purpose and audience.

- Purpose: to persuade his audience that privatization and professionalization of youth hockey is having a negative impact on the values of the sport

- Audience: based on my previous research of the publication, his audience is on the political left and would likely oppose privatization; they are also likely a well-educated audience interested in debating such an issue; they may or may not be familiar with hockey, but if they are choosing this article based on the title, it's likely that they have some interest in and knowledge of the sport

STEP 2: Determine your focus of the analysis. Which of the following will you focus on?

- Connotation (terms that have been specifically chosen for their persuasive merit)

- Terms that the author overtly defines

STEP 3: Gather evidence for your area(s) of focus. If you chose connotations as your focus, gather examples of words that have been chosen because of the connotations they possess. Then, describe the connotation of each word and the context in which it is used.

LOADED LANGUAGE	CONNOTATION	CONTEXT
Relic (par. 1)	Very old and no longer relevant	Used to describe what privatization is doing to minor hockey
Juggernaut (par. 1)	Massive, relentless, damaging	Used to describe privatization of minor sports
Hyper-specialized (par. 2)	Extremely or abnormally specialized	Used to describe the current state of minor sports
Fantasies (par. 12)	Not real; impossible to achieve	Used to describe the attainment of expertise and "mak[ing] it to the pros" (par. 12)
Distorting (par. 16)	Deforming	Used to describe what professionalization is doing to "the value of sport and competition"

STEP 4: Determine the author's tone based on your evidence.

The vocabulary the author uses when describing the privatization and professionalization of minor hockey is very negative, so his tone can be defined as negative or even grim. All of this negative vocabulary, however, is used only when talking about privatization and professionalization. When he talks about minor hockey from his own childhood, he avoids such language.

STEP 5: Make an evaluative claim about the author's language and tone as it relates to the author's purpose and audience. Do the language and tone serve the purpose and audience well?

Decosse's language and tone are appropriate for his purpose and audience.

STEP 6: Write your critical analysis of the author's language and tone. Make sure you include your evaluative claim and your reasons and evidence for it.

Decosse's language and tone are appropriate for his audience (those interested in hockey and opposed to corporatization) and for his purpose (to persuade his audience that privatization and professionalism are having a negative impact on the values of youth hockey). Whenever Decosse talks about privatization or professionalization, he uses language with very negative connotations. For example, he describes privatization of minor hockey as a "juggernaut," which emphasizes the massive destruction it will inflict on the sport. His use of this term implies there is absolutely no silver lining to privatization. He also describes the professionalization of minor hockey as being responsible for creating "fantasies" (par. 12). In other words, he is emphasizing that professionalization encourages unachievable goals that will only let players down. His description of professionalization as "*distorting* the value of sport and competition" (par. 12, emphasis mine) also points to wreckage as opposed to just change. This carefully chosen vocabulary helps Decosse paint a negative picture of privatization and professionalization of minor hockey, which contrasts very well with his neutral description of the minor hockey from his past.

▶ Apply the Skill

Critical Analysis of an Author's Language and Tone

1. Mark up the above critical analysis paragraph by doing the following:

   a. Underline the evaluative claim and circle the terminology that indicates the components being analyzed *and* that indicates the writer's evaluation of the components.

   b. Draw a box around the evidence that supports the evaluative claim.

   c. Draw a wavy line under any sentence that explains the evidence and its connection to the evaluative claim.

2. Write a critical analysis paragraph that evaluates the use of language in another reading from this textbook. Be sure to begin with a topic sentence that states your evaluative claim and be sure to provide strong reasons and evidence to support your claim. Keep in mind the reading's purpose and audience.

3. Complete Question 1 again, but this time mark up your own critical analysis paragraph to ensure your analysis is complete and effective.

Focus on Structure and Organization: Writing a Critical Analysis Essay

Throughout this chapter, you have been writing critical analysis paragraphs. The final step of a critical analysis is to piece these paragraphs together into a coherent critical analysis essay. A typical critical analysis essay has four components: introduction, summary, critical analysis, and conclusion. You were introduced to elements of an essay, such as introductions, body paragraphs, and conclusions, in Chapter 2.

Introduction

The introduction to a critical analysis can take on many forms. At minimum, your introduction should have a hook that draws the reader into your analysis, a reference to the article you are critically analyzing (at minimum, identify the author, title, and thesis), your overall evaluation of the article (this is *your* thesis), and your approach to analysis (i.e., what you will focus on—author and publication; claims, evidence, and reasoning; language and tone; all of the above) as seen in Figure 8.5.

Summary

To provide context for your analysis, you should present a summary of the article before you analyze it. Instead of writing a complete summary, some writers prefer to write an abstract, or a brief summary, that states only the claims being analyzed and evaluated

FIGURE 8.5
MINIMUM REQUIREMENTS FOR A CRITICAL ANALYSIS ESSAY INTRODUCTION

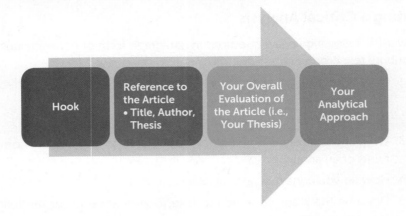

Hook | Reference to the Article • Title, Author, Thesis | Your Overall Evaluation of the Article (i.e., Your Thesis) | Your Analytical Approach

by the writer. If you choose this method, make sure you are not deliberately selecting claims that support a biased critical analysis: the claims selected for an abstract need to provide good representation of the article.

Some writers prefer to write the summary or abstract as a single paragraph directly after the introduction, which is typically used for a macro critical analysis and is known as the block method; others prefer to split it up among the critical analysis paragraphs, using a point-by-point structure, which is typically used for a claim-by-claim critical analysis (see Figure 8.6). In the point-by-point structure, each critical analysis paragraph begins by explaining the idea in the article that is being evaluated before the evaluation is articulated. This type of structure is best used for critically analyzing claims, evidence, and reasoning because it allows you to present the claim before critically analyzing its development. You were introduced to both the block and point-by-point structures in Chapter 3.

FIGURE 8.6
OPTIONS FOR SUMMARY OR ABSTRACT COMPONENT

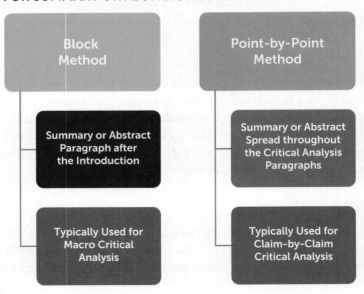

Block Method
- Summary or Abstract Paragraph after the Introduction
- Typically Used for Macro Critical Analysis

Point-by-Point Method
- Summary or Abstract Spread throughout the Critical Analysis Paragraphs
- Typically Used for Claim-by-Claim Critical Analysis

Critical Analysis Paragraphs

The critical analysis paragraphs form the body of your essay. The goal is to carefully connect all your points of analysis, which will require you to pay attention to the unity and coherence strategies you learned about in Chapter 2. This is also the section in which you will employ the quotation and explication strategies you learned about in Chapter 5.

Conclusion

The conclusion of a critical analysis essay, like the introduction, can take on many forms as you learned in Chapter 2. As shown in Figure 8.7, a good conclusion should remind your reader of your overall evaluation of the article and should reiterate how your evaluation is important. How does your critical analysis further the discussion of the issue addressed in the article? How does it contribute to critical thinking in the topic area?

FIGURE 8.7
WHAT YOUR CRITICAL ANALYSIS CONCLUSION SHOULD DO

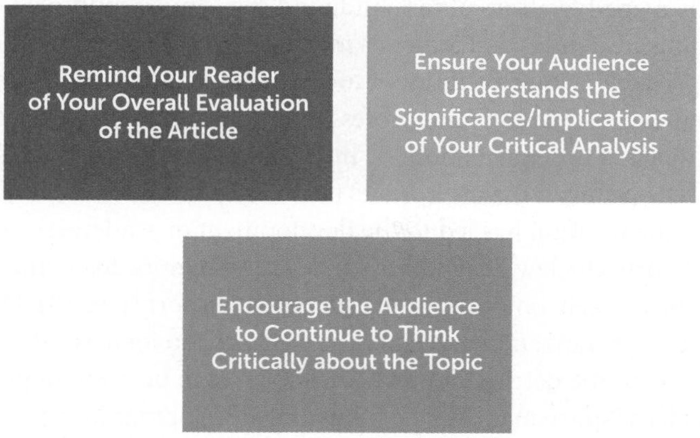

Remind Your Reader of Your Overall Evaluation of the Article

Ensure Your Audience Understands the Significance/Implications of Your Critical Analysis

Encourage the Audience to Continue to Think Critically about the Topic

---

▶ Apply the Skill

Critical Analysis Essays

The piece of writing below is an essay that critically analyzes "Corporate Hockey's Home-Ice Advantage: How Privatization and Professionalization Are Remaking the Sport I Love." It synthesizes many of the paragraphs you have already seen in this chapter, and it includes an introduction, summary paragraph, and conclusion. Read the essay, and then answer the questions that follow it.

A CRITICAL ANALYSIS OF STEFAN DECOSSE'S "CORPORATE HOCKEY'S HOME-ICE ADVANTAGE: HOW PRIVATIZATION AND PROFESSIONALIZATION ARE REMAKING THE SPORT I LOVE"

The world's largest sports organizations, such as FIFA, the NFL, and the NHL, are all for-profit organizations that bring in millions of dollars each year. While society has come to accept these sports organizations as private businesses driven by the professionalization of their sports, this acceptance has yet to become as widespread in the world of minor or youth sports. In "Corporate Hockey's Home-Ice Advantage: How Privatization and Professionalization Are Remaking the Sport I Love," former youth hockey player and current youth hockey coach Stefan Decosse argues that "privatization and professionalism of our sport [hockey] has made us lose sight of what matters" (par. 17). In other words, it is putting too much focus on single-sport expertise and winning to the detriment of whole-person development in areas such as fitness, collaboration, and fair play (par. 16). Decosse's thesis seems reasonable, but the means by which he justifies his thesis are largely ineffective. After providing a summary of Decosse's argument, I will describe the shortfalls of the article in terms of its credibility, claims, and evidence. I will conclude with a positive evaluation of Decosse's attention to diction to demonstrate that the writing, despite its shortfalls, does have some merit.

To begin his argument about the negative impacts of privatization and professionalization of hockey, Decosse explains how the hockey season has now transformed into a year-round duty and how the term *athlete* will no longer refer to someone who is good at many sports but rather someone who attains expertise in a single sport (par. 2). He then explains the shift from the publicly owned facilities of his childhood that served multiple purposes in developing academics and athletics in young people (par. 5) to the more common privately owned facilities of today that encourage profit-driven "supplementary instruction" and professionalization in a single sport (pars. 11–12). As part of his explanation, he mentions Canlan Ice Sports Corporation and the profits it makes from its facilities (par. 9). He also mentions how professionalization has led to the development of academies, such as the Canadian Sports Hockey League, which he argues ignore academic achievement and focus solely on professional success in a sport (par. 15). Decosse concludes that privatization and specialization are too focused on "tangible outcomes" to the detriment of what he believes to be more important lessons, such as "sportsmanship, healthy body development, teamwork and co-operation" (par. 16).

Stefan Decosse's experience as a competitive hockey player (par. 4) and coach (par. 17) make him a credible voice for the sport of hockey. His choice of publication, *Canadian Dimension,* also enhances his credibility since it is a magazine that has been around for 53 years (*About Us*) and has a built-in peer review process (*Writer's Guidelines*). On the specific topic of privatization and professionalization of hockey, however, both Decosse and *Canadian Dimension* demonstrate bias. Most of Decosse's article is based on his own experience, and he does not provide the points of view of those involved in the privatization or professionalization of hockey. He talks about how much money some of these companies, such as Canlan, make (par. 9), but he does not actually explain their point of view on the matter. Furthermore, he puts a negative spin on everything to do with privatization and professionalization, even considering "supplementary instruction" to be a bad thing just because it helps companies make money (par. 11). Decosse's publication choice also demonstrates bias. Because *Canadian Dimension* is a self-proclaimed left-wing publication (*About Us*), it is evident that there would be a bias against corporatization.

In addition to the problem of bias, Decosse makes a number of unsound claims while trying to justify that privatization and professionalization are negatively impacting the values of youth hockey. One such claim is that "the concept of the hockey 'season' is . . . becoming antiquated" (par. 2). This claim is unreasonable, as the term "hockey season" is very much still commonplace among the hockey community, and so too is the term "off-season." While he may be right that hockey is now a year-round activity, that does not mean it is played competitively year round. The term "season" refers specifically to the time at which competitive games are played, not the time at which players train to play in these games. There is still a distinct hockey season, and hockey players know exactly when that season is. The NHL has a distinct season that runs from October to April—not year round; therefore, this claim is not even representative of the world's most popular hockey league. Finally, there is no indication that "[t]he concept of the hockey 'season'" (par. 2) and the value of the sport have any connection, let alone a cause-and-effect relationship whereby the length of the hockey season negatively impacts the value of the sport. Therefore, this claim does not relate to Decosse's thesis about the negative impact of privatization and professionalization on youth hockey values.

Much of Decosse's evidence is also problematic. While the evidence Decosse provides is current, well-varied, and appropriate for his audience, it seems to lack relevance. He claims that privatization and professionalization have "made us lose sight of what matters" when it comes to hockey (par. 17), but none of the evidence demonstrates this loss of sight. He provides an example of how The Burnaby 8 was transformed by Canlan Ice Sports Corporation into a complex that now has "an indoor soccer field, a restaurant complex and cutting edge gym facilities" in addition to its "six HNL-sized rinks" (par. 8); this does not, however, prove that privatization makes us lose sight of the values hockey can provide. He also provides details about Canlan's earnings in 2014 (par. 9), which again does not prove that the company has negatively impacted the value of hockey. The only thing the evidence seems to prove is that hockey is becoming more expensive, and cost is not relevant to his argument. Yes, rising prices are a negative consequence of privatization, but this consequence is not related to the attainment of "sportsmanship, healthy body development, teamwork and cooperation" in hockey—the values that Decosse argues are being destroyed (par. 16). It is related only to accessing the sport.

One strength that Decosse's article demonstrates is attention to diction. Decosse's language and tone are appropriate for his audience (those interested in hockey and opposed to corporatization) and for his purpose (to persuade his audience that privatization and professionalism are having a negative impact on the values of youth hockey). Whenever Decosse talks about privatization or professionalization, he uses language with very negative connotations. For example, he describes privatization of minor hockey as a "juggernaut," which emphasizes the massive destruction it will inflict on the sport. His use of this term implies there is absolutely no silver lining to privatization. He also describes the professionalization of minor hockey as being responsible for creating "fantasies" (par. 12). In other words, he is emphasizing that professionalization encourages unachievable goals that will only let players down. His description of professionalization as *"distorting the value of sport and competition"* (par. 12, emphasis mine) also points to wreckage as opposed to just change. This carefully chosen vocabulary helps Decosse paint a negative picture of privatization and professionalization of minor hockey, which contrasts very well with his neutral description of the minor hockey from his past.

Decosse highlights a significant conundrum in the world of sports: at what point should the line between recreation and professionalization be crossed, if at all? However, the approach he has undertaken may not lead to valuable debate on this issue. He should have taken a balanced rather than biased approach. Doing so would provide a bigger picture of the debate and would allow for more meaningful discussion within it. The claims and evidence should also focus more on how privatization and professionalization actually inhibit "sportsman-ship, healthy body development, teamwork and co-operation" (par. 16). If these are the important values at risk of being lost, then there needs to be a focused discussion on where this loss may be happening with privatization and profes-sionalization. It is not clear from the article as to why someone cannot learn "teamwork" and "co-operation" in a professionalized setting—after all, these are values desired by most professions. In short, the debate on the privatization and professionalization of sport is significant because of the relationship among sports, human development, and social relationships. The way to carry on this debate is to look specifically at those values that may become lost if privatization and professionalization remain unquestioned.

Works Cited

"About Us." *Canadian Dimension*. Canadian Dimension, canadiandimension.com/about. Accessed 2 Jan. 2016.

Decosse, Stefan. "Corporate Hockey's Home-Ice Advantage: How Privatization and Professionaliza-tion Are Remaking the Sport I Love." *Canadian Dimension*, vol. 6, no. 2, Spring 2016. *Academic OneFile*, go.galegroup.com.ezproxy.humber.ca/ps/i.do?p=AONE&u=humber&id=GALE%-7CA453721714&v=2.1&it=r&sid=summon&authCount=1. Accessed 2 Jan. 2017.

"Writer's Guidelines." *Canadian Dimension*. Canadian Dimension, canadiandimension.com/about/guidelines. Accessed 2 Jan. 2016.

1. Does the writer include all minimum requirements for the introduction of a crit-ical response essay? Label them directly on the essay.

2. Has the writer used a block style or point-by-point style for the summary? Is the chosen style appropriate for the writer's approach to critically analyzing the article?

3. Has the writer ensured unity and coherence both within and between para-graphs? What particular strategies has the author used: transitions, repetition, pronouns, or a combination of all three?

4. Does the writer present enough evidence to justify his evaluation?

5. Does the writer explain the connection between his evidence and his evaluative claims clearly?

6. Has the writer followed good citation practices?

7. Does the writer's conclusion remind the reader of his evaluation, ensure his audience understands the significance/implications of his critical analysis, and encourage his audience to continue thinking critically about the issue? How so?

8. Circle the vocabulary in the critical analysis that identifies a component for analysis.

9. Draw a box around the evaluative vocabulary in the critical analysis (e.g., *weak, strong, problematic, effective*).

10. What aspects of this critical analysis essay would you want to incorporate into your own critical analysis essay? Why? What aspects would you want to avoid? Why?

Review

Critical Analysis Essay Structure

Answer the following review questions in paragraph form or generate ideas to contribute to a group or class discussion:

1. What are the minimum requirements for the introduction of a critical analysis essay?
2. What are the two approaches for writing the summary component of a critical analysis essay?
3. How do you ensure unity and coherence within and between the body paragraphs of a critical analysis essay?
4. What are the key functions of a critical analysis essay's conclusion?

▶ **Did You Know?**

USING COLONS AND SEMICOLONS

The colon (:) and semicolon (;) are two punctuation marks that can enhance the clarity of your writing and help you demonstrate relationships between ideas. While these two punctuation marks look similar, their functionality is different.

Colons in Sentences

In Chapter 5, you learned that a colon is used after an independent clause to introduce a quotation. A colon can also be used after an independent clause that introduces a list, a definition, or a clarification, as in the following example from this chapter:

A typical critical analysis essay has four components: introduction, summary, critical analysis, and conclusion.

Note how, in this example, the part after the colon helps to define or clarify the part before the colon. You can think of the part after the colon as filling in the blanks left by the information before the colon. You can also think of the colon as speaking the words *that is, they are,* or *namely.*

Colons that are used within sentences *must always be preceded by an independent clause.* Therefore, you need to avoid the trap that some writers fall into of using colons to introduce all lists. In particular, avoid using a colon after the words *are, such as,* and *including.*

Incorrect	The sports I like to play are: hockey, soccer, and volleyball.
	I like to play many sports, such as: hockey, soccer, and volleyball.
	I like to play many sports, including: hockey, soccer, and volleyball.
Correct	The sports I like to play are hockey, soccer, and volleyball.
	I like to play many sports, such as hockey, soccer, and volleyball.
	I like to play many sports, including hockey, soccer, and volleyball.
	I like to play the following sports: hockey, soccer, and volleyball.

Note how none of the colons in the incorrect sentences are preceded by an independent clause. Contrast these examples with the final example in the correct sentences in which the colon is preceded by an independent clause.

Colons in Titles and Headings

In the reading you have been working with throughout this chapter, you will notice that a colon forms part of the title "Corporate Hockey's Home-Ice Advantage: How Privatization and Professionalization Are Remaking the Sport I Love." Colons are often used in titles to separate a main title from a subtitle, or to separate a "hook" title (intended to capture the audience's attention) from a more descriptive title (intended to more accurately summarize what the reading is about). Similarly, colons are often used in headings, such as in a list of steps in a process. You have seen this pattern through this chapter (e.g., "Step 4: Determine the author's tone based on your evidence").

▶ **Apply the Skill**

Using Colons

Examine the use of colons in the article at the end of this chapter entitled "Top 10 Scandals That Define FIFA's Tarnished Legacy." For each colon that you find, describe why the author has used it. If there are any colons that you think have been used incorrectly, explain why.

Semicolons

You have already seen that semicolons can be used to connect two independent clauses when the two independent clauses bear a close relationship, such as one of cause-effect or contrast. When the relationship between the two independent clauses is self-evident, a semicolon can connect them on its own, as in this cause-effect example:

> Decosse uses hyperbolic language to express his distaste for privatization and professionalization; he seems to use it to cause panic in his readers.

If the relationship requires some clarification through the help of a conjunctive adverb, then a semicolon can be placed before the conjunctive adverb (of more than one syllable) and a comma after it, as in this contrast example:

> In a critical analysis, your goal is not to present your opinion on the issue the author is discussing; instead, your goal is to present your opinion on how the author addresses the issue.

The other less common use of a semicolon is for complex items in a list. As you already know, you usually use *commas* to separate items in a list. However, if each item in the list has its own punctuation embedded within it, then using commas may cause confusion, as in the following example:

> Canada has NHL teams in seven different locations: Vancouver, British Columbia, Calgary, Alberta, Edmonton, Alberta, Winnipeg, Manitoba, Toronto, Ontario, Ottawa, Ontario, and Montreal, Quebec.

As you can see, someone who isn't familiar with Canada would be confused: it looks as though 14 locations are listed, when in fact there are only seven cities with their corresponding provinces. Note how separating the locations with semicolons helps clarify the list:

> Canada has NHL teams in seven different locations: Vancouver, British Columbia; Calgary, Alberta; Edmonton, Alberta; Winnipeg, Manitoba; Toronto, Ontario; Ottawa, Ontario; and Montreal, Quebec.

▶ Apply the Skill

Using Semicolons

1. The following two quotations are from "Top 10 Scandals That Define FIFA's Tarnished Legacy" by Jake Smith. For each of the quotations, do the following:

   a. Explain why Smith uses a semicolon instead of a period.

   b. Identify the logical relationship between the two independent clauses that the semicolon connects. Is it cause-effect? Comparison? Contrast? Explanation and example?

   c. Explain why a conjunctive adverb after the semicolon is not necessary.

Quotation 1: "To say that FIFA is a powerful organization would be more than an understatement; each World Cup event generates billions of dollars of revenue for the world's largest football association" (par. 2).

Quotation 2: "Migrant workers are treated like slaves; they aren't allowed to leave their filthy, sewage-soaked work sites even though construction companies are too cheap or lazy to haul away garbage" (par. 11).

▶ Questions for Writing and Discussion

Read the article below, "Top 10 Scandals That Define FIFA's Tarnished Legacy" by Jake Smith. Then, answer the following questions:

1. What are the purpose and audience for Jake Smith's article? Are they similar to or different from the purpose and audience for Stefan Decosse's article? How are Jake Smith's article and Stefan Decosse's article related in terms of their theme?

2. What is Jake Smith's thesis and supporting ideas? Write them in a one-paragraph summary of the article.

3. Compare and/or contrast Jake Smith's tone and Stefan Decosse's tone. Is one more persuasive than the other? Is there a relationship between the authors' tones and their respective publications?

4. How would you evaluate Jake Smith's overall use of evidence? Is it varied, appropriate, and reliable? Be sure to include ample evidence and thorough explanations to justify your evaluation.

5. Select a claim from Jake Smith's article and evaluate how effectively he supports that claim with evidence and explanations.

6. Write an essay that critically analyzes "Top 10 Scandals That Define FIFA's Tarnished Legacy." Choose an approach that suits the article and your own preferences best. Be sure to include ample evidence and thorough explanations to justify your evaluation. Your answers to the previous questions will help you generate content.

OR

Write a critical analysis essay that compares and contrasts the argumentative effectiveness of "Top 10 Scandals That Define FIFA's Tarnished Legacy" with "Corporate Hockey's Home-Ice Advantage: How Privatization and Professionalization Are Remaking the Sport I Love." Focus on at least three strategies that both of the authors use. Evaluate each author's use of the strategy, and determine which author uses it best. Be sure to include ample evidence and thorough explanations to justify your evaluation.

TOP 10 SCANDALS THAT DEFINE FIFA'S TARNISHED LEGACY

Jake Smith

1 Given FIFA's well-known culture of corruption and ethical problems, it's almost a miracle that Sepp Blatter was finally convinced to resign in June of 2015. But FIFA's accountability problems aren't a recent development. FIFA is not exactly an organization that's a stranger to scandal. The recent Sepp Blatter scorcher was only the latest in a long line of ethical problems for one of the world's largest, most influential and most notorious sports organizations.

2   As the saying goes: absolute power corrupts absolutely. To say that FIFA is a powerful organization would be more than an understatement; each World Cup event generates billions of dollars of revenue for the world's largest football association. By far, television and marketing rights are the biggest money maker for the company. But FIFA's soulless corporate partners don't mind the scandals—they are all more than happy to throw money at FIFA, so long as their advertising messages continue to be broadcast worldwide during commercial breaks.

3   Perhaps FIFA is just too big to control. Soccer is the most popular sport in the world and FIFA nearly has a monopoly over it. FIFA has more member countries than the United Nations and its yearly net profit figures are comparable to Luxembourg's GDP. Its headquarters are in Zurich, so the association must abide by Swiss laws—but policing an organization with over a billion dollars of cash reserves isn't a simple task.

4   Insiders have known about corruption at FIFA for years, but it took an intervention by the United States FBI to get the ball rolling in the Blatter case. Allegedly Blatter's plots were hatched on U.S. soil and dirty money flowed through U.S. banks, making it possible for American authorities to intervene. Further U.S.–Swiss cooperation might lead to more revelations, but it could very well be that the punishments inflicted on FIFA executives won't be enough to change FIFA's corporate culture in any significant ways. After all, this is an organization whose 111 year history is more than checkered—it's absolutely sordid. FIFA executives always seem to be up to something nefarious: lining their own wallets with stolen cash, buying re-election votes, supporting tyrants around the world, ignoring human rights issues and discriminating against minorities are just a few of their most notable offenses.

10. Institutionalized Ticket Scalping

5   FIFA officials have special access to tickets, but when they are caught scalping them FIFA always looks the other way. In Rio de Janeiro, an unnamed FIFA official was caught working with local hustlers to illegally re-sell tickets for multiple times their listed value during the 2014 World Cup. The hustler—an Algerian by the name of Mohamadou Lamine Fofana—had been meeting with the unnamed FIFA official at the Copacabana Palace Hotel. Back in 2006, FIFA official Ismail Bhamjee of Botswana was caught by British police selling 12 tickets for triple the price. In the aftermath of the scandal, Bhamjee was sent home and he later resigned his position.

9. Fake It Until You Reform It

6   There have been multiple attempts to reform FIFA over the years, but none of them have been very serious. Michael Garcia, a lawyer from the United States, spent multiple years looking into corruption around the World Cup bidding process. He presented a 430- page report in 2014, which was then presented to the public as a "summary" that left out all the shocking details of his investigation. Garcia quit FIFA shortly after the summary was released. Swiss prosecutor Mark Pieth also investigated FIFA back in 2011, but his report was also watered down and then ignored by FIFA executives. Clearly, attempts at reform at FIFA are nothing more than PR stunts.

8. FIFA'S Filthy Modern Father

7   Most experts agree that former FIFA president João Havelange is the man responsible for modernizing the organization. In particular, Havelange was able to understand the importance of sponsorship and its potential for profit. Under Havelange's watch, FIFA grew into a multibillion dollar sports empire—but it also devolved into a cesspool of financial corruption. In 2012, a Swiss prosecutor finally caught Havelange with his hand in the cookie jar. After being charged with accepting over $23 million in bribes from marketing companies in the 1990s, Havelange was forced to resign. Shortly afterwards, Havelange was replaced by his infamous protegé, Sepp Blatter.

7. No Blacks or Asians, Please

8   Sir. Stanley Rous of England was president of FIFA before Havelange. Rous wasn't as greedy as Havelange—he wasn't involved in any scandals involving money,

at least as far as the public knows—but he also lacked business acumen. Instead of expanding FIFA and promoting soccer outside of Europe, he actually fought to keep the association smaller. In the 1966 World Cup tournament, there was only one spot for Asia and Africa—effectively guaranteeing that at least one team from Europe would always make it to the championship game. Additionally, Rous allowed apartheid South Africa to play FIFA soccer and ignored critics who accused his organization of supporting institutionalized racism.

6. Cash for Votes: FIFA'S Uncontrollable Blatter Problem

9   Blatter continued FIFA executives' hallowed modern era tradition of accepting bribes from marketing companies. In June of 2015, the U.S. Department of Justice found Blatter guilty of accepting over $150 million in bribes from companies interested in FIFA broadcasting rights—but that was just the tip of the iceberg. Other allegations against Blatter claimed he had accepted bribes from Russia and Qatar during the World Cup bidding process. He also paid for the votes that got him elected as FIFA president in the first place, back in 1998. Shockingly, Blatter managed to get reelected as president of FIFA in the midst of the 2015 investigations, only to resign after further details began to emerge.

5. That'll Be $15 Billion, Please

10   Presidents Blatter and Havelange were willing to allow developing countries to play FIFA soccer, but only as long as they were willing to pay the price. FIFA provided nothing in the way of funds to help Brazil and South Africa set up World Cup caliber stadiums. As a result, the impoverished citizens of those nations were faced with increased taxes and benefit reductions. South Africa shelled out $4 billion in 2010 and Brazil spent $15 billion on World Cup construction. Protests in Brazil over the misleading way that the World Cup was sold to the people (at first the government said that no public money would be used to construct the arenas, but in the end Brazilians paid for almost everything) were ignored by FIFA.

4. Fixed Exhibition Matches

11   A FIFA investigation revealed that referees from South Africa were bribed into fixing at least 15 exhibition games. The report was quite detailed and a referee was named in being the primary person involved in the scandal—yet, not one person was fired as a result of the investigation. The most basic job of a sports association is to ensure that the basic rules of the game are being followed. With their non-reaction, FIFA is sending the message that as long as people are still showing up to stadiums in droves and tuning in on TVs to lay eyeballs on advertisements, FIFA doesn't really care if the games are actually real or not.

3. The Most Pathetic Match in the History of Football

12   In 1973, Chile played the easiest game of their lives. The other team (the U.S.S.R.) decided to stay home that day. The problem was political in nature. The new Chilean dictator Augusto Pinochet was not only torturing his communist opposition, he was using the World Cup soccer stadium as the venue for their detainment. In response to outrage from the Soviets, FIFA performed a superficial investigation of the arena—a lackadaisical once-over that didn't even include a

full inspection of the entire premises. If the inspectors hadn't "forgotten" to look in the basement, they would have discovered thousands of gagged prisoners being held there at gunpoint.

13   FIFA's limp-wristed investigation didn't satisfy the Russians, so the U.S.S.R team didn't show up to play in the qualifying play-off game. A lack of an opponent, however, didn't stop the Chilean players from running across the field to kick a symbolic goal into the net, thus "winning" the game and a spot in the 1974 World Cup for Chile. Writer Eduardo Galeano called it "the most pathetic match in the history of football." FIFA allowed it to happen.

2. Torture, Rape and Kidnapping Condoned: Argentina's Dirty War and the 1978 World Cup

14   FIFA cooperated with another ruthless dictator once again in 1978, this time in Argentina. The political situation was similar to Chile's in 1974, except the torture inflicted by the government against the socialist opposition was even more extreme. Prisoners were hung on hooks for days or raped with metal rods and then electrocuted, according to an ESPN report. In response to allegations of human rights violations, the Argentinian government came up with this slogan: "We Argentines are both right and human." Every year, more and more shocking details about the Dirty War emerge. Yet, FIFA continues to strike an oblivious pose. In 2013, FIFA president Sepp Blatter had this to say regarding the 1978 World Cup: "I was happy Argentina won. This was kind of a reconciliation of the public, of the people of Argentina, with the system, the political system, the military system at the time."

1. Qatar's Lethal, Inhumane World Cup Construction Project

15   Qatar's desert climate and filthy, dangerous working conditions virtually guarantee that thousands of migrant workers will die during their World Cup construction project. Migrant workers are treated like slaves; they aren't allowed to leave their filthy, sewage-soaked work sites even though construction companies are too cheap or lazy to haul away garbage. Accidents are under-reported and injured laborers are sent home if they are unable to continue working. Amnesty, Human Rights Watch and the International Trade Union Confederation have all confirmed that conditions at the labor camps guarantee that thousands will die during the construction of the World Cup stadiums, but so far FIFA has done nothing to force Qatar to take better care of their migrant labor (or strip them of the World Cup entirely).

Source: Smith, Jake. "Top 10 Scandals That Define FIFA." *TheSportster*, 24 June 2015. www.thesportster.com/soccer/top-10-scandals-that-define-fifas-tarnished-legacy/. Reproduced by permission of Valnet Inc.

09
CHAPTER

WRITING A RESPONSE TO A TEXT

BY THE END OF THIS CHAPTER, YOU WILL BE ABLE TO

- Distinguish among various levels of response.
- Write a claim that indicates agreement or disagreement with a text.
- Develop support for a response to a text by questioning claims, writing from diverse perspectives, and incorporating evidence.
- Create a coherent, unified essay that responds to a text.

▶ WHY IS THIS INFORMATION IMPORTANT?

In the previous chapter, you learned how to evaluate the quality of a persuasive text through a critical analysis of how well a writer presents the argument. This type of evaluation is often described as objective: your goal is to assess the writing fairly rather than respond subjectively to the issue the writer discusses. In this chapter, you will shift from an objective evaluation to a subjective response. In other words, you will now respond directly to the issue(s) a writer presents, explaining why you agree or disagree with the writer's argument(s).

When you write a response to a writer's arguments, you need to apply the critical analysis skills from the previous chapter to your own response writing.

Doing so will not only ensure that your own writing is sound and reliable but also allow you to learn more about how you are influenced by texts and how you react to texts. The more aware you are about your own thinking and the ways in which your brain responds objectively and subjectively, the higher the quality of your thinking. The higher the quality of your thinking, the more meaningful your contribution to the debates on key issues that impact the many communities to which you belong.

▶ Think about It!

In this chapter, you will read and write about issues surrounding health care. Here are some questions to consider as you move through this chapter and as you read the following essay.

1. Why are some people hesitant to discuss health care topics such as treatment for individuals who use illicit drugs or end-of-life options for the terminally ill?

2. What role *does* or *should* government have in making decisions about individuals' health and wellness preferences?

3. What are the concerns regarding the creation of policies that change drug abuse and physician-assisted suicide from a criminal perspective to a public health perspective?

In the following reading, the authors describe what they believe to be positive changes to policies surrounding illicit drugs. They also stress that more needs to be done as Canada is currently experiencing a drug overdose epidemic. While they recognize multiple solutions are required, they emphasize that the starting point for addressing the epidemic is recognizing substance abuse as "a public health issue, not a law enforcement issue" (par. 6). Read this essay and consider these questions:

1. What is the authors' main idea or thesis?

2. What overall pattern of organization do the authors use to make their argument? How do you know?

3. Overall, do you think the authors' claims are sound and reliable? Why or why not?

4. Overall, do you think the authors' evidence is varied, appropriate, and reliable?

5. Do you agree with the authors' thesis? Why or why not? Do your answers to Questions 3 and 4 influence your point of view?

DRUG POLICY SHOULD FOCUS ON HARM REDUCTION

By Katrina Pacey and Donald MacPherson

1   The flurry of new initiatives introduced by the federal government signals a major philosophical shift on drug policy issues.

2   First, Health Minister Jane Philpott approved the Dr. Peter Centre's application to continue operating a supervised injection site in Vancouver, giving hope that similar sites in other parts of the country might also be welcomed by the government. Then, Minister Philpott visited Insite, Vancouver's other

supervised injection facility, which she described as "having a huge impact on people" and "incredibly moving." That was closely followed by news that Health Canada would fast-track the process of changing the status of naloxone to a non-prescription drug, making it easier to access this life-saving medication that's administered during overdoses.

3   Together, these measures not only provide a desperately needed expansion of this country's harm-reduction initiatives that are needed to address the drug overdoses plaguing our communities, they also represent a shift toward a drug policy that puts people's lives first.

4   The Harper government viewed illicit drug use as a criminal justice matter, a perspective that consistently led to punitive and stigmatizing measures being taken against people who use illegal drugs. The new government,[1] on the other hand, has started to shift Canada's drug policy towards a public health and harm reduction approach, which is grounded in scientific evidence and human rights. This shift was further reinforced when, this week,[2] the Canadian delegation to the United Nations Commission on Narcotic Drugs in Vienna articulated the government's commitment to advance evidence-based policies in considering all drug policy initiatives.

5   We should celebrate this stated commitment to evidence-informed policy development and the tentative but important first steps. But we should also recognize that much more needs to be done.

6   Alberta, Ontario and British Columbia have all reported staggering increases in the number of overdoses and overdose-related deaths over the past two years. These increases can be linked directly to a steady rise in the availability of fentanyl, an opiate drug regularly passed off as heroin by street dealers, but dangerously more potent.

7   The statistics lay bare what public health officials have known for some time: we are in the midst of an epidemic. Instead of ignoring this national health crisis as the previous government did, however, the federal Liberals appear to be open to solutions, including ending the proliferation of new laws that punish drug users and create barriers to health services meant to support them.

8   Another promising initiative is a Liberal MP's private member's bill that would grant amnesty to those reporting an overdose. Fear of prosecution has proven to be a barrier for people to call for help when they are with someone who's having an overdose. Only 46 per cent of respondents to a Waterloo Region Crime Prevention Council survey said they would call 911 during an overdose situation. Seconds matter in these cases and saving a life shouldn't be weighed against facing a potential drug possession charge. Granting amnesty to Good Samaritans is a simple answer. The Liberals should move to pass this bill as quickly as possible.

9   Measures like the ones the federal government has introduced to date have their limits, however. They don't stem the tide of dangerous, unregulated drugs that are readily available on our streets, nor do they address the myriad of reasons why people consume drugs in the first place.

10   Larger—and, importantly, more impactful—solutions are still necessary, including reversing dozens of mandatory minimum sentence laws related to drug use and repealing The Respect for Communities Act, which was introduced by the Conservatives as a means of creating barriers to opening supervised drug consumption facilities.

11   Innovative, scientifically proven substitution therapies to address the harms caused by addiction to illicit substances should also be encouraged. This includes clearing the way for physicians to offer heroin-assisted treatment in cases where methadone maintenance treatment has failed.

12   When we recognize that all substance use is a public health issue, not a law enforcement issue, the blueprint for the way forward is to ensure that Canada's drug policies are based on the best available evidence and aligned with the Charter of Rights and Freedoms.

---

[1] Refers to the Liberal party government, elected in October 2015.
[2] A week in March 2016.

Source: Pacey, Katrina, and Donald MacPherson. "Drug Policy Should Focus on Harm Reduction." 16 Mar. 2016. *National Post*, https://nationalpost.com/opinion/pacey-macpherson-drug-policy-should-focus-on-harm-reduction. Accessed 19 August 2018. Reproduced by permission of the authors.

Response Writing: An Overview

The purpose of response writing is to articulate your own point of view on an issue another writer has discussed. Writing a response is different from writing a critical analysis. While a critical analysis requires that you evaluate how the writer presents an issue, a response requires that you agree or disagree with the writer's viewpoints on the issue. Writing a response is also different from writing an academic argument (a genre you will learn about in Chapter 10). In an academic argument, your own claims drive the argument and the texts of other writers are used as support. On the other hand, in a response, you are required to discuss the issue as part of a conversation with one writer's specific text. In other words, the writer's claims—not your own claims—drive the argument. Everything you say about the issue needs to be tied to what the writer has said. Table 9.1 clarifies the differences among a critical analysis, a response, and an academic argument.

TABLE 9.1

THE DIFFERENCES AMONG CRITICAL ANALYSIS, RESPONSE, AND ACADEMIC ARGUMENT

CRITICAL ANALYSIS	RESPONSE	ACADEMIC ARGUMENT
Evaluates how effective a writer's argument is presented	Converses with a text by agreeing or disagreeing with the claims presented in it	Presents the writer's own argument supported by the claims and evidence of other texts

Writing a Response Claim

A response claim tells your reader the degree to which you agree or disagree with the writer's perspective on a specific topic or issue. Your response claim is subjective because it presents your own opinion based on your own background and experiences. It is a perspective held by you for your own reasons. Some people may hold the same perspective for the same or different reasons. Conversely, others may not hold the same perspective at all.

Your response claim must address the writer's claim directly, and it must indicate your agreement or disagreement with it. Table 9.2 provides you with some vocabulary that you can use to express your response to a writer's claim.

TABLE 9.2
TERMINOLOGY TO INDICATE AGREEMENT OR DISAGREEMENT

AGREEMENT		DISAGREEMENT
Agree		Disagree
Correct		Incorrect
Right		Wrong
Sensible		Problematic
Approve		Disapprove
Believe		Do not believe

Your response claim requires, at minimum, a *reference* to the author's claim, as well as your *agreement or disagreement* with that claim. Here is an example:

> I agree that Canadian drug policies should be evidence-based and created from the perspective that "all substance use is a public health issue, not a law enforcement issue" (par. 11).

If you want, you can expand your response claim to clarify your opinion of the author's supporting claims, as well:

> I agree with Pacey and MacPherson that Canadian drug policies should be evidence-based and created from the perspective that "all substance use is a public health issue, not a law enforcement issue" (par. 12). However, I disagree with some of the supporting claims they provide.

▶ Apply the Skill

Vocabulary for Agreement and Disagreement

Write three different thesis statements for an essay that responds to Pacey and MacPherson's thesis in "Drug Policy Should Focus on Harm Reduction." In each statement, circle the words that indicate your agreement or disagreement with Pacey and MacPherson's thesis.

Developing Support for a Response

Developing appropriate support for a response is a critical skill. To achieve a strong response, you will need to consider three criteria as seen in Figure 9.1: questioning claims, writing from diverse perspectives, and strengthening support with evidence.

QUESTIONING CLAIMS

Your first step in developing your response is to identify the supporting claims the writer uses to justify her main claim. In other words, you need to produce a summary of the writer's argument. Once you have identified each of the supporting claims, you need to

FIGURE 9.1
DEVELOPING SUPPORT FOR A RESPONSE

thoroughly question each one to determine whether you agree or disagree as seen in Table 9.3. This questioning will help you develop your explanations for justifying your point of view about the main claim.

TABLE 9.3
QUESTIONS TO ASK ABOUT EACH SUPPORTING CLAIM

TYPE	QUESTIONS
"Who" Questions	Who does the claim involve? Are these the right people? Is anyone being excluded who should not be excluded?
Reasoning Questions	Is the claim one of cause-and-effect, one of comparison, or one of contrast? Is it reasonable? Why or why not?
Assumptions Questions	What underlying assumptions does the claim depend on? Do you actually share those underlying assumptions?

An *assumption* is an implied point of agreement between you and the writer that the writer takes for granted. You learned about recognizing assumptions in Chapter 7. Now, you can put your skills to use in developing support for a response. In order for you to agree with a writer's claim, you must agree with all of its underlying assumptions. In other words, you must agree with all the other sub-claims that the writer's claim implies.

Example of claim:

It is unfair for the police force to use unmarked police vehicles to catch drivers who are speeding.

Underlying assumptions:

Fairness is a desired quality.

Law enforcement should always be distinguishable from other citizens.

Speeding is not a serious offence.

Your decision to agree or disagree with a claim depends on whether you agree or disagree with its assumptions. In fact, when a writer tries to support a claim, the writer's job is to convince you to agree with all of the assumptions of that claim. If there is even just one assumption you disagree with, then you will likely disagree with the claim. For example, if you think that speeding is, in fact, a serious offence, then you would likely disagree that it is unfair to use unmarked police vehicles to catch drivers who are speeding.

You can see, then, how questioning supporting claims and their assumptions can provide you with the evidence and explanations you need when responding to a main claim. Just as you gather your evidence and formulate your explanations before being able to make an evaluative claim for a critical analysis, so too do you need to gather your evidence and formulate your explanations before being able to put into words your subjective response to a text's claims. Answering the questions above will help you do just that, as you can see in the example below.

RESPONDING TO A CLAIM THROUGH QUESTIONING

The following is a step-by-step example of how to articulate and support a response to one of the claims in "Drug Policy Should Focus on Harm Reduction" by Katrina Pacey and Donald MacPherson.

Step 1: Determine the supporting claim you are responding to.

I will respond to the following claim:

> Amnesty should be granted "to those reporting an overdose" because "[f]ear of prosecution has proven to be a barrier for people to call for help when they are with someone who's having an overdose" (Pacey and MacPherson par. 8).

Step 2: Ask questions of the supporting claim and provide answers.

"Who" Questions

- Who does the claim involve?
  - Parties in possession of illegal drugs
  - One of the parties has overdosed
  - One of the parties has not overdosed but needs to figure out how to respond to the party who has overdosed
  - Law enforcement
  - Illegal drug users who are not reporting a friend's overdose because they fear being arrested
  - Health field professionals who would be helping the person who has overdosed if the overdose were reported
- Are these the right people?
  - Yes, these are the right people. The debate is about whether the solution to the drug overdose problem lies with public health or with law enforcement. This particular claim addresses all three parties involved: the drug users, public health, and law enforcement.
- Is anyone being excluded who should not be excluded?
  - No.

Reasoning Questions

- Is the claim one of cause-and-effect, one of comparison, or one of contrast?
  - It's cause-and-effect
  - If amnesty were granted "to those reporting an overdose" (par. 8), then people would be more likely to report the overdose. "Fear of prosecution" would no longer deter them from reporting it (par. 8).
- Is it reasonable? Why or why not?
  - Most people would consider the cause-and-effect relationship logical. If people do not have to fear being arrested for drug possession if they call authorities for help, then they are more likely to call for that help. If someone risks his own freedom by calling for help for a friend, he would be less likely to call for that help.

Assumptions Questions

- What underlying assumptions does the claim indicate? Do you share those underlying assumptions?
  - The claim assumes that drug possession is not as serious as other crimes. I tend to agree because it usually causes harm to only the person possessing the drugs rather than to others.
  - The claim assumes that granting amnesty is acceptable in certain situations. I do not share this assumption. Society has agreed that laws need to be put in place for the protection of the majority, so making exceptions for certain lawbreakers throws the whole legal system into question. Exceptions can lead to loopholes that end up harming society rather than helping it.
  - The claim assumes that those who have a drug overdose are deserving of medical help. I share this assumption as all human beings deserve access to medical help.

Step 3: Use your answers from Step 2 to write your response to the claim. You may or may not want to incorporate *all* of the answers.

I disagree with Pacey and MacPherson that amnesty should be granted to illegal drug users who alert medical professionals when they are with someone who has suffered an overdose (par. 8). While it is likely that more people would report an overdose if they did not fear being arrested, granting amnesty sends the message that it is acceptable to break the law in certain situations. Society has agreed that laws need to be put in place for the protection of the majority, so making exceptions for certain lawbreakers throws the whole legal system into question. Exceptions can lead to loopholes that end up harming society rather than helping it. The better solution is to revisit the law itself to determine if it is doing what it was originally intended to do: protect people from harm. If the laws against drug possession are not reducing harm, then these laws need to change rather than be circumvented. A change in a law sends the message that a society is in agreement that the law no longer protects us from harm. A circumvention of the law, however, sends the message that people can get away with disobeying the rules that society has agreed upon are necessary for its safety.

In the example above, you will note that the writer not only explains why he disagrees with Pacey and MacPherson's claim. He also provides an alternative: revisiting the law rather than granting amnesty for some individuals who break it. A good response writer always offers alternatives, whether he agrees or disagrees with the writer (see Figure 9.2). If the writer is in agreement, the goal is not to reiterate everything the author has said: it is to provide new explanations and evidence that support what the author has said. If the writer is in disagreement, the goal is not to just point out faults: it is to provide an alternative claim that is more sound and reliable.

FIGURE 9.2
WHAT A GOOD RESPONSE DOES

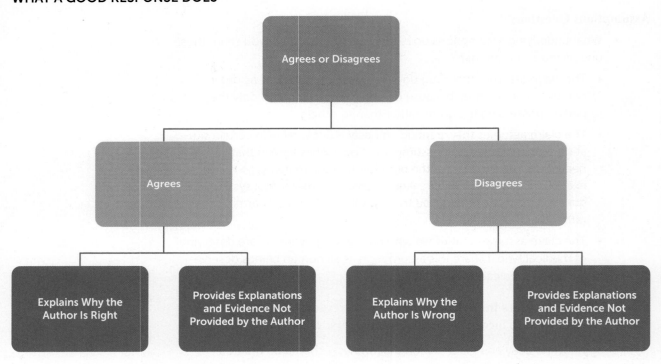

▶ Apply the Skill

Evaluating a Response

1. Evaluate the response paragraph example in the section "Responding to a Claim through Questioning."

2. In your evaluation, focus on the support for the writer's claim. Is the writer convincing? Does he justify his response well?

3. The writer of the response paragraph does not provide concrete evidence to support the claim. Instead, the writer relies on reasoning alone. Is a lack of evidence in this context problematic? Why or why not?

4. Revise the response paragraph in the example above by adding evidence to support the claim.

5. Write your own response paragraph to the claim about granting amnesty for someone who reports an overdose. You can choose to either agree or disagree with this claim. If you choose to disagree, use reasoning that is different from the reasoning used in the example above. When you are done, do the following:

   - Circle the word(s) in your response paragraph that indicate your agreement or disagreement with the claim.

   - Draw a box around any evidence you use to support your point of view.

   - Underline the explanations that connect your evidence to your claim.

   - Draw a wavy line under any reasoning that you use that does not require specific evidence.

WRITING FROM DIVERSE PERSPECTIVES

To maintain momentum in your response to a text and to demonstrate a high level of critical thinking, you should consider the responses and accompanying reasoning you provide from diverse perspectives (see Figure 9.3). In the sample response paragraph above, the writer's reasoning focused on the relationship between the claim and society. He disagreed with the claim because of the negative implications it has for the way that society constructs and enforces the laws that protect society. This is not the only approach the writer could have taken. Instead, the writer could have chosen to focus on personal implications of the claim. In other words, he could have explained the negative impact that granting amnesty for certain lawbreakers would have on his own life or that of his family.

FIGURE 9.3
MULTIPLE PERSPECTIVES TO CONSIDER FOR A RESPONSE

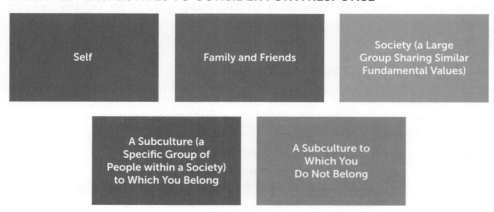

Responding to claims from diverse perspectives has the potential for changing one's response to a claim. Think once again about the amnesty argument. Let's say that from the perspective of society, the writer disagrees with "grant[ing] amnesty to those reporting an overdose" (par. 8) because of its negative implications on law and order. However, let's say that the writer had a friend or family member who passed away from a drug overdose because the people who were with that friend or family member were too afraid to call for help. They thought they would be arrested. This personal experience may influence the writer to respond differently to the claim. From this perspective, the writer may choose to actually agree with it, reasoning that the well-being of a person should not be put at risk because of a certain law. This example helps you see how viewing a claim from different perspectives can result in different responses, which is why addressing multiple perspectives throughout a response demonstrates a higher level of critical thinking.

▶ Apply the Skill

Responding from Multiple Perspectives

Select a supporting claim from "Drug policy Should Focus on Harm Reduction" by Katrina Pacey and Donald MacPherson. Write three different response paragraphs for this claim: one that uses support focusing on yourself or your family and friends, one that uses support focusing on society at large, and one that uses support focusing on a specific subculture. Evaluate the quality of your response paragraphs. Which of the three paragraphs presents the strongest response? Why do you think this paragraph is the strongest?

STRENGTHENING SUPPORT WITH EVIDENCE

As you saw in the example response paragraph from earlier in this section, a response can be quite effective with solid reasoning strategies that are not actually supported by evidence. That being said, evidence always strengthens a response because it helps readers clarify or visualize the writer's reasoning, and it enhances the writer's credibility.

In the previous chapter, you learned that strong evidence is varied, appropriate, and reliable. You need to keep this in mind as you search for and incorporate your own evidence to support your response. The search for evidence can be challenging, but if you use Table 9.4 to help you, you should be able to find the varied, appropriate, and reliable evidence you need. Notice how the table is organized by the perspectives you just learned about.

TABLE 9.4
FINDING EVIDENCE TO SUPPORT YOUR RESPONSE

PERSPECTIVE	WHERE TO LOOK FOR THE EVIDENCE
Self, family, or friend	Think about your lifestyle, your demographic, your career, etc. Interview family members or friends.
Society	Read newspapers or watch the news online or on TV. Read magazine or journal articles. Interview community or governmental leaders.
Subculture	Read publications written by members of the subculture. Interview prominent members of the subculture. Survey people from the subculture. Read newspapers or watch the news online or on TV. Be familiar with certain texts or artefacts that represent the subculture.

Finding Evidence to Support Your Response

Write a response paragraph to Pacey and MacPherson's claim that safe injection facilities "are needed to address the drug overdoses plaguing our communities" (par. 3). Use Table 9.4 to help gather evidence that you can include in your response paragraph.

Review

Responding to Claims

Answer the following review questions in paragraph form or generate ideas to contribute to a group or class discussion.

1. How is a response different from both a critical analysis and an academic argument?
2. What is a response claim and what must it include?
3. What questions should you ask about the supporting claims of a main claim? What is the purpose of asking such questions?
4. What is an assumption? Why is it important in response writing?
5. What are the different perspectives from which you can respond to a text?

Focus on Structure and Organization: Writing a Response Essay

Throughout this chapter, you have been writing response paragraphs. Most responses to texts, however, are much more detailed and come in the form of an essay. A typical response essay has four components: introduction, abstract, response paragraphs, and conclusion. Before putting these components together, however, you need to select an approach for your response.

Approaches: Macro Level or Micro Level

As with critical analysis, there are two ways to approach a response: at a macro level and at a micro level. At the macro level, you respond to the writer's central claim—i.e., the thesis. In doing so, you address some of the supporting claims as well, thus engaging in a broad discussion of the issue. On the other hand, at the micro level, you focus on only *one* of the writer's supporting claims. In doing so, you discuss a particular component of the issue rather than engaging in a more holistic discussion of the issue. The decision to engage in a macro response versus a micro one will come down to your purpose and audience for writing.

► **Apply the Skill**

Distinguishing between Micro and Macro Responses

Each of the following sentences is a thesis statement for an essay responding to the two readings in this chapter: "Drug Policy Should Focus on Harm Reduction" and "Self-Checkout." Identify whether the thesis statement indicates a macro-response essay (MAC) or a micro-response essay (MIC).

_____ 1. Pacey and MacPherson are absolutely right that drug abuse should be perceived as an issue of public health rather than as an issue of criminal justice.

_____ 2. Trying to grant amnesty for certain individuals who break the law is a very slippery slope.

_____ 3. I agree with Sarah Kerr that we will all live more fulfilling lives if we start talking about the choices we have at the end of them (Wiart par. 9).

_____ 4. Wiart is right to argue that discussing our end-of-life choices is important.

_____ 5. I disagree with Wiart that "[m]ortality for millennials is conceptually different from what it has been for our elders" (par. 7).

Approaches: Text-Centred or Writer-Centred

In addition to selecting a macro level or a micro level for your response, you need to decide whether you will use a *text-centred* or *writer-centred* approach (see Figure 9.4). A text-centred approach works best at the macro level, particularly if the text you are responding to is short. In a text-centred approach at the macro level, you work hand-in-hand with the text as you go about responding to the writer's thesis. You structure your response around the writer's supporting claims. These supporting claims become the organizing principle for your response. They drive your own claims and support. Essentially, you are engaging in a back-and-forth conversation with the writer, but you are spending more time on your side of the conversation as you justify your own point of view with strong evidence and clear explanations.

A writer-centred approach works well at either the macro level or the micro level. In a writer-centred approach at the macro level, you still work closely with the text, but rather than using the text's supporting claims as the conversational starting point for each of your paragraphs or sections, you use your own claims. This type of structure does not resemble a back-and-forth conversation. Instead, it resembles a debate structure whereby you focus on your own perspective on the issue, reminding the reader of the points with which you agree or disagree with your opponent whenever and wherever you see fit. Your claims, rather than the writer's claims, structure the response. You use the text's thesis as a springboard for your response and you continually reference the text throughout your essay, but you organize your essay by your own claims rather than by the text's claims.

FIGURE 9.4
TEXT-CENTRED VERSUS WRITER-CENTRED RESPONSE

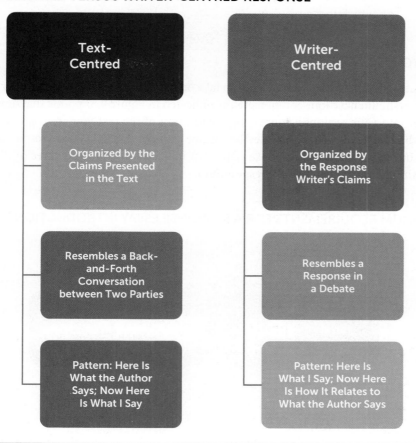

▶ Apply the Skill

Distinguishing between Text-Centred and Writer-Centred Responses

Read each of the following statements, all of which are responses to "Drug Policy Should Focus on Harm Reduction." Identify whether the statements signal a text-centred (TC) or writer-centred (WC) response.

_____ 1. The second claim I strongly disagree with is granting amnesty to illegal drug users who alert medical professionals when they are with someone who has suffered an overdose (Pacey and MacPherson par. 8).

_____ 2. I agree with much of what Pacey and MacPherson say, but I do not think they have framed the issue appropriately.

_____ 3. I understand where Pacey and MacPherson are coming from, but here is my take on the issue.

_____ 4. Pacey and MacPherson argue that Health Canada's intention to "fast-track the process of changing the status of naloxone to a non-prescription drug" (par. 2) is a good thing. I disagree. As soon as a non-prescription drug that counteracts the negative side effects of a dangerous, illicit drug is made readily available, the use of the illicit drug will skyrocket.

_____ 5. Another area that Pacey and MacPherson avoid exploring is the impact that removing sentencing for drug offenders would have on the communities in which these offenders live.

Introduction

The introduction to a response essay can take on many forms. At minimum, your introduction should have four components, as indicated in Figure 9.5: a hook that draws the reader into your response; some contextualization of the text you are responding to, including the text's writer and title; the specific claim of the text you are responding to; and your thesis (i.e., your response claim that indicates whether you agree or disagree with the claim to which you are responding).

FIGURE 9.5
MINIMUM REQUIREMENTS FOR A RESPONSE ESSAY INTRODUCTION

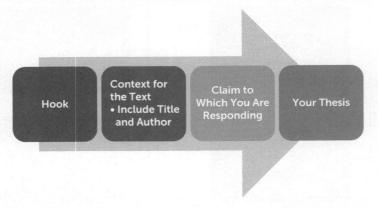

There are a variety of concrete strategies for writing an effective hook and thesis statement for introductions to response essays.

THE HOOK

A good hook captures the attention of your readers by giving them a taste of the topic at hand—without actually revealing the specifics of your response. Table 9.5 provides a review of some of the strategies for hooks you learned in Chapter 2, in addition to some new strategies. It also provides an example of those strategies at work from the various articles in this textbook.

TABLE 9.5
STRATEGIES FOR HOOKS

STRATEGY	EXAMPLE
Impactful Fact A statistic or fact relevant to the topic that the audience will find shocking, intriguing, or surprising	"Becoming an air traffic controller is one of the country's most gruelling career paths: an ordeal of interviews, personality assessments, math exams and pattern-recognition tests that take place over months." (From "One Man's Fight to Help Jets Fly—Despite Mental Illness" by Charlie Gillis [in Chapter 4 of this text].)
Story A story relevant to the topic that is suspenseful or thought provoking	"On a clear morning in early May, Brian Lathrop, a senior engineer for Volkswagen's Electronics Research Laboratory, was in the driver's seat of a Tesla Model S as it travelled along a stretch of road near Blacksburg, Virginia, when the car began to drift from its lane." (From "Learning to Trust a Self-Driving Car" by Simon Parkin Gillis [in Chapter 4 of this text].)

(Continued)

STRATEGY	EXAMPLE
Question A question relevant to the topic that incites the reader to start thinking about an issue or that ends up being addressed by the author throughout the essay	"What if PTSD is located not in the trauma of combat, but in the transition back to modern life?" (From the subhead of "Homecoming Trauma: What Do We Really Know about PTSD?" by Brian Bethune [in Chapter 2 of this text].)
Startling Statement An unexpected, controversial, or thought-provoking perspective relevant to the topic	"The purpose and meaning of education is widely misunderstood and wrongly presented." (From "An A+ Student Regrets His Grades" by Afraj Gill [in Chapter 1 of this text].)
Advice or Warning A recommendation to think or act in a certain way; the recommendation is relevant to the topic	"You hear a lot of talk about how universities and teachers are expensive dinosaurs and how the future of teaching lies online. Don't believe a word of it." (From "There's No Online Substitute for a Real University Classroom" by Clifford Orwin [in Chapter 1 of this text].)
Quotation Topic-related testimony from an expert or non-expert	"A student who is a 'New Canadian' was talking one day about the wonders of Canada. *'You know,'* he said, *'Canada is such a rich country. It has education, housing, lots of food in the stores and goods to buy. But the one thing that Canada is very short of is—TIME.'* (From "Cultural Messages about Time" by Joan Fleet and Denise Reaume [in Chapter 2 of this text].)
Interesting Comparison An unexpected, controversial, or thought-provoking comparison of two people, events, etc.	"TORONTO—The fatal shooting of teenager Michael Brown by a police officer in Ferguson, Missouri happened 1,000 kilometres from, and a year after, teenager Sammy Yatim was fatally shot by an officer in Toronto." (From "What Canadian Police Are Doing So Ferguson Doesn't Happen Here" by Erika Tucker [in Chapter 3 of this text].)

▶ Apply the Skill

Identifying Strategies for Hooks

Each of the following sentences is a hook from articles in this textbook. Identify which of the strategies from Table 9.5 the author is employing.

1. "The local public ice rink and the non-profit minor hockey association are fast becoming relics." (From "Corporate Hockey's Home-Ice Advantage: How Privatization and Professionalization Are Remaking the Sport I Love" by Strefan Decosse [in Chapter 8 of this text].)

   Hook Strategy:

2. "Given FIFA's well-known culture of corruption and ethical problems, it's almost a miracle that Sepp Blatter was finally convinced to resign in June of 2015." (From "Top 10 Scandals That Define FIFA's Tarnished Legacy" by Jake Smith [in Chapter 8 of this text].)

   Hook Strategy:

3. "We were all in our early twenties, all healthy, living in the primes of our lives. But when we gathered that night, the discussion was focused on one thing: how we wanted to die." (From "Self-Checkout" by Nikki Wiart [in this chapter]).

   Hook Strategy:

4. "Virtual reality appears poised to become at least as widespread, sophisticated, powerful and subversive as any other form of transformative media—television, video games or the Internet." (From "Should Virtual Reality Be More Regulated than Video Games?" by Doug Bierend).

   Hook Strategy:

THE THESIS

When writing a thesis to articulate your response to your chosen claim, you should indicate your response to both the claim and its sub-claims. If you are writing a macro response, this would mean commenting on both the writer's thesis and the main ideas the writer uses to support this thesis. If you are writing a micro response, this would mean commenting on both the main claim you are responding to and the other claims that support it. Figure 9.6 helps you visualize the four perspectives you can have when responding to a text. Figure 9.7 then provides thesis statement suggestions corresponding to each of these perspectives.

FIGURE 9.6
FOUR PERSPECTIVES FOR A RESPONSE TO A TEXT

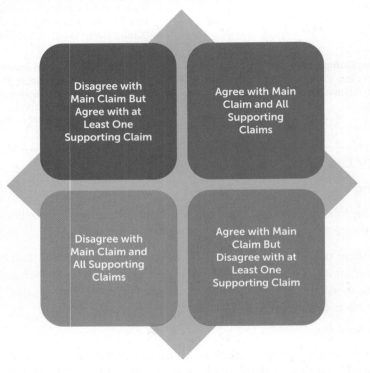

▶ Apply the Skill

Writing Thesis Statements for Response Essays

For each reading in this chapter, write four different thesis statements for macro-response essays that correspond with the four perspectives for a response described in Figure 9.6. Use the templates in Figure 9.7 to help create your eight thesis statements.

Abstract

To provide context for your response, you should provide an abstract of the supporting claims that you will be responding to throughout your essay (see Figure 9.8). In a text-centred approach, the abstract is typically scattered throughout the essay; the supporting claims you are responding to usually appear in the topic sentences for

FIGURE 9.7
POTENTIAL THESIS STATEMENTS FOR A RESPONSE TO A TEXT

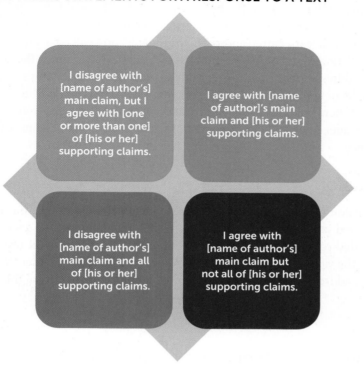

each of the response paragraphs (this is known as the point-by-point method that you encountered in Chapters 3 and 8). This placement is logical in a text-focused approach since the text's claims organize and drive your response. In a writer-centred approach, on the other hand, the abstract is typically written as a single paragraph directly after the introduction (this is known as the block method that you encountered in Chapters 3 and 8). This placement allows the rest of the paragraphs to be more flexible in their focus, which helps you organize the paragraphs according to your own claims.

FIGURE 9.8
OPTIONS FOR PLACEMENT OF ABSTRACT

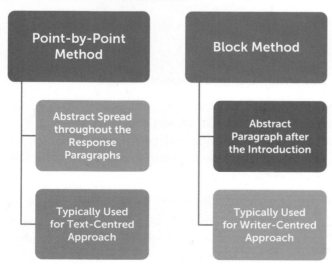

Response Paragraphs

The response paragraphs form the body of your essay. The goal is to carefully connect all your response paragraphs together to form a coherent essay that responds to the text. If you are taking a text-centred approach, the organization will typically depend on the text's organization: you should try to address each supporting claim in the same order in which it is addressed in the text and in your abstract. If you are taking a writer-centred approach, the organization will depend on your own claims and how they build upon one another. Remember to use the unity and coherence strategies from Chapter 2 to help your reader understand the connections among all of your claims, explanations, and evidence.

Conclusion

The conclusion of a response essay, like the introduction, can take on many forms as you learned in Chapter 2 (see also Figure 9.9). That being said, a good conclusion should remind your reader of your overall response to the claims in the text and should emphasize the value of your response. How does your response further the discussion of the issue addressed in the article? How does it contribute to critical thinking in the topic area?

FIGURE 9.9

WHAT YOUR RESPONSE CONCLUSION SHOULD DO

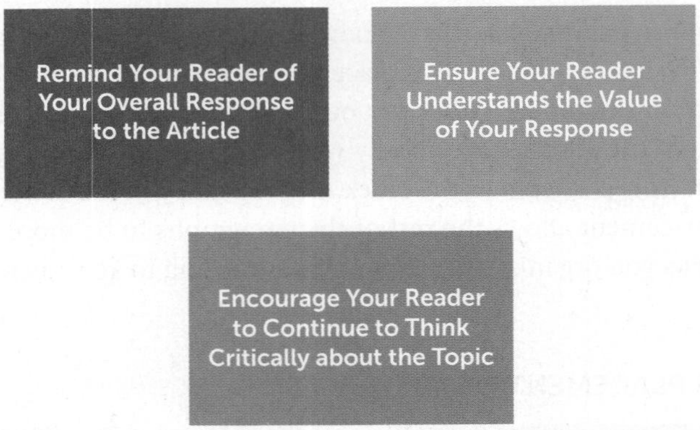

Remind Your Reader of Your Overall Response to the Article

Ensure Your Reader Understands the Value of Your Response

Encourage Your Reader to Continue to Think Critically about the Topic

▶ Apply the Skill

Macro Text- and Writer-Centred Response Essays

Below are two short essays, both of which respond to "Drug Policy Should Focus on Harm Reduction" by Katrina Pacey and Donald MacPherson. The first response essay is done at a macro level, using a text-centred approach. The second response essay is done at a macro level, using a writer-centred approach. Read both essays, and then answer the questions that follow.

Example 1: Macro Text-Centred Response Essay

Canada saw a surge in the number of deaths resulting from drug overdose in 2016. In "Drug Policy Should Focus on Harm Reduction," authors Katrina Pacey and Donald MacPherson argue that the way to reduce bodily harm caused by overdosing on illegal substances is to create evidence-based policies that position substance use as "a public health issue, not a law enforcement issue" (par. 12). I agree that an evidence-based approach to health care is necessary to improve the well-being of those who use illicit drugs. Some of Pacey and MacPherson's supporting claims to support this approach, however, are highly problematic.

According to Pacey and MacPherson, one policy that needs to be put in place to reduce the harmful effects of illegal drugs is granting amnesty to illegal drug users who alert medical professionals when they are with someone who has suffered an overdose (par. 8). While it is likely that more people would report an overdose if they did not fear being arrested, granting amnesty sends the message that it is acceptable to break the law in certain situations. Society has agreed that laws need to be put in place for the protection of the majority, so making exceptions for certain lawbreakers throws the whole legal system into question. Exceptions can lead to loopholes that end up harming society rather than helping it. The better solution is to revisit the law itself to determine if it is doing what it was originally intended to do: protect people from harm. If the laws against drug possession are not reducing harm, then these laws need to change rather than be circumvented. A change in a law sends the message that a society is in agreement that the law no longer protects us from harm. A circumvention of the law, however, sends the message that people can get away with disobeying the rules that society has agreed upon are necessary for its safety.

I also think Pacey and MacPherson make a mistake when commending Health Canada's intention to "fast-track the process of changing the status of naloxone to a non-prescription drug" (par. 2). Naloxone is certainly proven to "stop or reverse the effects of an opioid overdose" (Health Canada) and is thus an important step to combating the opioid crisis. However, there are two problems with this solution. One problem that Pacey and MacPherson do express is that naloxone does not actually solve the problem of addiction—it solves the problem of potentially dying from an opioid overdose (par. 8). A problem that they do not consider, however, is that making the drug easily accessible can potentially encourage opioid use rather than discourage it. If people know that they can take opioids more safely, they will likely be encouraged to do so. It is the same argument that those who oppose injection sites make: normalizing the behaviour leads to the acceptance and perpetuation of it.

Overall, Pacey and MacPherson are correct in arguing "that all substance use is a public health issue" and that the way to address it is with evidence-based solutions (par. 12). If Canada continues down the path of simply charging and incarcerating those suffering from substance abuse problems, then those individuals will be taken down an even darker path that could exacerbate their health problems rather than treat them. More investment needs to be made in counselling these individuals to discover the sources of their addiction. As Pacey and MacPherson argue, the best way to improve the dire situation of drug overdose is to discover and address the root causes. Rather than focusing on providing easier access to life-saving drugs and granting amnesty for those helping their friends while breaking the law in the process, we all need to find ways to connect substance abusers with the people in their communities who can genuinely help them overcome—rather than "deal with"—their addiction.

Works Cited

Health Canada. "Notice—Availability of Naloxone Hydrochloride Nasal Spray (NARCAN®) in Canada." *Health Canada*, 6 July 2016, www.hc-sc.gc.ca/dhp-mps/prodpharma/activit/announce-annonce/notice-avis-nasal-eng.php.

Pacey, Katrina, and Donald MacPherson. "Drug Policy Should Focus on Harm Reduction." *National Post*, 16 March 2016, news.nationalpost.com/full-comment/pacey-macpherson-drug-policy-should-focus-on-harm-reduction.

Example 2: Macro Writer-Centred Response Essay

The line between the health-care system and the legal system can be blurry when it comes to the topic of illegal drugs. In "Drug Policy Should Focus on Harm Reduction," Katrina Pacey and Donald MacPherson argue that the best way to combat the rise in deaths resulting from drug overdose is to create more policies that focus on harm reduction, which can be done only if the drug overdose problem is viewed as a medical rather than criminal issue (par. 11). While I agree with Pacey and MacPherson that substance abuse is a health-care issue, I still think substance abuse lies in the middle of the health-care and legal spectrum. Perhaps Pacey and MacPherson oversimplify the issue.

The purpose of laws against the use of illegal drugs is to keep society safe. Those who are arrested for possession of illicit drugs are incarcerated not only as a deterrent for themselves but also as a deterrent for others who are thinking about substance abuse. The goals of these laws are to discourage people from using illicit drugs that can have harmful effects on themselves or on others. Pacey and MacPherson are right that these laws are "punitive and stigmatizing" for drug users (par. 4), but that is not necessarily a bad thing. It's the punitive and stigmatizing element that will discourage others from following that same path. The law—and society as a whole—does not give those involved in fatal drunk driving incidents a free pass to avoid stigmatizing the driver who may have an alcohol addiction, so why should such a thing be applied to those who use drugs illegally?

Illicit drug use should not be treated as its own issue that is granted exemptions from certain laws. Instead, it should be treated as any other complex issue of addiction; the legal system and the health-care system need to work together for the safety of both the addict and the individuals the addict encounters. Many people who suffer from addiction can be dangerous to those around them, which is why incarceration is unfortunately necessary. Beyond protecting the rest of society, though, incarceration is also a deterrent that encourages drug abusers to get clean. Once drug abusers have the desire to get clean, the health-care system needs to step in to actually help these individuals overcome their addictions. That is why these two systems—legal and health-care—work better hand-in-hand rather than in isolation from each other. Pacey and MacPherson are trying to draw a distinct line between "public health" and "law enforcement" (par. 12), but this kind of distinction would result in more problems than it would solve.

The public health system on its own does not offer the same kind of deterrent that law enforcement offers, while law enforcement does not actually address the addiction problem, which is where the public health system needs to step in.

In the end, it is obvious that drug abuse is a health issue, but Pacey and MacPherson are wrong to try to completely isolate it from the legal system. If Canada does not provide a deterrent for drug abuse, then more and more people will start to use illicit substances at dangerous levels. The solution is to investigate how the legal system and health-care system can work together to target both the causes and consequences of substance abuse. Pacey and MacPherson state, "the blueprint for the way forward is to ensure that Canada's drug policies are based on the best available evidence and aligned with the Charter of Rights and Freedoms" (par. 12). I completely agree, but with the added caveat that the legal system is a critical source of "available evidence" and is a necessary entity for ensuring that policies are "aligned with the Charter of Rights and Freedoms" (par. 12).

Work Cited

Pacey, Katrina, and Donald MacPherson. "Drug Policy Should Focus on Harm Reduction." *National Post*, 16 March 2016, news.nationalpost.com/full-comment/pacey-macpherson-drug-policy-should-focus-on-harm-reduction.

Questions

1. A good title for a response essay highlights the issue being discussed, the writer's opinion on the issue, and the specific text the writer is responding to. What title would you assign to Example 1? What title would you assign to Example 2? Could you assign the same title to both? Why or why not?

2. In both examples, underline the sentences that indicate the writers' responses to Pacey and MacPherson's thesis statement. Draw a box around the part of the writers' thesis statements that indicates their response to Pacey and MacPherson's supporting claims. Is the response to the supporting claims explicit in Example 1? What about Example 2?

3. Circle all of the words in the essays that indicate agreement or disagreement with Pacey and MacPherson.

4. Evaluate the two essays. Do they include all the components of a response essay? Are the writers convincing? Have the writers demonstrated sound and reliable claims? Do the writers provide evidence that is varied, appropriate, and reliable? Do the writers have conclusions that remind the reader of the overall response to the article, ensure the reader understands the value of the response, and encourage the reader to think critically about the topic?

5. What would you do to improve the essays? Describe three substantive changes you would make to each essay and explain why you would make them.

Review

Response Essays

Answer the following review questions in paragraph form or generate ideas to contribute to a group or class discussion.

1. What is the difference between a macro-level approach in response writing and a micro-level approach?
2. What is the difference between a text-centred response essay and a writer-centred response essay?
3. What are the four components of a response essay? Describe the function of each one.
4. What subcomponents form the introduction of a response essay?
5. What are some strategies for writing the hook of a response essay?
6. What are the four perspectives for responding to a text? How do they impact the thesis statement for the response?
7. What are the two methods for writing the abstract of a response essay, and how do these methods intersect with the text-centred and writer-centred structures?
8. What three goals should the conclusion of a response essay achieve?

▶ Did You Know?

SENTENCE VARIETY

You may have heard the word *flow* used to describe a piece of writing. A text that flows is one that sounds good to the reader's ear: it has a rhythm that helps the reader digest the text with ease. This rhythm is the result of sentence variety. You may also have heard the words *choppy* or *longwinded* used to describe a piece of writing. These words refer to a text that lacks flow: the sentences are either all too short (choppy) or all too long (longwinded).

Because flow is so important for a reader's ability to process information and to continue to be engaged in a text, you need to know how to achieve sentence variety in your writing, both in terms of length and sentence structure. Table 9.6 provides strategies for achieving this variety.

TABLE 9.6
STRATEGIES FOR ACHIEVING FLOW-THROUGH SENTENCE VARIETY

STRATEGY	EXPLANATION
Use different sentence lengths.	Use a combination of short, medium, and long sentences throughout your piece of writing; avoid using too many sentences of one specific length in a row (e.g., five short sentences in a row).
Use different sentence types.	In earlier chapters, you learned about the four sentence types: simple, compound, complex, and compound-complex. Your piece of writing should include a combination of these four sentence types.

(Continued)

STRATEGY	EXPLANATION
Use different clause or phrase orders.	In earlier chapters, you learned about clauses and phrases. You also learned that adverb clauses can move to different places in a sentence. Try to achieve a variety of placements for clauses and phrases. For example, if you put a dependent adverb clause at the beginning of one sentence, try to put it in the middle or end of a subsequent sentence.
Vary the starts and ends of your sentences.	Avoid starting or ending consecutive sentences with the same word or phrase.

▶ Apply the Skill

Strategies for Achieving Flow-Through Sentence Variety

1. The paragraph below is from "Self-Checkout" by Nikki Wiart, which is the reading at the end of this chapter. Read the paragraph (par. 4) and then describe the strategies Wiart has used to achieve sentence variety.

When my guests arrived at 7 pm, we sat on the floor around my living room table, snacking on crackers and cheese, talking about our lives: Mark and Selena mentioned their upcoming wedding; Sarah was uncertain about her career and where her life was headed; Dan talked about a new relationship; Kevin had worked a long day and was asleep on the couch. Normally death wouldn't be on any of our minds, and it wasn't an easy topic to broach. So I broke the ice. "Do you believe in reincarnation?" I asked.

Source: Wiart, 2016.

2. Read the paragraph below that responds to Wiart's idea that "we all need to embrace the simultaneous discomfort and luxury of talking about our [end-of-life] preferences with our loved ones" (par. 11). Explain the ways in which the paragraph lacks sentence variety. Then, rewrite the paragraph, maintaining the content but altering the sentence variety. When you are done, justify the changes you made.

I agree with Wiart that we should speak openly with our friends and family about our end-of-life choices. It is important. Everyone agrees on "bodily" autonomy in life (par. 6). Everyone should agree on bodily autonomy in death. "Bodily autonomy" is lifelong, from birth to death (par. 6). If people are in pain, they should get to end their life how and when they want to. They should talk to their families. They need to help their families understand their choices. These families must accept their decision. Families are for support. Death will be more comforting when everyone knows that the person has died as per his or her own wishes. It will make the grieving process easier.

▶ Questions for Writing and Discussion

1. Wiart uses narrative to make her argument about the importance of discussing end-of-life choices. Do you think this is an effective rhetorical (i.e., persuasive) strategy?

2. Wiart implies that discussing our wishes for our own deaths is more important than thinking about death from a religious perspective (par. 6). Do you agree with this claim? Why or why not?

3. Wiart claims the following:

> [W]e were born into a world guaranteeing legal access to safe abortions; we've witnessed the legalization of same-sex marriage and the increasing acceptance of trans individuals. We live our lives by the mindset "my body, my choice," and see no reason why our deaths should be any different. (par. 6)

These statements refer specifically to her and her friends, who are all Canadian.

a. What are all the assumptions Wiart makes in this claim?

b. Do you agree or disagree with this claim?

c. Some other countries in the world have not provided "legal access to safe abortions' (par. 6), have not experienced the "legalization of same-sex marriage" (par. 6), and have not seen an "increasing acceptance of trans individuals" (par. 6). How might Wiart's claim here be received in countries other than Canada? How might her overall argument about the need to discuss end-of-life choices be perceived outside Canada?

4. Respond to one of the following writing prompts:

a. What does Wiart mean by "[t]he sanitization of death" (par. 7)? Do you agree that this "sanitization" has resulted in us talking about death less (par. 7)? Do you agree that millennials think about death differently from their parents and grandparents (par. 7)?

   OR

b. Wiart describes the ability to discuss one's end-of-life choices as a "simultaneous discomfort and luxury" (par. 11). Do you agree that discussing end-of-life choices is both a "discomfort" and a "luxury"?

5. Write a response essay to "Self-Checkout." Use some of your answers to the previous questions to help you generate content. In addition, think carefully about whether you want to take a macro- or micro-level approach and whether you want to structure the essay as text-centred or writer-centred. When you are done, perform a critical analysis of your own essay to ensure it is effective.

6. In "Drug Policy Should Focus on Harm Reduction," Pacey and MacPherson grapple with how substance abuse can be viewed from either a health-care or criminal justice perspective. "Self-Checkout" also focuses on a sensitive issue that has been a tug-of-war between the health-care system and the legal system: people's ability to choose the how and when of their own deaths. Write an essay that argues whether end-of-life choices should be positioned as a health issue, a criminal justice issue, both, or neither. When you are done, perform a critical analysis of your own essay to ensure it is effective.

SELF-CHECKOUT

With Canada set to enact new right-to-death legislation, Nikki Wiart argues that we all need to get comfortable talking about end-of-life choices.

By Nikki Wiart

1   APRIL 13, 2016—Last November, I invited six friends to my Ottawa home for a dinner party. On the menu was chicken that had been clucking only months earlier. It was then fattened, killed, scalded, gutted, plucked, frozen, thawed, seasoned, cooked and eaten. There was also red wine that, not long ago, thrived as purple, juicy grapes. They were subsequently picked, squished, strained, aged, filtered, bottled, bought, sold, uncorked and drank.

2   We were all in our early twenties, all healthy, living in the primes of our lives. But when we gathered that night, the discussion was focused on one thing: how we wanted to die.

3   I was taught that death—like sex, religion and politics—is not proper dinner-table conversation. But after reading about events such as Death Cafe and Death Over Dinner, both of which bring people together over food and drinks to talk about mortality and end-of-life choices, I was intrigued, and knew that my friends would open up to the idea as well.

4   When my guests arrived at 7 pm, we sat on the floor around my living room table, snacking on crackers and cheese, talking about our lives: Mark and Selena mentioned their upcoming wedding; Sarah was uncertain about her career and where her life was headed; Dan talked about a new relationship; Kevin had worked a long day and was asleep on the couch. Normally death wouldn't be on any of our minds, and it wasn't an easy topic to broach. So I broke the ice. "Do you believe in reincarnation?" I asked.

5   We all had answers for how we'd like to be reincarnated: a tree, an eagle, a monkey. But, as it turned out, our choices didn't much matter; for the most part, we all shared the belief that nothing follows death except oblivion. This is in line with the prevailing beliefs of our generation—an Angus Reid poll in early 2015 found that 44 percent of Canadians between eighteen and thirty-four neither embraced nor rejected religion and 28 percent rejected it completely.

6   With the religious talk out of the way, we settled into discussing the more important question: how we wanted our own personal deaths to occur. We all have faith in bodily autonomy and quality of life: we were born into a world guaranteeing legal access to safe abortions; we've witnessed the legalization of same-sex marriage and the increasing acceptance of trans individuals. We live our lives by the mindset "my body, my choice," and see no reason why our deaths should be any different.

7   In Western countries, mostly safe, mostly free from violence, we typically associate death with illness and age. Mortality for millennials is conceptually different from what it has been for our elders: many of our grandparents survived a brutal war, one that killed friends and family members. Many of our mothers and fathers were raised by these survivors, and they were the ones ducking and covering during the subsequent Cold War, thinking about all the ways to survive a seemingly unavoidable nuclear armageddon. When morticians promised a kind of death that appeared clean and hands-free—one disguised in make-up,

expensive suits, limousines, formaldehyde and everything-happens-for-a-reason proverbs—our elders found it appealing. The sanitization of death removed it not just from the home, but from our social dialogue. Death became easy to forget—it was something that would happen someday, but that someday was always in the future. We learned to ignore death until it was suddenly and unavoidably upon us.

8   As of 2012, 86 percent of Canadians had not heard of advanced-care planning or made plans in the event they become legally incapable of directing their own healthcare wishes. Less than half of those had discussed their wishes with friends or families, and fewer than one in ten had discussed them with a healthcare provider. But discussing end-of-life care isn't just about the question of autonomy. Sarah Kerr, a death midwife in Calgary, says it's "an exercise of bringing death into awareness."

9   My own desire to confront death came thanks to Kerr, who first introduced me to the concept of the death dinner. Kerr helped facilitate the home death of one of my family members, giving us the chance to be part of the process by communicating our grief through a series of rituals including traditional sage smudging and rattling. Over the past three years, Kerr says she's seen the conversation around death grow. For her, this shift has been powered by baby boomers, who comprise the vast majority of people seeking her services. "The move to a new cultural pattern around dying is being driven by people who have death in their face," Kerr says. "Millennials have a lot to offer if they can hopscotch a little bit and not wait until they're old and grey and their friends are dying." By talking about death well before it comes, she says, it can become a companion, or a teacher, making life itself more vibrant.

10   Inviting my friends over for dinner wasn't just about sharing our wishes with one another. It was a practice run, something to offer us the courage to approach our loved ones not with an "if" but with a "when." To find this courage, we'd need to embrace our generation's oh-so-typical urge to share—specifically, to share our fears. Sarah went first. "I think we fear dying. Not death," she said. Most of us agreed: we feared the pain and the unknown that follows. We feared the grief we would inflict on our families. We feared dying young and missing out on our potential. But then the conversation started to shift, and we spoke of what we wanted out of our deaths and the decisions we would like to make before that final moment came. We all wanted to leave some kind of legacy beyond an abandoned Facebook profile. We talked about donating our organs, from our hearts to our skin to our eyes; some mentioned forgoing a traditional burial or cremation for something greener, like Dan, who said he wanted to be buried under a tree, not a tombstone—something living that would provide for future generations.

11   By 2031, all of the baby boomers will have crossed into seniorhood and Canada will have had fifteen years of experience legislating doctor-assisted dying. That's fifteen years to work out the kinks and close loopholes; to learn from what is and isn't working in other jurisdictions; to recognize abuses in the system and learn how to avoid them. This choice—the ability to select the when and where of our inevitable end—is one that wasn't readily available to generations past. To take advantage of this new autonomy, we all need to embrace the simultaneous discomfort and luxury of talking about our preferences with our loved ones.

12   Once our chicken dinner was reduced to scraps of bones and skin, it swam in a large pot, accompanied by carrots, celery, onions and herbs. The meal we'd eaten was no more, but it would soon become broth, used to flavour new rices and soups. The wine bottles, now empty, would be taken away and repurposed too, maybe turning into fibreglass insulation or garden mulch.

13   As the party wound down, Amanda had her coat on, ready to jump into a waiting car. "I had reservations about coming tonight," she told us. She was worried everyone was more prepared to talk about death than she was, that she hadn't thought about it enough. But, she said, our conversation had left her "enlightened." In fact, she thought about going home to her boyfriend and asking him what he wanted when he died, just in case she needed to know. They were a millennial couple after all—a millennial couple who would, as death midwife Kerr hopes, confront their ends before they are old and grey and have no time left to say anything other than "goodbye."

Source: Wiart, Nikki. "Self-Checkout." *Maisonneuve Magazine*, 13 April 2016. https://maisonneuve.org/article/2016/04/13/self-checkout/. Reproduced by permission of the author.

WRITING AN ARGUMENT

BY THE END OF THIS CHAPTER, YOU WILL BE ABLE TO

- Identify an appropriate issue for argumentation.
- Determine the best approach to writing an argument.
- Develop an argument that is supported with original, unbiased, sound, and concrete details.
- Refine an argument through the strategic use of rhetorical appeals and rhetorical modes.
- Describe the role of critical analysis and response in the delivery of an argument.

▶ WHY IS THIS INFORMATION IMPORTANT?

An argument is the means by which you not only articulate a viewpoint on a particular issue but also demonstrate the knowledge, experience, and critical thinking skills you have gained through engaging deeply with the issue in question. In an academic setting, this writing task is typically done near the end of a unit, course, or research project as it requires you to create an innovative, unique piece of writing resulting from analysis, evaluation, and synthesis of all the information you have amassed.

Informed arguments are the means by which individuals in academic settings communicate with one another and engage in critical discussions that lead to new ways of thinking and doing. That is why arguments are so important: they encourage divergent thinking that can produce important solutions to complex problems.

While you may not write a formal argument outside an academic setting, the information in this chapter will provide you with essential strategies for making a persuasive case in any type of setting. Persuasion involves using sound arguments to convince others to think or behave in a certain way. Without the critical thinking, reading, and writing skills required to craft a sound argument, you will have significant difficulty in persuading people to think or act in ways that will result in positive solutions to problems within your community, for example. Moreover, the ability to craft a sound argument can help you persuade an audience to question and challenge manipulative persuasive messages—propaganda made for personal gain by individuals who tend to persuade through emotion rather than through sound reasoning and evidence.

▶ Think about It!

In this chapter, you will read and write about the impact of digitization on the music industry. As a consumer of music, you likely recognize that the way you access your music has changed considerably over the last few years. You likely access much of your music in digital formats—possibly through digital downloads or streaming services. This change in access to music affects not only you as the consumer but also the songwriters, artists, and music labels responsible for bringing you music. Collectively, these parties form the music industry that has struggled to adapt to the digital era in terms of financial security and fairness. Consider the following questions as you move through this chapter and as you read the following essay.

1. What are the means by which you consume and search for music? Why have you chosen these means?

2. What impact has digitization had on your listening habits and preferences?

3. In what ways have apps and streaming services changed the landscape of the music industry?

In the following reading, the author describes the benefits and challenges that streaming services have brought to the music industry. While these services have helped the industry recover a bit from loss of revenues experienced since the introduction of Napster, there is still concern that the industry is not picking up as quickly as it should be and that streaming is causing other modes of music consumption to decline. Read the article, and then answer the following questions.

1. What is the difference between a "[l]icensed subscription streaming service" and an ad-supported streaming service? What are the implications of this difference?

2. Why might songwriters and artists be skeptical of streaming services?

3. In what ways is making an album available on one exclusive streaming service beneficial to an artist? In what ways might this exclusivity be detrimental?

4. Would you classify this article as argumentative or expository? Justify your answer.

5. How would you evaluate the sources the author has cited in this article? Are they reliable, varied, and relevant? Do they enhance or take away credibility?

STREAM ON

Why the Music Industry's Not Celebrating Its Big Digital Windfall Just Yet

By Josh O'Kane

1   Two decades ago, Canadian indie darlings Sloan released One Chord to Another to huge fanfare, racking up the best sales of the band's career. Today, the Halifax-turned-Toronto group is touring in support of that album's 20th anniversary—and can no longer depend on sales alone.

2   "We've really realized touring is our bread and butter," songwriter-guitarist Jay Ferguson said from his tour bus. The band has put out a few "boutique" releases in the past few years—most recently, a special vinyl box set of One Chord—"which we can take on tour, and make money that way." It's a helpful strategy, because now that fans are streaming music instead of buying it, he said "we've noticed less money" than ever before from record sales.

3   Streaming started as [a] trickle, and now it's leading a sea change: Last year, services such as Spotify and Apple Music helped push the global recorded music industry into significant year-over-year revenue growth for the first time since the Napster-led industry crash. But this growth has been at the expense of both physical and digital music sales.

4   So the International Federation of the Phonographic Industry (IFPI), a lobby group, is making a plea to legislators worldwide to take action against music services that don't adequately compensate rights holders—artists and the companies that bankroll them—with hopes that the record industry can return to the kind of sustainable revenue it had in the sales-heavy nineties.

5   Licensed subscription streaming services, such as Spotify and Apple Music, have been difficult for the industry to adjust to, with artists generally earning fractions of pennies per stream. IFPI is arguing for a greater share of income from free on-demand services that rely on ads to make money—including YouTube, which often sees unlicensed content uploaded from users—as they generally pay musicians and rights holders even less than subscription services.

6   In its Global Music Report, released Tuesday, IFPI contends that nearly 900 million people find music on such ad-supported services; yet, they contribute to only 4 per cent of global music revenue. This, in turn, draws users away from properly licensed services, whose subscription tiers brought in an estimated $2-billion (U.S.) in revenue last year.

7   "While the development is positive, we should be growing much faster, as the streaming business is exploding," Edgar Berger, Sony Music Entertainment's international chief executive officer, said during a Tuesday conference call with reporters. "If we continue to recover at the same speed as last year, it would take us more than 10 years to reach the market level of predigital disruption."

8   Both IFPI and Music Canada released their 2015 revenue numbers on Tuesday. Worldwide, recorded music income rose 3.2 per cent to $15-billion after flat

growth in 2014, while Canada saw even better growth, at 8.3 per cent year-over-year—the first positive growth here since 2011.

9   It's too early to celebrate this sudden success, said Amy Terrill, executive vice-president of Music Canada—especially given a "rough" 2014, which saw year-over-year revenue fall by 11 per cent.

10   "We had been a very underserved market in terms of premium subscriptions, so 2015 was the first year with much stronger offerings," she said in an interview, referring to the entry of both Spotify and Apple Music.

11   Canada continued to punch above its weight in global visibility. Justin Bieber, Drake and the Weeknd were among the top 10 global recording artists.

12   IFPI representatives said they arrived at the 3.2-per-cent growth figure by recasting 2014 revenue in last year's weaker currency. What had been $14.97-billion in sales was revised down to $14.5-billion, making this year's sales look rosier by comparison.

13   Digital music analyst Mark Mulligan, a frequent skeptic of reported industry figures, said he's wary of the report's accuracy because of this and "a whole bunch of anomalies," including discrepancies in revenues for different types of streaming services.

14   Catherine Moore, a New York University music-business professor, noticed similar discrepancies, chalking them up to the constant change in measuring tools for music consumption. "I think that's partly why they're reluctant to say, 'Oh look, it went up, it'll continue to go up,'" she said.

15   The last time the global music industry had significant, measurable growth was 1998, IFPI representatives said, at 4.8 per cent.

16   Worldwide, 68 million people now pay for streaming music services, usually at $10 a month. Digital-music revenue rose 10 per cent worldwide last year, for the first time outpacing revenue for physical discs and vinyl, in large part thanks to a 45-per-cent rise in revenue from streaming services. (Including the high-flying vinyl sector, physical sales accounted for 39 per cent of revenue, versus digital's 45 per cent.)

17   Streaming, though, has come at a cost. Despite the record-breaking sales success by Adele, physical-sales revenue fell 4.5 per cent and downloads plummeted 10.5 per cent in 2015—the same year that Apple, the world's largest music retailer, launched a streaming service of its own.

18   Its arrival in Canada, with the addition of Spotify in 2014, pushed streaming revenue here up nearly 150 per cent, according to Music Canada.

19   Income from paid streaming services far outweighs the revenue from the ad-supported free versions that some companies offer. In the case of Spotify, this number can be glaring when compared with its user numbers: more than 75 million people use the service, but only 30 million pay for it. And, according to IFPI, these "freemium" tiers and services such as YouTube are estimated to contribute no more than 10 per cent of 2015's $2.89-billion in global streaming revenue.

20   Music Canada plans to address these discrepancies when the Copyright Modernization Act comes up for review in 2017. In the United States, hundreds of artists, including Arcade Fire and Neko Case, recently put their voices together to ask for changes to the Digital Millennium Copyright Act for fairer compensation.

21   The organization has long been an advocate for fairer music copyright legislation. "I don't think we have, as a community, really united on the issue until now," Ms. Terrill said. "There's definitely a growing consensus to get this fixed."

22   Last year also brought forward a curious trend that may encourage piracy or slow the adoption of streaming: withholding albums from some or all services. Adele almost entirely avoided streaming for *25*, the world's bestselling album last year, with 17.4 million units sold. Taylor Swift, on the other hand, gave preference to Apple Music for *1989*. And, for more than a month earlier this year, Kanye West's *The Life of Pablo* was available exclusively on the high-definition audio streaming service Tidal.

23   Asked by The Globe and Mail about exclusive releases, record executives on the IFPI conference call acknowledged that they were a concern, but inevitable. "Short-term [exclusivity] windows associated with marketing campaigns can be part of the positive market development story we're seeing with [streaming] services, but in general I think we all really want to see that music subscribers are getting access to most of the music they care about," said Michael Nash, Universal Music Group's executive vice-president of digital strategy.

24   "We are advocating music be as widespread as possible," Sony's Mr. Berger said.

Source: O'Kane, Josh. "Stream On: Why the Music Industry's Not Celebrating Its Big Digital Windfall Just Yet," *The Globe and Mail*, 12 April 2016. www.theglobeandmail. com/arts/music/after-surprising-growth-in-2015-music-industry-seeks-fairer-revenues/article29604379/. Reproduced by permission of The Globe and Mail.

Writing an Argument: An Overview

All the work you have done in the previous chapters will help you construct an informed argument (see Figure 10.1). In fact, you need to have a thorough understanding of every chapter in this book in order to write an argument that is convincing and well structured. Specifically, you must have a solid grasp of fundamental reading and writing strategies (Chapter 1); the ability to distinguish among and to develop main ideas, major supporting details, and minor supporting details (Chapters 2 and 3); the skills required to effectively summarize any information you read (Chapter 4); a clear research methodology for both finding and integrating research (Chapter 5); the ability to analyze and evaluate the writer, publication, language, and argumentation of multiple texts, including those you produce on your own (Chapters 6 to 8); and the skills to develop meaningful, logical, and well-supported responses to the arguments of others (Chapter 9).

In an argument, you express your point of view in the form of a limited and focused thesis statement that distinguishes you from others who have written on the same topic. You then systematically and logically convince your reader of the relevance, significance, and reliability of this viewpoint through supporting claims that are in turn supported by detailed explanations and concrete evidence. As you present your reasoning and evidence, you need to think carefully about the claims of those who may oppose your viewpoint so that you can respond to those claims skillfully by refuting (arguing) or accepting (conceding) them. It is also critical that you incorporate the testimony of others who have made significant contributions to the discussion of the topic, whether you agree or disagree with what those individuals have said. Figure 10.2 summarizes these key components of an informed argument.

FIGURE 10.1
SKILLS REQUIRED TO WRITE AN INFORMED ARGUMENT

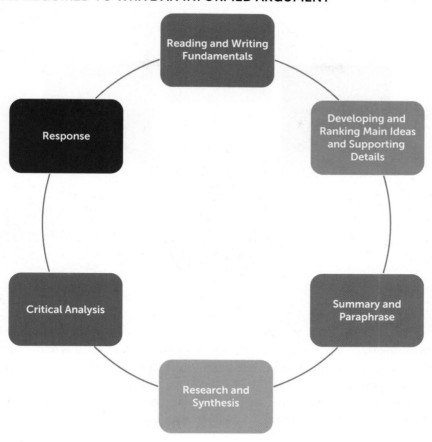

▶ Apply the Skill

Identifying the Key Components of an Informed Argument

Read the argumentative article entitled "Will Streaming Music Kill Songwriting?" by John Seabrook, which you will find at the end of this chapter. Complete the following chart based on the article.

COMPONENT	EXAMPLE FROM "WILL STREAMING MUSIC KILL SONGWRITING?"
Unique, focused thesis statement	
One claim to support the thesis	
One supporting detail for the claim indicated above	
One counterargument and refutation	
Testimony	

FIGURE 10.2
KEY COMPONENTS OF AN INFORMED ARGUMENT

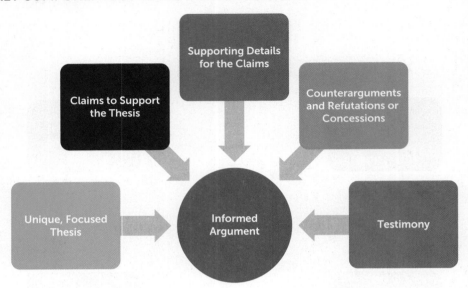

Planning an Argument

The planning stage sets the tone and direction for your argument. It is important that you spend a significant portion of your time at this stage as it will impact how the rest of the writing process progresses. It is also the stage at which you ensure you have fully understood the purpose and audience for your argument, so that you can shape the argument in a way that will appeal to and persuade people.

Determining an Appropriate Issue

Any argument needs to start with a debatable or controversial issue, as you learned when you were introduced to argumentation in Chapter 7. In some of your post-secondary classes, a controversial issue will be assigned to you. In others, you will be responsible for finding your own. A good place to start is the opinion pages—or perhaps even the front page—of a reputable newspaper. Almost all newspapers are now online, so they are easy to access. Opinion pages contain columns by seasoned journalists who weigh in on the most popular debates of the day. Opinion pages also usually provide some good context for the debate, providing you with a sense of the key issues at play.

Whatever issue you select, be sure it is one that has not been overdone. Examples of issues that have been exhausted include capital punishment and abortion. That does not mean these are not still important issues that people are still debating; it just means that it is difficult to create and develop a unique perspective on these issues since they have been widely debated. Current events are usually better for debate and informed arguments. The issue presented in this chapter—the impact of digitization on the music industry—is still highly debatable since digitization is relatively new and constantly evolving. Yesterday there were digital MP3 downloads, while today the focus seems to be on streaming. New ways of being and of doing are valuable topics for debate.

Engaging in Preparatory Research

Whether you are assigned a topic or select your own, you need to research what has already been debated about the issue. The research skills you learned about in Chapter 5 are vital in the planning stage of your argument. These skills will help you determine what will be your unique contribution to the discussion.

AUDIENCE AND RESEARCH

Once you have determined, through research and self-reflection, the stance you want to take on a particular issue (your thesis), you will need to determine your audience. Once again, your research will help you determine this. Which audiences have already been addressed by others? Is it helpful to address the same audience? Would it be better to address a different audience? The answers to these questions will all depend on where the debate has already been and where it needs to go.

Just as your research helps you determine your audience, so will your audience help you determine further research. The relationship is symbiotic: the audience and the research depend on each other as seen in Figure 10.3. It is important to be strategic about the research you do before as well as after determining your audience. Before determining your audience, you should adopt the research strategy you learned in Chapter 5 that involves searching for texts that provide overviews on the issue, such as encyclopedias and textbooks. After determining your audience, you should look at in-depth sources, as you will have a much better sense of what those sources should be after general research. Don't forget to create a graphic organizer as you conduct your research, so that you have a visualization of how the texts you read relate to one another. You learned about using graphic organizers to aid your reading in Chapter 4.

FIGURE 10.3
RESEARCH, THESIS, AND AUDIENCE

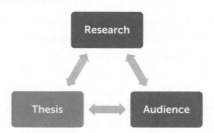

Choosing How to Present the Argument

The more you know about your audience, previous debates on the issue, and your own point of view, the more knowledge you will have about how best to present your argument. Figure 10.4 depicts three considerations to keep in mind when planning your argument.

PLACEMENT OF THESIS

One presentation element to take into consideration is the placement of your thesis (Table 10.1). As you know from Chapter 1, some writers put the thesis near the beginning of the argument so that their readers understand the central idea right from the beginning. The rest of the essay then explains, clarifies, and justifies the soundness and reliability of that particular perspective. This approach is usually effective for arguments that are less complex. If you are at the beginning of your academic studies, you will likely find this approach the most appealing because it is relatively straightforward. You state your overall

FIGURE 10.4
CONSIDERATIONS FOR CHOOSING HOW TO PRESENT YOUR ARGUMENT

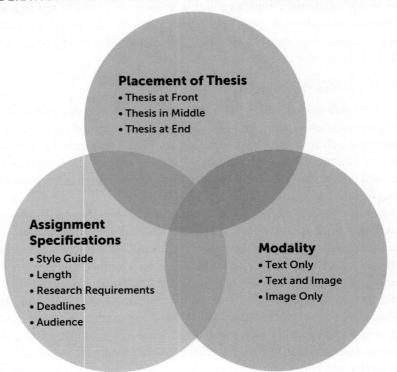

Placement of Thesis
- Thesis at Front
- Thesis in Middle
- Thesis at End

Assignment Specifications
- Style Guide
- Length
- Research Requirements
- Deadlines
- Audience

Modality
- Text Only
- Text and Image
- Image Only

point of view and then go on to provide the support that defends it. Each body paragraph or group of paragraphs presents one more reason why you believe what you believe.

The other common option for placing a thesis statement is near the end of the argument. This placement allows you to carefully build your case, claim by claim, throughout the essay before delivering your final perspective on the issue. This approach is usually effective for more complex arguments or arguments that may seem particularly controversial. Such an approach can slowly bring the audience on board with the underlying claims and assumptions of the argument, making the audience more receptive to the conclusion that these claims and assumptions point toward. A thesis near the end of an argument also helps to build suspense, which may give your thesis a more forceful punch.

A less common, but still effective, approach is to place the thesis somewhere in the middle. Doing so offers the advantages of both late placement and early placement thesis statements. You have the opportunity to start building the argument, making your audience more and more agreeable to its underlying claims before revealing the most

TABLE 10.1
PLACEMENT OF THESIS STATEMENT

EARLY	LATE	MIDDLE
Effective for less-complex arguments	Works well for complex arguments or those that are particularly controversial	Allows you to build trust in some of the supporting claims before revealing your thesis, while still allowing you to provide more support afterward
Encourages a straightforward structure	Allows you to build trust in your supporting claims, making your audience more receptive before delivering your overall point of view Builds suspense to give your thesis statement a greater punch	Encourages a straightforward structure but offers the opportunity for some complexity

important claim. At the same time, you still have plenty of room to defend the thesis statement after it has been stated.

MODALITY

In the past, arguments were presented in academic institutions in written form. It has now become more commonplace, however, to incorporate images in these texts to help clarify or illustrate certain components of the argument. In non-academic contexts, it is not unusual to see an argument being made solely by a visual—or by a visual with limited text.

You learned how to incorporate visuals in Chapter 5 when doing expository writing; the same principles apply to incorporating visuals in an argument. The key is to use the visual only if it will enhance the soundness or reliability of your argument. Use visuals sparingly, and only for the purpose of emphasizing a claim that cannot be stated more artfully in words. Always check with your instructor to determine whether visuals are permitted for your particular assignments. In some contexts, arguments must be made using text alone.

ASSIGNMENT SPECIFICATIONS

When writing an informed argument as part of an assignment for a course, you need to pay special attention to the guidelines provided by your instructor. These guidelines will typically indicate information about the style guide you need to follow for your writing (e.g., APA or MLA), page or number counts, research requirements, deadlines, and so forth. In some cases, the instructor will even ask you to consider a particular audience to write for. All of these guidelines will shape your approach to your writing task, so you need to be aware of them right from the start.

You should try to make presentation decisions before drafting your essay because they will help provide a roadmap for your argument. Of course, during the drafting and refining stages, you still have the opportunity to revisit and revise your plan.

Generating and Organizing Your Ideas

Now that you've determined your issue, engaged in research, and decided on how you will present your argument, you are ready to start generating and organizing your ideas. You will remember from Chapter 1 that there are a number of ways to engage in this type of prewriting: freewriting, graphic organizers, outlines, and journalling. Because this is still a part of the planning stages, do not get caught up in sentence-level details. The goal here is to figure out what, precisely, your thesis statement is and how you will go about defending it. This part of the argument writing process should also reveal the overall organizational pattern your informed argument will follow. Informed arguments typically focus on one of the patterns that analyze. You learned about these patterns in Chapter 3: classification, cause–effect or problem–solution, and compare–contrast.

▶ Apply the Skill

Preparing to Write an Informed Argument

1. What are three emerging issues currently being debated in your community, country, or worldwide? On which of these issues would you choose to write an informed argument? Justify your choice.

2. Write an annotated bibliography consisting of three secondary sources that would provide you with effective support in an argument essay based on your chosen issue in Question 1.

3. Explain how you would present your argument for the issue you selected in Question 1 if you were asked to limit your argument to just 1200 words. Consider the placement of your thesis and whether or not you would include visuals. Justify your choices.

4. Decide on the overall pattern of organization you would use for an argument essay on the issue you selected in Question 1. Justify your choice.

Review

Planning an Argument

Answer the following review questions in paragraph form or generate ideas to contribute to a group or class discussion.

1. What skills are required to write an informed argument?
2. What are the key components of an informed argument?
3. How do you determine what issue to argue about?
4. Describe the relationship among research, thesis, and audience.
5. What do you need to consider when choosing how to present your argument?

Drafting an Argument

After you have determined your issue, engaged in research, decided on how you will present your argument, narrowed your thesis statement, and chosen your overall pattern of organization, you are ready for the drafting stage. Drafting is the point at which you begin articulating your argument in the form of sentences and paragraphs, ultimately creating an essay.

Introduction and Context

As you already know, an essay typically begins with an introduction that provides context for the essay. Context is the surrounding information that clarifies the topic and why you are writing about the topic. You have already written different types of introductions throughout this book, including the introduction to a critical analysis essay and a response essay. These particular introductions put into context what a single writer wrote in a single text. In an argument, you put into context what more than one writer wrote in more than one text. Table 10.2 provides concrete strategies for setting the context for an argumentative essay.

TABLE 10.2
WAYS TO CONTEXTUALIZE AN ISSUE

STRATEGY	DESCRIPTION
Summarize multiple viewpoints	An excellent way to contextualize the issue is to describe the variety of viewpoints.
Outline the viewpoint of an expert	If there are too many viewpoints to provide, try providing just one detailed viewpoint with which you either agree or disagree.
Provide a narrative	Stories related to the issue are a good way to get the audience invested in the argument. People relate well to real-life stories. A narrative is a good way to develop a reader's empathy for your argument.
Refer to a current event	If the issue is directly related to a current event, describe that event as a springboard for your own opinion on the issue.

Depending on the length of your argument, you may have an introduction that spans more than one paragraph. No matter the length, make sure you provide your reader with a good grounding in the issue.

Thesis Statement

Because your thesis statement represents your overall viewpoint of the issue, you need to take great care in crafting it. A strong thesis statement for an argument is debatable and focused. If the thesis statement is not debatable, then you are not writing an argument at all. If the thesis statement is not focused, then you may end up arguing for an issue much too large for your context, or you may end up presenting an unoriginal or over-simplified argument. You may recall completing an Apply the Skill activity in Chapter 7 in which you were presented with a number of claims that you needed to identify as being debatable and/or focused. Now you need to write your own claims and ensure they are controversial (debatable) and nuanced (focused).

To ensure your thesis is controversial or debatable, try to write a claim that opposes it. If you cannot think of an oppositional claim, then your thesis is not controversial. Consider, as an example, that your potential thesis is the following statement:

YouTube should start charging a fee for its streaming services.

Can you write a claim that opposes this thesis? Yes:

YouTube should not charge a fee for its streaming services.

Because there is a clear opposing viewpoint, you know that the thesis is controversial.

The next question, then, is whether the thesis is sufficiently focused. Determining the focus is much more difficult, as many different elements come into play: the length of the essay, the depth of the research, and even the audience. Assume that for this particular essay on the issue of YouTube streaming, your essay is 1800 words, you are required to integrate three secondary sources, and your audience is amateur musicians. Is the thesis statement, "YouTube should not charge a fee for its streaming services" focused enough? Table 10.3 provides an analysis that will help answer that question.

As you can see, having a clear understanding of an assignment's parameters will shape your thesis statement. Given the parameters in the example above, a focused thesis statement might be, "YouTube should not charge a fee for streaming amateur music videos."

TABLE 10.3

ANALYSIS OF A THESIS STATEMENT'S FOCUS: YOUTUBE SHOULD NOT CHARGE A FEE FOR ITS STREAMING SERVICES

PARAMETER	WHAT IT MEANS
1800 words	In 12-point, Times New Roman font, 1800 words is equivalent to just six pages. Therefore, the thesis statement needs to be much more specific about the charges and the specific streaming services. Is it a flat charge? Is it a pay-per-stream charge? Is it for streaming all videos? Or is it for only professionally produced videos?
Three secondary sources	If the research is limited to just three secondary sources, then the thesis statement needs to be very specific. It means that it is being written as part of a smaller conversation about the issue: the smaller the conversation, the more precise the thesis statement needs to be.
Audience: amateur musicians	If the audience for your essay is amateur musicians, then focus on streaming *amateur music videos* on YouTube, specifically, as this will interest the audience. The thesis statement should mention this type of music video.

Keep in mind that in the drafting stage, there will be many opportunities for you to continue to refine your thesis statement. You need to start with a working thesis to guide your writing, but remember that one of the purposes for writing about an issue is to learn more as you write. You will remember the phrase *writing to learn* from Chapters 4 and 5. The more you learn as you write, the more you will likely revisit and reshape the thesis statement to accurately reflect your developing point of view.

▶ Apply the Skill

Introducing an Issue and Crafting a Thesis

1. Go back to the issue you selected in the previous Apply the Skill activity, "Planning an Informed Argument." What strategy would you use to contextualize it? Why?

2. Write a controversial and focused thesis statement on the issue you selected in the previous Apply the Skill activity. Explain how you know the thesis statement is focused and controversial.

3. Examine the introduction of the essay at the end of this chapter, "Will Streaming Music Kill Songwriting?" Explain how the author has chosen to contextualize his argument, and identify his thesis statement. Then, evaluate the quality of both the contextualization and the thesis statement.

Supporting Claims

After you have written your thesis and introduction, you are ready to start writing and developing your claims. You may end up going back to your introduction and thesis statement for revisions, which is fine—that is why writing is considered a recursive process. You may also start changing your mind about where to position the thesis—beginning, middle, or end. That's fine, too. Your goal is to draft sound supporting claims. Then, you will need to provide explanations and evidence in the form of major and minor supporting details to justify these supporting claims. Figure 10.5 reminds you of this structure of an argument.

FIGURE 10.5
THE STRUCTURE OF AN ARGUMENT

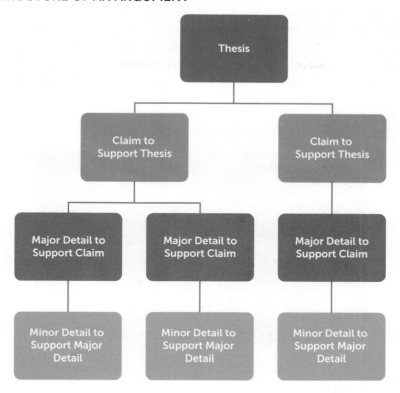

Keep in mind that the number of claims, major supporting details, and minor supporting details is flexible. Figure 10.5 demonstrates only one possible version.

Writing a supporting claim is similar to writing a thesis. The goal is for the claim to be debatable and nuanced. You also need to pay attention to relevance. In other words, you need to make sure that the claim actually supports the thesis.

Earlier, you considered the following thesis statement: "YouTube should not charge a fee for streaming amateur music videos." Can you think of a supporting claim to help justify this statement that is debatable, nuanced, and relevant? Analyze the following claim in terms of its effectiveness as support for the thesis:

> The free advertising amateur artists receive by having their music videos on YouTube is a form of compensation.

Is this claim debatable? Yes. One could argue that advertising is not the same as compensation. Is the claim nuanced? Yes. It examines the issue of charging fees from the perspective of having to pay musicians for their work. Is the claim relevant? Yes. It clearly focuses on one reason charging for streaming is not necessary: the artist does not need monetary compensation.

A final question to ask is whether the claim is logical or reasonable. Remember that you will think a claim is logical if you agree with its hidden assumptions, which you learned about in Chapter 7. So what are the hidden assumptions for the supporting claim above? One assumption is that if musicians are not getting paid, then charging a fee for streaming is unnecessary. The problem with this assumption is that streaming fees typically go to not only the artist but also the streaming company. Another assumption, which is not so hidden, is that the exposure these musicians get will lead to profits for them at some point in the future. This assumption is also problematic because if these artists are not recognized by somebody who will actually pay to listen to their music, then they will just end up in a cycle of performing for free. If you agree that these assumptions are problematic, that means your claim is illogical or unreasonable. Therefore, you need to change it. If, on the other hand, you think these hidden assumptions are reasonable, then you can conclude that your supporting claim is also reasonable. The key components of a strong supporting claim are summarized in Figure 10.6.

FIGURE 10.6
CHARACTERISTICS OF A STRONG SUPPORTING CLAIM

▶ **Apply the Skill**

Drafting Supporting Claims

1. Go back to the thesis statement you wrote in the previous Apply the Skill activity, "Introducing an Issue and Crafting a Thesis." Write three supporting claims you would use to justify and develop your thesis. Then, explain how each of these claims is debatable, focused, relevant, and reasonable.

2. Select one supporting claim from "Will Streaming Music Kill Songwriting?" by John Seabrook. Evaluate this supporting claim based on the degree to which it is debatable, focused, relevant, and logical/reasonable. Be sure to justify your evaluation.

Major and Minor Supporting Details

You may recall from Chapters 8 and 9 that it is often necessary to gather details before being able to craft the claim that those details support. Your supporting details make or break your argument. Whether you write them before or after you construct your claim, they will determine whether or not you will be successful in getting the audience to agree with or accept your perspective on an issue. If you cannot justify your supporting claims through strong evidence and careful explanations, then these supporting claims will fall apart. If these supporting claims fall apart, then your thesis, too, will fall apart; it won't have anything left to stand on.

Supporting details are perhaps the most difficult part of the argument to draft because they require you to synthesize your ideas with those of all the sources you have researched. You learned how to integrate and explain other sources for expository writing in Chapter 5, but now you need to think carefully about how to present your sources in a way that clearly displays *your* train of thought and highlights the legitimacy of *your* supporting claims. You need to make sure you draft supporting details that are original, unbiased, sound, and concrete (see Figure 10.7).

FIGURE 10.7
CHARACTERISTICS OF EFFECTIVE SUPPORTING DETAILS

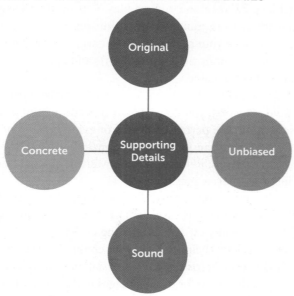

ORIGINALITY

Originality is key when drafting supporting details. After all, there is no point in providing the same evidence and explanations that someone else has already provided. Some novice writers believe that supporting ideas are original only if they come from their own knowledge or experiences, but that is not the only source of original support.

Originality refers to not only a unique claim or piece of evidence but also a unique perspective on one or more claims or pieces of evidence that already exist. That is why synthesizing, or integrating, your research is important: you are putting together new combinations of ideas and evidence, finding new relationships, and presenting these relationships as they have never been presented before. These new combinations actually produce new evidence and new explanations. They advance the debate on the issue, providing a unique perspective that you have had a hand in creating. Ultimately, if you can take these combinations and apply your own knowledge and experience to develop the new claim(s) these combinations have created, you are on your way to producing a truly original argument.

What does it mean to integrate ideas in order to make a new, original idea? Think about the two issues presented in the articles in this chapter. In the first article, the issue is about the degree to which music streaming has both benefitted and challenged the music industry. In the second article, the issue is focused more specifically on what happens to the songwriters of the music industry, and the outlook is much more bleak. When you take these ideas together, you can develop an informed, nuanced idea about streaming in the music industry: those artists and music labels that believe streaming may yield financial gains need to advocate for the songwriters they depend on. You would not be able to come this conclusion unless you read both articles: you need to understand that streaming can be good for artists and labels but that it is always bad for songwriters.

LIMITING BIAS

Limiting bias when writing supporting details will help strengthen your supporting claim. While all claims are, by default, biased because you are supporting one particular point of view, the reasoning and evidence does not necessarily have to be biased too.

In order to achieve balance and reduce bias, you need to ensure you produce evidence and explanations from multiple viewpoints on the issue. If you present only the testimony that agrees with your perspective, your argument will be viewed as biased. However, if you present testimony that both supports and opposes your argument, you will be seen as unbiased and reliable.

Do not be afraid to acknowledge claims or evidence that support a viewpoint other than the one you hold. At worst, you may have to concede a point or two. At best, you will be able to assert why those particular claims or evidence are not as significant or legitimate as your own. If you can refute a point, make sure you do so with plenty of evidence and clear explanations. Refutation is a powerful tool that not only limits bias but also carries a lot of persuasive merit.

Another way to limit bias and strengthen your supporting details is to make the assumptions underlying your claims explicit. The more you show your audience, the more likely your audience will view you as a strong critical thinker and trusty source. Clarifying the underlying claims helps to build your credibility. Even if one of the underlying assumptions may come across as controversial, you need to address it. In any argument, there will be advantages or disadvantages to the point of view. It is better to be honest about the disadvantages than to ignore them.

SOUNDNESS

You must ensure that your supporting details provide sound reasoning and evidence for your claim. In Chapter 7, you learned that supporting details are sound if they are reasonable, relevant to the claim they are supporting, compatible with one another, and representative of the bigger picture. Be sure to assess each of your supporting details using these criteria.

CONCRETENESS

When you start drilling down to minor supporting details, in particular, you need to provide your readers with evidence they can visualize. They need to see the evidence in their minds' eye. Abstract reasoning is important in terms of establishing logic and a strong foundation for critical thinking and debate, but many arguments are won by an individual's ability to draw attention to concrete examples that bring the reasoning to life—that make it real.

Consider the following claim:

The free advertising amateur artists receive by having their music videos on YouTube is a form of compensation.

To help prove this claim, you could explain how the free exposure helps an artist build up a larger fan base, and these fans will then pay the artist to see him in concert. So, while YouTube itself doesn't compensate the artist, the people who access the music through YouTube will eventually compensate the artist. To help *show* that this is actually the case, however, you should provide a specific example. If you can actually track a particular artist's progression from YouTube to increased concert sales, you validate your line of reasoning. You show how that reasoning manifests itself in reality. On YouTube, there are many artists whose fortunes can be traced back to posting music videos. Canadian artists Shawn Mendes and Justin Bieber are two popular examples. Putting images to your reasoning gives your argument more weight. It shows that your argument has real-life implications.

▶ Apply the Skill

Drafting Supporting Details

1. In the Apply the Skill activity "Drafting Supporting Claims," you wrote three supporting claims for a thesis. Draft supporting details for each of those supporting claims. When you are done, evaluate your own supporting details based on how original, unbiased, sound, and concrete they are.

2. Select one supporting claim from "Will Streaming Music Kill Songwriting?" by John Seabrook. Examine the details he uses to support the claim. Evaluate these supporting details based on how original, unbiased, sound, and concrete they are.

Conclusion

A conclusion for an academic argument has the same characteristics of conclusions for writing critical analysis or response essays. In your conclusion, you should summarize the most important points you made throughout your argument. Then, if you have not made your thesis statement explicit, this is the perfect place to do so. You also need to be clear about how your claims and support have made a significant and unique contribution to the discussion of the issue. Finally, you need to encourage your audience to continue debating the issue. These key points for an effective conclusion are summarized in Figure 10.8.

FIGURE 10.8
CRITERIA FOR A CONCLUSION

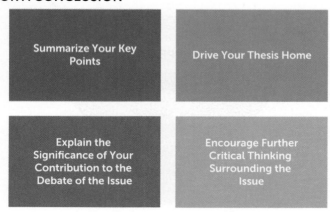

Summarize Your Key Points

Drive Your Thesis Home

Explain the Significance of Your Contribution to the Debate of the Issue

Encourage Further Critical Thinking Surrounding the Issue

Evaluating Conclusions

Evaluate the author's conclusion in "Will Streaming Music Kill Songwriting?" Be sure to explain how well the author summarizes the key ideas, drives his thesis home, explains the significance of his contribution to the debate over streaming, and encourages further critical thinking on the issue.

Refining an Argument

As you can see, drafting an argument is hard work: it requires you to apply all the skills you have learned throughout this book. What you have learned about so far in this chapter will help you write an argument that is well researched and logically sound. However, to maximize the impact of your academic argument, you also need to spend a lot of time refining it. Critically analyzing your own argument and proofreading it carefully are two excellent strategies for refining your argument. Two others are paying attention to your use of rhetorical appeals and rhetorical modes.

Using Rhetorical Appeals

In Chapter 7, you learned about the three rhetorical appeals: *logos, ethos,* and *pathos*—three methods to persuade someone to accept your point of view. You will remember that *logos* refers to persuasion through logic, *ethos* refers to persuasion through establishing credibility and common ground, and *pathos* refers to persuasion through emotion.

A strong argument will weight these three rhetorical appeals strategically (see Figure 10.9). The best arguments tend to be those that focus on *logos* the most, *pathos* the least, and *ethos* somewhere in the middle. The reasoning behind this is quite logical. Most people are receptive to logical explanations, particularly if the logic is indisputable, as in the case of deductive arguments. Emotion, on the other hand, will not move everyone in the same way. Moreover, arguments made on the basis of emotion alone are usually made to satisfy one person's agenda. This does not mean that arguing by emotion is ineffective. Unfortunately, much propaganda is based on how well emotional persuasion works. In an academic context, however, an argument's strength is

FIGURE 10.9
THE WEIGHTING OF RHETORICAL APPEALS

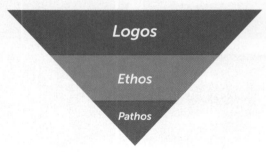

not measured by the number of people who are moved emotionally. Instead, it is defined by its ability to persuade through soundness and reliability—by its ability to engage individuals in critical thinking as opposed to emotional thinking. The component of reliability is where *ethos* comes in. The more you can establish yourself as a reliable source through the research you have done, your experiences, and your attention to grammar and mechanics, the more you will be trusted as an important contributor to the discussion of the issue.

Using Rhetorical Modes

While rhetorical appeals refer to the type of content you use to persuade your audience, rhetorical modes refer to how that content is packaged. In fact, many writers consider rhetorical modes the argumentation-specific terminology for patterns of organization, which you learned about in Chapter 3. In the context of an academic argument, you should pay attention to the following rhetorical modes that can help you deliver your persuasive content. This is not an exhaustive list of the modes: these are simply the ones that are used most often and to the greatest effect.

FIGURE 10.10
FOUR IMPORTANT RHETORICAL MODES

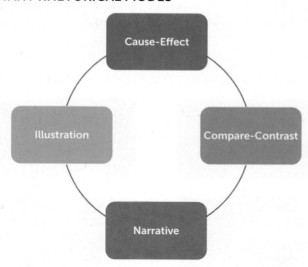

CAUSE–EFFECT

Many arguments and claims are written on the basis of cause-effect. If you think about the thesis "YouTube should not charge a fee for streaming amateur music videos," you will notice that it is actually an argument of cause-effect. The writer does not want YouTube to charge for streaming amateur music videos *because* of the specific effects that such a decision would yield. In fact, part of the writer's argument may also explain why YouTube decided not to charge fees in the first place. These reasons would be considered causes—the factors that led YouTube to not want users to pay for the service. Another common rhetorical structure is a variation of cause–effect: problem–solution. In this case, typically one or multiple problems call for one or multiple solutions.

COMPARE–CONTRAST

Explaining how two people, places, events, decisions, and so forth are either similar or different can be an effective persuasive strategy. In particular, illustrating a key difference between two very similar entities or illustrating a key similarity between two very different entities can have an effective impact on your argument. Just as with cause–effect, compare–contrast can be used at the level of claims or at the level of supporting details.

A comparison or contrast can be delivered following one of two patterns: point-by-point or block, discussed in Chapter 2. You may also remember this terminology from the context of the summary portion of the response essay in Chapter 9. When it comes to comparison or contrast writing, a point-by-point pattern organizes the text by the *points of comparison* (POC), also known as the *qualities* or *characteristics* being compared. In other words, you alternate back-and-forth between the two entities being compared, focusing on each similarity or difference one at a time. A block pattern, on the other hand, organizes the comparison or contrast by the *entities* being compared. In other words, you discuss all the points about the first entity and then all the points about the second entity.

To aid your understanding of these patterns, think about comparing music streaming with digital downloads—these would be the entities. In conducting this comparison, you need to choose what, precisely, you would like to compare. For example, you could compare streaming and digital downloads by price to the consumer, payment to the artist, and quality of the sound—these would be the points of comparison. Figure 10.11

FIGURE 10.11
EXAMPLE OF POINT-BY-POINT VERSUS BLOCK PATTERNS

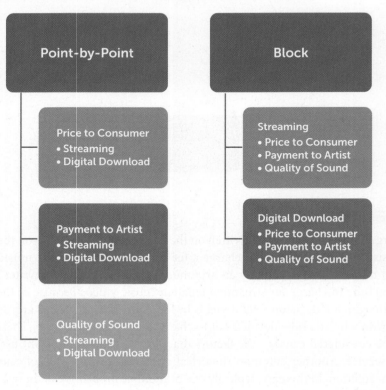

demonstrates what the point-by-point and block patterns would look like for this particular comparison.

How you choose to present your comparison or contrast is up to you. The point-by-point pattern is typically effective for extended comparisons, as it helps the reader keep track of the specific similarities and differences. The complication with this approach is that you have to continuously transition back and forth between the two entities. The opposite is true for the block pattern. In the block pattern, it is more difficult for the reader to keep track of the specific similarities and differences. However, the writer does not have to engage in that constant back-and-forth transition.

Analogy is a subset of comparison that can help you clarify an unknown aspect of your claim or evidence by comparing it to something your reader knows quite well. For example, if your reader does not understand what streaming actually means, you could compare it to going to see a movie at a theatre. While the experience of streaming a video and going to see a movie at a theatre are quite different, there is a key similarity that can help your reader understand the concept of streaming: in both cases, the viewer does not own the actual content. Viewers can watch the content as many times as they would like, but they can't own the content.

NARRATIVE

A narrative is the telling of a story. You read about this in relation to arguments in the section about contextualizing an argument. Often narratives can be used to establish your own experience and therefore your credibility. They can also be used to make an emotional appeal. If you get your audience invested in the life of a particular person, for example, their empathy for that person may make them more amenable to accepting an argument in favour of that person. Of course, a narrative can also aid in clarifying logical reasoning you provide. If, for example, you presented the story of how Shawn Mendes moved from a YouTube star to a respected mainstream musician, you would be using narrative to support the claim examined earlier regarding free advertisement as compensation.

ILLUSTRATION

Illustration is sometimes referred to as an extended example because it is a method typically used for evidence. The purpose of an illustration is to immerse your reader in the evidence. This type of immersion can help the reader actually see your argument come to life and, more importantly, how he is immediately involved in the implications of your argument. A good illustration will provide plenty of concrete descriptions, which means it will incorporate the description pattern of organization. It may also draw on the patterns of classification, sequence order, definition and example, and problem–solution.

As with the appeals, finding a balance of rhetorical modes is the key to arguing effectively. While one mode will dominate your writing, using others as well serves to strengthen your argument. You should also be aware that the lines between these modes are not distinct. An illustration may include comparison, a cause–effect statement may include a narrative, and so forth. You need to use these modes in concert with one another in a way that effectively presents the complexity but also clarity of your argument.

Rhetorical Appeals and Rhetorical Modes

Fill in the right column of the chart below by paraphrasing or quoting a supporting detail from "Will Streaming Music Kill Songwriting?" that corresponds to the description provided in the left column.

TYPE OF SUPPORTING DETAIL	EXAMPLE FROM "WILL STREAMING MUSIC KILL SONGWRITING?"
Persuades through logic	
Persuades through emotion	
Builds the author's credibility	
Presents a cause–effect relationship	
Persuades through comparison or contrast	
Persuades through storytelling	
Persuades through illustration	

The Roles of Critical Analysis and Response in Argument

In Chapters 8 and 9, you learned how to write a critical analysis of and response to an argument. You had to recognize strategies of argumentation, critique the strategies of argumentation, and agree or disagree with the claims presented by the writer. You did this all in the context of a single article. When writing an argument, you apply these skills to multiple articles at the same time—the articles that you use to explain and justify your argument.

In order to develop a unique point of view on an issue, you need to synthesize the views of others. This means you need to understand how others have made their arguments—what support they have used, whether that support is of high quality, and whether you agree or disagree with their claims. In order to use the strategy of counterargument and refutation, for instance, you need to be able to identify a claim and its support, and you also need to be able to discern a flaw—with soundness or reliability, for example. Examining a flaw through critical analysis will direct you toward a specific response to the claim and combining such analysis and response across multiple articles helps you articulate your argument. Notice these key components of argumentation in Figure 10.12.

FIGURE 10.12
ARGUMENT REQUIRES CRITICAL ANALYSIS AND RESPONSE

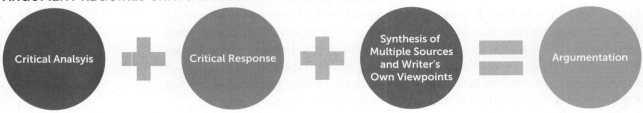

Critical Analsyis **+** Critical Response **+** Synthesis of Multiple Sources and Writer's Own Viewpoints **=** Argumentation

Critical analysis and response not only help make your argument unique and your support varied but also lend credibility to your argument. One pitfall that novice writers fall into when writing an argument is forcing research into the argument. In other words, some writers simply "drop" a quotation or paraphrase into their argument to satisfy a research requirement for an assignment. This is problematic for a number of reasons: it can misrepresent your own point of view; it can disturb the logic and flow of your argument; it can make your argument sound artificial rather than sincere; it can provide weak support for your argument; and, worst of all, it can lead to inaccurate representation of another writer's ideas—an academic offence. It is of utmost importance, then, to critically read your sources before attempting to integrate any part of them into your essay.

In Chapter 5, you learned how to write an annotated bibliography. Constructing an annotated bibliography for an academic argument is an excellent way of ensuring your argument is well researched with sound, reliable sources. It will also help you plan out how the sources might be used and integrated within your own argument. As a planning tool, annotated bibliographies help shape the direction of your argument, so they should be an instrumental component of your planning stage.

Pulling It All Together

You can see that writing a strong argument is a complex task, requiring skilful application of every chapter in this textbook. In the appendix on documentation, you will see how one student has applied the skills of this textbook to craft an effective argument. As you read through the argument, make note of how the writer has woven together all the skills presented in this textbook.

▶ Apply the Skill

Analyzing an Academic Argument

Read the argumentative essay in the appendix on documentation. Then, write an essay that analyzes the argumentative essay from each of the following perspectives. Each perspective should form one or more paragraphs of your analytical essay. Your instructor may also ask you to *evaluate* the quality of the argumentative essay.
   Perspectives:

1. **Purpose and audience.** Define who the purpose and audience are and how you know.

2. **Main ideas.** Summarize the argument by paraphrasing its main ideas and describe whether the main ideas are explicit, implied, or a combination of both.

3. **Unity and coherence.** Describe the strategies the writer has used to ensure unity and coherence.

4. **Patterns of organization.** Describe the overall pattern of organization the essay employs, as well as the patterns of organization of the essay's subsections. Explain, as well, how these patterns contribute to your understanding of the essay's supporting details.

5. **Research.** Provide examples of the research the student has done in order to craft the argument. Comment on whether she used primary sources, secondary sources, or a combination of both.

6. **Language and tone.** Explain how the language used throughout the essay indicates a particular tone, and describe the connection between this tone and the argument the writer is trying to make.

7. **Claims and support.** Select one of the claims in the essay and describe the support used to justify the claim. What types of support does the writer use? Does the support lead to a sound claim?

8. **Rhetorical appeals.** Which rhetorical appeal does the writer use the most? How do you know? Provide an example of the most-used appeal.

9. **Response.** Provide an example of when the writer is responding to someone else's position on an issue. Is the response macro or micro? How does this response contribute to the essay's thesis?

10. **Critical analysis.** Determine whether the writer incorporates critical analysis into the argument. If so, how does the critical analysis help support the thesis? If not, how does leaving out critical analysis impact the argument?

Review
Drafting and Refining an Argument

Answer the following review questions in paragraph form or generate ideas to contribute to a group or class discussion.

1. What are four different strategies for contextualizing an issue?
2. What are the characteristics of a strong argumentative thesis statement?
3. What are the characteristics of a strong supporting claim?
4. What are the characteristics of effective supporting details?
5. What should you accomplish in the conclusion of your argument?
6. How should rhetorical appeals be weighted in an academic argument? Why?
7. What four rhetorical modes can be used to package your argument?
8. What role do critical analysis and response play in argumentation?

▶ Did You Know?

USING ACTIVE VOICE AND PASSIVE VOICE TO REFINE YOUR ARGUMENT

All English sentences are written in either the active voice or passive voice. Active voice sentences place the focus on who or what is performing the action in the sentence.

Passive voice sentences, on the other hand, place the focus on the recipient of the action—the doer is less important.

Take a look at this pair of sentences to visualize and understand the difference between active and passive voice:

YouTube should charge subscription fees.

Subscription fees should be charged by YouTube.

The first sentence is in the active voice. The subject is "YouTube," which is the *doer* of the action. YouTube should perform the action of charging subscription fees. The verb is *should charge*, and the direct object is *subscription fees*. The second sentence is in the passive voice. The subject is "subscription fees," which is the *recipient* of the action—not the doer. They are what are being charged. They are not doing the charging—YouTube is.

Choosing between Active and Passive Voice

When writing an academic argument or other persuasive text, you should use the active voice as much as possible. The active voice sets a more immediate tone, and places emphasis on the key players whose actions impact the issue. It also shows that you are well informed about the issue, as it forces you to assign a subject to an action. In passive voice, you can usually remove the doer of the action, which is why some people use it if they lack knowledge of an action's source. For this reason, an academic argument should not use passive voice. Instead, the passive voice should be used in an academic argument only when the recipient of the action is more important than the doer of the action. Table 10.4 summarizes the differences between active and passive voice.

TABLE 10.4
ACTIVE VERSUS PASSIVE VOICE

CHARACTERISTIC	ACTIVE	PASSIVE
Sentence Pattern	Doer + action + recipient	Recipient + action + doer (optional)
Usage	Sets a tone of immediacy Emphasizes the people whose actions impact the issue Demonstrates depth of knowledge	Emphasizes the people or things impacted by the issue Allows for the doer of the action to remain hidden, for better or for worse (good if the doer is unimportant; bad if the doer is purposefully being obscured to avoid blame or to cover up lack of knowledge)

How to Change from Active to Passive Voice and Vice Versa

Because there is an important relationship between the active and passive voice and the message you are trying to get across to your reader, you need to know how to change an active voice sentence to a passive voice sentence and vice versa.

Take another look at the example sentences from above:

YouTube should charge subscription fees.

Subscription fees should be charged by YouTube.

Notice how the subject of the active voice sentence becomes an object of the preposition "by" in the passive voice sentence. Similarly, the direct object from the active voice sentence becomes the subject of the passive voice sentence. The other change is the form of the verb. In the passive voice, you always need to have a form of the verb *be* followed by the past participle of the main verb. Make sure the auxiliary verb *be* agrees with the subject that precedes it, in terms of person and number. In other words, make sure you choose whether *am, is, are, was,* or *were* is required. If you are preceding the verb with a modal, as in the example above, just use the base form of *be*. To move back from passive to active, simply reverse the changes.

▶ Apply the Skill

Active versus Passive Voice

1. Find three examples of the use of passive voice in "Will Streaming Music Kill Songwriting?" Then, explain why you think the author has chosen passive voice instead of active voice for these statements.

2. Rewrite the three sentences you identified in Question 1, changing them from passive voice to active voice. For each sentence, explain how the change impacts the focus or tenor of the author's message.

3. Overall, does the author of "Will Streaming Music Kill Songwriting?" prefer active voice or passive voice? How does this preference impact the persuasiveness of his argument?

▶ Questions for Writing and Discussion

1. In "Will Streaming Music Kill Songwriting?" is Seabrook's argument controversial and focused? Provide three examples that demonstrate Seabrook's commitment to providing concrete details to support his claims.

2. What role does testimony play in the author's argument in "Will Streaming Music Kill Songwriting?" Are the sources of this testimony credible? Has the author chosen them strategically? Justify your response.

3. In "Will Streaming Music Kill Songwriting?" how does Seabrook build his *ethos* (credibility)? Provide three specific examples from the article to support your answer.

4. Seabrook uses the rhetorical mode of illustration when describing the impact of Spotify on copyright holders. Is this illustration effective at supporting his thesis statement? Think about originality, limiting bias, soundness, and concreteness.

5. Compare and contrast Seabrook's article to "Stream On: Why the Music Industry's Not Celebrating Its Big Digital Windfall Just Yet" by Josh O'Kane. What do the articles have in common? How are they different? Think about both the content and the way in which it is presented. Would you argue that one is more persuasive than the other? Why or why not?

6. Write your own argumentative essay about the impact of streaming on the music industry. Be sure to take a unique approach that you arrive at after you have done more research on the topic. Before writing your essay, construct an annotated bibliography of five secondary sources. Use the two articles from this chapter as two of your sources.

WILL STREAMING MUSIC KILL SONGWRITING?

As the music industry has been slowly and agonizingly stretched across the rack of the digital age, the songwriter's comfortable spot amid music's royalty flow has steadily slipped away.

By John Seabrook

1   FEBRUARY 8, 2016—For many songwriters, the wake-up call comes when they have their first streaming hit. For Michelle Lewis, an indie-rock singer-songwriter who now writes primarily for other artists, it was the song "Wings," which she co-wrote for the British girl group Little Mix. Lewis and her writing partner, Kay Hanley, the former lead singer of the band Letters to Cleo, had been busy working on a Disney show (children's TV relies heavily on alt-rock music), and at first she didn't realize how popular the song had become.

2   "We were emerging from this bubble," she told me, "and I realized, 'I have this hit. This is going to be good! Nearly three million streams on Spotify!' And then my check came, and it was for seventeen dollars and seventy-two cents. That's when I was, like, 'What the fuck?' So I called Kay."

3   "And I said, 'What the fuck?'" Hanley recalled.

4   Lewis was one of fourteen people credited for the song (some of whom had bigger shares than others). The discrepancy between the stream count and her earnings surprised her. The numbers from other services were similar.

5   "We started reading and talking to our friends and fellow-songwriters," Lewis said. Eventually, they found their way to Dina LaPolt, a music lawyer in Los Angeles, who specializes in copyright and songwriter issues.

6   Lewis: "And Dina said to us, 'Where the fuck have you bitches been?'"

7   Hanley: "She literally said that."

8   LaPolt told them that unless streaming rates were changed and the music-licensing system were overhauled for the digital age, the profession of song-writing was on its way to extinction. And they were on their own, she added, because, while everyone loves a songwriter, members of the profession have no actual bargaining power, whether via a union or another powerful institution, and so, when the money in the industry dries up, they're in serious trouble.

9   "Our jaws were on the floor at the end of talking to her," Lewis said. "And then it was, like, 'We have to tell our friends.'"

10   If streaming is the future of music, songwriters may soon be back to where they started. Stephen Foster, America's first professional songwriter, was also the first to die broke. His songs, which include "Oh! Susanna," "Camptown Races," "Old Folks at Home" (a.k.a. "Swanee River"), "My Old Kentucky Home," and "Jeanie With the Light Brown Hair," made lots of money for other people—music publishers, music-sheet sellers, minstrel-show promoters, concert-hall owners, and star performers. But not very much of that money reached the

chronically impecunious Foster, who died, in 1864, in New York City, at the age of thirty-seven, with three pennies in his pocket, some Civil War scrip, and a scrap of paper on which the songwriter had written "Dear friends and gentle hearts." His best-known melody, "Beautiful Dreamer," came out only after his death.

11   Over the next century and a half, American songwriters' prospects improved dramatically, largely thanks to the Copyright Act of 1909 and subsequent government intervention. Under the regime that emerged in the first half of the twentieth century, composers own the "publishing" rights to their songs—the copyright on the song's words and melody, as they exist on paper. Most song-writers assign part of these rights to a music publisher in exchange for an advance and for marketing services. If the music publisher succeeds in getting a song recorded, the songwriter then grants the backers of the recording—a record label, generally—what's known as a "mechanical license." (The word "mechanical" derives from the days when player-piano rolls were the primary commodity of the nascent record business.) With each copy of the record sold, the owners of the master recording, as the audio copyright is known, pay a mechanical royalty to the owners of the song's publishing rights. Today, that royalty rate works out to about nine cents per copy.

12   Songwriters also earn performance royalties when a record is played in a large commercial venue, such as a restaurant or a theater. With the spread of broad-cast radio, in the nineteen-twenties and thirties, performance royalties became a significant part of a songwriter's potential income. Generally, when a song plays on the radio, the station pays the publishing-rights holders a fixed rate that represents a percentage of the station's advertising revenues. The owners of master recordings, on the other hand, don't make anything from radio play, nor do the performers. The reasoning behind this bizarre arrangement, which apart from the U.S. exists only in Iran, North Korea, and China, is that the promotional value of radio play is recompense enough; the labels and performers can make up the difference with record and ticket sales.

13   In 1941 the Justice Department issued what's known as the Consent Decree, which allowed performing-rights organizations (P.R.O.s, or collecting societ-ies) to process the licensing fees for large numbers of songwriters, collectively, for obvious reasons of efficiency. In return for an exemption from what would normally be treated as an antitrust issue—private owners banding together to set prices—the music publishers agreed to let a federal court set the royalty rates, if the parties disagree on them. The Consent Decree also mandated compulsory licensing, requiring songwriters to make their entire catalogues available to whoever pays the licensing fee. Accordingly, songwriting is now the most heavily regulated of the creative arts. Seventy per cent of a songwriter's income comes from rates set by the government, rather than by the songwriters and publishers, on the free market.

14   Regulation helped to insure [*sic*] that songwriters avoided Stephen Foster's fate and were paid fairly for their work. Today, the system supports perhaps a million American songwriters. (The estimate is based on the memberships of the two largest collecting societies, ASCAP and B.M.I., and a guess about the much smaller SESAC, which doesn't publish its numbers.) It offers a decent living for many in the trade, and the prospect of extraordinary wealth for a few. Indeed,

the amount of money that a hit song can earn for its composers is staggering. Court papers in a recent infringement dispute involving Pharrell Williams, Robin Thicke, and the estate of Marvin Gaye have revealed that the song "Blurred Lines" earned almost seventeen million dollars in under two years, mainly from radio play, with Thicke and Williams each getting more than five million dollars. And a long-running suit launched by the family of Randy California, the former front man of the band Spirit, whose 1968 song "Taurus" is alleged to sound a lot like "Stairway to Heaven," calculated that the Led Zeppelin song, which was released in 1971, had earned *half a billion dollars* by 2008. Since copyrights last for up to seventy years, depending on when the song was released, the rights to a couple of hit songs can support an entire family for several generations.

15   The remarkable worldwide popularity of American music is often ascribed, rightly, to the talent and diversity of the country's artists and musicians. But it also happened because of a system that inspired and allowed songwriters to devote themselves full time to their craft. (Of the top ten most-downloaded songs in the U.S. in 2015, according to Nielsen, only one, Fetty Wap's "Trap Queen," was written solely by the artist.) The system not only rewarded proven talents; it also let promising novices secure advances against future earnings, affording them the time to learn their craft gradually, until they too had a hit and could begin nurturing the next generation of talent.

16   But as the music business began to be slowly and agonizingly stretched across the rack of the digital age, the songwriter's comfortable spot amid music's royalty flow started slipping away. The steep decline in album sales—the result of a shift from brick-and-mortar distribution to digital retail, and now to streaming—has dealt a blow to songwriters' mechanical-royalty income. (In the album era, even a throwaway track on a best-selling LP earned as much for a songwriter as the hits that made people purchase the album in the first place.) And, as Lewis's experience demonstrates, the performance-royalty rates that songwriters command from streaming services such as Pandora, Spotify, YouTube, Amazon Prime, and Apple Music are in most cases far lower than the ones they get for terrestrial-radio plays—the entire royalty payout, remember. Typically, under terms that the record labels worked out with the streaming services (and somehow persuaded the federal rate courts to sign off on), when a song is streamed, sixty per cent of the income goes to the owners of the sound recording, thirty per cent goes to the service itself, and ten per cent goes to songwriters and publishers. When a song is streamed on an Internet radio site—Pandora is by far the largest—the holders of publishing copyrights receive a thousandth of a cent per stream.

17   Why are streams worth so much less than radio spins? The standard reason given is because a stream is generally a one-to-one transaction, whereas a spin goes out to thousands or even millions of people at a time. But if millions of people hear your song on YouTube, and you still haven't received a check, you begin to sense that something is amiss. Also, why is the value of the publishing copyright worth so much less, relative to the sound-recording copyright, in the streaming world? There appears to have been a digital land grab by the record labels, who own most of the master recordings for the U.S. catalogue. Having lost out, historically, on income derived from performance royalties and sound recording for terrestrial radio, they were careful, in the digital era, to guarantee themselves income, and in some cases equity interest, from streaming.

18   Kara DioGuardi, a longtime songwriter known for her turn as a judge on "American Idol," told me recently, "I'll be at a party and I'll hear a friend's song, and then I'll realize it's being streamed. And I'll think, 'Wow, that sucks,' because I know the songwriters aren't getting paid what they deserve." For songwriters, there are both big, sweeping rationales and smaller, more nuanced reasons to hate streaming services. Perhaps the greatest outrage, apart from the primal sense that the services are picking their pockets, is directed at the corporations benefitting most from streaming music—Google, Amazon, Apple. These companies, which are among the wealthiest on earth, use music to draw traffic to their sites and keep people within their ecosystems, but for them, the business end of music is hardly more than a rounding error. In 2015, for example, the global music-copyright industry brought in twenty-five billion dollars, barely more than a tenth of Apple's revenues for the year. What makes the situation positively Kafkaesque is that under the terms of the Consent Decree, which was created in part to prevent songwriters from monopolizing the market, composers are now often compelled to license their songs to these monopolistic behemoths at absurdly low rates.

19   As for the more nuanced reasons, some streams are worse than others. Spotify's free, ad-supported platform has been the source of much complaint, as has YouTube's. Spotify's total revenues from its ad-supported tier in the first half of 2015 were a paltry hundred and sixty-two million dollars, sixty million *less* than the revenues from the sales of vinyl albums and EPs over the same period. Revenues from the company's paid tier are usually marginally better than from its ad-supported one, but it's still having issues with publishing royalties there. It appears that while the company was assiduous about getting the licenses for the audio-recording copyrights from the labels, it was less thorough about obtaining all of the necessary mechanical-publishing licenses, partly because the metadata needed to identify the rights holders is missing from many song files. Spotify is holding about seventeen million dollars in royalties in a segregated account until these copyright holders can be identified (publishers say that the number should be closer to twenty-five million), and is in the process of building a database that will make it easier to identify them.

20   In late 2015, David Lowery, the frontman of Cracker and Camper van Beethoven, and a persistent industry gadfly, filed a class-action lawsuit against Spotify, charging the company with willfully infringing the mechanical rights to a number of his songs, and those of others, and seeking up to a hundred and fifty million dollars in damages. According to TechDirt's breakdown of the suit, Lowery is arguing that Spotify is failing to obtain the necessary mechanical licenses for many of the compositions in its database, including some of his; the case may hinge, among other issues, on whether the company properly complied with technical requirements for situations in which it didn't know who the copyright holders were. (A second lawsuit was filed by the singer-songwriter Melissa Ferrick in early January.)

21   Certainly the missing names did not slow co-founder Daniel Ek's quest to license all the world's music. However, it's not entirely clear whether Spotify even needs a mechanical license to stream music. A stream isn't a copy in the same way that a download is—in many ways, it is more like a performance. The Copyright Act of 1976 is too dated to provide much useful statutory guidance.

22   Amid all of the anger and uncertainty, last year LaPolt, the copyright lawyer, brought together Lewis, Hanley, and some hundred other songwriters, and inspired them to found an education and advocacy organization, Songwriters of North America (SONA), that seeks major reforms in the song-licensing system, to better suit the digital era. There are already a few legislative initiatives under way, nationally—among them the Songwriter Equity Act, a bill first introduced by Doug Collins, a Republican from Georgia, and Hakeem Jeffries, a Democrat from New York, and then in the Senate by, among others, Orrin Hatch, who is himself a prolific songwriter. (Copyright issues make for strange political bedfellows.) It would amend two sections of the Copyright Act of 1976, to raise the rate songwriters get from streaming services. Another effort, the Fair Pay, Fair Play Act—which would require terrestrial-radio companies to begin paying royalties to audio-recording-rights holders, as well as to songwriters, alongside some reforms to the digital-music industry—was introduced in the House of Representatives in 2015.

23   In LaPolt's view, the best hope for real change is a major revision of the Copyright Act of 1976. Bob Goodlatte, a Republican congressman from Virginia and a techie, has made copyright reform a signature issue of his tenure as chairman, for the past two years, of the House Judiciary Committee, holding twenty subcommittee hearings on the issue, and inviting a number of songwriters, including Rosanne Cash and Sheryl Crow, to appear. LaPolt thinks it is unlikely that Goodlatte would leave the chairmanship (in 2017) without at least trying to effect significant reform.

24   Songwriters have never really had to organize before, but they're learning, Lewis said. "It's because we've been doing fine. As long as the checks showed up it was, like, 'This has nothing to do with me.' But about two years ago people started saying, 'Hey, who moved our cheese?'" Even now, she added, some writers are loath to complain, because "the psychology is, 'I can't believe they're paying me to do this at all, and I'd better not rock the boat or they'll find out about my scam!'"

25   Savan Kotecha, whose "Love Me Like You Do," was recently nominated for a Grammy, told me that songwriters are increasingly aware of the stakes. "It affects how you plan for the future and whether you invest in new talent, because in the streaming world you won't necessarily see any return on your investment. For now, terrestrial radio is holding out. But radio could go away, because everyone has phones. And once streaming gets into cars in a big way, it's over."

26   Indeed, music listeners continue to embrace streaming. On-demand streaming-service usage rose ninety-three per cent in 2015, with three hundred and seventeen billion songs streamed, in all. Adding YouTube and other unpaid services pushes the total into the trillions. Meanwhile, album sales, the longtime mainstay of the business, continued their decline, in spite of the record-breaking success of Adele's "25", which accounted for three per cent of the entire U.S. album market in 2015, according to Billboard. For a songwriter, taking a stand against streaming can seem like taking a stand against your own future.

27   Performers are facing many of the same challenges, but they, at least, have the option of going on tour. Without royalties, songwriters will have only dear friends and gentle hearts to support them. That didn't work out so well for Stephen Foster.

Source: Seabrook, John. "Will Streaming Music Kill Songwriting?" *The New Yorker*, 8 February, 2016. www.newyorker.com/business/currency/will-streaming-music-kill-songwriting. Reproduced by permission of the author.

APPENDIX: DOCUMENTATION

Overview

What Is Documentation?

When you write an essay, it is important to give credit to the sources you have used. Crediting these sources formally in writing is called documentation.

What Is the Purpose of Documentation?

Documentation is crucial to protect you against serious consequences of plagiarism (presenting ideas you learned from others without acknowledging the source). Also, documentation allows your reader to access your sources for fact checking and their own further research.

Which Information Needs Documentation?

Any information from another author that you *quote* (copy directly) or *paraphrase* (write in your own words) must be documented. If you are not sure whether an idea needs to be documented or whether it is simply common knowledge, check with your professor. When in doubt, it is better to document the source to be safe.

How Do I Document Sources?

Keep track of the secondary sources you draw from when you are putting your paper together. A secondary source is a published source, such as an article, a book, a webpage, etc. The guidelines outlined below will show you the basics on how to document secondary sources.

There are various styles of documentation, each with their own set of particular formatting rules. Two of the most common styles are *APA* (American Psychological Association) and *MLA* (Modern Language Association). In general, APA is used for the social sciences, and MLA is used for literature and humanities. When your instructor assigns a research paper, check which style she prefers you to use. One style must be used consistently throughout the paper.

Two Essential Parts of Documentation

Whichever formal documentation style you use, you must document each source that you quote or paraphrase both *within the text* of your paper and *in a list of sources at the end* of your paper. In other words, you must include both these parts for any source you document:

1. *In-text citation* (a short documentation within parentheses in the text of your paper)
2. *Bibliographic entry* (a full documentation in a list of sources at the end of your paper)

An in-text citation is short, so it does not interrupt the flow of your paper. The purposes of an in-text citation are (1) to show your reader where in your paper a source has been used, and (2) to signal your reader to the full reference information for that source at the end of the paper. Never include a URL to cite a quote or paraphrase within the text of your paper. Instead, use the proper format for an in-text citation either in APA or MLA style, as shown in the sections that follow.

APA Style

Follow the guidelines below to format your paper in APA style. Also, see the sample essay in APA style near the end of this appendix.

General formatting (font, spacing, etc.): Use these features throughout the paper, from title page to references: 12 pt. Times New Roman font, double spacing, and 1-inch margins. Indent each paragraph (except the abstract).

Running head: Include a "running head" at the top of every page. This includes the title of your paper (or a shortened version that is no more than 50 characters) and the page number. On the title page only, include "Running head:" before your title. For a sample of how the running head should look, see the sample essay in APA style near the end of this appendix.

To create a running head, insert page numbers top right in your page header. Then type "[TITLE OF YOUR PAPER]" to the left of the page number and press enter until the title is top left. Within your word-processing programs, try choosing "Different First Page" to do so.

Here are the main parts to include in an APA-style paper:

Title page: Start with a cover page that includes the *title* of your paper, *your name*, and your *school's name*. However, your professor may ask you to include other information as well, such as her name, the course code, and the date of submission. Be sure to check the assignment instructions and include what your professor requires.

- Centre everything horizontally and vertically. Do not use underlining, bold, or italics.
- Capitalize key words in the title. Do not use quotation marks around your title.

Abstract (if required by your professor): If an abstract is required, include it on a separate page after the title page. An abstract is a one-paragraph summary of your paper, 150–250 words long. Do not indent the paragraph. Centre the title "Abstract" above the paragraph.

Main body: Start with the title, capitalized and centred above your first paragraph. Use APA-style in-text citations in the body of your paper wherever necessary.

References: Start a new page at the end of your paper where you will list your sources. Use APA-style bibliographic entries (references).

In-Text Citations in APA Style

For information that you quote or paraphrase, you must include an in-text citation.

When you quote (copy an author's words exactly), you must

- include quotation marks (" ") around the quoted text
- cite the following three items, in order:
  - *author's last name* (never cite the first name only)
  - *year* of publication in parentheses
  - *page number(s)* of the quoted text in parentheses (preceded by "p." or "pp.")

Here are three correct ways to incorporate these elements in an in-text citation:

> It has been argued that "participating in regular art therapy sessions has great potential to positively affect one's mental health" (Miller, 2017, p. 64).

> According to Miller (2017), "participating in regular art therapy sessions has great potential to positively affect one's mental health" (p. 64).

> Miller (2017) stated that "participating in regular art therapy sessions has great potential to positively affect one's mental health" (p. 64).

Note that all three items can be placed inside parentheses after the quotation. Alternatively, the author's name (year) can be placed before the quotation in an introductory phrase. Either way, the year always belongs in parentheses directly after the author, and the page number always belongs in parentheses directly after the quotation. Also, note the particular placement of commas, periods, and spaces, and follow this format when you create your citations.

When you summarize or paraphrase, you must still cite the author's name and year. You are encouraged to cite the page number, but it is not required. Also, do not include quotation marks.

> Art therapy has undeniably had a positive impact on those experiencing mental health problems (Malchiodi, 2013).

> According to Malchiodi (2013), art therapy has undeniably had a positive impact on those experiencing mental health problems.

WHAT IF A SOURCE HAS NO AUTHOR'S NAME? NO YEAR? NO PAGE NUMBER?

If any of the three items listed above are missing from the source, do not simply leave them out of your citation. Instead, use the following alternatives in their place.

No author: If there is no person's name, the author might be an organization.

(Statistics Canada, 2016)

If there is no individual or organization as author, use a shortened version of the title.

("Art Therapy Effects," 2014) or (*Art Therapy Works Wonders*, 2012)

Put titles of articles, chapters, and websites in quotation marks.

Put titles of books and reports in italics.

No date: Use "n.d.":

(Grewal, n.d.,)

No page number: For most electronic sources, like web articles, there will be no page number. Instead, cite the paragraph number preceded by "para."

(Kleiner, 2018, para. 1)

Here is an example of a source with no author, no date, and no page number:

("How to Make Money," n.d., para. 3)

WHAT IF A SOURCE HAS MORE THAN ONE AUTHOR?

Two authors: cite both last names. (Hughes & daSilva, 2011, p. 612).

Three to five authors: cite all author's names in the first citation. If you cite the same work again, use the first author's name followed by "et al.", which means "and others."

(Hughes, daSilva, & Mankus, 2015) … then (Hughes et al., 2015).

Six or more authors, use the first author's name plus "et al." for all citations.

(Uttley et al., 2015)

WHAT IF I AM QUOTING OR PARAPHRASING A SOURCE WITHIN ANOTHER SOURCE?

For indirect sources, precede the citation with "as cited in."

Example: Walker argued that changes in emotion and behaviour were the key focus (as cited in Miller, 2017, p. 67).

In other words: While reading Miller, you learned about Walker. Miller is the entry in your References List (not Walker).

WHAT IF I NEED TO OMIT OR ADD WORDS TO A QUOTE TO MAKE IT FIT SMOOTHLY IN MY OWN TEXT?

To omit words, use "…" to replace any words you leave out.

To insert words, use "[ ]" around any words you insert.

Bibliographic Entries in APA Style (References List)

There is a specific way to include the full bibliographic information for each source, and this will vary depending on the type of source (book, online article, etc.). Examples for several types of sources are included in the sample essay near the end of this appendix. Pay close attention to punctuation, capitalization, italics, spacing, etc. Remember to double space.

> **Tip:** Many citation tools exist (e.g., on library websites, within word processing programs, etc.) that can produce a reference electronically. Note, however, that these tools often have flaws, so if you use them, check that the resulting reference matches proper APA style as outlined below, and make any adjustments necessary.

Follow these *basic rules* to format your References list overall.

- Start the references list on a new page at the end of your paper.
- Centre the title "References" at the top. Do not bold, underline, etc.
- List your entries in alphabetical order, by the first word of each entry.
- Use a hanging indent for each entry. This means that the second and subsequent lines of each entry should be indented.

- Give the author's last name followed by initial(s) of first name(s). If a source has multiple authors, present the author's names in the order they appear in the source. (Do not use alphabetical order within an entry; use it only between entries.)
- When referring to books, chapters, articles, or webpages, capitalize only the first letter of the first word of a title, the first word after a colon or a dash in the title, and proper nouns.
- Italicize titles of works that contain articles, etc. such as books, journals, and websites.
- *If there is no author,* use either the organization as the author or the full article title in the author position.
- *If there is no date,* use "(n.d.)" in the date position.

Here are two examples of full reference entries in APA style:

Online article from a newspaper or magazine website:

Author's Last Name, Initial(s) of First Name(s). (Year, Month Day). Title of article. *Title of Source Containing the Article*. Retrieved from http://copy_paste_homepage_url

Kolczak, A. (2017, December 8). Five trends influencing the future of our cities. *National Geographic*. Retrieved from https://www.nationalgeographic.com

Online article from a scholarly journal:

Author, A. A., & Author, B. B. (Date of publication). Title of article. *Title of Journal, volume number* (issue number if available), page range. doi:0000000/000000000000

Wooldridge, M.B., & Shapka, J. (2012). Playing with technology: Mother–toddler interaction scores lower during play with electronic toys. *Journal of Applied Developmental Psychology, 33*(5), 211–218. doi.org/10.1016/j.appdev.2012.05.005

MLA Style

Follow the guidelines below to format your paper in MLA style. Also, see the sample essay in MLA style near the end of this appendix.

General formatting (font, spacing, etc.): Use these features throughout the paper: 12 pt. Times New Roman font, double spacing, and 1-inch margins.

Header: Create a header that includes your last name, followed by a space and then the page number, placed at the top right of each page of your paper.

Here are the main parts to include in an MLA-style paper:

First page: Do not start with a title page unless your professor specifically requires one. Type the following information flush left at the top of your first page, directly under the header.

Your name

Your professor's name

Your course

Date of submission

Below this information, type the title of your paper and centre it on the page. Do not use underlining, bold, italics, or quotation marks around the title. Begin your first paragraph directly under the title. Remember to double space.

Main body: You may choose to use numbered headings to divide your paper into sections. Check with your professor if this is required. Make sure to use MLA-style in-text citations in the body of your paper wherever necessary.

Works cited: Start a new page at the end of your paper where you will list your sources. Use MLA-style bibliographic entries (works cited).

In-Text Citations in MLA Style

For information that you quote directly or paraphrase, you must include an in-text citation. *When you quote* (copy an author's words exactly), you must

- include quotation marks (" ") around the quoted text
- cite the following two items, in order, with no punctuation in between:
  - *author's last name* (never cite the first name only)
  - *page number* of the quoted text

Here are two correct ways to incorporate these elements in an in-text citation:

> It has been argued that "participating in regular art therapy sessions has great potential to positively affect one's mental health" (Miller 64).

> Miller stated that "participating in regular art therapy sessions has great potential to positively affect one's mental health" (64).

Pay close attention to the punctuation and spacing, and follow this in your citations.

When you summarize or paraphrase, do not include quotation marks, but do cite the author's last name and page number(s).

> Art therapy helps people through its process and product (Malchiodi 28–31).

> According to Malchiodi, art therapy helps people through its process and product (28–31).

WHAT IF A SOURCE HAS NO AUTHOR'S NAME? NO PAGE NUMBER?

No author: If there is no person's name, the author might be an organization.

(Canadian Blood Services 48) or (CAMH 23)

If there is no individual or organization as author, use a shortened version of the title.

("Art Therapy Effects") or (*Art Therapy Works Wonders* 146)

Put titles of short works (articles, chapters, etc.) in quotation marks.

Put titles of longer works (books, reports, websites, etc.) in italics.

No page number: For most electronic sources, like web articles, there will be no page number. In this case, cite the author's name only.

(Miller) or (CAMH)

WHAT IF A SOURCE HAS MORE THAN ONE AUTHOR?

Two authors: cite both last names. (Hughes and daSilva 612).

Three or more authors: cite the first author's last name followed by "et al.", which means "and others."

(Uttley et al. 318) or (Uttley et al.)

WHAT IF I AM QUOTING OR PARAPHRASING A SOURCE WITHIN ANOTHER SOURCE?

For indirect sources, precede the citation with "qtd. in":

Example: Walker argued that changes in emotion and behaviour were the key focus (qtd. in Miller 67).

In other words: While reading Miller, you learned about Walker. Miller is the entry in your Works Cited list (not Walker).

WHAT IF I NEED TO OMIT OR ADD WORDS TO A QUOTE TO MAKE IT FIT SMOOTHLY IN MY OWN TEXT?

To omit words, use "…" to replace any words you leave out

To insert words, use "[ ]" around any words you insert

Bibliographic Entries in MLA Style (Works Cited List)

There is a specific way to include the full bibliographic information for each source, and this will vary depending on the type of source (book, online article, etc.). Examples for several types of sources are included in the sample essay near the end of this appendix. Pay close attention to punctuation, capitalization, italics, spacing, etc.

> **Tip:** Many citation tools exist (e.g., on library websites, within word processing programs, etc.) that can produce a reference electronically. Note, however, that these tools often have flaws, so if you use them, check that the resulting reference matches proper MLA style as outlined below, and make any adjustments necessary.

Follow these *basic rules* to format your Works Cited list overall.

- Start the Works Cited list on a new page at the end of your paper.
- Centre the title "Works Cited" at the top. Do not bold, underline, etc.
- List your entries in alphabetical order, by the first word of each entry.
- Use a hanging indent for each entry. This means that the second and subsequent lines of each entry should be indented.
- Give the author's last name followed by first name. If the author uses a middle initial, include it after the first name.
  - If a source has *two authors,* use this format:
    First author's last name, first name and second author's first name last name.
    (E.g., Green, Eric. J., and Athena A. Drewes.)
  - If a source has *three or more authors,* list the first author's name followed by "et al." (E.g., Green, Eric J., et al.)

- Capitalize the first letter of key words in titles of books, articles, websites, etc. (Do not capitalize function words like "a," "the," "in," etc.)
- Use quotation marks around titles of shorter works such as articles, chapters, etc.
- Use italics for titles of larger works (that contain shorter works like articles) such as books, journals, and websites.
- *If there is no author,* use either the organization as the author or the full article title in the author position.
- *If there is no date of publication or page number,* just skip this information.
- *Include the last date you accessed the source,* if you accessed it electronically, at the end of the entry. (E.g., Accessed 12 Apr. 2018.)

Next are two examples of full works cited entries in MLA style.

BOOK

Author's Last Name, First Name Middle Initial (if given). *Title of Book.* Publisher, Location, Publication Date.

Guo, Shibao, and Lloyd Wong. *Revisiting Multiculturalism in Canada: Theories, Policies and Debates.* Sense Publishers, Rotterdam, 2015.

ONLINE ARTICLE FROM A NEWSPAPER, MAGAZINE, OR OTHER TYPE OF WEBSITE

Author's Last Name, First Name. "Title of article." *Title of Source Containing the Article,* Date Month Year, www.copy_paste_full_url. Accessed Date Month Year.

Kolczak, Amy. (2017, December 8). "Five trends influencing the future of our cities." *National Geographic*, 8 Dec. 2017, www.nationalgeographic.com/environment/urban-expeditions/green-buildings/design-trends-sustainability-cities-wellness-climate-change/. Accessed 3 Feb 2018.

Sample Research Paper

An example of a research paper is presented on the following pages. The essay "Treating Mental Illness with Art Therapy" by Madeleine Luvisa is shown first in APA style and then in MLA style.

> **Note:** This sample research paper demonstrates the correct usage of the APA and MLA styles of documentation. The paper shown here is typeset according to the textbook's design. For word-processed documents, APA recommends that your essay be typed, double spaced, on 8.5" x 11" paper, with 1" margins on all sides. You should use a clear font that is highly readable. APA recommends using the Times New Roman font at 12 pt size. MLA recommends that whatever font you select be set in 12 pt type. Consult with your instructor for more information on formatting to be sure you understand his or her requirements.

Sample Research Paper in APA Style

APA style requires only your name and your school name, but your professor may ask you to also include the course code, professor's name, submission date, etc. Always follow your professor's instructions carefully, and check with him if you need clarification on any part of the paper.

Treating Mental Illness with Art Therapy

Madeleine Luvisa

Mohawk College

Treating Mental Illness with Art Therapy

"In any given year, 1 in 5 Canadians experiences a mental health problem" (Centre for Addiction and Mental Health [CAMH], n.d., para. 2). This is a staggering statistic, especially considering the fact that it only reflects the reported cases in our country. Mental health is a widespread issue; every individual is impacted by it, whether directly or indirectly, at some point in their lives. However, the conversation surrounding mental illness and the treatment it requires is often discouraged and dismissed. This is no topic from which to shy away; in fact, the more we create conversation about mental health, the more people will begin to understand it, be aware of it, and be courageous enough to seek the treatment they require. And perhaps, through this open conversation, people will begin to consider trying new treatments to which they have not yet been exposed. One of many fairly new treatments that is being introduced to the field of mental health is art therapy. Although it is still quite new, art therapy has undeniably had a positive impact on those experiencing mental health problems (Malchiodi, 2013). Art therapy has two essential elements: process and product. As a process, it as an opportunity to engage in self-expression, which can lead to some kind of transformation. As a product, the art is a means of communicating issues and emotions symbolically (Finnerty, 2013). It is essential that art therapy continue to be used on a greater scale as a treatment for mental health problems because it helps individuals work through their prob-lems healthily, it provides a way for people to relax, and it allows indi-viduals to express themselves in ways verbal communication cannot achieve.

According to Marygrace Berberian, a clinical assistant professor of art therapy, "Research has shown that art making can have a profound impact on a person's physical and psychological well-being" (as cited in Kvarnstrom, 2017, para. 5). While the healing properties of art have been valued by artists for thousands of years, art therapy started to form officially during the middle of the 20th-century, when doctors noticed people suffering from mental illness expressing themselves through artwork and started to explore this as a healing strategy (Cherry, 2018). Art therapy allows people to immerse themselves in the creative process as a step towards creating new thoughts, emotions, and behaviours. As a result, art therapy has come to be recognized as an evidence-based treatment for various mental health issues. In a study that reviewed the clinical effectiveness of art therapy, it was found that art therapy had a significant positive effect on depression, anxiety, trauma, distress, inability to cope, and low self-esteem (Uttley et al., 2015). Instead of using negative coping mechanisms, such as substance abuse or self-injury, people who experience mental illness can access other ways to manage without causing harm to themselves or others. This can allow them to regain a sense of control over their lives.

For some people, art therapy is a good alternative or complement to talk therapy. It can sometimes be very difficult to search for the correct words to explain to somebody else what you are thinking and feeling; this may create a feeling of resentment and avoidance toward standard counselling. However, art therapy goes beyond verbal communication skills, and taps into our ability to be present in the moment and experience it as wholly as possible. As argued by Pizarro (2004), "individuals who lack the skills to communicate through writing, or are uncomfortable about verbal expression, may be encouraged to disclose by first engaging in an art project" (p. 6). For people who find it difficult to communicate their life experiences verbally, art therapy provides "'safe space' to express difficult emotions," and some say it "is more relaxing and fun than other forms of verbal therapy" (Hughes & da Silva, 2011, p. 612). Art therapy helps people find ways to express their feelings without having to use words.

Art therapy can be beneficial for children as well. Introducing various coping skills to children and adolescents puts them on a path towards stronger mental health. According to Green and Drewes (2014), art therapy provides youth psychoanalytic, developmental, and cognitive-behavioural benefits. They reviewed research in the area, noting that "Art therapy research suggests that it can be an effective modality for treating a variety of issues and circumstances of childhood and adolescence" (p. 49). They reported that art therapy has been associated with a decrease in symptoms of post-traumatic stress disorder (PTSD) and hyperactivity and with an increase in self-esteem, assertiveness, and coping ability.

There is also compelling anecdotal evidence of art therapy's value for both youth and adults. For example, one teenager shared her story of seeing a therapist for depression during her sophomore year of high school, during which she was encouraged to let out her feelings through making art. She ended up creating art on the canvas of over seventy pairs of shoes and feeling better over time (Children's Hospital Colorado, 2014). In another case, a textile artist found that making fabric collage helped her through depression and PTSD, and six years later she developed a program through CAMH called Art Cart, which "brings career artists who have experienced mental health and addiction in to the hospital to do art with patients who are recovering" (Bruno, 2017, para. 6). People in the program have reported that they are comforted by the fact that they don't have to have art skills to do expressive art therapy, and that the chance to make art in a group setting allows them to feel relaxed and grow (vanKampen, 2017). Another individual who suffers from depression and anxiety discovered art therapy while hospitalized and said, "I drew for my life" (Kleiner, 2018, para. 1). He has continued to use art to feel better for a decade.

To conclude, the further integration of art therapy in the field of mental health treatment would be beneficial because it allows people to cope with their struggles in a more healthy and productive manner, it creates an opportunity for people to relax and de-stress, and it provides a chance for individuals to express themselves and their emotions in ways words cannot. Art opens the door to a new aspect of healing. Although art therapy may not be a successful treatment for all who try it, it would undoubtedly help many people make progress on their path to recovery. It is time for us all to bring more awareness to the benefits of art therapy for mental health.

References

Online article (*newspaper*)

Bruno, N. (2017, April 14). Art Cart is a crafty idea to improving mental health. *Toronto Star*. Retrieved from https://www.thestar.com

Webpage (*with organization as author*)

Centre for Addiction and Mental Health. (n.d.). Mental health statistics. Retrieved from CAMH: http://www.camh.ca

Online article (*website*)

Cherry, K. (2018, June 11). How art therapy is used to help people heal. *Verywellmind*. Retrieved from https://www.verywellmind.com/what-is-art-therapy-2795755

Online video

Colorado Children's Hospital. (2014, September 21). *How art therapy changed my life* [Video file]. Retrieved from https://www.youtube.com/watch?v=Rhw4spxVqN0

Audio podcast

Finnerty, T. (Host). (2013, February 4). Mental health day podcast #5: Art therapy with Cathy Malchiodi. *Mental Health Day Podcast: Art Therapy*. Podcast retrieved from https://www.cathymalchiodi.com/resources/audio-podcasts/

Book (*with two authors, 1st edition*)

Green, E. J., & Drewes, A. A. (2014). *Integrating expressive arts and play therapy with children and adolescents* (1st ed.). Hoboken, NJ: Wiley.

Online scholarly journal article

Hughes, E. G., & da Silva, A. M. (2011). A pilot study assessing art therapy as a mental health intervention for infertile women. *Human Reproduction*, 26(3), 611–615. doi:https://doi.org/10.1093/humrep/deq385

Kleiner, G. (2018, January 25). Re: Psychological benefits of art therapy. [Blog comment]. Retrieved from https://www.ccpa-accp.ca/psychological-benefits-of-art-therapy/

Kvarnstrom, E. (2017, July 14). Using art therapy to create freedom from depression. [Blog post]. Retrieved from https://www.bridgestorecovery.com/blog/using-art-therapy-to-create-

Malchiodi, C. (2013, February 27). Yes, Virginia, there is some art therapy research. *Psychology Today*. Retrieved from https://www.psychologytoday.com

Pizarro, J. (2004). The efficacy of art and writing therapy: Increasing positive mental health outcomes and participant retention after exposure to traumatic experience. *Art Therapy*, 21(1), 5–12. doi:10.1080/07421656.2004.10129327

Uttley, L., Scope, A., Stevenson, M., Rawdin, A., Taylor Buck, E., Sutton, A., . . . & Wood, C. (2015). Systematic review and economic modelling of the clinical effectiveness and cost-effectiveness of art therapy among people with non-psychotic mental health disorders. *Health Technology Assessment*, 19(18), 1–120. doi:10.3310/hta19180

vanKampen, S. (2017, October 14). Healing invisible wounds with the Art Cart. *CBC News*. Retrieved from https://www.cbc.ca/news/entertainment/camh-healing-art-cart-1.4354472

Online web comment (*posted in comment section of blog*)

Blog post

Online article (*magazine*)

Online scholarly journal article

Online scholarly journal article (*more than seven authors*)

Online article (*news website*)

Sample Research Paper in MLA Style

MLA style does not require a separate title page, but your professor may ask you to include one. Always follow your professor's instructions carefully, and check with him or her if you need clarification on any part of the paper.

Madeleine Luvisa
Professor Amy Santiago
COMM 19999
27 July 2018

Treating Mental Illness with Art Therapy

"In any given year, 1 in 5 Canadians experiences a mental health problem" (CAMH). This is a staggering statistic, especially considering the fact that it reflects only the reported cases in our country. Mental health is a widespread issue; every individual is impacted by it, whether directly or indirectly, at some point in their lives. However, the conversation surrounding mental illness and the treatment it requires is often discouraged and dismissed. This is not a topic from which to shy away; in fact, the more we create conversation about mental health, the more people will begin to understand it, be aware of it, and be courageous enough to seek the treatment they require. And perhaps, through this open conversation, people will begin to consider trying new treatments to which they have not yet been exposed. One of many fairly new treatments that is being introduced to the field of mental health is art therapy. Although it is still quite new, art therapy has undeniably had a positive impact on those experiencing mental health problems (Malchiodi). Art therapy has two essential elements: process and product. As a process, it is an opportunity to engage in self-expression, which can lead to some kind of transformation. As a product, the art is a means of communicating issues and emotions symbolically (Finnerty). It is essential that art therapy continue to be used on a greater scale as a treatment for mental health problems because it helps individuals work through their problems healthily, it provides a way for people to relax, and it allows individuals to express themselves in ways verbal communication cannot achieve.

According to Marygrace Berberian, a clinical assistant professor of art therapy, "Research has shown that art making can have a profound impact on a person's physical and psychological well-being" (qtd. in Kvarnstrom). While the healing properties of art have been valued by artists for thousands of years, art therapy started to form officially during the middle of the 20th century, when doctors noticed people suffering from mental illness expressing themselves through artwork and started to explore this as a healing strategy (Cherry). Art therapy allows people to immerse themselves in the creative process as a step towards creating new thoughts, emotions, and behaviours. As a result, art therapy has come to be recognized as an evidence-based treatment for various mental health issues. In a study that reviewed the clinical effectiveness of art therapy, it was found that art therapy had a significant positive effect on depression, anxiety, trauma, distress, inability to cope, and low self-esteem (Uttley et al. 87). Instead of using negative coping mechanisms, such as substance abuse or self-injury, people who experience mental illness can access other ways to manage without causing harm to themselves or others. This can allow them to regain a sense of control over their lives.

For some people, art therapy is a good alternative or complement to talk therapy. It can sometimes be very difficult to search for the correct words to explain to somebody else what you are thinking and feeling; this may create a feeling of resentment and avoidance toward standard counselling. However, art therapy goes beyond verbal communication skills, and taps into our ability to be present in the moment and experience it as wholly as possible. As argued by Pizarro, "individuals who lack the skills to communicate through writing, or are uncomfortable about verbal expression, may be encouraged to disclose by first engaging in an art project" (6). For people who find it difficult to communicate their life experiences verbally, art therapy provides "'safe space' to express difficult emotions," and some say it "is more relaxing and fun than other forms of verbal therapy" (Hughes and da Silva 612). Art therapy helps people find ways to express their feelings without having to use words.

Art therapy can be beneficial for children as well. Introducing various coping skills to children and adolescents puts them on a path towards stronger mental health. According to Green and Drewes, art therapy provides youth psychoanalytic, developmental, and cognitive-behavioural benefits. They reviewed research in the area, noting that "Art therapy research suggests that it can be an effective modality for treating a variety of issues and circumstances of childhood and adolescence" (49). They reported that art therapy has been associated with a decrease in symptoms of post-traumatic stress disorder (PTSD) and hyperactivity and with an increase in self-esteem, assertiveness, and coping ability.

There is also compelling anecdotal evidence of art therapy's value for both youth and adults. For example, one teenager shared her story of seeing a therapist for depression during her sophomore year of high school, during which she was encouraged to let out her feelings through making art. She ended up creating art on the canvas of over seventy pairs of shoes and feeling better over time (Children's Hospital Colorado). In another case, a textile artist found that making fabric collage helped her through depression and PTSD, and six years later she developed a program through CAMH called Art Cart, which "brings career artists who have experienced mental health and addiction in to the hospital to do art with patients who are recovering" (Bruno). People in the program have reported that they are comforted by the fact that they don't have to have art skills to do expressive art therapy, and that the chance to make art in a group setting allows them to feel relaxed and grow (vanKampen). Another individual who suffers from depression and anxiety discovered art therapy while hospitalized and said, "I drew for my life" (Kleiner). He has continued to use art to feel better for a decade.

To conclude, the further integration of art therapy in the field of mental health treatment would be beneficial because it allows people to cope with their struggles in a more healthy and productive manner, it creates an opportunity for people to relax and de-stress, and it provides a chance for individuals to express themselves and their emotions in ways words cannot. Art opens the door to a new aspect of healing. Although art therapy may not be a successful treatment for all who try it, it would undoubtedly help many people make progress on their path to recovery. It is time for us all to bring more awareness to the benefits of art therapy for mental health.

Works Cited

Bruno, Natasha. "Art Cart is a crafty idea to improving mental health." *Toronto Star*, 14 Apr. 2017, www.thestar.com. Accessed 15 July 2018.

Centre for Addiction and Mental Health. "Mental Health Statistics." *CAMH*, www.camh.ca. Accessed 13 July 2018.

Cherry, Kendra. "How art therapy is used to help people heal." *Verywellmind*, 11 June 2018, www.verywellmind.com/what-is-art-therapy-2795755. Accessed 20 July 2018.

Colorado Children's Hospital. "How art therapy changed my life." *YouTube*, uploaded 21 Sept. 2014, www.youtube.com/watch?v=Rhw4spxVqN0. Accessed 18 July 2018.

Finnerty, Timothy, host. "Mental Health Day Podcast #5: Art Therapy with Cathy Malchiodi." *Mental Health Day Podcast: Art Therapy*, 4 Feb. 2013, www.cathymalchiodi.com/resources/audio-podcasts/. Accessed 20 July 2018.

Green, Eric. J., and Athena A. Drewes. *Integrating Expressive Arts and Play Therapy with Children and Adolescents*. 1st ed., Wiley, 2014.

Hughes, Edward G., and Alicia Mann da Silva. "A Pilot Study Assessing Art Therapy as a Mental Health Intervention for Infertile Women." *Human Reproduction*, vol. 26, no. 3, 2011, pp. 611–615, doi:https://doi.org/10.1093/humrep/deq385. Accessed 13 July 2018.

Online article (*newspaper*)

Webpage (*organization as author*)

Online article (*website*)

Online video

Audio podcast

Book (*two authors, 1st edition*)

Online scholarly journal article

Online web comment (*posted in comment section of blog*)

Kleiner, Gary. Comment on "Psychological benefits of art therapy." Canadian Counselling and Psychotherapy Association, 25 Jan. 2018, 2:02 p.m., www.ccpa-accp.ca/psychological-bene-fits-of-art-therapy/. Accessed 15 July 2018.

Blog post

Kvarnstrom, Elisabet. (2017, July 14). "Using art therapy to create freedom from depression." *Bridges of Recovery*, 14 July 2017, www.bridgestorecovery.com/blog/using-art-therapy-to-cre-ate-freedom-from-depression/. Accessed 22 July 2018.

Online article (*magazine*)

Malchiodi, Cathy. "Yes, Virginia, there is some art therapy research." *Psychology Today*, 27 Feb. 2013, www.psychology-today.com. Accessed 14 July 2018.

Online scholarly journal article

Pizarro, Judith. "The efficacy of art and writing therapy: Increas-ing positive mental health outcomes and participant retention after exposure to traumatic experience." *Art Therapy*, vol. 21, no. 1, 2004, pp. 5–12. doi:10.1080/07421656.2004.10129327. Accessed 13 July 2018.

Online scholarly journal article (*more than two authors*)

Uttley, Lesley, et al. (2015). "Systematic Review and Economic Modelling of the Clinical Effectiveness and Cost-effectiveness of Art Therapy Among People with Non-psychotic Mental Health Disorders." *Health Technology Assessment*, vol. 19, no. 18, 2015, pp. 1–120. doi:10.3310/hta19180. Accessed 13 July 2018.

Online article (*news website*)

vanKampen, Stephanie. (2017, October 14). "Healing invisible wounds with the Art Cart." *CBC News*, 14 October 2017, www.cbc.ca/news/entertainment/camh-healing-art-cart-1.4354472. Accessed 24 July 2018.

INDEX

text annotation, summarizing information, 100–102
text-centred/writer-centred approaches, 260–262, 266–269
text marking, 13
text *vs.* image, 285
"There's No Online Substitute for a Real University Classroom," 12–13
thesis
    audience, 8–9
    implied main ideas, 42
    location of, 8–10
    placement of, 283–285
    response writing/essay, 264
    statement, 6–7, 287–288
    topic, 5–6
tone
    analyzing language, 166–168
    definition, 162, 166–168
    elements, 162
    sentence structure, 163
    writing analysis, 172–174
topic
    clues for reading, 5
    sentence, 6
topic sentences
    at beginning and end of paragraph, 38
    end of paragraph, 38
    at paragraph beginning, 37–38
    at paragraph middle, 38
    phrases and words, 37
    topic and locating topic sentences, 38–39
"Top 10 Scandals That Define FIFA's Tarnished Legacy," 244–247
Tucker, Erika, 90–92

U

unified paragraph, 23

W

"What Canadian Police Are Doing So Ferguson Doesn't Happen Here," 90–92
"Why the Music Industry's Not Celebrating Its Big Digital Windfall Just Yet," 278–280
Wiart, Nikki, 273–275
"Will Streaming Music Kill Songwriting?" 303–307
writing
    critical analysis (*see* critical analysis)
    drafting and revising, 23–25
    editing and proofreading, 25–26
    incorporating visuals, 141–142
    integrating and citing sources, 138–140
    paraphrasing, 106–113
    prewriting stage
        choosing methods, 22–23
        freewriting, 18
        graphic organizing, 20–22
        journalling, 18
        outlining, 18–20
    purpose of, 4
    question–answer relationships, 27–29
    subjects and verbs, 29–30
    survey data integrated into report, 142–144
    thesis
        location of, 8–10
        statement, 6–7
        topic, 5–6
writing prompt, 27
writing structure
    audience, 80
    compare–contrast essay
        block method, 82
        point-by-point method, 81–82
    organizational pattern, 81
    purpose, 80
    thesis, 80
    topic, 80